Ajax and REST Recipes

A Problem-Solution Approach

Christian Gross

Ajax and REST Recipes: A Problem-Solution Approach

Copyright © 2006 by Christian Gross

ISBN-13 (pbk): 978-1-59059-734-7

ISBN-10 (pbk): 1-59059-734-6

Printed and bound in the United States of America 9 8 7 6 5 4 3 2 1

Lead Editor: Chris Mills
Technical Reviewers: Nick McCollum, Bernhard Seefeld
Editorial Board: Steve Anglin, Ewan Buckingham, Gary Cornell, Jason Gilmore, Jonathan Gennick, Jonathan Hassell, James Huddleston, Chris Mills, Matthew Moodie, Dominic Shakeshaft, Jim Sumser, Keir Thomas, Matt Wade
Project Manager: Beth Christmas
Copy Edit Manager: Nicole Flores
Copy Editors: Nicole Abramowitz, Nicole Flores
Assistant Production Director: Kari Brooks-Copony
Production Editor: Laura Esterman
Compositor: Kinetic Publishing Services, LLC
Proofreader: Liz Welch
Indexer: Ann Rogers
Artist: April Milne
Cover Designer: Kurt Krames
Manufacturing Director: Tom Debolski

Distributed to the book trade worldwide by Springer-Verlag New York, Inc., 233 Spring Street, 6th Floor, New York, NY 10013. Phone 1-800-SPRINGER, fax 201-348-4505, e-mail orders-ny@springer-sbm.com, or visit http://www.springeronline.com.

For information on translations, please contact Apress directly at 2560 Ninth Street, Suite 219, Berkeley, CA 94710. Phone 510-549-5930, fax 510-549-5939, e-mail info@apress.com, or visit http://www.apress.com.

The source code for this book is available to readers at http://www.apress.com in the Source Code/Download section. You will need to answer questions pertaining to this book in order to successfully download the code.

Contents at a Glance

Contents

About the Author

 Many people say that by looking at a person's dog, you can tell what the person is like. Well, the picture of me is my dog Louys, an English Bulldog. And yes, my English Bulldog and I have many common characteristics.

But what about my biography? It's pretty simple: I am a guy who has spent oodles of time strapped to a chair debugging and taking apart code. In fact, I really enjoy this business we call software development. I have ever since I learned how to peek and poke my first bytes. I have written various books, including *Ajax Patterns and Best Practices* and *How to Code .NET*, all available from Apress.

These days I enjoy coding and experimenting with .NET, as it is a fascinating environment. .NET makes me feel like a kid opening a present on Christmas morning. You had an idea what the gift was, but you were not completely sure. And with .NET, there is no relative giving you socks or a sweater. It's excitement all the way!

About the Technical Reviewers

 **NICK MCCOLLUM** has more than 18 years of experience designing and developing enterprise applications on a variety of platforms. He is a principal consultant for NuSoft Solutions, Inc., and is currently the architect and lead developer for http://www.spout.com. Nick has acted as a technical editor for the following publications: *C# COM+ Programming* by Derek Beyer (John Wiley & Sons, 2001) and *Pro Ajax and the .NET 2.0 Platform* by Daniel Woolston (Apress, 2006). He is a Microsoft Certified Solution Developer and frequently speaks at Microsoft events and local user group meetings in the West Michigan area.

BERNHARD SEEFELD cofounded the Swiss search engine http://search.ch in 1995, where in October 2004, he released the first worldwide Ajax mapping application, http://map.search.ch. Bernhard holds an MSc in theoretical physics from the University of Berne, Switzerland.

Introduction

I wrote this, and I have a good feeling about it. It's an odd way to begin a book, but I like this book because of what it represents; the building of Asynchronous JavaScript and XML (Ajax) applications using Web services. I have been developing Web service-based applications since 1999. With Ajax, Web services has found its killer combination.

This book focuses on practical solutions for implementing Ajax, JavaScript, and Representational State Transfer (REST)–based Web services and functionality. I want to promote the development of applications that are decoupled (client code is separate from the server code), applications that can be adequately tested and maintained, and code that can be used by clients outside of the Ajax context. I believe in Ajax, but I also believe that if you can develop Ajax code that non-Ajax clients can access, then your application has a distinct advantage over others.

This book features the following chapters:

- Chapter 1—Getting Started: The focus of this chapter is on understanding the definitions of Ajax, REST, Web services, and service-oriented architecture (SOA). I've based the definitions on opinions in the industry, and understanding the definitions makes it simpler for you to understand the context of Ajax/REST and the rest of this book. This first chapter also covers how to test your Ajax/REST application using JavaScript. It shows you how to test Web service contracts and JavaScript client code.

- Chapter 2—JavaScript Recipes: The focus of this chapter is on explaining how to write more advanced JavaScript functionality. This chapter covers the following techniques (among others): using delegates that allow multiple methods or functions to be called, using functions as objects with state, and using functions to initialize and make decisions.

- Chapter 3—Dynamic Content Recipes: The focus of this chapter is on illustrating how you can build user interfaces that process dynamic content. Typically, dynamic content is form-based content, but not always. This chapter illustrates validation techniques, dynamic layout, and state-management techniques.

- Chapter 4—Implementing an SOA Architecture: The focus of this chapter is on explaining the topics of SOA and REST-based Web services in detail. This chapter discusses the details of how to use the various HTTP verbs (such as GET and POST), how to test a Web service, and how to upgrade an already existing system to expose its functionality using REST.

- Chapter 5—Implementing a Universal Web Service Architecture: The focus of this chapter is on using a REST-based Web service in a general context. This chapter illustrates the techniques necessary to implement Web services that you can integrate into a mashup, to generate multiple data formats, and to integrate dynamic URLs into static HTML pages.

- Chapter 6—Implementing Web Services for Large or Slow Data Sets: The focus of this chapter is on implementing REST-based Web services for situations where you have many results, or the results take a long time to generate. The recipe in this chapter focuses on solving one problem and illustrates how to describe the data, implement the URLs, and execute tasks on the server side.

- Chapter 7—Implementing an Ajax Shopping Cart: The focus of this chapter is on the general problem of the online shopping cart. In the abstract sense, the problem with current implementations of the shopping cart is the association of data with a specific user. This chapter illustrates how you can define and access non-user-associated URLs using authorization control.

- Chapter 8—Don't Submit Your Forms—Ajax Them: The focus of this chapter is on solving the dreaded back-button submit problem. The recipe illustrates how to manage the form submittal process and associate state with an HTML page, allowing for a more sophisticated content display.

■ ■ ■

CHAPTER 1

Getting Started

The focus of this chapter is to provide solutions to some common, general problems and questions that are bound to arise before or during development of Asynchronous JavaScript and XML (Ajax) and Representational State Transfer (REST) applications. These common questions are not always technical in nature, often leaning more toward theory or philosophy of development. The problem with these kinds of questions is that once you begin to think about them, you keep going in a circle and end up where you started. The trick to figuring out the answers is not to keep going in a circle, but to stick with the assumptions and make a decision.

Understanding the Definition and Philosophy of Ajax

Jesse James Garrett at Adaptive Path coined the original definition[1] of Ajax. Quoting the original definition, Ajax incorporates the following features:

- Standards-based presentation using Extensible HyperText Markup Language (XHTML) and Cascading Style Sheets (CSS)

- Dynamic display and interaction using the Document Object Model (DOM)

- Data interchange and manipulation using Extensible Markup Language (XML) and Extensible Stylesheet Language Transformations (XSLT)

- Asynchronous data retrieval using XMLHttpRequest

- JavaScript to bind everything together

In a nutshell, Ajax is a style of Web development that requires a Web browser. The user interface of the Web browser is dynamically modified using a programming language that retrieves data only when necessary, rather than the traditional approach of refreshing the whole page every time a request is made. I want to highlight the terms *dynamically* and *only when necessary*, because those terms are the essence of Ajax. Ajax and JavaScript are examples of *duck typing*[2] and *latent-type programming*.

---

1. http://www.adaptivepath.com/publications/essays/archives/000385.php

2. http://www.artima.com/weblogs/viewpost.jsp?thread=131502

Duck-typed programming is about writing code where the definition of the classes is not known ahead of time, but you know the object has some specific behavior. Reuse is made possible by cloning and assembling the objects dynamically at runtime. Classical object-oriented programming is about defining the behavior of the type before execution.

The following source code is for an example Dynamic HTML (DHTML) and JavaScript application that illustrates the essence of duck-typed programming.

Source: /website/ROOT/gettingstarted/PrototypeBased.html

```
<html>
<head>
    <title>Prototype-based Programming</title>
<script language="JavaScript" type="text/javascript">
function Variation1() {
    document.getElementById( "output").innerHTML = "Ran Variation 1";
}

function Variation2() {
    document.getElementById( "output").innerHTML = "Ran Variation 2";
}

var obj = new Object();

function RunVariation() {
    obj.runIt();
}
</script>
</head>
<body>
    <input type="button" value="Variation 1"
        onclick="obj.runIt = Variation1; RunVariation()" />
    <input type="button" value="Variation 2"
        onclick="obj.runIt = Variation2; RunVariation()" /><br/>
    <div id="output">Nothing yet</div>
</body>
</html>
```

In the example, the bold code segments illustrate the duck-typed programming constructs. When the Web browser loads the code, it will be parsed from top to bottom. When the code has been parsed, the following types and object instances will be active:

- Definition of the functions Variation1, Variation2, and RunVariation

- Instantiation and definition of the variable obj, which references a plain vanilla Object instance

- Definition of two buttons (Variation 1 and Variation 2) that execute some JavaScript when clicked

- Definition of an HTML div element that has the identifier output

Calling the function RunVariation generates an exception, because obj is a plain vanilla object instance and has no method implementation for runIt. A classical programming language such as Java, C#, or C++ is not able to compile the JavaScript code, because the function RunVariation executes a method on a type that is not defined to possess the method.

When an object method is called, as in the source code, it is called latent typing. Latent typing is the identification of the type associated with a variable during the runtime of the application. In the case of the source code example, that means the exact behavior of obj is not known until the application is executed. Hence, RunVariation may or may not work.

In the example code, when the input buttons are pressed, the property obj.runIt is assigned to either Variation1 or Variation2. After the property has been assigned, the input buttons call the function RunVariation, which in turn calls the property obj.runIt. As the property has an assigned value, the function Variation1 or Variation2 is called. The assigning of the property to a function is the essence of duck-typed programming.

This raises the question, if a programming language employs latent programming techniques, does that imply duck-typed programming? And if it does not, what are the differences? If a programming language supports latent typing, it does not imply duck-typed programming. But if a programming language supports duck-typed programming, it must support latent typing. C++ is an excellent example of a language that supports latent types but does not support duck typing. The following source code illustrates latent typing:

```
class LatentTypeCaller< T> {
    public void CallIt( T t) {
        t.LatentDefinedMethod();
    }
}
```

In the example code, T is a type that belongs to a C++ template. In the implementation of CallIt, the method t.LatentDefinedMethod is called. From the source code, the type of T is not apparent, but whatever it is, the method LatentDefinedMethod must be supported. C++ does not support duck typing, because T cannot have the method LatentDefinedMethod assigned dynamically.

With the inclusion of template type functionality in .NET 2.0 and in Java 5.0 called generics, you might be tempted to believe that generics support latent typing. The code as written in C++ is not possible in either .NET or Java, as the compilers would complain about unconstrained types. To get rid of the compiler errors in C# or Java, you must constrain T to a type that supports the method LatentDefinedMethod.

A common argument against duck-typed programming and latent typing is that you don't know what the code will do until you execute it. In contrast, the C++, .NET, and Java programming environments, which require explicit definition or static typing of types, make for stable and robust code. At least, that is the argument promoted by individuals who support static typing. Static typing ensures that a program compiles and fits together, but it does not guarantee that the program does what is expected. Consider the following code, which illustrates how static typing can be fooled:

```
class Math {
    public long add( long value1, long value2) {
        return value1 - value2;
    }
}
```

In the example, a class Math is defined, and Math has a single method add that is supposed to add two numbers together. If a program uses Math, the compiler will verify that Math is instantiated properly and that the method add is called properly. However, the compiler won't verify that two numbers are added properly. To do that, you need to create an explicit test to verify that the numbers have been added properly. A well-written test can quickly catch the fault of add and realize that a subtraction operation is being performed. The point of the argument is not to mock a constrained language, but to illustrate that the compiler cannot verify the correctness of a program.

Another illustration of the supposed advantage of a constrained language is IntelliSense. IntelliSense makes it possible to type in the name of a variable, hit the period keyboard button, and see all of the object's associated methods, properties, and data members. With IntelliSense, you can code quicker, because you're not left wondering how many parameters a method has. However, Charles Petzold makes an interesting argument[3] against IntelliSense, saying that it causes the mind to rot. His main argument is that because of IntelliSense, .NET contains 5,000 classes, 45,000 public methods, and 15,000 properties. This begs the question, can a developer actually understand all of this complexity? Petzold illustrates the problem using verbose but cryptically named types.

A final downside of using IntelliSense is the tendency it causes developers to create programs using bottom-up techniques. Bottom-up techniques are required because IntelliSense cannot work if the types have not been defined. Thus, top-down programming techniques have become rare, as developers get used to IntelliSense and writing bottom-up code.

Putting the two arguments together, you're probably thinking, "Why on earth are we still writing code using constrained languages? Constrained languages, simply put, constrain us." The answer is that constrained languages, along with the proper IDEs, give us a warm and fuzzy feeling of being able to define programmatic contracts and types and make sure everything is working properly.

The reality, though, is not black and white, and there are times when using a constrained language or a duck-typed language makes sense. In a nutshell, constrained languages are useful for implementing logic that has been precisely defined. For example, calculating a mortgage is a known science, and rules are associated with the calculation. It isn't difficult to associate with the calculation a number of requirements that define the exact behavior.

Duck typing—or more aptly put, dynamic languages—is well suited for those situations when you want flexibility in a system, such as creating a mortgage calculation application. Bankers like to create special mortgage packages, such as ones that show clients how they can pay less upfront and more later, or pay a large amount upfront, nothing for a while, and then the rest later. In these examples, the math used to calculate the mortgage is identical. What changes is how the calculations are assembled.

You can use a constrained language for all problems, and you can use a duck-typed language for all problems. You can also mix and match using Web services or compatibility layers. When you're writing JavaScript and Ajax code, you're writing duck-typed code. It's important to realize that Ajax is not just about XML, JavaScript, and DHTML. It's about the ability to dynamically create content and code that can be injected and executed. This ability to create content and code dynamically is possible in a constrained language, but is incredibly difficult and tedious. To illustrate the point, take a look at this simple click-me application, which is extended dynamically to include a second click-me button:

---

3. http://charlespetzold.com/etc/DoesVisualStudioRotTheMind.html

```java
public class MainFrame extends JFrame {
    public MainFrame() {
        initialize();
        setTitle(titleText);
        getContentPane().setLayout(new BorderLayout());
        getContentPane().add(panel1, BorderLayout.CENTER);
        button1.addActionListener(new ActionListener() {
                public void actionPerformed(ActionEvent e) {
                    label1.setText("hello world");
                }
            }
        );
    }

    public void show() {
        pack();
        setSize(new Dimension(
            Math.max(getWidth(), windowSize.width),
            Math.max(getHeight(), windowSize.height)));
        setLocationRelativeTo(null);
        super.show();
    }

    private String getLocalizedText(String text) {
        return text;
    }

    private JButton button1; // Button,Click Me,1,,,1
    private JPanel panel1; // Panel,Title
    private JTextArea label1; // Text,,1

    // Implementation (X-develop Swing designer code)
    ...
    // End of Implementation (X-develop Swing designer code)
}
```

The example Java source code is used only as an illustration, as .NET offers the same approach. A large amount of code can be labeled as infrastructure. For example, from the declaration of the three data members button1, panel1, and label1, you have no idea what they're supposed to be doing. You can't even deduce the dependencies or hierarchy of the data members.

You can figure out the nature of the data members by looking at the method calls setLayout, add, setSize, and setLocationRelativeTo, and at the large amount of code that has been removed that relates to the GUI designer. The illustrated code, with its data members and various methods, highlights the fact that a constrained language requires explicitly telling the system everything you want to do in painstaking detail. In contrast, let's implement the same functionality using DHTML and JavaScript technologies:

```html
<html>
<head>
    <title>Title</title>
</head>
<script language="JavaScript" type="text/javascript">
function ClickMe() {
    document.getElementById( "output").innerHTML = "hello world";
}
</script>
<body>
    <div id="output"></div>
    <input type="button" value="Click Me" onclick="ClickMe()" />
</body>
</html>
```

The functionality as implemented in DHTML and JavaScript is simpler, because there are fewer lines of code, and the code is explicit in that it is used to implement functionality, not infrastructure. Another feature of duck-typed languages is that the order of the code can be very important. Going back to the Java example, the location of the data members in the class is irrelevant. However, the location of the input and div HTML elements is extremely important, as it defines the layout and functionality. The advantage of a simpler and explicit programming model is that you as a designer are in control of how things appear and function.

Let's extend the HTML/JavaScript and Java examples and change the requirements so that instead of a simple text field, the output is generated into a table. This time, the DHTML and JavaScript code is shown first:

```html
<html>
<head>
    <title>Title</title>
</head>
<script language="JavaScript" type="text/javascript">
function ClickMe() {
    document.getElementById( "output").innerHTML = "hello world";
}
</script>
<body>
    <table border="1">
        <tr>
            <td id="output"></td>
        </tr>
    </table>
    <input type="button" value="Click Me" onclick="ClickMe()" />
</body>
</html>
```

In the example source, to change from a text panel to a table, only the HTML GUI code needs changing. The JavaScript logic and the HTML button logic remain exactly the same, because with latent typing, the text panel and table cell share a common contract property called innerHTML.

In contrast, Java would require at least two major changes: a new data member to be defined as a table, and new logic to iterate the table and find the cell used to assigned the value "hello world". What makes this development process in Java so frustrating is that the types and properties used to assign the value may or may not be the same.

When trying to understand the definition and philosophy of Ajax, remember the following points:

- The biggest advantage to Ajax and its associated technologies is its ability to act in a dynamic fashion using duck typing.

- Using Ajax, you need to stop thinking of data and the GUI as static elements. The data and GUI can and should be extended at runtime, allowing you to combine and extend functionalities on the fly.

- The biggest advantage to Ajax is also its biggest disadvantage—that is, dynamic code needs well-defined tests. Without a set of well-defined tests, there is no guarantee that the code will be used correctly or behave properly.

Understanding the Definition and Philosophy of Web Services and SOA

Wikipedia offers the following definition of Web services:[4]

> The W3C defines a Web service as a software system designed to support interoperable machine-to-machine interaction over a network. This definition encompasses many different systems, but in common usage the term refers to those services that use SOAP-formatted XML envelopes and have their interfaces described by WSDL. For example, WS-I only recognizes Web services in the context of these specifications.

Interestingly, like the pure Ajax definition, a Web service is defined to a large degree using technical terms such as Simple Object Access Protocol (SOAP), Web Services Description Language (WSDL), and so on. It leads you to believe that in order to build a Web service, you must use SOAP and WSDL.

What is misleading is that a Web service is directly related to the technology being used. For example, the REST way of building Web services may not involve XML, WSDL, or SOAP. Thus, is REST a Web service? The answer is that REST is indeed a Web service if the following more succinct definition[5] is used:

> Web services [instead] share business logic, data and processes through a programmatic interface across a network.

---

4. http://en.wikipedia.org/wiki/Web_Services

5. http://www.webopedia.com/TERM/W/Web_services.html

What is preferable with this definition is the reference to business logic, data, and processes and the exposing of those items using a programmatic interface. With this definition, Web services need not be a machine-to-machine interaction, as a Web browser in the context of Ajax has the ability to call a Web service. It's important to realize that in the context of Ajax, the programmatic interface may generate an interface definition that is intended to be processed by a human—for example, a link or button that is pressed to generate new content.

With a generalized definition of Web services, let's look at a definition of service-oriented architecture (SOA):[6]

> *In computing, the term service-oriented architecture (SOA) expresses a perspective of software architecture that defines the use of loosely coupled software services to support the requirements of business processes and software users. In an SOA environment, resources on a network are made as independent services that can be accessed without knowledge of their underlying platform implementation.*

This time, instead of a definition that uses technical terms, abstract terminology is used to describe an SOA. Looking at the definition of SOA, you might consider a network printer as an SOA. Yet, is that what the definition of SOA intends? Is a Web service an SOA, and is an SOA a Web service? JP Morgenthal[7] says it best:

> *An SOA is a service with a contract.*

Morgenthal's comment is simple, succinct, and expresses exactly what an SOA is: An SOA is a service with a contract. What makes an SOA unique is that somebody who has no knowledge of a system can ask an SOA, "What services do you offer?" and the SOA will respond, "Here is what I offer and here is how you call me." Therefore, since Web services provide a description of their interface, a Web service is an SOA. A file server is an SOA, if a client is able to query the file server for its contract in order to ask for data.

Keep the following facts in mind when trying to understand the philosophy and definition of Web services and SOA:

- An SOA can be a Web service, and a Web service can be an SOA.

- When building robust, scalable, and extendable Ajax applications, write the client code to only make Web service calls. Don't use the traditional Web application architecture, where pieces of HTML are cobbled together to make a functioning HTML page.

- Don't get too caught up with the details of the definition of a true Web service or a true SOA. Theory is good, but pragmatics solves problems.

- A Web service is a programmatic interface to business logic, data, or processes across a network.

- An SOA is a service (a programmatic interface to business logic, data, or processes across a network) with a contract.

---

6. http://en.wikipedia.org/wiki/Service-oriented_architecture

7. http://www.avorcor.com/

Understanding the Definition and Philosophy of REST

REST is a controversial topic among Web service enthusiasts, because it's considered to stand for the opposite of what Web services and SOA are trying to achieve. The problem with this thinking is that REST is not in contradiction with the abstract definition of SOA and Web services. REST is in contradiction with technologies such as SOAP, WSDL, and WS-* specifications.

The following offers a quick definition of REST:

REST is about database design, and SOAP is about API design.

The definition in itself is controversial, as many point out that SOAP can be used to create document-based Web services. However, they miss the fact that REST does not refer to the data sent between the client and the server. It refers to how to address and send or receive the data.

Let's say you're writing a SOAP Web service, which means you'll be designing a WSDL document. WSDL itself implies the definition of an access point with operations, or in programming language terms, APIs. The APIs may support the transfer of documents, but the WSDL operations are APIs. This is not a bad thing, just a reference point to say that SOAP is about APIs.

REST is about using the HTTP protocol to manipulate state indicated by a resource. The SQL programming language is used to manipulate relational data. In the SQL language, verbs, such as INSERT, SELECT, UPDATE, and DELETE, perform actions on the data. REST uses these verbs, but they're HTTP verbs: PUT, POST, GET, and DELETE. Everything that you need to do to the data can be expressed in those verbs, regardless if you're using HTTP or SQL.

Another difference between database design and API design is that with database design, you're working with sets. The sets may have no, one, or many elements. The count does not matter. With APIs, the number of elements does matter, because you need to explicitly create APIs that manipulate either no, one, or multiple elements. None of these comparisons are meant to say that one is good and the other is bad. Instead, they are meant to illustrate that REST and SOAP are very different in their approaches.

All of this theory sounds like hand waving, so the best way to explain the theory is to implement a service using REST. The example calculator application starts with a traditional API approach, converts the application into a preliminary REST approach, and then transforms the preliminary solution into a full-fledged REST solution. The preliminary REST solution is illustrated to demonstrate that not all REST solutions take advantage of all of the features of REST.

The simple calculator only supports memory and the addition of two numbers. Figure 1-1 shows the front end of the calculator using traditional Web technologies.

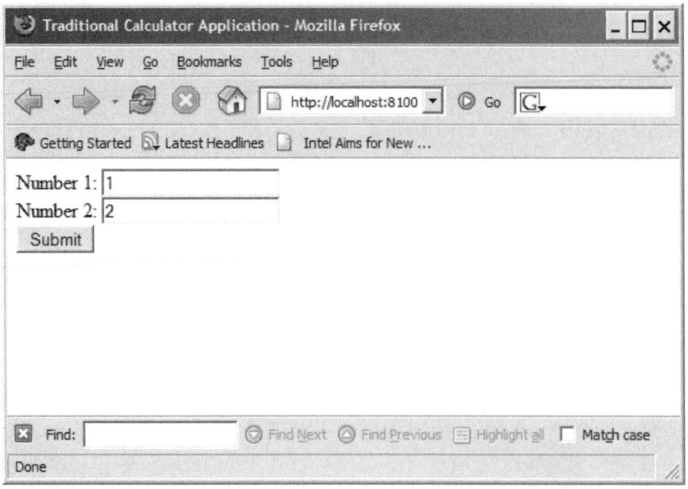

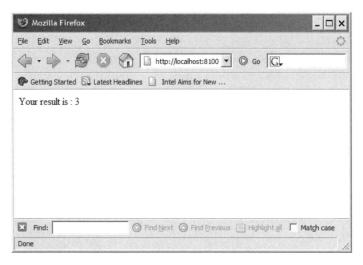

Figure 1-1. *Calculator front end using traditional Web technologies*

The calculator contains two text boxes, where each text box represents a number. Users click the Submit button on the HTML page to submit the numbers to the server, which adds the two numbers together and returns a result, as illustrated in Figure 1-2.

Figure 1-2. *Generated result of adding two numbers*

The server adds the two numbers together and generates a result. To add a new set of numbers, you need to click the Back button and enter two different numbers. From a processing perspective, Figure 1-3 represents the flow between calling the HTML page, sending the data to the server, and then generating the result.

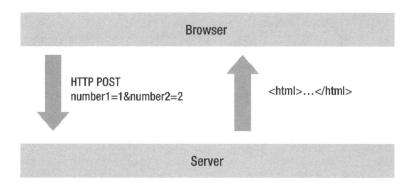

Figure 1-3. *Calling sequence of a traditional Web application*

In a traditional Web application, when the user clicks the Submit button, the data from the HTML form (meaning the contents of the two text boxes) is gathered and sent to the server using an HTTP POST. The server reads and processes the data to generate the response in the form of an HTML page.

The results of the POST are fixed. This means that any HTML page with an HTML form can call the server-side generation page, but the result is predefined. In the example, the result has to be an HTML page that can be generated in an HTML page. The problem is that to generate a proper result, the server has to take into account style sheets as well as other look-and-feel attributes. If you think about it, the general purpose of the server-side POST is to generate a result to a query. Of course the server could employ some techniques to generate the correct data in the correct context. That has led to sophisticated frameworks that attempt to "fix" the problem of posting content.

This is what makes Ajax such a compelling argument when developing Web applications. Ajax focuses on sending and receiving the necessary content, not the extra bits that have nothing to do with the content. When using Ajax, the initial page is still downloaded, but the nature of the HTTP POST changes. The same HTTP POST is sent, but the response doesn't have to include HTML codes necessary to create a complete HTML page. When using Ajax, the HTTP POST changes into a Web service call that asks for chunks of content to inject. The quirky Web application changes back to a traditional client/server application, where you can query and retrieve specific pieces of content.

When creating Ajax applications, how server-side logic is called becomes important. Imagine if the Ajax application were using a remoting technology such as Remote Method Invocation (RMI), Distributed Component Object Model (DCOM), or .NET Remoting. When using those technologies, a great deal of thought goes into which objects are exposed and how they are called. In an Ajax application, the same happens, except that instead of thinking in remoting terms, you think in terms of REST. REST is a way of organizing how to present data that the Ajax application can manipulate.

Let's go back to the calculator example and go through a preliminary version of converting the application into Ajax and REST. Figure 1-4 shows the Ajax-enabled sample application.

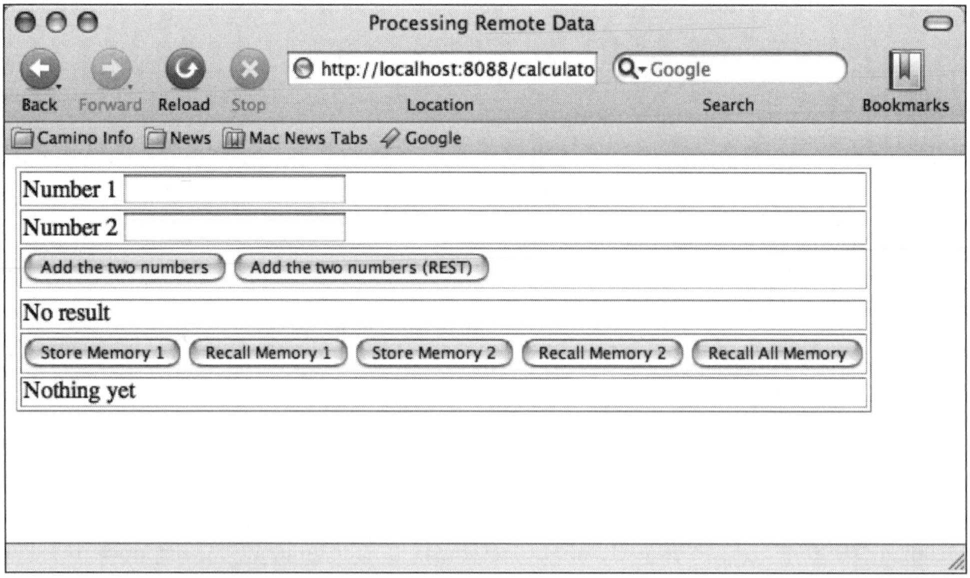

Figure 1-4. *Ajax-enabled calculator application*

The Ajax-enabled calculator application is more complicated than the traditional Web application. It features the added functionality of being able to store and retrieve data values like the memory of a calculator. The client implements some HTML GUI logic and then calls the server using REST. The server needs to expose the features used on the client using URLs, which are illustrated in Figure 1-5.

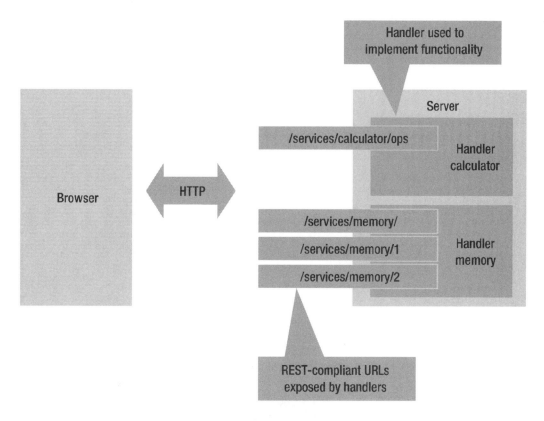

Figure 1-5. *Illustrative REST URLs used to implement calculator and memory logic*

The browser uses HTTP and URLs to reference logic exposed by the server. The HTTP server itself doesn't implement the logic, but instead uses the concept of a handler. A handler is a general cross-platform and language concept that is a cross-reference of a URL and some logic. For example, in Figure 1-5, if the URL /services/calculator/ops is called, then the handler Calculator is executed. A single URL doesn't have to be associated with a single handler. A handler could process multiple URLs, as is the case of the Memory handler.

The URLs in Figure 1-5 are REST-compliant because they reference some resource on the server. For example, the URL /services/memory references the resource of all memory locations. The URLs /services/memory/1 and /services/memory/2 are specific references to memory resources—specifically, memory location 1 and 2. The URL /services/calculator/ops is used to access a resource that adds two numbers together.

In a REST implementation, the important rule is that the URL defines the resource. A single URL cannot be used to expose multiple functionalities. Instead, a single URL can be used to expose multiple representations of the resource. In the case of calculator service /services/calculator/ops, the format of the numbers to be added and the result depends on what the client indicates and the server can support. What is indicated and sent are HTTP headers in the HTTP POST.

For comparison purposes, let's consider how a SOAP-based Web service would expose its functionality. Figure 1-6 illustrates an example SOAP Web service.

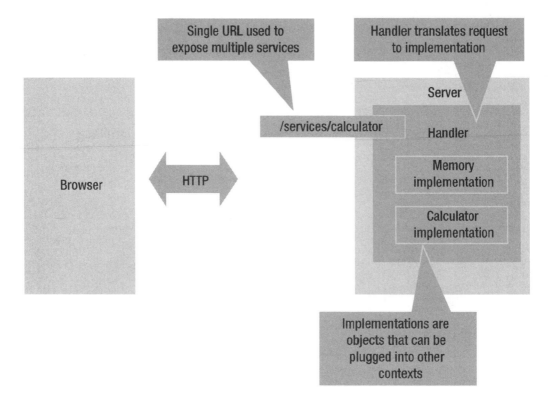

Figure 1-6. *Illustrative SOAP URLs used to implement calculator and memory logic*

The SOAP implementation exposes a single URL, which is managed by a single handler. There are multiple implementations in the context of a handler. The handler knows which implementation to call depending on the information sent to the URL. It calls the method add for addition, and it calls the method memory to store or retrieve memory. In the case of the memory retrieval, which piece of memory is stored or retrieved is a parameter. The data that is returned is packaged as a SOAP message. SOAP, in contrast to REST, offers multiple functionalities and representations in a single URL.

Earlier, it was stated that REST is more akin to a database, and SOAP is more akin to an API. This is understandable because of the way each approach exposes its URL, and the data that is sent and received. The semantics of what the data is and represents at the URL is very different for SOAP and REST. In a REST approach, if you use HTTP PUT to save data on the server, then you assume to get the same data when calling HTTP GET. In a SOAP approach, if you use HTTP PUT, you don't assume to get the same data when calling HTTP GET. In fact, using SOAP, you have no idea what data you'll get, because SOAP requires some type of semantics that is associated with HTTP PUT and GET using a contract defined in a WSDL file.

The difference between a database and API approach becomes clearer by evolving the calculator example. In Figures 1-5 and 1-6, the calculation operations and memory operations are two separate operations. To be able to store the results of an addition, you would need an explicit operation to save the data, because an API approach offers no facility to save old operations automatically.

Originally, the REST application used a set of URLs, but the URLs were wrong because they fitted an API approach on top of a resource approach. For example, the memory URL is `/services/memory/1`. The URL looks correct, but is in fact completely incorrect. As the URL is defined, the memory location `/services/memory/1` is shared by everybody. To distinguish between the different users, most Web application frameworks use cookies. And cookies, again, are the completely wrong answer. Imagine writing an application where you save some value that you want to share with somebody else. If you give to the other person the URL that you used to store the data, that person could not access the data because his cookie identifier would not be compatible with your cookie identifier.

The problem is that the state of the resource as defined by the URL is dependent on the URL and a cookie identifier. This violates REST principles. REST principles state that if memory is stored at the URL `/services/memory/1`, then the same state is retrieved regardless of who accesses the URL. A cookie can be used for authorization purposes. Using a cookie, a server can identify whether a request is authorized to view the representation of the resource. The solution is to think in data terms and consider the memory location identifier as an arbitrary row identifier that references a memory location. This results in the addition being both a calculation and a memory operation.

You can extend the solution of assigning an arbitrary value to the addition operation, as illustrated in Figure 1-7.

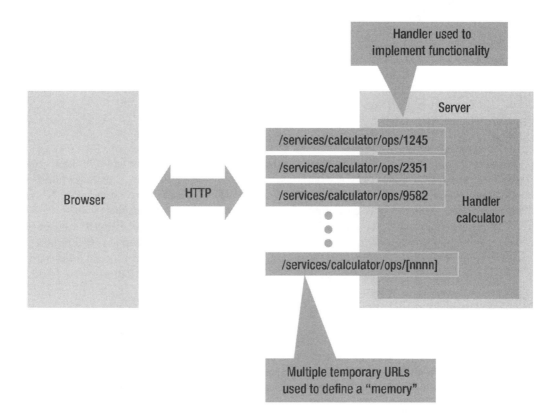

Figure 1-7. *Ideal REST calculator application*

Figure 1-7 shows only a single handler, which processes the calculator operations. Unlike Figure 1-5, an infinite number of URLs can be used to add two numbers. The numeric identifier is an arbitrary value used to reference a past calculation. Thus, a memory operation is not necessary because to reference a past calculation, you only need to reference the URL. If a calculation is to be shared among multiple users, then it is only necessary to bookmark the URL.

When writing your own REST application, remember the following points:

- REST is about managing data, and SOAP is about managing APIs.

- REST has dynamic contracts—that is, the resources are connected and described using links and the HTTP headers of the client. For example, one client can define the contract to be XML data, and another can define the contract to be HTML data. The server adapts to each by sending an appropriate representation for a resource.

- REST has a set of predefined semantics using HTTP GET, HTTP POST, URLs, resources, and representations.

- SOAP doesn't have a predefined set of semantics or contracts, as they're defined by the metadata (WSDL).

- REST manages URLs in a dynamic manner, where URLs are created dynamically.

- URLs in a REST approach represent references to a resource and not necessarily a file on a hard disk.

1-1. The Easiest Way to Get Started with Ajax and REST

Problem

You want to know the best way to get started with writing Ajax and REST.

Solution

When developing an Ajax and REST application, you must decide on the tools and frameworks you'll use. The choice is simple: Use whatever you're using today, and write some Ajax applications. You don't need to change the tools you're using today. Whether you're using ASP.NET, JavaServer Pages (JSP), PHP, Ruby, or Python, you can continue with those tools.

Ajax uses JavaScript, DHTML, and the XMLHttpRequest object, but ASP.NET, PHP, and similar technologies don't hinder you from writing HTML pages that make use of Ajax techniques. If your technology does hinder you from writing Ajax applications, then you should think hard about continuing using the technology. After all, you're reading an Ajax and REST recipe book, so I assume that you plan on implementing Ajax and REST solutions.

Next, you want to decouple the client from the server, as illustrated in Figure 1-8.

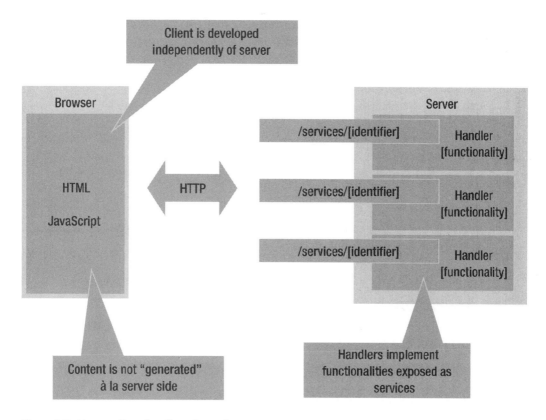

Figure 1-8. *Decoupling the client from the server*

When decoupling the client from the server, you can create the content on either side independently. You can develop the client using technologies such as DHTML and JavaScript. Within the client, you can code references to services offered by the client. The client-side code provides an infrastructure where the content generated by the services can be injected. The client and server interact with each other using contracts. Using contracts, you can develop the client independently and test it using mock objects. Using contracts, you can develop the server independently and test it using tests from a test suite. Then when the client is combined with the server, the application will work without requiring a large amount of further testing. Of course, this assumes that the tests for the client and server are implemented properly—normal testing is often also required.

Having decoupled the client from the server, you can easily modularize and delegate the implementation work to individual team members. Allowing each team member to focus on the task makes it possible to specialize and create innovative content. For example, delegating the database work to the server allows a client developer to make more use of graphics and innovative representations of the data generated by the service. Delegating the UI work from the server to the client side makes it possible for the server developer to focus on database optimization and access speeds.

Having decoupled the client from the server, you can make use of specific frameworks to make it simpler to implement specific pieces of logic. For example, a client-side developer could use the Prototype[8] or Dojo[9] frameworks. Which toolkit you end up using is your choice, and there is no right or wrong answer. You need to investigate what you need and see if the framework offers that functionality.

When getting started with Ajax and REST, remember the following points:

- You can use Ajax and REST today with existing technologies. You generally don't need to throw out old technologies and replace them with new ones.

- Ajax and REST are about decoupling the client from the server and making using of Web services.

- Ajax and REST frameworks can make it simpler for you to implement your applications, but because there are so many frameworks, you need to inspect them to see if they fulfill your needs.

1-2. Implementing an Ajax and REST Application Using Test-Driven Development Techniques

After you're convinced that you want to develop Ajax and REST applications, you'll want to execute some testing routines.

Problem

You want to know the best way to test your Ajax and REST applications.

Solution

This recipe explains the different layers of test-driven development techniques.[10] There are different layers because an Ajax and REST application involves both client-side and server-side code. To put it simply, you don't hire a few users to test an Ajax and REST application and get them to try out application scenarios.

As stated earlier, the server side and client side are decoupled from each other. This is a good approach for testing purposes, because you can develop and test the client and server independently of each other. An architect has the ability to define a contract between the client and server, enabling each to work independently of each other. Figure 1-9 illustrates the testing architecture of an Ajax and REST application.

---

8. http://prototype.conio.net/

9. http://dojotoolkit.org/

10. If you are unfamiliar with test-driven development, read the materials on this Wikipedia page: http://en.wikipedia.org/wiki/Test_driven_development.

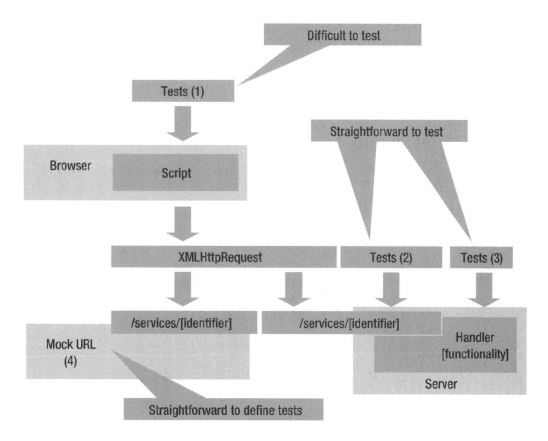

Figure 1-9. *Testing structure for an Ajax and REST application*

Figure 1-9 contains three layers of tests and one layer of mock URLs. The four layers range in implementation complexity from complicated to straightforward. Each layer, which is explained as follows, is associated with a numeric identifier:

- GUI-level tests involve testing the Ajax and DHTML user interface.

- REST-level tests test the REST and Web service interfaces for correct implementation of the defined contracts.

- Server-side class-level tests test the implementation of the functionality using test-driven development techniques.

- Mock URL-level tests are not actually tests, but rather implement the contracts defined by the REST and Web service interfaces. The mock implementations allow you to test the GUI without needing a completed server-side implementation.

Each layer requires using a different testing toolkit, as each layer tests a different aspect of the Ajax and REST application. However, this raises a question: Do you start developing with the server side or the client side? Do you develop using top-down techniques or bottom-up techniques?

You could develop all the layers at once using agile techniques, though it's not a good idea. The problem is that by using agile techniques on all of the layers at once, you instantly create a communications overhead and defeat the purpose of decoupling the client from the server. In a complete agile manner, the client, contract, and server are all developed at once. If the client has a problem, that might cause a change in the contract and the server, causing the client and server to become coupled.

It is not to say that you shouldn't develop using agile techniques. What you need to do is direct the agile techniques so that the client and server are decoupled from each other. Thus, the first thing you should develop are the contracts that the client uses and the server provides. Figure 1-10 illustrates how to convert the Ajax application into an agile development model.

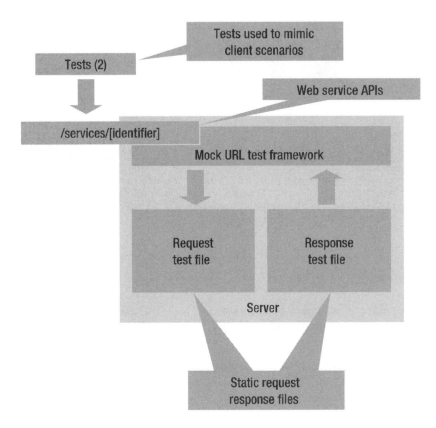

Figure 1-10. *Architecture of developing the contracts using agile techniques*

Figure 1-10 contains a testing layer 2 and a Mock URL layer. The idea behind this architecture is to test and implement a complete user case without actually implementing the client or server. The testing layer 2 represents a set of tests used to verify that the server-side implementation is complete. The Mock URL layer represents a set of tests used to verify that the client-side implementation is complete. By having the testing layer 2 verify the data generated by the Mock URL layer, the contracts for completeness are verified.

Practically speaking, you could use a programming language such as Java to make a series of Web service calls that define a contract. These Web service calls represent scenarios that the client implementation would execute. You would implement the scenarios using agile techniques defined by application use cases. For example, if a use case is to open a bank account, then you would create a test that would make the appropriate Web service calls to open a bank account.

A test cannot function without some implementation. And since you don't have an implementation, you must fake the request and response or, more appropriately, use the Mock URL framework. The role of the Mock URL framework is to anticipate the client tests. When a test is underway, the Mock URL framework verifies the data sent by the test and then generates the appropriate response. The verification and generation are the result of performing some logic and loading and sending pregenerated application data. It is important that the Mock URL not implement business logic, but rather use canned logic and pregenerated requests and responses as much as possible.

When the contracts are implemented properly, the tests should not be able to tell if a live implementation is generating the data or if some layer has faked the data. Appropriately, the Mock URL framework should not be able to tell if it is being called by a series of tests or if it is live client implementation. The combination of tests and Mock URLs allows you to use agile and test-driven techniques to create the contracts that the client and server need to implement. If you feel that creating a complete mock layer is too much work, then you could create an implementation that has canned returned values.

Having defined the contract, the implementations of the client and server know what they need to do. In order for you to use agile techniques to implement the client and server, the tests have to be a finer granularity than the contracts. The implementation tests need to be extensive and go beyond the contract and may include other aspects such as data initialization and presentation. For example, the test layers 1 and 3, as illustrated in Figure 1-9, are not related directly to the contracts and are used to test the client- and server-side implementations.

Starting with layer 3, you use the tests to test the functionality of the implemented server-side logic. From a programmatic perspective, this means that a clear separation exists between the implemented logic and the technology used to present that logic using the HTTP protocol. Figure 1-11 illustrates the architecture.

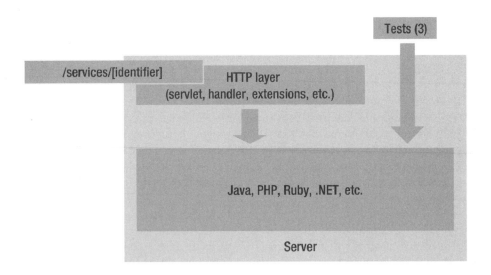

Figure 1-11. *Test layer 3 tests server-side logic.*

The test layer 3 doesn't depend on or care about how the logic is exposed to the HTTP protocol. The tests in layer 3 focus on making sure that the server-side logic is implemented correctly. The contracts that the tests verify are not exposed externally, and the client doesn't care what the tests are. Because the tests are private, the server developer can define their class structure, using whatever technology desired without affecting the client.

Testing the server requires using the correct test framework; a few of these frameworks are outlined as follows:

- *JUnit* (http://www.junit.org): Java test-driven development framework. JUnit is the original unit-testing tool.

- *NUnit* (http://www.nunit.org): .NET unit-testing framework that uses .NET attributes.

- *PyUnit* (http://pyunit.sourceforge.net/): Python unit-testing framework.

- *PHPUnit* (http://www.phpunit.de/wiki/Main_Page): PHP unit-testing framework.

- *Test::Unit* (included with Ruby distribution): Ruby unit-testing framework.

If your programming language is not mentioned, do a search for the term "[Insert your language] unit test". Regardless of the programming language, the unit-testing framework and approach are the same. You use agile and test-driven techniques to implement server-side logic.

Test layer 1 is used to test the client-side code. Figure 1-12 illustrates the detailed client-side architecture.

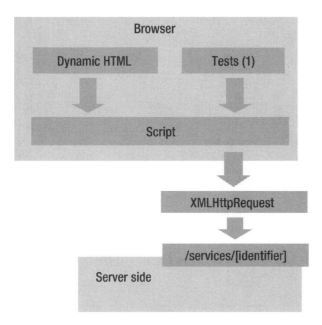

Figure 1-12. *Test layer 1 tests client-side logic.*

In the architecture of testing the client-side logic, most if not all of what's tested is the correctness of the JavaScript code. Notice in the architecture how the test layer 1 tests the scripts and not the DHTML user interface. This is on purpose and relates to the complexities of testing DHTML user interfaces.

When JavaScript and DHTML are combined, you get a mostly predictable user interface. Contrast that to a traditional user interface, where elements are designed to occupy fixed areas. Knowing that a user interface has to look a certain way makes it possible to use GUI test tools that take image snapshots and compare them to each other. While it's possible to control the exact look of a DHTML user interface, it is not recommended because it contradicts the purpose of DHTML. Remember that DHTML contains the word *dynamic*, which indicates the ability to determine the layout of a user interface at runtime.

Therefore, you cannot use classical user-interface testing techniques. Instead, you need to employ a thin-layer testing approach.[11] Using a utility such as JsUnit,[12] you could write a series of scripts for the server side and to execute user-interface logic. The test scripts would exercise the client logic and ensure that the application works properly. However, this solution is not ideal, because any logic that is embedded into the DHTML is not tested, so errors could potentially occur.

---

11. One possible solution is to implement the Model View Presenter pattern as originally defined (`http://msdn.microsoft.com/msdnmag/issues/06/08/DesignPatterns/`). This pattern has been expanded into two other patterns (`http://www.martinfowler.com/eaaDev/ModelViewPresenter.html`), and the reader is expected to investigate which is best for them.

12. `http://www.jsunit.net`

When figuring out how to implement test-driven development techniques, remember the following points:

- An Ajax application contains four main test layers: client side, server side, contract, and Mock URL.

- The contract and Mock URL tests are developed simultaneously using agile development techniques, and they implement application use cases.

- You can use the contract and Mock URL tests for REST, SOAP, and other protocols.

- The client- and server-side tests are specific to the client or server and are used to implement test-driven development.

- The client side should not be dependent on the implementation details of the server, and the server should not be dependent on the implementation details of the client.

1-3. Coding the Contract Using Test-Driven Development Techniques

Coding the contract using agile and test-driven development techniques requires writing a number of tests and implementing a Mock URL layer.

Problem

You want to code the contract using these development techniques.

Solution

To demonstrate, let's define a use case, implement the use case as a contract, write a test case(s) to implement the contract, implement the contract in the Mock URL, and finally run the test.

The example is XMLHttpRequest-based, as you'll most likely be using XMLHttpRequest for your testing purposes. However, the contract and mock URLs are not integrated explicitly into the client or server code, so that you can verify any client. This book is about building Web services, and you can call Web services by an XMLHttpRequest client, by a mashup client, or by some server-side Web service aggregator.

The example features a calculator application that contains only a single operation used to add two numbers together. What makes the calculator operation unique is that it uses temporary URLs to keep a history of past additions. The use case is the addition of two numbers, but two things must happen to carry out the use case: redirection and addition.

The details of managing redirections aren't covered here but will be covered in the following section entitled "Testing a Dynamic Contract." How the temporary URL is determined falls into the category of pixie dust, so let's focus on the details of the contract that performs the addition. The following represents the HTTP request used to perform an addition:

```
POST /services/calculatorrest/operations/2364564565 HTTP/1.1
Content-type: application/json
User-Agent: Jakarta Commons-HttpClient/3.0
Host: localhost:8100
Content-Length: 25

{"number2":2,"number1":1}
```

In the request, an HTTP POST is executed, and the URL used is the temporary URL found in the redirection test. The HTTP headers Content-type and Content-Length are not optional and are used to define the type and length of the content sent with the POST request. The body of the request contains a buffer encoded using JavaScript Object Notation (JSON).[13] Two data members are defined in the JSON request: number1 and number2. These two data members represent the numbers to be added.

The following shows the appropriate response:

```
HTTP/1.1 200 OK
Content-Type: application/json
Content-Length: 14
Server: Jetty(6.0.x)

{"result":3}
```

The headers Content-Type and Content-Length describe the content that is returned, which is encoded using JSON and contains a single data member. The single data member result is the result of adding two numbers together.

As you look at the requests and responses and do some mental math, you'll know that adding 1 and 2 results in the sum of 3. From the perspective of the contract, it would seem that everything is OK and that the system is implemented and works. In reality, however, the illustrated HTTP conversations were all faked. This leads to the following question: when developing a contract, how do you physically define the contract?

A purist might say, "The contract is defined using some sort of tool that the client and server programmers then implement." The purist answer sounds good and would be great if such a tool existed. Unfortunately, no tool allows you to design REST-based HTTP conversations that can serve as the basis of the test and Mock URL layer.

Faced with the fact that you don't have such a tool, using an editor to generate the HTTP conversation manually is incredibly error-prone and tedious. I don't suggest that anybody should do that. However, you still need to define a contract, but you can't do it without a tool or an editor. Without any sort of documentation, the contract literally remains a figment of your imagination. And figments of imagination are rather difficult to create test cases for.

The solution is to write the tests that make up the contracts, even though writing a bunch of tests does not make a contract. The tests have to serve a dual purpose—that is, they have to provide tests as well as act as documentation for how the contracts are called and used. Therefore, it's important that you structure the tests clearly and make them verbose.

For programming purposes, you can code the test framework in any particular language that makes you comfortable. For the scope of this solution and this book, I use JavaScript and JsUnit to write my test scripts. However, there's nothing stopping you from using Java, a .NET language, PHP, or Ruby.

You can start the contract in one of two ways: You can implement the client side first, or you can implement the Mock URL layer first. If you implement the client side first, you'd be using a top-down approach, and if you implement the Mock URL side first, you'd be using a bottom-up approach. I've chosen a top-down approach and have implemented the client side first. Of course, many say that top-down is the best, but I try not to be so picky about it.

---

13. http://www.json.org

The important thing is that you start with one, do a bit of coding, and then move to the other. Don't code all of one and then implement the other. Remember that you're trying to develop the contract in an agile manner using test-driven development techniques.

To make it easier to write your own tests, take a look at Figure 1-13, which shows an example template HTML page that contains all of the essentials you need to write your contract tests.

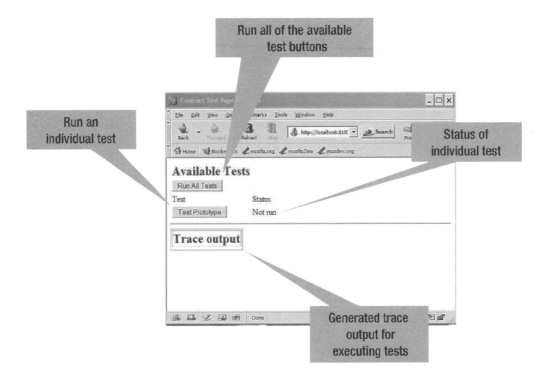

Figure 1-13. *Appearance of the template test page*

The generated HTML page contains two buttons. You use the topmost button Run All Tests to run all available tests on the HTML page. You use the lower button Test Prototype to run a particular test. When you click the button, the status of the test is generated to the right of the button. In the example, the status of the test is "not run." Below the button is trace output, which is used to display any messages or errors that occur as the tests are running.

The source of the HTML page is defined as follows.

Source: /jaxson/trunk/website/ROOT/scripts/templates/testcontract.html

```
<html>
<head>
    <title>Contract Test Page</title>
    <script language="JavaScript" src="/scripts/common.js"></script>
    <script language="JavaScript" src="/scripts/Synchronous.js"></script>
    <script language="JavaScript" src="/scripts/commontest.js"></script>
```

```
        <script language="javascript" src="/scripts/jsunit/jsUnitCore.js"></script>
</head>
<body>
<script language="javascript">
// Setup the output generator
setJsUnitTracer( new jsUnitTraceGenerator( "traceoutput"));

// Start of defined contract URLs
// Potentially define a URL as
// var baseURL = "/my/url";

// End of defined contract URLs

var testsToRun = {
        // Start JavaScript code for test cases here
        testPrototype : function() {
        // Synchronous functions identically to Asynchronous
        // but Synchronous waits for the request to complete
        // Good for testing, but bad for production as the browser hangs
        var request = new Synchronous();

        request.complete = function( statusCode, statusText,
            responseText, responseXML){
            // Do something with the result

            // Indicate that you are done, and define the output element
            testManager.success( "statusPrototype");
        }
        // Do something with the request
    }
    // End JavaScript code for test cases
};

testManager.setTestCases( testsToRun);

</script>

<table>
    <tr>
        <td><h2>Available Tests</h2></td>
        <td></td>
    </tr>
    <tr>
        <td>
            <input onclick="testManager.runAll()"
             type="button" value="Run All Tests" />
        </td>
        <td></td>
```

```
    </tr>
    <tr>
        <td>Test</td>
        <td>Status</td>
    </tr>
    <!-- Insert GUI for test cases here -->
    <tr>
        <td>
            <input onclick="testManager.testPrototype()" type="button"
                value="Test Prototype" />
        </td>
        <td id="statusPrototype">Not run</td>
    </tr>
    <!-- End test cases here -->
</table>
<hr />
<table border="1">
    <tr>
        <td><h2>Trace output</h2></td>
    </tr>
    <tr>
        <td id="traceoutput"></td>
    </tr>
</table>
</body>
</html>
```

The code is relatively long, so I've highlighted the important pieces to make it simpler to understand. The test code uses the script tag to include a number of JavaScript files that provide the basis of the test code. After you load the base script, the first piece of highlighted code setJsUnitTracer redirects the generated warnings and informational and debug messages to the current HTML page. Specifically, the output is generated in the table element with the id traceoutput, which is shown in bold at the bottom of the HTML code.

The other bold source code is the variable baseURL, which represents a variable that references the contract URLs that will be used in the test script. It's important to define all contract URLs in this area so that it's clear which URLs need to be supported. If a URL cannot be determined ahead of time because of its dynamic nature, then you declare a variable and assign an empty string.

The next pieces of bold text represent a variable (testsToRun) and a function (testPrototype). The function testPrototype is an example of how you could write a test. Remember these two important steps: Use Synchronous, and call the method testManager.success. Synchronous is a helper class that makes a synchronous XMLHttpRequest call. Normally, in your applications you would use the Asynchronous class, which makes asynchronous XMLHttpRequest calls.

Let's take a look at the differences between asynchronous and synchronous requests and discuss why you'd choose either. When XMLHttpRequest is used to make a synchronous request, XMLHttpRequest waits for a response before returning control to the browser. Having XMLHttpRequest wait for an answer is a problem, because JavaScript is not multithreaded, causing the browser to lock. For a better user experience, you should always use asynchronous requests. Using asynchronous requests has its own problems. An asynchronous request doesn't wait for the response and returns control to the JavaScript. When running tests, asynchronous requests are a problem because tests are executed sequentially, not concurrently. When writing Ajax and REST code, use the following rule of thumb: use asynchronous requests for applications, and use synchronous requests for testing.

Getting back to the example function `testPrototype`, each test function must indicate whether or not the test was successful. This is required because when the test manager runs all tests, the next test will run only when the current test was successful. In the example, a success is when the method `testManager.success` is called. Calling the method `failed` indicates a failure, and the method `waiting` indicates that the test involves multiple steps and needs to wait for an answer before determining success or failure.

Moving on, in the example HTML source code file, the method `testManager.setTestCases` associates the tests with the test manager. The test manager iterates through all of the tests defined in the variable `testsToRun` and creates a proxy that is an encapsulation to the originally defined method. You can read more about this in Chapter 2. When running tests, don't reference the variable `testsToRun`, but rather the test manager variable `testManager`.

After the test manager method `setTestCases` completes initialization, you can execute the tests. In the example HTML source code, tables (`<table>`) are dynamically defined to contain references to the tests. The first table contains buttons used to execute the tests as a group or individually. To run all of the tests, call the method `testManager.runAll()`. To run an individual test, execute the method `testManager.[testname]`. The second table is used for generating the logging output.

Let's first test the redirection and addition, as illustrated by the following code snippet.

Source: /jaxson/trunk/website/ROOT/calculator/testcontract.html

```
var entityURL = "";

var testsToRun = {
    testVerifyAdd : function(){
        info( "testVerifyAdd", "Running testVerifyRedirection first");
        testsToRun.testVerifyRedirection();
        info( "testVerifyAdd", "Finishing running testVerifyRedirection");
        var state = new Object();
        state.number1 = 1;
        state.number2 = 2;

        var buffer = JSON.stringify( state);
        info( "testVerifyAdd", "JSON Buffer (" + buffer + ")");
        var request = new Synchronous();
        request.complete = function( statusCode, statusText,
                responseText, responseXML) {
            var response = JSON.parse( responseText);
            info( "testVerifyAdd.complete", "Add Result (" + responseText + ")");
            assertEquals( "JSON result", 3, response.result);
            testManager.success( "addTest");
        }
        request.post( entityURL, "application/json", buffer.length, buffer);
```

```
    }
};
...
    <tr>
        <td>
            <input onclick="testManager.testVerifyAdd()"
                type="button" value="Test Add" /></td>
        <td id="addTest">Not run</td>
    </tr>
```

The code snippet illustrates the JavaScript code that contains the test, and the HTML snippet shows how to call the test defined by the JavaScript. The variable `entityURL` references the contract URL used to perform an addition. The variable is not assigned a predefined URL, because the URL is created dynamically in another test not illustrated in the snippet. Contained within the definition of the variable `testsToRun` is a function `testVerifyAdd` that represents the test used to perform an addition.

To run the test, the test manager calls the dynamically defined method `testManager.testVerifyAdd`, which calls `testsToRun.testVerifyAdd`. The purpose of creating a proxy to the test is to enable the test manager to manage the test harness that calls the test.

In the implementation of `testVerifyAdd`, the not-illustrated test `testVerifyRedirection` is called. The `testVerifyRedirection` executes to verify that the variable `entityURL` will reference a valid URL. Notice how the not illustrated test is referenced using the variable `testsToRun` and not `testManager`. Earlier, I stated that you should call `testManager` to run a test, and not the test directly. That rule of thumb only applies if you want to run a test and are not already running a test. The main reason why you wouldn't use `testManager` is that if an exception is generated, you want the currently running test to exit. Calling a test using `testManager` within a test results in the exception being caught and the current test continuing as if everything went OK. Of course, this doesn't mean that you might not want this behavior, and you could call a test from `testManager`. The choice is yours, but it's more important to understand the reason for calling each.

Having called the not-illustrated `testVerifyRedirection` test, the test of performing an addition has started. The test will verify that adding 1 and 2 results in the value of 3. The data is stored in a JavaScript object instance state that you instantiate and assign. You serialize the state of the object to the JSON format using the method `JSON.stringify`.

Once you convert the state into a string buffer, you send it to the server using the method `request.post`. The method `request.post` is an HTTP POST request, fulfilling the requirements of REST. When the `request.post` method responds, the method `request.complete` is called. In the anonymous method implementation of `request.complete`, the returned buffer is formatted using JSON. To convert the JSON buffer into a state, you call the method `JSON.parse`. You assign the returned state to the variable response. The state contains the value of the addition, and the value is tested using the method `assertEquals`. If the value is not 3, then the testing framework triggers, catches, and processes an exception.

Without going into the details of the server side yet, and assuming that the server side is working, Figure 1-14 shows the results of running the tests.

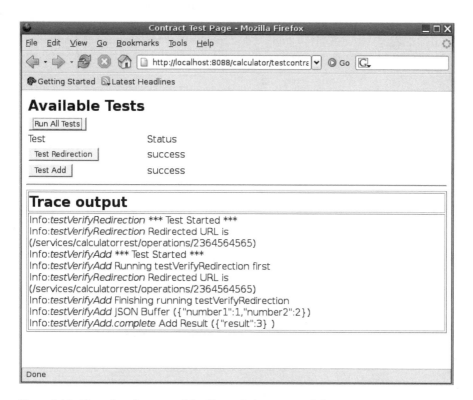

Figure 1-14. *Running the tests with all tests being successful*

Figure 1-15 illustrates what a failed test looks like.

Figure 1-15. *Running the tests with one of the tests failing*

With either example, you can see which tests were successful and which tests failed. When a test fails, an error states why the test failed. Additionally, informational messages are generated so that you know what your tests are doing and what data is being sent.

The test is written as a single test and doesn't constitute a complete contract test. When you implement the client-side tests of your contract, you'll want to employ test-driven development techniques that include tests that succeed and tests that fail.

Now let's shift focus from the client side to the server side. You don't want to implement a complete working server-side implementation, but rather implement the Mock URL layer. For the scope of this solution, Java is used.

The purpose of the Mock URL layer is to imitate and implement server-side functionality. Imitating and implementing server-side functionality is tricky, because you can only implement targeted test cases. In the case of the example, that means implementing the case of adding 1 and 2. Of course, the addition of 1 and 2 is trivial, and in the case of the Mock URL, you could implement it within seconds. However, there are more complicated cases, so you shouldn't be tempted to provide a solution.

The focus of the Mock URL layer is to provide correct requests and responses for specific tests. By implementing logic, you're setting yourself up for an error because the logic needs to be tested. Let's put it this way: Imagine implementing the trivial addition of two numbers. How do you know that your implementation will work properly? The answer is that you write tests. However, that doesn't answer the question properly, because how do you know that the tests are implemented properly? The answer is that you don't, and that is the purpose of the Mock URL layer.

The following source code implements the request and response of the add contract.

Source: /jaxson.java.tests/devspace/jaxson/tests/calculator/mockurl/DoMockAdd.java

```java
public class DoMockAdd extends MockUrlTestCaseBase {
    public void processRequest(HttpServletRequest request,
        HttpServletResponse response) throws ServletException {
        assertAreEqualJSONObject( request, "requestadd.json");
        try {
            FileWriter.writeFileObject( "application/json",
                response, "responseadd.json");
        }
        catch( Exception e) {
            throw new ServletException( "Could not write file response", e);
        }
        response.setStatus( 200);
    }
}
```

Two method calls are shown in bold. The method assertAreEqualJSONObject compares the sent data stored by the Java servlet to the file requestadd.json. If the sent data matches the contents of the file, then the next method call writeFileObject is executed. The purpose of writeFileObject is to send the contents of the file responseadd.json to the client. The files requestadd.json and responseadd.json represent predefined contracts used to add two numbers together.

The class DoMockAdd has no idea what the purpose of the operation is. It only knows that if the request matches a file, then a response based on another file is sent. The Mock URL layer implementation is simple but can only deal with a single case of adding two specific numbers and generating a single response. In the Mock URL layer example, you perform multiple tests to see which test case is matched. If a test case is matched, then the appropriate response is sent. If no test cases matches, then no response is sent, and an error is generated.

The method assertAreEqualJSONObject compares the JSON data that is sent to the JSON data in a file. Don't be misled into believing that a byte-to-byte comparison is performed. The method assertAreEqualJSONObject performs a logical comparison based on the format of the data. This is important because otherwise, whitespace or other characters that don't influence the state of the data could cause a test to fail. You don't want a test failing because of a different formatting, unless of course you desire testing a specific formatting of the data. For example, XML is another technology where most likely you don't want whitespace to cause the test to fail.

After you've created the Mock URL layer, you can test the client scripts, which will verify the contracts. Based on the working client and server side, subbing in a working client or server implementation should not change the behavior. If the behavior is changed, then the client test scripts and Mock URL implementations are inconsistent. You want neither the client nor the server to know if it's running against a test or an actual implementation.

You should remember the following points when creating contracts:

- The Mock URL layer represents the definitive contract between the client and server.

- The Mock URL layer implements the contracts using predefined files for requests and responses.

- The Mock URL layer can only test targeted test cases and should not use any code that will be used in implementation, since the logic might have bugs.

- When comparing the sent data with the data in the file, use a logical comparison and not a byte-to-byte comparison. A byte-to-byte comparison could cause whitespace, which has nothing to do with the state of an object, and would cause a test to fail. The exception to this rule is if the test requires verifying the whitespace.

- The Mock URL layer performs multiple tests on which request is being sent and sends the appropriate response. In most cases, the request is tested using a file, and the response is based on another file.

- If you must implement logic in the Mock URL layer, make sure that it's extremely well tested and stable, as that implementation will serve as a reference for how the contract between the client and server functions.

- The client-side tests that test the contract represent an implementation of how to use the contract and are used to verify the correctness of the server-side implementation.

- You develop the client-side contract tests and Mock URL layer together using test-driven development techniques.

- You can implement the client-side contract tests in any programming language, but since this book and most likely your application are JavaScript-based, it makes sense to use JavaScript.

- Neither the client- nor the server-side implementations or tests should ever have any dependencies on each other. This way, you can replace the client tests with the client implementation without causing problems in the Mock URL layer or server implementation.

1-4. Testing a Dynamic Contract

The previous example, which illustrated how to create a contract, didn't cover the dynamic aspect of the contract and the problem of redirection in particular. Redirection was not covered because redirection is a part of a bigger problem that is part of the Ajax and REST paradigm.

Problem

You want to test a contract that is dynamic.

Solution

The "Understanding the Definition and Philosophy of Ajax" section argued that Ajax allows you to create and manipulate content dynamically. The dynamism extends to the contract, which can involve the following techniques:

- Definition of a specific URL based on a general URL

- Definition of specific content based on a specific URL

In either example, a general URL or general content reference is hard-coded or referenced in the client side. The hard-coded general reference is then converted into a specific reference. To understand what is involved, let's focus on the calculator example and the redirection part of the addition operation. The following code represents the HTTP request that the client would make to convert the general addition operation URL into a specific addition operation URL:

```
GET /services/calculatorrest/operations HTTP/1.1
User-Agent: Jakarta Commons-HttpClient/3.0
Host: localhost:8100
```

An HTTP GET is executed, and the URL /services/calculatorrest/operations is called using the HTTP 1.1 protocol. This part of the request is required. In the example, the HTTP headers are not required, but to implement the Permutations[14] pattern, the headers most likely are required. For this test, the required response is as follows:

```
HTTP/1.1 201 Redirecting+a+user
Location: /services/calculatorrest/operations/2364564565
```

The response looks a bit odd, because the HTTP code 201, and not 307 or 302, is returned. For those readers who have no idea what the response codes mean, let me clarify. If you make a request and the server wants to redirect you to the real temporary URL, then you use a response code in the 3xx series. In the case of the calculator application, the redirect is temporary, as many addition operations could be performed. Therefore, the appropriate response would be either 307 or 302. However, that is not the correct answer for multiple reasons.

Returning either a 307 or 302 is not correct in this case for the following reasons:

- The browser makes the redirection automatically and thus doesn't give the XMLHttpRequest object the redirected URL.

- Doing an automatic redirection is not useful, because you may want to execute multiple queries and would not want to perform multiple redirections.

- When making a request on the base URL, you're not doing a redirect to a known resource, but rather creating a resource that you need to redirect to.

In the World Wide Web Consortium (W3C) HTTP 1.1 specification, the 201 response code is used to indicate that calling the original URL has created a new resource that can be referenced at the new URL, which is defined in the Location HTTP header. Therefore, even though you could have used 307 or 302, the more appropriate answer is 201.

---

14. Christian Gross, *Ajax Patterns and Best Practices* (Berkeley, CA: Apress, 2006), p. 111.

From an implementation perspective, the identifier 2364564565 is generated dynamically and cannot be predicted. From a testing perspective, this is a problem because you cannot write a test for the identifier 2364564565. If you were to do so, you'd violate the principle of being able to substitute the Mock URL layer for a server implementation. The reason is because the client test would expect a specific identifier that the server implementation cannot, nor should, generate.

The solution is not to test for a specific identifier, but rather to test for the existence and format of the identifier, as illustrated by the following test.

Source: /jaxson/trunk/website/ROOT/calculator/testcontract.html

```
var baseURL = "/services/calculatorrest/operations";
var entityURL = "";

    testVerifyRedirection : function(){
        var request = new Synchronous();

        request.complete = function( statusCode, statusText,
            responseText, responseXML){
            if ( statusCode != 201) {
                fail( "Expected 201 received " + statusCode);
            }
            entityURL = this._xmlhttp.getResponseHeader( "Location");
            if ( entityURL == null || entityURL.length <= baseURL.length) {
                fail( "Redirected URL cannot be null");
            }
            info( "testVerifyRedirection", "Redirected URL is (" + entityURL + ")");
            testManager.success( "urltest");
        }
        request.get( baseURL);
    },
```

In the test, the hard-coded reference URL is stored in the variable baseURL. The dynamically created URL is stored in the variable entityURL, which is assigned an empty string. The test testVerifyRedirection has a single purpose and that is to call the hard-coded general reference. Calling the hard-coded general reference returns the specific dynamic reference. To implement the contract, you must test two things. The first is the return of the status code 201, and the second is the generation of the identifier. Testing for the status code 201 is simple and involves a decision.

Testing for the dynamic identifier is a bit more complicated, but the approach taken in the test is simple. The test contains two verifications to test the existence of the dynamically generated identifier. The two verifications are the two lowest layers of testing a dynamic identifier. The following lists the verifications from the lowest to highest level of verifiability:

- *Testing for the existence of the data*: Typically, testing for the existence is a *null* or *not-null* test. If the test is not null, it doesn't mean that the data is correct, but it does verify that there is data. The test assumes that the data contains the dynamic identifier.

- *Testing for the existence of the identifier in the data*: Testing for the existence means knowing about the nature of the dynamic identifier. Typically, that means knowing what the original data is and how the dynamically generated data should appear.

- *Testing the formatting of the dynamically generated identifier*: Testing the formatting means knowing something about the format of the identifier. This could mean knowing that the identifier is numeric, a certain length, or must contain certain characters. The calculator example doesn't test for the correct formatting of the dynamically generated identifier, but if it had, the test would have been length-based and numerically based. Be careful when testing for the formatting, as the dynamic generation of temporary data might switch from one version to another.

When testing dynamic data, start at the lowest level and perform the tests incrementally. Don't start at the highest level right from the start. Doing so makes a dangerous assumption that dynamic data exists. For example, if you only test for correct formatting, you won't be able to discern between the test failure of missing dynamic data and incorrectly formatted dynamic data.

The following code illustrates a Java implementation of the URL redirection:

```
public class RedirectionImplementation extends MockUrlTestCaseBase {

 public class RedirectionImplementation extends MockUrlTestCaseBase {
    public void processRequest(HttpServletRequest request,
        HttpServletResponse response) {
      this.generateRedirection( response, 201,
          request.getRequestURI() + "/2364564565");
    }
}
```

The bold code illustrates how the redirection is implemented. Notice that the dynamic identifier is hard-coded. There is no logic. If the same client called the redirection multiple times, it would receive the same identifier. This appears to be a violation of the contract, yet it is not a violation. The contract for the calculator says to redirect to a resource that you can use to perform a calculation. The client cannot make assumptions, but the server can, because the server is in control of generating the dynamic identifiers. To turn the table, if the client has the responsibility to define the dynamic identifier, then the server must accept the dynamic identifier from the client and use it for Mock URL purposes.

You could generate the dynamic identifier dynamically, but how would you test the correctness of the contract? This goes back to the problem illustrated in the previous section, which said the Mock URL layer has a dual role of defining what the contract needs to look like. If the Mock URL layer contains logic that is reused in the server implementation, then a correctness problem can exist. Therefore, if you must have variety in dynamic identifiers, create a few of them and then use a random number algorithm to choose between them.

When testing dynamic contracts, remember the following points:

- Figure out who is responsible for generating the dynamic data and who consumes the dynamic data.

- The generator of dynamic data can define specific test cases and make assumptions about how the data is formatted.

- The consumer of the dynamic data is responsible for receiving the dynamic data and applying three levels of verification when verifying the correctness of the data.

- Test cases don't always support dynamic data. For example, the provider might not support a reference made to a data format. In this case, the generator of the dynamic data must generate an error, and the consumer must verify that an error is generated. Don't attempt to accommodate with warnings or informational messages. You would never expect a plumber to know how to fix a broken tooth.

1-5. Testing the Client-Side Logic

Problem

You want to effectively test your application's client-side logic.

Theory

Testing GUI code tends not to be a productive task because of the complications that arise. The main complication is how to test the correctness of a user interface. Imagine a situation where clicking a button causes a table to be filled with data. Now imagine that when a check box is checked and the button is clicked again, a different table is filled with content. The fact that clicking the same button results in two different generated outputs is frustrating and complicates GUI testing.

One of the main reasons why testing a GUI is complicated is because the GUI is a black box, and the user cannot access the individual GUI elements. Figure 1-16 illustrates an example application that is a black box.

Figure 1-16. *RealPlayer application that is a black box*

In Figure 1-16, RealPlayer is used to play some media file. Imagine running a media-file generation service. Testing the format of the media is not a problem and is akin to testing the contract. You also need to test if a client such as RealPlayer can consume, process, and display the media. Figuring this out requires taking a snapshot and then checking if the bits and bytes are displayed properly. However, something as simple as taking a snapshot is difficult, because the utility to take a snapshot in Figure 1-16 kept blacking out the content. Thus, you're left wondering how to test the functionality of your data stream when played in RealPlayer.

The simplest but probably most expensive and error-prone solution is to have a human look at RealPlayer and say, "Yes, the content is being played," or "No, the content has problems." A human could carry out the same tests repeatedly and then verify whether the tests worked. The problem with getting a human to do this is that humans make errors when doing the same thing over and over again. Humans are not incapable of doing the same thing over and over again, but they get bored and the mind wanders. Humans are much better at spotting problems if the menial work is replaced with automation.

Automating the testing of RealPlayer is difficult, because RealPlayer is not under your control. It is programmed using a traditional programming language. Traditional programming languages create black boxes that a user cannot get around. In the old days of Windows 3.1, an application could access another application's window handles. That ability made it possible to do interesting things, but the cost was that hackers could wreak havoc on an application. Today, applications are not allowed to access another application's GUI elements willy-nilly.

Solution

The only effective way to test a GUI is to have access to the source code and test the layer that the GUI calls. The idea is not to test the GUI, but rather to test the logic that the GUI calls. Of course, this only works if the GUI layer contains absolutely no logic and no state. This is more complicated because it means that the GUI is a copy of the state held in memory. Many developers consider this a good thing, and I'm not about to debate the merits or problems of this strategy. Instead, I want to highlight that Ajax and DHTML applications are unique in that they allow you to have your cake and eat it too.

With DHTML, two completely unrelated HTML pages can communicate with each other and slice and dice each other's data. In a traditional programming approach, you wouldn't like to have other applications changing your look and feel to suit their needs. Yet this is an inherent behavior of DHTML. This feature can be put to good use when creating tests. Specifically, a controller HTML page will load and manipulate the HTML page to be tested. From an architecture perspective, it looks similar to Figure 1-17.

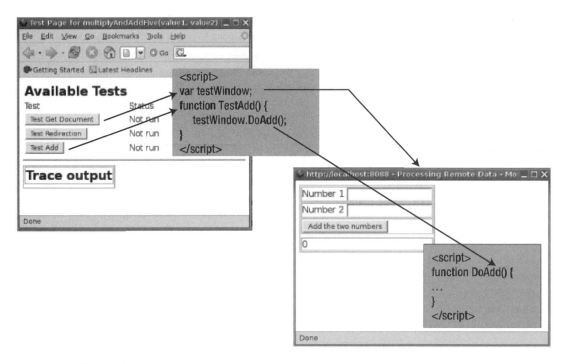

Figure 1-17. *Test controller architecture*

The browser window in the upper left-hand corner is the test controller, which contains a number of buttons used to test individual features. The test controller button Test Get Document is used open a new instance of the HTML window to be tested. It assigns the instance to the script variable testWindow. When clicked, the button Test Add executes the method TestAdd, which then calls a method DoAdd defined in the new instance of the HTML window. This is a unique feature of DHTML, in that one HTML window can reference elements in another HTML window even though both windows are unrelated.

The test controller uses the identical testing routines as outlined in the "Coding the Contract Using Test-Driven Development Techniques" section. The test controller example uses the calculator example.

To be able to test the calculator application, copy and modify the empty template file that represents a test. Add the three tests used to verify the correctness of the calculator. There were two unique contracts in the contract recipe. The additional test is the test to open a new window that will load the initial HTML page used to add two numbers.

The modification of the template test page involves adding some tests, as well as some user interface elements used to instantiate the tests. I won't focus on the user interface elements, as the details have already been explained in the "Coding the Contract Using Test-Driven Development Techniques" section. Instead, I'll focus on the tests that are executed, as they are unique in that they don't use the XMLHttpRequest object directly. The tests execute functionality in the other HTML page.

In the following implementation of the testsToRun variable, note that the declaration has been abbreviated for clarity purposes.

Source: /jaxson/trunk/website/ROOT/calculator/testcalculator.html

```
var testsToRun = {
    testOpenWindow : function() {
    },
    testVerifyRedirection : function() {
    },
    testVerifyCalculation : function() {
    },
    performCalculation : function( event) {
    }
}
```

The code shows four test functions, though I mentioned only three. The additional function is part of a single test and is required due to the asynchronous nature of the HTTP requests. If all tests were run, then the order would be testOpenWindow, testVerifyRedirection, performCalculation, and then testVerifyCalculation. The order is important, because the code first opens the calculator window, then verifies that the operation's URL has been redirected, and finally carries out the addition operation.

The first test is the function testOpenWindow, which is used to open the HTML window that contains the calculator application. The source code for the test is as follows:

```
testGetContent : function() {
    var url = "/calculator/calculatorajaxrest";

    if (!testWindow.closed && testWindow.location) {
        testWindow.location.href = url;
    }
    else {
        testWindow =window.open(url,'name','height=400,width=550');
    }
    if (testWindow && testWindow.baseURL) {
        testManager.success( "createwindow");
    }
    else {
        testManager.failed( "createwindow");
    }
}
```

The variable url references the root URL, which is used to load the HTML page to be tested. Think of it as the URL you would type in an HTML browser to load the HTML page to perform the calculation. To open a new window, call the method window.open. If the testWindow is already open, use the property testWindow.location.href to navigate to the HTML page. Verifying that the page loaded properly is a bit more complicated and requires a two-step verification. First, check if the variable testWindow references something. Second, test if the variable testWindow.baseURL exists. This example assumes a local area network, where the loading of the page happens quickly. If it takes time to load the page, put a timer into the code and wait for the page to load.

The second step says, "If a variable declaration exists, the HTML page must be the one that I'm interested in." This is an effective test, but can easily be broken. The existence of a variable declaration proves nothing other than the declaration of the variable. It doesn't prove that the HTML page is what it is supposed to be. Therefore, when verifying the identity of an HTML page, come up with some type of unique identifier convention and use it for your application infrastructure.

Running the `testOpenWindow` test results in something similar to Figure 1-18.

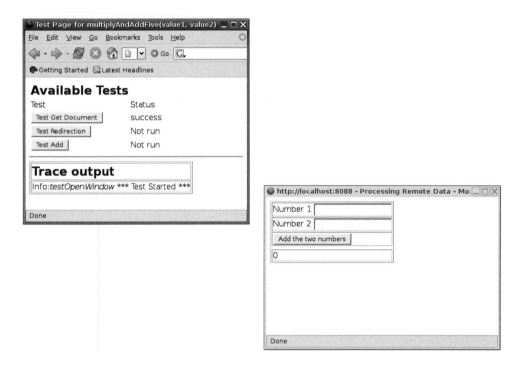

Figure 1-18. *Running the* `testOpenWindow` *test*

Running the `testOpenWindow` test results in the lower right-hand corner window being opened. When the test completes successfully, the result success is generated in the test controller window.

The next test, which is implemented in the test function `testVerifyRedirection`, is to verify that the URL has been redirected.

```
testVerifyRedirection : function() {
    var origURL = "/services/calculatorrest/operations";
    document.getElementById( "urltest").innerHTML = "<b>Failed</b>";
    if ( testWindow.calcURL == null ||
        testWindow.calcURL.length <= origURL.length) {
        fail( "Test URL Verification");
    }
    testManager.success( "urltest");
},
```

The verification test routine references the variable calcURL, which is defined in the HTML page. The test is the same as the one used in the "Testing a Dynamic Contract" section. Again, in this test example, the internal state of the HTML page is used to perform a verification. Many programmers would consider this a fragile test, because you could easily change the variable name and break the test. This is correct, but when using test-driven development, it quickly becomes obvious that a test is not working.

The last test is used to test the addition of two numbers and is implemented as follows:

```
testVerifyCalculation : function() {
    var state = newwindow.document.getElementById(
        'htmlform').morphing.getState();
    assertEquals( "Test Number addition verification", 3, state.result);
    testManager.success( "addTest");
},
performCalculation : function( event) {
    var state = new Object();
    state.number1 = 1;
    state.number2 = 2;
    newwindow.document.getElementById(
        'htmlform').morphing.setState( state);
    newwindow.DoNavigation( event);
    testManager.waiting( "addTest");
    window.setTimeout( "testManager.testVerifyCalculation()", 4000);
}
```

The test addition of two numbers has two functions because of the way an addition is performed. A user would enter two numbers into the text boxes of Figure 1-18 and then click the Add Two Numbers button. However, the result of adding the two numbers might not be given right away, because the answer is generated asynchronously. The test routine needs to wait, so you need to use the method window.setTimeout. Use the function performCalculation to execute the calculation, and call the function testVerifyCalculation shortly thereafter to verify the calculation.

Both the functions performCalculation and testVerifyCalculation illustrate how a contract defined by the HTML page can be created using the Representation Morphing[15] pattern. Using a contract the HTML page can be integrated into a bigger application using component technologies.

When implementing the tests for a client, remember the following points:

- Implement a test controller that controls the page to be tested. Avoid embedding the test controller into the page to be tested, as that will complicate your development.

- HTML pages that will be tested need to expose a contract that the test controller or other HTML pages can use.

- HTML allows other pages to inspect its structure, which is a good thing, but be careful of referencing specific variables, as that will create fragile references.

- Develop your test controller and HTML page using test-driven development. Ideally, you won't ever need to click any buttons in your application.

---

15. Christian Gross, *Ajax Patterns and Best Practices* (Berkeley, CA: Apress, 2006), p. 197.

1-6. Managing Ajax Security and Intellectual Property

Problem

You need to know which security and intellectual property issues exist with Ajax applications and how to manage them effectively.

When developing Ajax applications, developers often ask if any security and intellectual property measures exist. The quick answer is, no!

Solution

If you're developing Ajax applications, then anyone can view whatever JavaScript you write. As much as I'd like to say that you can somehow disable view source, you can't. Even if you did manage to disable the context menu, users can simply use a tool such as `curl` or `wget` to get the content manually. My advice is to get over it and accept the fact that Ajax applications by default are source-available applications.

If you wish to control access to the server-side logic, then remember that Ajax is a Web service–oriented technology. By granularizing the client, you can keep certain pieces of logic private on the server. If you're concerned about protecting your intellectual property, then a Web service strategy is the best strategy. Also, don't fool yourself into believing that if your application were coded in C++ or Java or some other language, you'd be safe from reverse engineering. The matter of the fact is that you are not, and there is no way to protect yourself. Using some kind of toolkit to decrypt your encrypted code doesn't work, because toolkits define standard APIs that can be easily traced. In the original PC DOS days, you would statically compile into your application all the libraries you needed. These days, you use shared libraries, which make it easy to intercept API calls, which in turn make it easy to reverse engineer any application. It is trivial.

Of course, you might not care about protecting the intellectual property and might be more concerned about protecting your security. Using the proper communication channels, you can protect your security with Ajax. You can use one of two approaches: Secure Socket Layer (SSL) or a private communications channel. It is assumed that all pages and script references use relative URLs, so that if an SSL connection is used for the main page, everything else will be loaded using the SSL connection.

The SSL approach is common and involves using encryption managed by the HTTP server. Figure 1-19 illustrates the request that the client would make to use SSL.

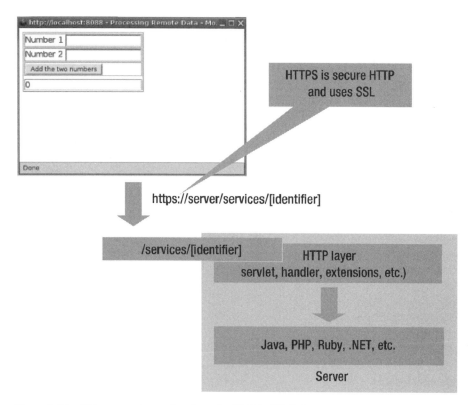

Figure 1-19. *SSL request is made when the URL is HTTPS.*

When the browser makes a request that is prefixed with the identifier HTTPS, then SSL is implied. To be able to make SSL requests, the server has to make an SSL port available. This involves getting a server certificate and is an administrative issue. With SSL, your communication is mostly secure because anybody listening would see traffic with encrypted packets. With SSL, it is possible to execute a man-in-the-middle attack. Without getting into the details of encryption, this is possible because SSL doesn't manage who can access your service.

I'm not trying to make SSL seem insecure, because it is not. For example, when they use SSL, most browsers verify the identity of the server. This means that if you access a server that identifies itself as being Amazon, then you can be certain it is Amazon. Problems arise when applications don't look closely at the server identifier. And believe me, not many people verify the certificates. Often this means tightly controlling which certificates can be added and manipulated in the browser. Again, this is an administration issue.

Using access control identifiers to control access to a Web service is a good idea, but it does open you up to hackers. Alternatively, you could create a secure channel, as illustrated Figure 1-20.

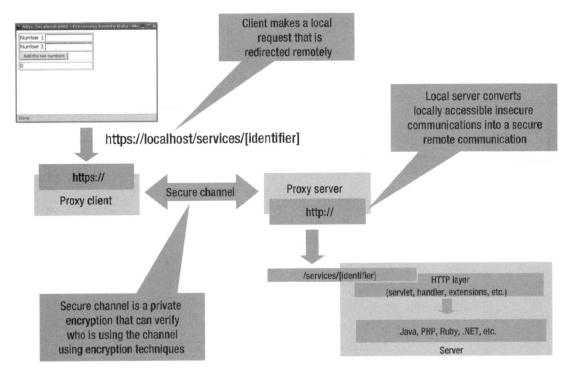

Figure 1-20. *Secure channel request*

The client doesn't make a remote request, but rather makes a local request. A locally running process captures the local request and securely packages the request, which is sent to a remote process. The remote process unwraps the package and makes a local request. The communication between the two processes is a secure channel that the client and server applications don't influence. For each, it appears that the request is local.

The advantage of this technique is the ability of the paired running processes to verify each other and allow only authorized and authenticated communications. The paired process approach is a secure approach, so long as the keys are exchanged properly. Again, that is an administrative issue. To realize the paired process approach, you could use one of the following open source software technologies: SSH, Stunnel, or OpenVPN.

There is another approach to exchanging data securely, but I don't recommend it. You could implement your own encryption using publicly available encryption libraries, but I don't believe that you should manage your own security. Security is a complex topic, and some experts spend every working day of their lives figuring out how to secure systems. Even if you spend a week, a month, or even two months on the topic, you won't have come close to the issues relating to a secure system. Thus, leave security to the experts and use the available security. On the other hand, this doesn't mean that you cannot ask intelligent questions and suggest the type of system you would like.

When thinking about Ajax security and intellectual property, remember the following points:

- There is no intellectual property protection with an Ajax application.

- There is no intellectual property protection with traditional applications either.

- To keep your intellectual property private, use Web services.

- In most cases, SSL is good enough for managing security.

- Use a secured channel approach to strictly control access to your Web services.

- Don't try to manage security yourself, unless you happen to be an administrator or security specialist. Security is a complex topic that requires a good understanding of the issues.

CHAPTER 2

■■■

JavaScript Recipes

When you write an Ajax application, you use the JavaScript programming language. JavaScript is a duck-typed programming language, and one of the main questions when using it is how to best structure the code. Do you write your code using object-oriented techniques? Do you write your code using dynamic language programming techniques? Or do you use functions and no objects? The answer is that you use all of the aforementioned techniques and then some.

JavaScript represents an evolution in programming capabilities. Sure, some things do not work as they would in a traditional programming language, but that does not mean there is a problem. In fact, I would say JavaScript frees you up to write code that is more flexible and maintainable because it is more compact and easier to assemble. Think about it: what do you normally do in an object-oriented programming (OOP) language? Your main task in traditional OOP is sorting out the referencing, for example, how to make a dog class reference a person class without hard-coding it, but this is trivial in JavaScript—you just tell it.

JavaScript requires that you break certain traditional programming habits, and that is what the recipes in this chapter cover. In this chapter, you'll learn how to write reusable, maintainable code in JavaScript's dynamic, duck-typed, object-oriented way.

■**Note** Some things explained in this chapter will run counter to what you have learned or coded. But remember, this is JavaScript; it is an evolution in programming. In other programming languages, you would implement some of the techniques mentioned in this chapter because it would make maintenance and reusability an absolute nightmare, but these techniques work well in JavaScript.

2-1. Understanding JavaScript and Types

Problem

You want to work around the fact that JavaScript does not have types declared for its variables.

Theory

JavaScript code does not have any variables with a declared type. The lack of typed variables is apparent when you declare functions. That said, not having typed variable declarations does not mean JavaScript has no types or no type safety.

Let's start out with the simple declaration of a function, as illustrated by the following example.

Source: /website/ROOT/ajaxrecipes/javascript/expectations.html

```
function AddTwoNumbers(num1, num2) {
  return num1 + num2;
}
```

The AddTwoNumbers function has two parameters, num1 and num2, and represents two individual numbers. In the implementation of AddTwoNumbers, the two numbers are added together and the value is returned. This way of declaring and using a function is common in other programming languages.

The result of adding the numbers num1 and num2 is returned to the caller as follows:

```
assertEquals(4, AddTwoNumbers(2, 2));
```

The assertEquals function is used to verify that when the AddTwoNumbers function is called with 2 and 2, 4 is generated as a result. When you run the code, everything works as expected, but can you feel assured that everything is correct? The answer is no, you cannot feel assured, because some misleading assumptions are being made.

The AddTwoNumbers function declares two numbers, but the assumption that num1 and num2 are numbers is not reasonable. In JavaScript, variables are not type declared. Once assigned to a type, a variable is type-safe, but you don't know what the type is until the variable is assigned. Therefore, with respect to the function, the types num1 and num2 are not known.

Solution

A safer way to implement AddTwoNumbers is as follows.

Source: /website/ROOT/ajaxrecipes/javascript/expectations.html

```
function AddTwoNumbersDisplayTypes( num1, num2) {
  var val1 = parseInt( num1);
  var val2 = parseInt( num2);

  if( isNaN( val1) || isNaN( val2)) {
     throw new Error( "num1, (and/or) num2 are neither a number or string");
  }
  info( "AddTwoNumbersDisplayTypes", typeof( num1));
  info( "AddTwoNumbersDisplayTypes", typeof( num2));
  return val1 + val2;
}
```

In the modified implementation, the parseInt method, which is used to convert a string into a number, is applied to both num1 and num2. The result of parseInt is an integer value that allows num1 and num2 to be added together. The num1 and num2 parameters are verified to be numbers using the isNaN operator. The return value of isNaN is a true or false value. If either of the values returns false, then num1 or num2 is not a number and an exception is thrown. In this modified implementation, it would seem that very little could go wrong.

Looking at the implementation of adding two numbers, you may wonder how using a dynamic language like JavaScript is an advantage over using another programming language. The additional code used to verify whether or not the correct types are used would be tedious if that sort of logic was implemented for all functions. In other programming languages such as Java and C#, adding two numbers together safely is completely trivial. Granted, if you are going to perform a large number of numerical calculations, then JavaScript is probably not the most suitable programming languages. But when you need to write an application to get something done, and you don't want to mess around with the lower-level details of which type does what, JavaScript is the better choice.

The modified source code is an example of writing defensive code, which is a good practice, but don't take it too far and let it make you paranoid. You want code that does what it is supposed to do, and when it doesn't, it should generate explicit errors—in other words, you want code that screams when an error occurs. The code that captures the scream should then do something with it.

When writing functions, the objective is to write an implementation that has defensive code appropriate to the expectations of the function. When writing code in a dynamic language such as JavaScript, expectations and conventions play extremely important roles. When writing code using a programming language such C# or Java, programmers are expected to account for every situation that works and does not work.

Let's therefore rewrite our addition function to implement our expectations and use a convention. The first step is to write the tests and think about what is and isn't appropriate. The following implementation reflects our expectations.

Source: /website/ROOT/ajaxrecipes/javascript/expectations.html

```
classical_add_display_types : function() {
  assertEquals( 4, AddTwoNumbersDisplayTypes( 2, 2));
  assertEquals( 4, AddTwoNumbersDisplayTypes( "2", 2));
  try {
    AddTwoNumbersDisplayTypes( new Object(), 2);
    testManager.failed();
    return;
  }
  catch( e ) {
    info( "classical_add_display_types", "Expected error (" + e.toString() + ")");
  }
  testManager.success();
},
```

The first two `assertEquals` method calls reflect the expectation that we could add a number that is either a string or a numeric value. The expectation of adding two numeric values is obvious because typically you add two numbers together. The expectation of being able to recognize two buffers as numbers is appropriate because we are dealing with HTML forms. HTML form elements store their values as buffers. So when performing mathematical operations using data from HTML form elements, we expect the formulas to handle the conversion from buffers to numeric values.

After the method calls that implement tests of our expectations, the code within the exception block implements something we would expect not to work. Calling the addition with an object, where a property of the object might reference a number, is not something we expect the addition function to figure out. Here we expect an error to be generated. The code that is not expected to work, or at least can be expected to fail, is wrapped in an exception block. The role of the expectation is required in both the function and the caller of the function, as illustrated in the example.

In JavaScript, functions must meet certain expectations, so you should observe the following points when writing them:

- Variables are not declared using types, and when the variables are not assigned they are considered typeless.

- Once assigned, variables look, feel, and behave like types.

- When implementing functions, you are writing blocks of code that implement expectations.

- To properly meet expectations, you need to write tests.

- When expectations are not met, the errors should be obvious and their accompanying messages should be explanatory.

- If you want to verify what type a variable is, use `typeof`. Do not use a simple object or check.

- When implementing expectations, don't be paranoid and attempt to create a type system by verifying the exact details of every variable and every parameter.

2-2. Coding Using Conventions and Not Configurations

Problem

You want to make your JavaScript constructs more efficient by applying the Rails "convention over configuration" principle to them.

Theory

You may already be familiar with the programming platform Ruby on Rails, which is used to build Web applications. The focus of this recipe is not Ruby on Rails, but one aspect of Ruby on Rails—namely, convention over configuration (see `http://en.wikipedia.org/wiki/Ruby_on_Rails` for more on this).

Imagine writing tests and realizing that you use a same set of instructions over and over again. When you convert the code from the repeated code into generic code, you are creating a framework. The framework can be created in one of two ways. The first way is to create infrastructure and wire it together, and the second is to make assumptions about your code. Consider the following JavaScript JsUnit test:

```
var testsToRun = {
  // Start JavaScript code for test cases here
  testPlainVanilla : function() {
    // Some code
    testManager.success();
  }
```

```
  // End JavaScript code for test cases
};

testManager.setTestCases( testsToRun);
```

The details of what the variables and classes do are not relevant. What is relevant is how they are wired together. The testsToRun variable contains a number of methods that are used to execute particular tests. When each test has completed successfully, the testManager.success method is called. The testsToRun variable is not associated with any other method, data member, or function—simply put, testsToRun is hanging like a flag in the wind.

Of course, we don't want testsToRun to hang in the wind; we want the tests to be executed. The tests are executed by the testManager variable, and testManager has no knowledge of testsToRun. The challenge is figure out how to make testManager aware of testsToRun and, once it's aware, to execute the contained tests. The wiring of testManager to testsToRun can be a convention or a configuration.

In the preceding example, the solution used to make testManager aware of testsToRun is *configuration*. In classical programming terms, you can think of configuration as being a file on a hard disk with pieces of text that are parsed by an algorithm. That process is a configuration, but it's just one type of configuration. Another type known as *programmatic configuration* involves the source code telling the classes how everything is wired together. I am not going to cover the advantages and disadvantages of the different configuration types—suffice it to say that configuration is used to wire together unknown implementations to create a working system.

Configuration is often used because it is an easy way to create a working system. Configuration does not require a deduction algorithm; rather, it needs just an algorithm that can parse a configuration file or a programmer who can wire implementations together. In a nutshell, configuration requires the programmer or administrator to do some of the heavy lifting of figuring out what piece is wired to the other piece. If something doesn't work, then the system can say, "Oops, that doesn't work. Try again."

Convention can seem to be a more complicated way to create a working system that's more art than science. As an analogy, in the movie *I, Robot*, the actor Will Smith plays a policeman, Del Spooner, who doesn't like robots. During the robot interrogation scene, Spooner winks at another policeman leaving the questioning room. The robot asks Will what the wink meant, and Spooner explains that the wink is something that a human knows. At a later point in the movie, the robot uses a wink to send a message to Spooner. Spooner is surprised, but he knows what it means and acts appropriately.

So how does the wink relate to convention? To someone who knows what the wink is, it is a single simple piece of information that has many implications. To someone who doesn't know what the wink is, it is dismissed as irrelevant. A person who dismisses the wink is missing a piece of vital information and could be considered out of the loop of knowledge. The wink represents a complicated piece of information that requires a context to completely understand. One critique of Ruby on Rails is that it's more art than science, and thus not logical, since it uses convention—in other words, it's like the wink, and if you don't have the context to understand it, it doesn't make sense.

I would like to counter that configuration uses convention, and thus is a convention. In the simplest case, configuration is self-explanatory, but in the more complex case, a configuration file is a convention all on its own. To understand the configuration, you need to understand the convention of the configuration, which begs the question, why use a configuration? The answer is that sometimes a configuration is the appropriate solution because it offers *flexibility*; with convention, you do things according to a predetermined overall scheme. The reason configuration has become a convention is that in many cases, developers think they need to use configuration to gain flexibility, when in fact convention would have been good enough.

Implementing convention does require using reflection, because to make a decision based on convention, you need to know the current context. The big advantage of using convention is that you don't need to maintain configuration whenever changes occur—a convention automatically picks up the latest changes.

The following are some scenarios in which you would use convention over configuration:

- When you need to constantly update and manage cross-reference information (e.g., database columns that are mapped to class data members).

- When your configuration is only of importance to a developer and not an administrator. For example, you would expect an administrator to want to configure which database your application will connect to. But you would not expect your administrator to configure which model belongs to which view and which controller in a Model-View-Controller (MVC) architecture.

- When you can use reflection and call methods anonymously, without knowing the type information. It is possible to implement conventions using programming languages such as C# and Java, as they support reflection, but the ability to call methods anonymously is much more complicated. Using dynamic languages such as JavaScript and Ruby, it is very easy to call methods or properties on types.

- When you need to provide your users (and yourself) with hints if something goes wrong. When you use conventions, it is very important to clearly indicate what is wrong when something does not work. Ruby on Rails does a very good job of providing hints about what to do next when something goes wrong. This feature is important because writing code for a system that uses convention only works if you know the convention.

Solution

For this recipe, we'll convert the unit-testing framework described previously into a completely convention-based system. Then when writing unit tests, our only task will be to implement a series of tests in a structure, and the unit-testing framework will do the rest.

For illustration purposes, let's look at the template of the unit test again and identify the pieces that need to be converted from a configuration approach to a convention approach.

Source: /jaxson/trunk/website/ROOT/scripts/templates/testcontract.html

```
<html>
<head>
  <title>Contract Test Page</title>
  <script language="JavaScript" src="/scripts/common.js"></script>
  <script language="JavaScript" src="/scripts/Synchronous.js"></script>
  <script language="JavaScript" src="/scripts/commontest.js"></script>
  <script language="javascript" src="/scripts/jsunit/jsUnitCore.js"></script>
</head>
<body>
```

```
<script language="javascript">
  // Setup the output generator
  setJsUnitTracer( new jsUnitTraceGenerator( "traceoutput"));

  // Start of defined contract URL's
  // Potentially define a URL as
  // var baseURL = "/my/url";

  // End of defined contract URL's

  var testsToRun = {
    // Start JavaScript code for test cases here
    testPrototype : function() {
      // Synchronous functions identically to Asynchronous
      // but Synchronous waits for the request to complete
      // Good for testing, but bad for production as the browser hangs
      var request = new Synchronous();

      request.complete = function( statusCode, statusText,➥
        responseText, responseXML){
        // Do something with the result

        // Indicate that you are done, and define the output element
        testManager.success( "statusPrototype");
      }
      // Do something with the request
    }
    // End JavaScript code for test cases
  };

  testManager.setTestCases( testsToRun);

</script>

<table>
  <tr>
    <td><h2>Available Tests</h2></td>
    <td></td>
  </tr>
  <tr>
    <td>
      <input onclick="testManager.runAll()" type="button" value="Run All Tests" />
    </td>
    <td></td>
  </tr>
  <tr>
    <td>Test</td>
```

```
        <td>Status</td>
      </tr>
      <!-- Insert GUI for test cases here -->
      <tr>
        <td>
          <input onclick="testManager.testPrototype()" type="button"➥
            value="Test Prototype" />
        </td>
        <td id="statusPrototype">Not run</td>
      </tr>
      <!-- End test cases here -->
    </table>
    <hr />
    <table border="1">
      <tr>
        <td><h2>Trace output</h2></td>
      </tr>
      <tr>
        <td id="traceoutput"></td>
      </tr>
    </table>
  </body>
</html>
```

The bold lines in the preceding example represent configuration-based code that will be converted into convention-based code. When converting from configuration-based code to convention-based code, you can apply one of two approaches. The first approach is to rewrite the classes used by the unit-testing framework so that they become completely convention based. The advantage to this approach is that the classes are lean and solve the task. The second approach is to keep the configuration functionality, and write a layer on top that implements the convention functionality. The advantage of this approach is that multiple convention solutions can be applied, but the disadvantage is an additional overhead.

We'll implement the second approach here, and keep both the configuration and convention layer as lean as possible. Ideally, the configuration layer should contain only the functionality needed by the convention. Additional functionality in the configuration adds unnecessary baggage.

The base unit-testing file when converted into a convention file is similar to the following.

Source: /website/ROOT/ajaxrecipes/javascript/conventionconfiguration.html

```
<html>
<head>
  <title>Convention over Configuration</title>
  <script language="JavaScript" src="/scripts/jaxson/common.js"></script>
  <script language="JavaScript" src="/scripts/jaxson/commontest.js"></script>
  <script language="javascript" src="/scripts/jsunit/jsUnitCore.js"></script>
</head>
<body>
```

```
<script language="javascript">
  // Setup the output generator

  // ******************************************************
  function AddTwoNumbers(num1, num2) {
    return num1 + num2;
  }

  // ******************************************************

  var testsToRun = {
    // Start JavaScript code for test cases here
    plain_vanilla : function() {
      assertEquals(4, AddTwoNumbers(2, 2));
    },
    failed_test : function() {
      testManager.failed();
    },
    exception_failed : function() {
      obj.notexistent();
    }
    // End JavaScript code for test cases
  };
</script>
<div id="unittestoutput"></div>
<script language="JavaScript" src="/scripts/jaxson/conventiontest.js"></script>
</body>
</html>
```

The modified code includes three tests, but notice the drastic reduction in code in this example. Also notice that certain code constructs are implied and do not need to be written explicitly (e.g., testManager.success). From a user perspective, the reduction and simplification of the code is a good thing, but in fact there are many hidden aspects that you'll need to be aware of, because when something goes wrong, you need to know why it happened.

The details of how this code was implemented are not covered in the recipe—they are discussed throughout this chapter—but the following general concepts are implemented:

- The HTML code that contained the buttons is dynamically generated by a strategically placed include file (conventiontest.js). The file is placed where it is so that the variables will already have been declared and available for initialization.

- The testsToRun variable is an implied-to-exist variable and is inspected for available tests. For each test method, a button is generated, where the name of the button is the name of the test method.

- Each method uses a proxy to encapsulate and automatically handle errors or successful tests appropriately.

When creating your own convention-based code, keep in mind the following points:

- *Initialization*: In configuration-based code, you are responsible for initialization of the variables and objects; in convention-based code, the code is mostly responsible for initializing itself. It's like starting a car: you expect the car to feed fuel to the engine, and you just want to turn the key and be able to drive. The problem with initialization is that you don't always know the context.

- You have two ways to initialize. The first is to initialize and configure when the JavaScript is loaded, as illustrated by the XMLHttpRequest factory in Recipe 2-4. The second is to initialize when the first action takes place. In the second scenario, a flag indicating the status of initialization is set to false when the JavaScript is loaded. Then as the first action takes place, the initialization happens.

- *Error checking*: Convention systems expect certain variables or types declared, and if they are not declared, problems arise. A convention system must have error routines that catch every error and explain in detail what went wrong. Many developers might think that a convention system should be adaptable and work around not entirely correct code. This is a big misconception—providing workarounds makes for a sloppy developer. Convention-based code requires good coding practices, so that everybody codes to the same convention. Don't take shortcuts.

- *Naming consistency*: Whenever you label identifiers, you need to be consistent. The name of the identifier needs to be as obvious as possible. Don't try to be clever, slick, or cryptic. Ruby on Rails is successful for many reasons, one of which is that the naming conventions are obvious, consistent, and intuitive.

2-3. Using Parameterless Functions

Problem

You want to take advantage of parameterless functions in JavaScript.

Theory

JavaScript functions for the most part have parameters. You may think that the previous sentence states the obvious—after all, without parameters, what data could be passed to a function? JavaScript has the ability to declare functions that have no parameters, even though the caller of the function has passed parameters to the function.

For example, let's look at an addition function that uses the num1 and num2 parameters.

Source: /website/ROOT/ajaxrecipes/javascript/parameterlessfunctions.html

```
function AddTwoNumbers(num1, num2) {
  return num1 + num2;
}
```

The num1 and num2 parameters are added and the result is returned.

Solution

Another way to write the same function is to drop the parameters and use the `arguments` object, as follows:

```
function AddTwoNumbers() {
  return arguments[0] + arguments[1];
}
```

In this modified version of the function, there are no parameters, but the addition is still possible. And if the method is called like this, an addition occurs:

```
AddTwoNumbers( 2, 2);
```

Here the function is passed two parameters, but the function declaration has none. There can be one, two, or ten parameters—it does not matter. Maybe one, or two, or ten of all the parameters will be assigned, or maybe none of them will be assigned. This uncertainty poses an additional challenge because you are left wondering if the parameter is assigned or not.

For example, consider the following function declaration.

Source: /website/ROOT/ajaxrecipes/javascript/parameterlessfunctions.html

```
function TooManyParametersNotEnoughArguments( param1, param2, param3) {
  info( "TooManyParametersNotEnoughArguments", typeof( param3));
  assertEquals( "undefined", typeof( param3));
}
```

The `TooManyParametersNotEnoughArguments` function expects three parameters, but it is going to be called with only two parameters, as illustrated by the following calling code:

```
TooManyParametersNotEnoughArguments( 1, 2);
```

There is a disjoint between the caller and the function, and the third parameter is left dangling. To see if a parameter is left dangling, you use the `typeof` operator and test if the result is `undefined`. Do not test for a `null` value because the third parameter is not `null`; it is undefined. As a general rule of thumb, don't use `null` as a way of testing state. `null` is ambiguous and can mean different things in different contexts. The value of `undefined` is not ambiguous—it clearly indicates that the variable has not been assigned.

Another way of testing whether or not the third parameter has been assigned is to see how many arguments have been passed to the function, as illustrated by the following modified `TooManyParametersNotEnoughArguments` function:

```
function TooManyParametersNotEnoughArguments( param1, param2, param3) {
  info( "TooManyParametersNotEnoughArguments", typeof( param3));
  assertEquals( "undefined", typeof( param3));
  assertEquals( 2, arguments.length);
}
```

The bold code is an additional test of the `argument.length` property that verifies the caller of `TooManyParametersNotEnoughArguments` is passing in only two arguments.

The `arguments` object is defined locally in the context of the function, thus the `arguments` instance of one function call will not match the `arguments` call of another function. It's important to realize that arguments are arrays that you can manipulate.

When you implement functions that have no parameters, you should consider the following:

- If you implement a function and it is declared with three parameters, don't expect the function to be called with more or fewer parameters. Coding with JavaScript is about convention and expectations. Code with more or fewer parameters when a certain number is expected confuses the developer.

- If you are going to accept a varying number of arguments, then declare the function without arguments, meaning that you will use the `arguments` objects. Somebody who then reads the function understands that the function will accept a varying number of parameters, again fulfilling the expectations requirement when writing JavaScript code.

- If you declare a function without parameters, and you will be using one index of the `arguments` object throughout the function, consider assigning the index to a variable identifier so that the parameter's purpose is apparent.

- If you are going to accept a variable number of arguments, remember to generate explicit and verbose errors whenever you expect more or fewer arguments.

2-4. Treating Functions Like Objects

Problem

You want to take advantage of the fact that functions are objects (remember, *everything* is an object in JavaScript).

Theory

Many people think that a function is some keyword used in JavaScript. A function is also an object that can be manipulated. Knowing that a function is an object makes it very interesting from the perspective of writing JavaScript code, because the code can treat the function like another other object. This means you could assign functions to variables, class properties, and what have you.

Solution

One way of using this capability is to implement the Factory pattern to return a function object. For example, in Ajax you have two ways to instantiate the `XMLHttpRequest` object, and the method used depends on the browser. The Factory pattern is used to separate the interface from the implementation. Usually that means implementing an interface, but because JavaScript is a dynamic language, there is no real notion of an interface. In a dynamic language, an interface is not necessary because you can call a method directly without requiring a specific type.

In the case of the `XMLHttpRequest` object instantiation, the Factory pattern returns a function reference that can be used to instantiate `XMLHttpRequest` using the appropriate technique.

In JavaScript, a function is an object that can be assigned to a variable. A way of implementing the factory that instantiates XMLHttpRequest is to use function assignments. The complete implementation is as follows.

Source: /website/ROOT/ajaxrecipes/javascript/functionsareobjects.html

```
function InstantiateIEXMLHttpRequest() {
  return new ActiveXObject( "Microsoft.XMLHTTP");
}

function InstantiateOthersXMLHttpRequest() {
  return new XMLHttpRequest();
}

function FactoryXMLHttpRequest() {
  if( window.XMLHttpRequest) {
    return InstantiateOthersXMLHttpRequest;
  }
  else if( window.ActiveXObject) {
    return InstantiateIEXMLHttpRequest;
  }
  throw new Error( "Could not instantiate XMLHttpRequest");
}
```

In the preceding example, the FactoryXMLHttpRequest function is the implementation of the Factory pattern. Within the function implementation are two if statements that verify which browser is currently running. Depending on the browser, the return statement will return a reference to either the InstantiateIEXMLHttpRequest function or the InstantiateOthersXMLHttpRequest function. In both cases, the returned reference is a function that will instantiate the XMLHttpRequest object.

The code that uses the FactoryXMLHttpRequest method follows.

Source: /website/ROOT/ajaxrecipes/javascript/functionsareobjects.html

```
factory_function : function() {
  var InstantiateXMLHttpRequest = FactoryXMLHttpRequest();
  var xmlhttp = InstantiateXMLHttpRequest();
  assertNotNull( xmlhttp);
},
```

Notice in the example how the InstantiateXMLHttpRequest variable can be treated as a function. For illustrative purposes, the InstantiateXMLHttpRequest variable uses a mix of uppercase and lowercase letters to illustrate that when the variable is called, it looks like a function call. Based on the identifier and the context in which the variable is used as a function, you would not know that the variable is not a function. This is a very important point, because it illustrates that a function is just another object.

FactoryXMLHttpRequest is coded using a traditional approach: the code declares a function that when called will return an instance of a function. The behavior of the code is determined after the code has been parsed and initialized. With JavaScript, this is not necessary, because you can initialize the functions when the code is being parsed to optimize it. For example, you could rewrite the FactoryXMLHttpRequest code as follows.

Source: /website/ROOT/ajaxrecipes/javascript/functionsareobjects.html

```
<script language="javascript">
if( window.ActiveXObject) {
  InstantiateXMLHttpRequest = function() {
    return new ActiveXObject( "Microsoft.XMLHTTP");
  }
}
else if( window.XMLHttpRequest) {
  InstantiateXMLHttpRequest = function() {
    return new XMLHttpRequest();
  }
}
else {
  throw new Error( "Could not instantiate XMLHttpRequest");
}
</script>
```

In the modified implementation, the code used to assign the InstantiateXMLHttpRequest variable is executed as the HTML page is loaded. Thus, whenever the InstantiateXMLHttpRequest variable is referenced as a function, the appropriate way of instantiating XMLHttpRequest is executed. There is no need to call a factory and make a decision each and every time the function is called.

This ability to treat functions as objects adds an interesting coding facet, in that the behavior of the code can be determined at runtime. Where normally you would use a decision structure to determine the appropriate behavior, a dynamically assigned variable can be used.

Because a function is an object, there are some additional coding possibilities. For example, it is possible to dynamically assign properties and methods to a function, as shown in the following example.

Source: /website/ROOT/ajaxrecipes/javascript/functionsareobjects.html

```
function FunctionFunctionProperties(cmpval) {
  assertEquals(cmpval, FunctionFunctionProperties.value);
}

var VariableFunctionProperties = function( cmpval) {
  assertEquals( cmpval, VariableFunctionProperties.value);
}

var startIndex = VariableFunctionProperties.toString().indexOf( "{");
var endIndex = VariableFunctionProperties.toString().lastIndexOf( "}");
var buffer = VariableFunctionProperties.toString().slice( startIndex + 1, endIndex);
var InstantiatedFunctionProperties = new Function( "cmpval", buffer);
```

This example shows three function declarations, with each declaration illustrating a different way to declare a function instance. The first declaration, `FunctionFunctionProperties`, is the traditional approach. The second declaration, `VariableFunctionProperties`, uses a variable and an anonymous function. And the third declaration, `InstantiatedFunctionProperties`, is an explicit instantiation of the `Function` object, where the constructor parameters represent the declaration of the parameters, and the last parameter is the function body. The function body is a buffer of JavaScript code that is converted into executable JavaScript.

For each of the three function implementations, the name of the function is referenced and appended with a reference to the property value. With each and every function instance you can assign a property or, if you so desire, another function reference. You can think of properties as a way to declare a static variable that is associated with the function.

Because each of the three function declarations represents an object and a variable, they can be called in an identical fashion, as illustrated in the following example.

Source: `/website/ROOT/ajaxrecipes/javascript/functionsareobjects.html`

```
 function_with_properties : function() {
  VariableFunctionProperties.value = 10;
  VariableFunctionProperties( 10);
  FunctionFunctionProperties.value = 10;
  FunctionFunctionProperties(10);
  InstantiatedFunctionProperties.value = 10;
  InstantiatedFunctionProperties( 10);
  testManager.success();
},
```

Reading the code that calls the declared functions takes a bit of getting used to. Before each function call, the identifier is used as if it were an object. After the object is referenced, the object is called as a function. These examples clearly indicate that functions have a dual nature, where functions are objects and objects can be functions. This dual nature poses a problem: how does the function implementation know the instance of the function? The following code illustrates this problem.

Source: `/website/ROOT/ajaxrecipes/javascript/functionsareobjects.html`

```
function GetFunction() {
  return function( cmpvalue) {
    assertEquals(cmpval, unknownfunctioninstance.value);
  }
}
```

In the example, the `GetFunction` function has an implementation that returns a unique function instance each and every time `GetFunction` is called. If you wanted to reference a property of the function instance, you would be hard pressed to do so, because an anonymous function has no associated identifier. In the previous examples, the reference to the function instance was used to reference the properties and methods of the function object. Using this way of declaring the function, there is no associated instance identifier, and no way to be able to reference the property of the anonymous function. The solution is to use an internal variable that is referenced, as the following example demonstrates.

Source: /website/ROOT/ajaxrecipes/javascript/functionsareobjects.html

```
function GetFunctionFixed() {
  var inst = function(cmpval) {
    assertEquals(cmpval, inst.value);
  }
  return inst;
}
```

How the code that fixes the problem of the unknown instance actually even works may seem a bit mysterious at first. It involves the use of a programming technique commonly known as a *closure*. To understand how closures work, remember to think of a function as an object, not some function keyword construct. Here's what happens in a nutshell:

1. The caller calls GetFunctionFixed.

2. The implementation of GetFunctionFixed is executed.

3. An anonymous function is declared, and a Function object is instantiated.

4. The instantiated anonymous function is assigned to the local declared variable inst.

5. The anonymous function references inst, and the JavaScript processor understands this and creates a reference to the local declared variable.

6. The inst variable is returned to caller.

7. The garbage collector attempts to garbage collect inst, but it cannot because the anonymous function references inst as long as anonymous is referenced somewhere.

When you consider the steps in this process together with the fact that everything is an object, it becomes easy to see how this code works. When an object references another object, the objects can only be garbage collected if they do not reference anything.

When using functions and treating them as objects, keep the following points in mind:

- Functions are objects, and you can manipulate them like any other JavaScript objects. However, because functions are objects, using functions improperly or properties of functions improperly can cause *memory leaks*, where memory is referenced and not garbage collected, even though the script is not making use of the memory.

- A configuration of functions or methods is possible when the HTML page is being loaded. This saves processing logic, as the code does not need to determine what code should be executed.

- It takes a bit of time and experimentation to get used to the idea that the behavior of code is determined at runtime, and not while you're writing the code.

- Being objects, functions can reference properties or methods, enabling functions to define behavior at runtime. If you do assign properties or methods to functions, then do so with the understanding that the properties and methods are transient—that is, if a function is copied from one instance to another, do not assume that the properties are copied too.

2-5. Implementing an Error and Exception Handling Strategy

Problem

You want to implement a clean error and exception handling strategy in your applications, to make them run more smoothly.

Theory

When writing JavaScript code, you're going to be confronted with the problem of your code not doing what it should be doing. This is a fact, and there's nothing that you can do about it. Errors, bugs, things you've left out of the code, and things you did not know to include in the code can generate an exception as a result. Exceptions, when not caught, look as shown in Figures 2-1 and 2-2.

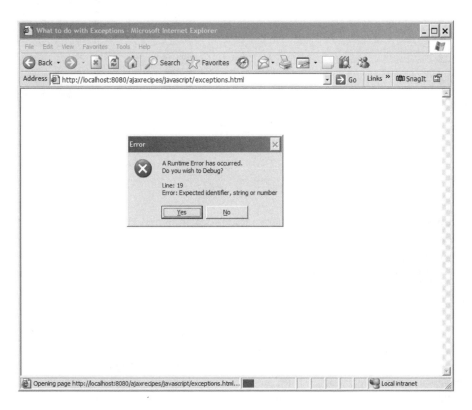

Figure 2-1. *Dialog box generated as the result of an error*

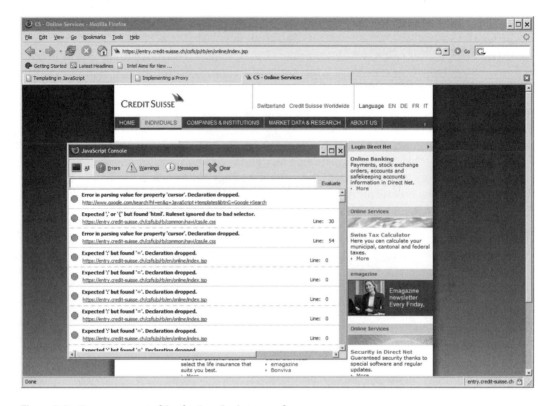

Figure 2-2. *Errors generated in the JavaScript console*

The errors shown in Figures 2-1 and 2-2 are not identical in nature. Of course, you might argue that one error is a dialog box and the other is generated in the JavaScript console. The fact that one browser uses a dialog box to show an error and the other does not is a browser issue, not an error issue. The difference between the errors in Figures 2-1 and 2-2 is that one is a *load* error and the other is a *runtime* error. A concise way of classifying the two errors is to say that one represents an HTML page *initialization* error and the other represents an HTML page *execution* error.

When implementing an error strategy, consider the technical implementation. At a technical level, when the first character is processed, the JavaScript runtime is executing and can generate an error. But if an error happens three characters in the processing, you are pretty much powerless to do anything about it. Until the HTML page has been completely processed, you should not enable error handling, because the error handling framework might not be properly initialized. And if an error does happen at that point, your error handling framework might go off half-cocked. Having an incomplete framework try to process an error will just confuse, not help.

Your objective should be to initialize and prepare the error handling framework when the HTML page has been completely processed. To know when to initialize the error handling framework, you need to know when HTML page initialization ends and HTML page runtime begins. Technically, HTML page initialization begins when the first character of the HTML page is processed. And technically, HTML page runtime begins when the `window.onload` event is called. The `window.onload` event is called after the HTML page has been processed, including frames and images, and it is the first piece of JavaScript code that when executing can expect the HTML page to be complete. An example implementation of the window.onload event could be as follows:

```
<html>
<head>
  <title>Implementing an Error Handling Strategy</title>
  <script language="JavaScript" src="/scripts/jaxson/common.js"></script>
  <script language="JavaScript" src="/scripts/jaxson/commontest.js"></script>
  <script language="javascript" src="/scripts/jsunit/jsUnitCore.js"></script>
</head>
<script language="javascript">
  window.onload = function() {
    window.onerror = function( msg, file, location) {
      info( "window.onerror", "Msg (" + msg + ") file (" + file +") location (" +➥
        location + ")");
    }
  }
</script>
<body>
```

In this example, window.onload is near the top of the HTML page, but the function could be put anywhere on the page. In the implementation of window.onload, the window.onerror method is assigned as a global catchall error handler. From a scripting perspective, it is the last point at which you can configure the browser before the browser begins its runtime execution of the HTML page. The window.onerror handler receives three parameters: msg, file, and location. These three parameters represent the message, the file, and the location in the file, respectively. Within the implementation of the window.onerror handler, the handler could repair and retry, generate a log, or do whatever else is desired. The example window.onerror implementation does not return a true or false value, resulting in the error being propagated to the browser. A false value will propagate and display the error, whereas a true value will not make the browser aware of the error.

The example implementation contains a problem, but it's not with the error handler. The problem is with the assignment of the window.onload function. As the code is written, there is only one function implementation for window.onload, and it initializes the window.onerror function. For an Ajax application of any complexity, it is not possible to assign a single window.onload method, as that would be hogging the method.

Solution

This solution involves creating a JavaScript delegate, as illustrated by the following source code.

Source: /website/ROOT/ajaxrecipes/javascript/functionsareobjects.html

```
<html>
  <head>
  <title>Implementing an Error Handling Strategy</title>
  <script language="JavaScript" src="/scripts/jaxson/common.js"></script>
```

```
<script language="JavaScript" src="/scripts/jaxson/commontest.js"></script>
<script language="javascript" src="/scripts/jsunit/jsUnitCore.js"></script>
</head>
<script language="javascript">
  ops.delegate(window, "onload", function() {
  window.onerror = function(msg, file, location) {
    info("window.onerror2", "Msg (" + msg + ") file (" + file + ") location (" +➥
      location + ")");
    }
  });
</script>
<body>
```

In the modified `onload` implementation, the `ops.delegate` function is used to create a delegate. For the moment, think of a delegate as a way to have a single method call result in multiple methods being called. (You can find more details about delegates in Recipe 2-17.)

The implementation of `ops.delegate` will test if a function is already is assigned to `window.onload`. If a function is assigned, then the existing function is converted to a delegate method, and the new function is associated with the delegate. Then when the browser calls `window.onload`, it will call both the original function and the new function.

In theory, an infinite number of functions can be associated with a delegate. The important thing to remember is that multiple functions can be associated with a single property, which is required for the `window.onload` method.

The following code tests the error handling routine:

```
var testsToRun = {
  throw_exception : function() {
    throw new Error("this is an error");
  }
};
```

When the `throw_exception` function is called, an exception is generated by instantiating the `Error` object and then throwing it using the `throw` keyword. In theory, you can throw any object—even one that looks like `Error`. Of course, using `Error` in this way is the most efficient choice, and this in essence is the basis of your error handling framework. You need something to capture an error, and you need to throw an error. How you capture and process the error is context-specific, so showing you something I or another programmer has implemented in another application is not going to help you here.

Another way to capture an error is through an exception handler, as follows:

```
function Generate() { throw new Error(); }
function CatchAll() {
  try {
    Generate();
  }
  catch( e) {
    // Do something with error
    throw e;
  }
}
```

In this example are two functions: Generate and CatchAll. Generate is used to generate an exception, and CatchAll is used to capture the exception. In JavaScript, you can capture an exception using the try and catch keywords, which catch all errors and exceptions that occur while the code in the try block is executing. When an exception is generated, the code within the catch block is executed. In the example, the error is generated by Generate and caught by the catch block, which then throws the error. When the error is thrown again, the exception will be caught in the window.onload method.

The try and catch block is extremely useful, because all errors and exceptions can be caught without the browser being any the wiser. But having a catchall mechanism can make debugging JavaScript more complicated, because errors that occur are processed without having the developer be any the wiser.

You might be tempted to use a try and catch block as a general programming technique, but that would be a bad idea. An error that is thrown is an exception, and an exception is something that should not have happened and is unpredictable. An exception should never happen, whereas an error could happen.

The best way to illustrate the difference between and error and an exception is the following example, which shows how an exception can be used to capture an error.

■**Note** This example could have written more succinctly using other keywords, but the point here is to simply show the difference between using a decision to test for an undefined variable and using an exception that executes if the variable happens to be undefined.

```
var func;

try {
  func();
}
catch( e) {
  func = Default;
  func();
}
```

The exception example illustrates how an exception handler (try and catch keywords) can be used to catch an exception if the func variable is not assigned to a method. Calling func will generate an exception and trigger the code in the catch block. In the catch block of the exception, the variable func is assigned a default function that works and is called.

Using an exception block in this manner is incorrect, because the code as it is written expects that func might not be assigned. If there is an expectation of func not being assigned, then the code should be written to reflect that. A better way to write the same code is as follows:

```
var func;
if( typeof(func) != "function") {
  func = Default;
}
func();
```

In the rewritten code example, the test of `func` checks to make sure that `func` is referencing a function. If `func` does not reference a function, then `func` is assigned the default function `Default`. Then when `func` is called, no exception will be generated.

When you write code, errors and exceptions will be generated, and you will need a strategy to deal with them. Keep the following points in mind when you are developing an error and exception strategy:

- Loading and processing an HTML page involves two phases: HTML page initialization and HTML page execution.

- During HTML page initialization, do not activate your error and exception strategy—doing so could have unpredictable results.

- Initialize your error and exception handling strategy in the `window.onload` method.

- Don't assume that you are dealing with only one piece of code that needs to be called by the `window.onload` method. Use a delegate to allow multiple functions to be called.

- Errors and exceptions are not the same thing. Errors can be anticipated and dealt with, but exceptions cannot.

- You can define a global exception handler by implementing the `window.error` method.

- To handle local exceptions, you can use a `try` and `catch` block.

2-6. Understanding the Behavior of Variables When Implementing Recursion

Problem

You want to implement recursion in JavaScript, and you also want to understand how variables will behave under those circumstances.

Theory

In JavaScript, you do not need to declare the variable type, or even declare the variable. For example, the following code works perfectly:

```
if( counter == 1) {
  buffer = "counter is 1";
}
document.getElementById( "result").innerHTML = buffer;
```

The `buffer` variable was not declared before the `if` block in the preceding code. The last line of the code uses the `buffer` variable to assign the `innerHTML` property. This sort of declaration is problematic because `buffer` might be `undefined`. JavaScript will not mention this as an error, and `innerHTML` will be assigned the value `undefined`.

This example illustrates that variables in JavaScript can behave in ways that a programmer with a Java or C# background may not be accustomed to. The focus of this recipe is on figuring out how a variable behaves in different contexts. One example context is the implementation of recursion in JavaScript.

Solution

Two example functions that implement recursion in JavaScript follow.

Source: /website/ROOT/ajaxrecipes/javascript/variablebehavior.html

```
function RecursionGlobal( counter) {
  info( "RecursionGlobal{localCounter}", typeof( localCounter));
  localCounter = counter;
  info( "RecursionGlobal{localCounter}", localCounter);
  if( localCounter < 3) {
    RecursionGlobal( localCounter + 1);
  }
}

function RecursionLocal( counter) {
  info( "RecursionLocal{localCounter}", typeof( localCounter));
  var localCounter = counter;
  info( "RecursionLocal{localCounter}", localCounter);
  if( localCounter < 3) {
    RecursionLocal( localCounter + 1);
  }
}
```

The example shows two methods: RecursionGlobal and RecursionLocal. Between the two methods there is a single difference, as shown in the bold code: the JavaScript keyword var. The single keyword var is the variation on how the localCounter variable is stored. The behavior of both methods when executed is identical and generates the same result.

You may think at first glance that the var keyword does not serve any purpose. But the var keyword does serve a purpose, which is illustrated by running the following program:

```
Info:recursion_global *** Started ***
Info:RecursionGlobal{localCounter} undefined
Info:RecursionGlobal{localCounter} 1
Info:RecursionGlobal{localCounter} number
Info:RecursionGlobal{localCounter} 2
Info:RecursionGlobal{localCounter} number
Info:RecursionGlobal{localCounter} 3
Info:recursion_local *** Started ***
Info:RecursionLocal{localCounter} undefined
Info:RecursionLocal{localCounter} 1
Info:RecursionLocal{localCounter} undefined
Info:RecursionLocal{localCounter} 2
Info:RecursionLocal{localCounter} undefined
Info:RecursionLocal{localCounter} 3
```

Notice that when the RecursionGlobal function executes, the type of the localCounter for the first call is undefined, and thereafter it is number. In contrast, when the RecurisonLocal function is called, the type of localCounter is undefined for each and every call. This means that var serves the purpose of declaring a variable that is local to the scope from which it is declared. If the variable is not associated with a var keyword, then the variable is declared in global scope. In the case of creating a recursion loop, you will need to use the var keyword for all cases; otherwise, there could be data corruption.

The following example illustrates how to reverse the contents of a stack using recursion. When using recursion, sometimes you will need to declare function parameters that serve no purpose other than as reference values.

Source: /website/ROOT/ajaxrecipes/javascript/variablebehavior.html

```
function RecursiveStackOldWay( arrayToProcess, processedArray) {
  info( "RecursiveStackOldWay", "---> Start");
  info( "RecursiveStackOldWay", "Recursive depth=" + (processedArray.length + 1));
  processedArray.push( arrayToProcess.pop());
  if( arrayToProcess.length > 0) {
    RecursiveStackOldWay( arrayToProcess, processedArray);
  }
  info( "RecursiveStackOldWay", "---> End");
}

var arrayToProcess = new Array();
arrayToProcess.push( "value1");
arrayToProcess.push( "value2");
var processedArray = new Array()
RecursiveOldWayStack( arrayToProcess, processedArray);
```

Here, the RecursiveStackOldWay function has two parameters: arrayToProcess and processedArray. The first parameter, arrayToProcess, is the array that will be reversed. The second parameter, processedArray, is the destination stack. The destination stack needs to be dragged along as a parameter for each recursion, so that the function can put the stack somewhere. The caller is responsible for instantiating the destination stack and passing it to the recursive function.

Often, though, when creating recursive functions, you will need to call the function with certain parameters that are defined in the first top-level call. These parameters have nothing to do with the initial call, yet the first top-level call needs to declare them (processedArray). In a nutshell, the problem is that when calling a recursive function, you need to initialize a set of variables that are then used by the recursion.

In the example, the initialization is a responsibility of the caller. The solution works, but it is far from optimal, because the developer needs to understand how certain parameters function, even though they might not be used by the caller. Another solution is to create a wrapper function to the recursion that initializes the parameters and then calls the recursion. The wrapper function will work, but now the programmer has to maintain the recursion function and the wrapper function.

JavaScript offers a third solution: let the recursion function initialize itself. The question is, how does the recursion function know it is being called for the first time? In a traditional programming language like Java or C#, a Boolean parameter would be defined and set to true to indicate the first call, and false to indicate any subsequent call.

The JavaScript solution does not require a flag or indicator, because the parameters themselves are indicators. For example, imagine if the RecursiveOldWayStack function implementation stays as is and the code that calls RecursiveOldWayStack resembles the following:

```
var arrayToProcess = new Array();
arrayToProcess.push( "value1");
arrayToProcess.push( "value2");
var processedArray  = RecursiveOldWayStack( arrayToProcess);
```

In the modified implementation, the caller is not responsible for instantiating the destination stack. That responsibility has been delegated to the RecursiveOldWayStack function. However, a problem arises because RecursiveOldWayStack needs to initialize and begin the recursion. The solution used by JavaScript is to determine whether the second parameter is defined, as illustrated in the following modified function called RecursiveStack.

Source: /website/ROOT/ajaxrecipes/javascript/variablebehavior.html

```
function RecursiveStack( arrayToProcess, processedArray) {
  info( "RecursiveStack", "---> Start");
  if( typeof( processedArray) == "undefined") {
    info( "RecursiveStack", "Initial");
    processedArray = new Array();
    RecursiveStack( arrayToProcess, processedArray);
    info( "RecursiveStack", "---> End");
    return processedArray;
  }
  else {
    info( "RecursiveStack", "Recursive depth=" + (processedArray.length + 1));
    processedArray.push( arrayToProcess.pop());
    if( arrayToProcess.length > 0) {
      RecursiveStack( arrayToProcess, processedArray);
    }
    info( "RecursiveStack", "---> End");
    return;
  }
}
```

In the modified implementation, the RecursiveStack function implements an expectation. The expectation is that if the function is called with a single parameter, then it is a caller doing the first call of the recursion; otherwise, a recursion is happening. The expectation of knowing whether a first call is happening is determined by the code in bold. If the second parameter, processedArray, is undefined, then the recursive function initializes itself and starts the recursion. If the second parameter is defined, then it is assumed a recursion is happening, and the function will process the data as such.

Before we continue, you might have caught the fact that RecursiveStack has two parameters, but is being called with one. Earlier I talked about expectations and that the caller needs to pass two parameters. This example does not say that that the caller does not need to pass two parameters; rather, the example says that if the caller does not pass two parameters, the function has the ability to compensate.

The same function can be used for the initialization and recursion based on an expectation. If, however, a caller defines the second parameter, that means the caller has taken on the responsibility to implement the initialization. With a caller-defined initialization, RecursiveStack will not perform an initialization and will jump directly to the recursion functionality. The advantage of this solution is that you have a multipurpose function without having to explicitly define a wrapper function. You may be thinking, "Of course this is possible using a language such as Java or C# using overloaded functions." Yes, it is possible using overloaded functions, but as mentioned earlier, an overloaded function is a wrapper function that calls the actual implementation, meaning two functions need to be written and maintained. In JavaScript, everything can be wrapped into one self-contained function.

Now that you've implemented recursion and know the difference between a locally scoped variable and a globally scoped variable, the next question is, what happens if there are two variables with the same name? Imagine defining a variable at a local scope that exists in a global scope—what happens to the globally and locally scoped variable declarations? The following code shows how a variable is defined globally in one function and then referenced in another function.

Source: `/website/ROOT/ajaxrecipes/javascript/variablebehavior.html`

```
function GlobalScope() {
  info( "GlobalScope{scopedVariable}", typeof( scopedVariable));
  scopedVariable = "globalscope";
  info( "GlobalScope{scopedVariable}", "scopedVariable=" + scopedVariable +➥
    " type=" + typeof(scopedVariable));
}

function TestScope() {
  info( "OtherScope{scopedVariable}", "scopedVariable=" + scopedVariable + " type="➥
    + typeof(scopedVariable));
}
```

scopedVariable is defined in GlobalScope and referenced in TestScope. Since there is no var-based declaration of scopedVariable in GlobalScope, scopedVariable is put into the global scope. Running TestScope after GlobalScope will result in scopedVariable being defined globally, as shown in the following generated output:

```
Info:GlobalScope{scopedVariable} undefined
Info:GlobalToLocalScope{scopedVariable} scopedVariable=globalscope type=string
Info:TestScope{scopedVariable} scopedVariable=globalscope type=string
```

In the generated output, GlobalScope is called, and at the beginning of the function implementation, scopedVariable is undefined. Then scopedVariable is assigned a buffer, and the generated output indicates that scopedVariable is not undefined and references a string. Calling TestScope illustrates that scopedVariable is global and is assigned a buffer.

Now consider the same example, except a globally scoped variable is redeclared as a local variable using the var keyword.

Source: /website/ROOT/ajaxrecipes/javascript/variablebehavior.html

```
function AlwaysLocalScope() {
  info( "GlobalToLocalScope{scopedVariable}", typeof( scopedVariable));
  scopedVariable = "AlwaysLocalScope";
  info( "GlobalToLocalScope{scopedVariable}", "scopedVariable=" + scopedVariable +➡
    " type=" + typeof(scopedVariable));
  var scopedVariable;
}
```

In the function implementation, scopedVariable is first assigned a buffer that does not use the var keyword. Thus, scopedVariable is declared at the global scope level. Or at least that is what you are led to believe. What happens is that the variable is declared at the local level because the last instruction of the function (in bold) declares the scopedVariable variable to be local.

It may seem odd that a variable is declared to be local if somewhere in the function the var keyword is used. It gets even odder, in that if the var keyword is used in a decision block that is never executed, the variable is still declared local.

To illustrate, first the AlwaysLocal function is called and then TestScope, which generates the following output:

```
Info:AlwaysLocalScope{scopedVariable} undefined
Info:AlwaysLocalScope{scopedVariable} scopedVariable=AlwaysLocalScope type=string
Warn:General error (scopedVariable is not defined)
```

When the AlwaysLocalScope function is called, scopedVariable will be undefined, meaning it exists in neither global nor local scope. Then when the variable is assigned, the generated output will have a value and type. When the TestScope function is called, an exception is raised because scopedVariable is not defined.

Now you know when a variable is declared in global scope and in local scope. The last test is to see what happens when a variable is declared in both global and local scope. The test involves calling the functions in the sequence: GlobalScope, TestScope, AlwaysLocalScope, and then TestScope. Calling this sequence generates the following output:

```
Info:GlobalScope{scopedVariable} undefined
Info:GlobalScope{scopedVariable} scopedVariable=globalscope type=string
Info:TestScope{scopedVariable} scopedVariable=globalscope type=string
Info:AlwaysLocalScope{scopedVariable} undefined
Info:AlwaysLocalScope{scopedVariable} scopedVariable=AlwaysLocalScope type=string
Info:TestScope{scopedVariable} scopedVariable=globalscope type=string
```

In the generated output, scopedVariable is declared and assigned in GlobalScope. The TestScope function verifies that scopedVariable exists. Then, when calling AlwaysLocalScope, var declares that any reference to scopedVariable within the function is a local variable reference. Thus, if there is a globally defined variable with the same name, it is not accessible within the scope of the function. You have two ways to reference a global variable: referencing via the window property or creating a function that is external to the executing function (meaning it's not an inline function) and assigning the globally scoped variable.

When a variable is not assigned, the typeof function returns undefined. Once you assign a variable, typeof will return another value. If a variable is defined in the context of a function, then each and every time the function is called, the variable before being assigned will be undefined. At the global level, a variable can be unset by using the delete operator, as follows:

```
delete scopedVariable;
```

Usually, the delete operator is used to reset the property of an object. When delete is used with an identifier, a global variable reference is deleted. You cannot remove a reference to a function using delete.

Let's test another variation of scope using dynamic code. In JavaScript, using the eval function will execute a JavaScript buffer, which tests when a variable will be considered global scope and when it will be considered local scope. The AlwaysLocalScope function will thus be modified.

For the first variation, AlwaysLocalScope will have a dynamic assignment:

```
function AlwaysLocalScope() {
  info("AlwaysLocalScope{scopedVariable}", typeof(scopedVariable));
  eval("scopedVariable = 'AlwaysLocalScope'");
  info("AlwaysLocalScope{scopedVariable}", "scopedVariable=" + scopedVariable +➡
    " type=" + typeof(scopedVariable));
  var scopedVariable;
}
```

The modified code is shown in bold, and the assignment of scopedVariable is executed. Using eval in this manner has no effect, and the dynamic execution of the code is the same as if the code had not been modified. The advantage with eval is that you can assign a piece of code to a text buffer, and then execute that buffer. The scope of scopedVariable has not been changed because the var keyword still exists in the function declaration. The declaration when parsed by the JavaScript processor will result in a local variable declaration.

One way to change the local declaration behavior is to embed the variable declaration in an eval statement, as shown in the following code modification:

```
function AlwaysLocalScope() {
  info("AlwaysLocalScope{scopedVariable}", typeof(scopedVariable));
  eval("scopedVariable = 'AlwaysLocalScope'");
  info("AlwaysLocalScope{scopedVariable}", "scopedVariable=" + scopedVariable +➡
    " type=" + typeof(scopedVariable));
  eval( "var scopedVariable;");
}
```

The modified code with respect to the original AlwaysLocalScope code is in bold. This time, both the assignment and the declaration of scopedVariable are dynamic, meaning that scopedVariable when assigned will be treated as a global variable. This is because when the first eval statement is executed, there is no declaration of scopedVariable, and the JavaScript runtime will store scopedVariable in the global space.

To change the behavior and declare scopedVariable as a local variable, AlwaysLocalScope needs to be modified one more time, as follows:

```
function AlwaysLocalScope() {
  info("AlwaysLocalScope{scopedVariable}", typeof(scopedVariable));
  eval( "var scopedVariable;");
  eval("scopedVariable = 'AlwaysLocalScope'");
  info("AlwaysLocalScope{scopedVariable}", "scopedVariable=" + scopedVariable +➦
    " type=" + typeof(scopedVariable));
}
```

In the latest modification, the first eval is the declaration of scopedVariable using the var keyword. The first eval call results in the declaration of scopedVariable as a local variable. The second eval call assigns a value to scopedVariable, which is scoped as a local variable.

When declaring variables in the context of functions or in global scope, keep the following points in mind:

- There are two scopes to a variable: local to a function and global.

- A local variable is declared using the var keyword, with the exception being the use of var in a global context. The use of var does not need to be at the beginning of a function.

- A global variable is declared when a variable is assigned without using the var keyword.

- It is good practice to declare variables at global level scope using the var keyword.

- Local and global variables with the same name do not overwrite each other. A locally declared variable hides a globally declared variable with the same name.

- When a variable is not declared, using typeof on the variable results in undefined.

- You can unset global variables using the delete operator.

- When using recursive functions, you should use locally declared variables.

- Recursion typically involves an initialization and an execution. Using JavaScript, the initialization and execution can be wrapped into a single function.

- Wrapping initialization and execution in a single function uses expectations, where the availability of variables is tested to determine a calling context.

- It is possible to use eval to dynamically declare local or global variables.

- Using eval causes the JavaScript processor to not perform a look-ahead when identifying local variables. Thus, to declare a local variable, the var keyword must be used before assigning a variable.

- Using the eval statement, a program could dynamically determine whether or not a variable should be declared at the local scope or the global scope.

2-7. Using Functions to Initialize and Make Decisions

Problem

You want to use functions to initialize and make decisions.

Theory

Usually when you write a piece of code where a change of logic needs to take place based on a context, you use a decision structure. For example, say you are implementing a light switch using a program. You turn on the light if the light is off, and you turn off the light if the light is on. The behavior of the program is determined by the conditions.

One example behavior that deserves a closer look is initialization. Initialization typically should happen only if it hasn't already. Initialization is important because the initialization logic creates the default framework for your application to properly function.

Solution

For illustrative purposes, let's go through an example where a function requires an initialization that is embedded within the function. The logic is to perform an initialization if it has not already occurred. The function that is called is defined as follows, and it embeds a call to the initialization.

■**Tip** You could use this type of code to implement a lazy initialization when writing convention-based code that does not perform an explicit initialization.

Source: /website/ROOT/ajaxrecipes/javascript/makingdecisionsinitialization.html

```
function ClassicalManipulateObject( obj) {
  info( "ClassicalManipulateObject", "Starting");
  if( !didInitialize) {
    DoInitialization( obj);
  }
  else {
    info( "ClassicalManipulateObject", "no initialization necessary");
  }
  assertEquals( 3, obj.value);
  info( "ClassicalManipulateObject", "Ending");
}
```

In the example, the bold code relates to the initialization functionality. didInitialize is a flag variable that can be either true or false. If the didInitialize variable is false, then initialization did not take place; if the didInitialize variable is true, then initialization did take place. If initialization did not take place, the DoInitialization function is called.

Notice that in the logic is a variable that represents whether initialization has taken place and a function to do initialization. This code is problematic because the variable has to be defined somewhere, and the variable has to be assigned properly somewhere. And somewhere there is a cross-reference between the variable state and the calling of the initialization functionality.

One solution is to embed much of the initialization logic in the context of the DoInitialization function. But the fact is that somewhere there is a variable, and somewhere there is an initialization function, and somewhere there is a cross-reference between the variable and initialization function. So where you put the logic is irrelevant in a "big picture" sense.

Another solution is to think of the initialization functionality not as a decision, but as a state. There is an initial state, which is to perform an initialization, and another state to perform no initialization. In a sense, the didInitialize variable is a representation of the state. Keeping that thought in mind, you know that JavaScript treats its functions as objects. Thus, the didInitialize variable could be a function and not a Boolean variable.

Treating the state as a variable that references a function makes it possible to simplify the function that requires an initialization. The implementation of the ClassicalManipulateObject function is changed to ManipulateObject, as illustrated in the following code.

Source: /website/ROOT/ajaxrecipes/javascript/makingdecisionsinitialization.html

```
function ManipulateObject(obj) {
  info( "ManipulateObject", "Starting");
  InitializeObject( obj);
  assertEquals( 3, obj.value);
  info( "ManipulateObject", "Ending");
}
```

In the modified implementation, the bold code again represents the initialization functionality. Here there is no decision—just a function call to InitializeObject. You might be thinking, "I could have done the same thing with the decision-based initialization, in that the decision is implemented in InitializeObject." But this is incorrect, because in the implementation of InitializeObject, there is no decision. The implementation of InitializeObject initializes the variable and then allows the processing to continue. If there is no decision on whether the initialization occurred, and InitializeObject represents a function to initialize the state, then for every call the state will be initialized you can't call this initialization functionality. The magic is in the fact that JavaScript treats functions as objects. The implementation of InitializeObject is as follows:

```
function InitializeObject( obj) {
  obj.value = 3;
  info( "InitializeObject", "doing initialization");
  InitializeObject = InitializeEmptyObject;
}
```

In the implementation of InitializeObject, the obj parameter is initialized to a value of 3, and the bold code shows the reassignment of the InitializeObject function. The reassigned InitializeObject references a function without body, which means that the first time InitializeObject is called, the initialization is carried out, but every call thereafter is an empty function call that does nothing.

This is the complete implementation of the initialization functionality without using a single decision or variable. One advantage of this approach is that you don't need to figure out which variable to cross-reference with the function. The function takes care of itself, and the caller can keep calling InitializeObject, knowing that everything will be taken care of.

Another advantage of this approach is that you are creating a state engine where the next state is determined by the execution of the current state. There is no centrally located decision block that determines the overall flow of execution and needs updating every time a new state needs to be integrated.

Normally when writing code in a language such as Java, C#, or C++, you don't go around reassigning the implementation of defined function. And because this behavior is engrained in the developers' minds, they don't even consider doing that. Yet there is absolutely no problem reassigning functions in JavaScript, because functions are objects. Functions are not unique identifiers with unique functionality, as you think of them when working with them in other languages.

The implementation of InitializeObject works and is a complete solution. But there is a little inconvenience in that once InitializeObject has been assigned to an empty function, the initialization functionality is lost until the HTML page is refreshed. For some problems, that is an acceptable solution. For example, you wrap XMLHttpRequest only once because you can instantiate XMLHttpRequest in only a certain browser-specific way. There are some instances, however, when you might want to reset and initialize again, and to be able to do that, you need to wrap InitializeObject into a function within a function, as demonstrated in the following example.

Source: /website/ROOT/ajaxrecipes/javascript/makingdecisionsinitialization.html

```
function ResetInitializeObject() {
  InitializeObject = function( obj) {
    obj.value = 3;
    info( "InitializeObject", "doing initialization");
    InitializeObject = InitializeEmptyObject;
  }
}


ResetInitializeObject();
```

The InitializeObject function is a variable that is assigned a function implementation in the ResetInitializeObject context. Recipe 2-4 shows that there is no difference in how a function is declared, even if it seems odd or out of place. To initialize InitializeObject, the ResetInitializeObject function is called, thus creating the InitializeObject function. And InitializeObject when called will reassign itself to an empty function. Calling ResetInitializeObject again resets the initialization, allowing InitializeObject to initialize the state and reset itself again.

From this example, you can see that a decision does not need to be implemented using an if statement. Another example that illustrates how a state engine could be implemented follows. The example implements a light switch, where if the light is on, it is turned off, and vice versa. Note that not a single if statement is used in this example.

Source: /website/ROOT/ajaxrecipes/javascript/makingdecisionsinitialization.html

```
function ToggleLight() {
  ToggleLight.on = function() {
    ToggleLight.curr = ToggleLight.off;
    return "on";
  }
  ToggleLight.off = function() {
    ToggleLight.curr = ToggleLight.on;
    return "off";
  }
  try {
    return ToggleLight.curr();
  }
  catch( e ) {
    info( "ToggleLight", "initialization..." );
    return ToggleLight.on();
  }
}
```

The function ToggleLight is called whenever you want to switch the light on or off. There is no parameter to indicate an on or an off; that functionality is embedded within the ToogleLight function. In the ToggleLight implementation there are two properties, on and off, both of which are functions. The on function assigns the curr property to off and returns an "on" buffer. The off function assigns the curr property to off and returns an "off" buffer.

To toggle the state, the curr property that is defined as a function is called. The calling of curr is embedded in an exception block, because curr will not be initialized the first time ToggleLight is called. Thus, an exception is generated, and in the catch part of the exception block, the on property (which is a function) is called. Calling on automatically assigns curr and initializes the state. It is important to remember that using an exception block and calling on is acceptable because it is a way of implementing lazy initialization.

When writing decision blocks and functions, think about state and the following aspects of this recipe:

- Your program does not need to include as many decisions, because decisions have been replaced by different states.

- You can reassign functions if you can break down the problem into a state engine problem.

- You can be more flexible with reassigned functions because behavior can be substituted dynamically. For example, if you require a two-stage initialization using a decision, that means additional if statements altered in a central location of source code. Using a reassigned function, you are creating a state engine where the behavior can be altered during runtime at the local level.

- When you read through this recipe's examples, you may have thought, "Why not use a class and object?" The answer is that a function is an object and the examples are object-oriented programming. The code looks odd because we normally assume a function is a feature used to create a class, and that classes typically are not functions. If the notation bothers you, my advice is to let this feature of JavaScript stew in your mind for a bit. You will surely come to see it is a powerful way of programming.

■**Note** For another example of using recursion instead of using decision blocks, take a look at Recipe 2-9.

2-8. Understanding the Ramifications of Duck-Typed Code

Problem

You want to understand where to best use duck typing and the issues you should be aware of when using it.

Theory

There is a difference between a *value type* and a *reference type* in JavaScript. Even for a reference type, there is a difference between defining the reference as a value or a pure reference. But should you even care about the difference? Is it something that you need to be aware of? It is when you are trying to do something specific.

JavaScript is a unique language in that it has duck type, latent type, and prototype characteristics. To create a type in JavaScript, you can define the type via a prototype definition, or you can define the methods and properties by assigning a class instance. In general, you have the ability to dynamically wire together types at runtime.

There are two ways to implement duck typing: value types and reference types. You need to be aware of both types, although in this book I mostly use value-type duck typing. I am not saying one is better than the other—just that each has advantages and disadvantages. Developers tend to choose one over the other based on their programming habits. For example, I prefer value duck typing because I tend to serialize objects for later use.

Solution

Let's go through an example of duck typing using reference values. Consider the following code, which is used to create a function without parameters that contains a state.

Source: /client/ajaxrestrecipes/javascript/valuevsreferencetypes.js

```
function CallMeReference(toCall, value) {
  return function() {
    toCall(value);
  }
}
```

In the preceding code, the CallMeReference function has two parameters: toCall, which is a function, and value, which is the state used to call the function toCall. The idea behind CallMeReference is to create a function that has no parameters, but is called using some state defined earlier.

The following code could be used to execute an example:

```
var func = CallMeReference(
  function( param) { info( "param is (" + param + ")"); }, "hello world");
  func();
```

In this example, the `func` variable is used to generate an encapsulated "hello world" message. The `func` variable can be called repeatedly, and the same message is generated. The variable could be assigned to other variables and the same message would be generated.

Because we are programmers, we will create functions that follow the Builder pattern and precreate functions with certain states. The following two functions implement the Builder pattern:

```
function Version1Reference() {
  return CallMeReference( function( param) { info( "Ver 1 is (" + param + ")"); },➥
    "hello world");
}

function Version2Reference() {
  return CallMeReference( function( param) { info( "Ver 2 is (" + param + ")"); },➥
    "hello world");
}
```

The `Version1Reference` and `Version2Reference` functions generate functions with slight differences. The resulting generated functions can be assigned to variables and then called as in the previous example.

Up to this point, everything that I have shown is something you could do using traditional programming languages such as C#, Java, and C++. Here, however, we are using JavaScript, which implements duck typing and prototype-based features, which means that if a function is assigned to a variable, we don't know how that assignment happened. This need to know who did what assignment does not matter in C++, C#, or Java, because the programmer defined the order and layout of the types ahead of time, and during runtime that order cannot be changed. In JavaScript, that order is not defined ahead of time—it is defined at runtime. For example, the following code is possible:

```
if( flag) {
  func = Version1Reference();
}
else {
  func = Version2Reference();
}
```

When `func` has been assigned, you don't know if it was assigned using the code from `Version1Reference` or from `Version2Reference`. When the assigned code is executed, you can logically determine from the behavior if the `Version1Reference` or `Version2Reference` function was used. The reason I say that you don't know which code was assigned is because when you serialize the variable `func`, the following code is generated:

```
function () { toCall(value); }
```

The generated code tells you that the `toCall` and `value` variables have been assigned, but you don't know to what. This can become problematic if you are trying to serialize an object that references the generated function. If you serialize the function and attempt to execute the function, an error would be generated because the `toCall` and `value` variables would not be defined. You can serialize the state of the data members, but serializing the methods causes state to be lost.

For example, imagine you are writing a mortgage application, and you are currently creating a client. The client has a certain age, address, and profile. In a traditional programming environment, you would associate the state with an object each and every time the state is loaded. This means each time the state is loaded, you have to execute various Builder pattern implementations to create the appropriate object type.

Using JavaScript, this is not necessary because the state of the object, including methods, could be serialized. This makes it possible to serialize a complete object, store it into a database, or execute it in another context. Dynamic functions need to use value types, which means `CallMeReference` has to be modified as follows:

```
function CallMeValue( toCall, value) {
  return eval( "function() { var func = " +➡
    toCall.toString() + "; func( '" + value.toString() + "'); } ");
}
```

The `CallMeValue` function is like `CallMeReference`, except that it serializes the function and value to string buffers that are concatenated and executed. The result of the execution is a function that when serialized generates the following buffer:

```
function () { var func = (function (param) {info("param is (" + param + ")");});➡
func("hello world"); }
```

The serialized function behaves exactly like the function created in `CallMeReference`, but the value function can be serialized and executed on another computer or in another context.

When writing code that dynamically wires together code, you need to think about whether to use reference or value programming techniques. When writing such code, consider the following rules of thumb:

- Reference duck types should be considered as transient types that live only for the extent of the JavaScript execution (e.g., an HTML page).

- Reference duck types are created using the Builder pattern.

- Once created, reference duck types have a slight performance advantage, as they do not need the overhead of running the `eval` statement in the Builder pattern implementation.

- Reference duck types can share instances with multiple object instances because you are assigning references.

- Value duck types should be considered as long-term serializable objects where the state and code can be serialized.

- Value duck types are created using the Builder pattern.

- Value duck types are slightly slower than reference duck types because the code is the result of serializing, building a buffer, and then evaluating the buffer.

- Value duck types do not have the side effect of having functions behave irregularly because of assigned object instances. Each call to a value duck type Builder pattern results in a clean-slate approach, where the variables are assigned the state given to the Builder pattern.

2-9. Implementing JavaScript "Generics"

Problem

You want to implement "generics" in JavaScript.

Theory

Programming languages such as Java and C# have a programming concept called *generics*. The idea behind generics is to write code in such a way that an identifier is defined as a general type that is manipulated in a class or method. For example, the following code would be a generic class in either Java or C#:

```
class Container<Type> {
  Type _managed;
}
```

The Container class has a generic parameter, Type, which can reference any other type. And in the declaration of Container, the _managed data member is the same type as the generic parameter. In an abstract notion, Container manages any type.

A JavaScript programmer might look at the code and think, "Hey, I have this already in JavaScript!" Here is the same code, this time in JavaScript:

```
function Container() {
  this._managed = /* whatever type */
}
```

As illustrated in Recipe 2-8, you can have reference-based duck typing or value-based duck typing. Implementing "generics" for JavaScript is like implementing a preprocessor, thus we want value-based duck typing.

The following code example shows what can go wrong when you mix value and reference duck typing together:

```
proxy : function(instance, funcIdentifier, newFunc) {
  if (!instance[funcIdentifier]) {
    throw new Error("Cannot proxy nonexistent method(" + funcIdentifier + ")");
  }
  eval( "var generatedOrigFunc = " + instance[funcIdentifier].toString());
  eval( "var generatedProxyFunc = " + newFunc.toString());
  instance[funcIdentifier] = function() {
    var origFunc = generatedOrigFunc;
    var proxyFunc = generatedProxyFunc;
    var args = new Array();
    for (var c1 = 0; c1 < arguments.length; c1 ++) {
      args.push(arguments[c1]);
    }
    args.push(origFunc);
    args.push(arguments);
    proxyFunc.apply(this, args);
  }
},
```

This source code is an example of how not to write a Proxy pattern implementation. The problem of the implementation is shown in the bold code. At the beginning of the bold code are two eval statements, which are generating the values of the generatedOrigFunc and generatedProxyFunc variables. In the embedded function instance[funcIdentifier], the variables are referenced, and due to closure, the origFunc and proxyFunc variables will reference the correct variables.

The concept of the Proxy pattern is that when a method is called, it first calls the function referenced by proxyFunc, which then calls the function referenced by origFunc. Because proxyFunc is called first, it has the ability to preprocess or postprocess the data. The code as written will work with a single application of the Proxy pattern, but it will fail if the proxy pattern is applied multiple times. For example, imagine the generated code embedding of the Proxy pattern on an already applied Proxy pattern.

Figure 2-3 shows two instances of the proxy code, and in one instance the generatedOrigFunc variable is referencing the other proxy code instance. This code is an example of a "gotcha" piece of code in JavaScript. Look closely at the declarations of the generatedOrigFunc and generatedProxyFunc variables—what are they referencing?

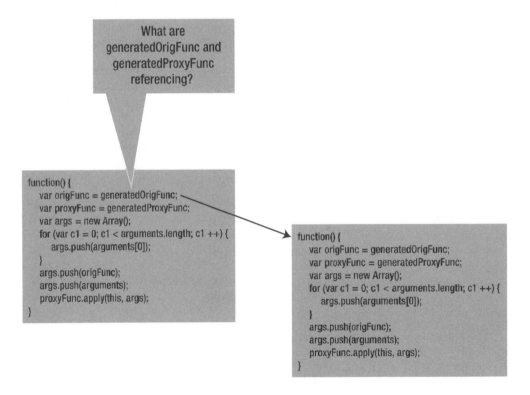

Figure 2-3. *Multiple embedding of the proxy pattern*

To understand the error, think of the proxy code on the left as proxy implementation 1 (PI1) and the code on the right as proxy implementation 2 (PI2). If a generic caller were to call PI1, the following sequence of events would take place:

1. PI1 is called.

2. PI1's proxyFunc is called.

3. PI1's origFunc is called, which is PI2.

4. PI2's proxyFunc is called, which is PI1's proxyFunc.

5. PI1's proxyFunc is called, calling PI1's origFunc.

Following these steps, you will notice that a recursion is taking place. The recursion is because of the way the generatedOrigFunc and generatedProxyFunc variables are declared. These variables are declared without any scope and because the proxy scope function is a mix of using references with eval code. This is a bad practice, because some variables will be serialized and others will not.

We want a solution like the C preprocessor, where "generics" represent the physical replacing of an identifier with a desired type. We don't want a templating system. A templating system would be described as follows:

```
<%for( var count = 0; count < 10; count ++) {%>
  series[<%=count%>] = GenSeries( <%=count%>)
<%}%>
```

This isn't what we want because the code readability decreases dramatically, and in general it is not necessary. JavaScript is a dynamic code language, and many of the templating constructs can be implemented in code. It's more difficult to implement the changing of a variable from using references to using values.

Solution

For illustration purposes, let's simplify the Proxy pattern to a single method with a single method call, as follows.

Source: /website/ROOT/ajaxrecipes/javascript/generics.html

```
function EmbeddedReplace() {
  var func = __toCall;
  info( "Replace", "hello");
  func();
}
```

The EmbeddedReplace function has declared a local variable, func. The func local variable references the __toCall variable. After the declaration of func is a call to the info function. The last function call is to func, which is a function call to __toCall. From looking solely at the usage of __toCall, you don't know much about the declaration other than it's a global variable.

For the scope of this recipe, __toCall is an identifier that will be replaced. A JavaScript expansion call would be as follows (I'll discuss the details shortly):

```
EmbeddedReplace = Generics.expand( EmbeddedReplace,
  { __toCall: function() { info( "replaced in Replace", "hello");}});
EmbeddedReplace();
```

The Generics.expand method has two parameters. The first parameter is the EmbeddedReplace function, which will have its implementation modified. The second parameter is the object structure that represents what identifiers will be replaced. The object structure is defined such that the property identifier defines the identifier to be replaced, and the value associated with the property is the replaced value.

■**Note** All of the code presented here uses standard JavaScript programmatic techniques. You don't need to use special buffers or tags that confuse editors and make it more complicated to build reliable, maintainable code.

When the Generics.expand method has finished executing, the following function declaration is generated:

```
function GeneratedEmbeddedReplace() {
  var func = (function () {
    info("replaced in Replace", "hello");
  });
  info("Replace", "hello");
  func();
}
```

The generated buffer is what we expect, and the behavior is what we expect. When GeneratedEmbeddedReplace is called, the embedded function is called. For comparison's sake, let's look at how this could have worked without expanding an embedded function:

```
function __toCall() {
  info("replaced in Replace", "hello");
};
function EmbeddedReplace() {
  var func = __toCall;
  info( "Replace", "hello");
  func();
}
```

Calling GeneratedEmbeddedReplace will call the __toCall function and behave, look, and feel like the expanded example. But why should you do this? The reference-based expansion is not an expansion at all. You have simply created a global variable (__toCall) that can be assigned at runtime. With a value-type expansion, you can have multiple functions with different functionalities that do not conflict with one another.

Because behavior is determined by assignment, you can run into the situation outlined in Recipe 2-14, where functions are shared. If functions are shared, then a conflict can arise if the functionality of the function is altered. Or you can have a situation where a function does one thing one time, and another thing another time. To illustrate the "do one thing now, but not later" problem, consider the following code scenario:

```
function __toCall() {
  info("replaced in Replace", "hello");
};
function EmbeddedReplace() {
  info( "Replace", "hello");
  __toCall();
}
function Caller() {
  EmbeddedReplace();
  __toCall = function() { }
  EmbeddedReplace();
}
```

When `Caller` is called, the first call to `EmbeddedReplace` results in some output. Then `__toCall` is reassigned, and calling `EmbeddedReplace` again results in other output being generated. Maybe this is the desired effect, but most likely it isn't. One way to solve the problem is to restrict your usage of the dynamic capabilities of JavaScript. However, at this point I would ask, why are you using JavaScript and Ajax? My opinion is that JavaScript and Ajax represent an evolution in programming and thus you should use their dynamic behavior capabilities.

Had `EmbeddedReplace` been expanded, then modifying `__toCall` would have had no effect on `EmbeddedReplace`. And this is what you need to consider when writing JavaScript code. Sometimes you will use references, and sometimes you will use expansions like those proposed by JavaScript generics.

I would like to add one more point. It is not a rule of thumb, but an idea that in specific contexts can have its place. Imagine writing an application where a payment is calculated based on the current daily interest rate. In most programming languages, the current interest payment would be a variable that would be loaded and assigned at runtime. Using JavaScript generics and behavior-based code, the following expanded code could be used:

```
function CalculateInterestPayment( amount) {
  return amount * 0.04;
}
```

This code is what other programming languages call *hard-coded*. It's considered hard-coded because the number 0.04 is compiled into the application and cannot be changed. But here is the advantage of the behavior-based code: using JavaScript generics, the hard-coded value is trivial to change, and keeping to a traditional programming model when you don't need to doesn't make any sense whatsoever.

You use a hard-coded programming strategy when the data is *read-mostly*, or when the data is read more often than it is written. Having the data hard-coded can be a performance gain, offer more flexibility, and simplify the algorithm. Using JavaScript generics today, the interest calculation is a simple number, but tomorrow the calculation could be a compound calculation that uses a sliding rule based on the amount that is processed.

Having explained the why, how, and when of JavaScript "generics," I'll now cover how JavaScript "generics" are implemented. It's a very simple process that involves searching and replacing an identifier in a buffer. The full implementation is as follows.

Source: /website/ROOT/scripts/common.js

```
var Generics = {
  expand : function(toProcess, itemsToInject) {
    var bufferToProcess = ops.singleSerialize(toProcess);
    for( itemToReplace in itemsToInject) {
      var recurFind = function(startIndex) {
        var offset = bufferToProcess.indexOf(itemToReplace, startIndex);
        if (offset == -1) {
          return;
        }
        var left = bufferToProcess.slice(0, offset);
        var right = bufferToProcess.slice(offset + itemToReplace.length);
        var middle = ops.simpleSerialize(itemsToInject[itemToReplace]);
        bufferToProcess = left + middle + right;
        offset ++;
        recurFind(offset);
      }
      recurFind(0);
    }
    var genBuffer = "var cls = " + bufferToProcess + ";";
    eval(genBuffer);
    return cls;
  }
}
```

To expand a JavaScript object, the object has to first be converted to a buffer. The ops.singleSerialize method converts any JavaScript object into a buffer, and in the case of the preceding example, it converts the toProcess parameter into a buffer. After the conversion to a buffer, the process of finding an identifier and replacing it using a loop is started. With each iteration of the loop stored in the itemToReplace variable is the identifier to replace in bufferToProcess.

In the loop, the recurToFind variable references a function that is called recursively. The purpose of the recursion is to incrementally search the buffer for the identifier to replace.

■**Note** Recursion strategy is covered in Recipe 2-6.

To find an identifier within bufferToProcess, the indexOf method is used. indexOf has two parameters: the first parameter is the identifier to find, and the second parameter is the index to start searching. If indexOf does not find an identifier, then a value of -1 is returned and the recursion stops. If indexOf finds the identifier, then the index of where the identifier starts is returned. Having found the identifier, the buffer is split into a left part and a right part. The left and right parts are combined with the text to be replaced, and a new bufferToProcess is created.

When no identifiers are found, the buffer is considered expanded. The last remaining step is to convert the buffer into an object instance. Converting the buffer is a problem because executing the `return eval( bufferToProcess)` command might lead to unpredictable scenarios. To make the conversion predictable, `bufferToProcess` is concatenated with an assignment to the `cls` variable. Then when the new buffer is executed using the `eval` statement, the local variable `cls` is instantiated, and it can be returned to the caller.

The code to expand and implement JavaScript "generics" is relatively simple, but the effects are profound. When using JavaScript "generics," keep the following points in mind:

- JavaScript references are easier to implement and, in many cases, good enough. However, as pointed out in Recipe 2-14, references do pose a "gotcha" problem.

- You have to make a decision between using references for everything and using `eval` for everything. "Everything" here doesn't refer to an entire application, but everything within the scope of a type or function. Don't mix references with the `eval` statement; doing so will cause problems.

- Overall, your code is more robust and stable if you use `eval`-like techniques. References work for simple cases, but if your code embeds code multiple times, then errors could result.

- With references, you run the risk that multiple pieces of code will reference the same code and the same variables. This can cause corruption and *should not be underestimated*.

- Using `eval`-like statements makes debugging easier, because if you serialize a function or object, you will get the current state of the code and thus be able to follow what the problem is. If you use references, you will need a debugger, and with code that determines its behavior at runtime, debugging can be tedious.

- Using JavaScript "generics" as described in this recipe is IDE-friendly because you are not creating buffers by hand, and you are not writing code with special tags that IDEs such as X-develop, Visual Studio, Komodo, and Visual SlickEdit do not understand.

2-10. Managing Runtime Behavioral Code

Problem

You want to effectively manage and debug your runtime behavioral code.

Theory

Using the `eval` keyword or dynamically assigning functions to object properties is a big part of dynamic programming. Dynamic programming involves code that exhibits a behavior at runtime, or *behavioral code*. Behavioral code is not a bad idea, but it does make for more complicated debugging.

The main problem with behavioral code is that the debugger has no idea what source it is debugging.

Solution

There are several solutions you can consider—here they are in brief:

- Implement test-driven development and perform in-depth testing in an incremental manner. Doing otherwise will cause errors to be generated in code pieces that do not have problems. Throughout this book, recipes use test-driven development techniques that you can inspect to understand how the code works. I highly advise that you take a moment now to explore how code is written, if you have not already done so. Take a look at these files, for example: /website/ROOT/ajaxrecipes/javascript/conventions.html, /website/ROOT/ajaxrecipes/javascript/proxy.html, and /website/ROOT/ajaxrecipes/javascript/variablebehavior.html.

- Generate the code into a buffer that is dumped to the HTML page text box. Take the dumped code and paste it into an HTML page for execution. The dumped code will contain the error that can be debugged. This solution is only advisable, however, if you are having persistent problems and cannot find the source.

- Use simple principles. I like dynamic and generated code as much as anybody else, but I stay away from code that is too clever and tries to solve too many problems at once. For example, I typically write verbose code and do not combine multiple operators into a single statement.

- Use a debugger. Mozilla and Firefox have fairly decent debuggers, and you should use them. With Microsoft Visual Studio 2005, it is possible to debug very complicated JavaScript code.

2-11. Putting XMLHttpRequest into a Factory

Problem

You want to put XMLHttpRequest into a factory.

Theory

When you are using XMLHttpRequest, the problem is how to instantiate XMLHttpRequest. Each browser has a different way of instantiating XMLHttpRequest. Here is what Mozilla and most other browsers use (this code will also work in Internet Explorer starting with version 7):

```
var xmlhttp = new XMLHttpRequest();
```

You use the following source code for Internet Explorer versions before 7:

```
var xmlhttp = new ActiveXObject('Microsoft.XMLHTTP');
```

The Microsoft.XMLHTTP buffer is a general identifier, as there are specializations available depending on the browser.

Solution

The short answer to the problem is that to instantiate XMLHttpRequest you need to use different techniques on different browsers.

To be able to instantiate the XMLHttpRequest object, you need to create an abstraction. The abstraction could be a class or a function, but which you choose does not matter. What does matter is that you create an abstraction or implement the Factory pattern.[1] In the Factory pattern implementation, the main challenge is to identify which browser is executing the script and then use the appropriate XMLHttpRequest instantiation.

The libraries jsolait, Prototype, Yahoo! patterns, and Dojo Toolkit all implement an XMLHttpRequest abstraction that is coded in the same manner. To illustrate the gist of how it is coded consider the following source code, which is from the Yahoo! Design Pattern Library (http://developer.yahoo.com/ypatterns).

```javascript
createXhrObject:function(transactionId)
{
    var obj,http;
    try
    {
        // Instantiates XMLHttpRequest in non-IE browsers and assigns to http.
        http = new XMLHttpRequest();
        // Object literal with http and id properties
        obj = { conn:http, tId:transactionId };
    }
    catch(e)
    {
        for(var i=0; i<this._msxml_progid.length; ++i){
            try
            {
                // Instantiates XMLHttpRequest for IE and assign to http.
                http = new ActiveXObject(this._msxml_progid[i]);
                // Object literal with http and id properties
                obj = { conn:http, tId:transactionId };
            }
            catch(e){}
        }
    }
    finally
    {
        return obj;
    }
},
```

The instantiations are wrapped in a series of try and catch blocks. A try and catch block in JavaScript is an exception block. The idea behind this form of abstraction is that you try executing some source code, and if it fails you do something else.

---

1. Erich Gamma, Richard Helm, Ralph Johnson, and John Vlissides, *Design Patterns: Elements of Reusable Object-Oriented Software* (New York: Addison-Wesley, 1995), p. 107.

The following steps are carried out in the source code:

1. Enter the first exception block.

2. Execute the XMLHttpRequest instantiation using the new keyword.

3. If the instantiation works, then the finally block is reached.

4. If the instantiation fails, an exception is generated and the catch block starts a loop.

5. The loop attempts to instantiate the Internet Explorer XMLHttpRequest using different identifiers referenced by the this._msxml_progid data member.

6. If the XMLHttpRequest object cannot be instantiated, an empty catch block captures the exception.

7. Regardless of what happens, the finally block is executed and returns the object instance stored in the obj variable.

The main idea of the abstraction is to execute the code, and if the browser does not support the functionality, an exception is generated. The exception is caught and causes a different instantiation sequence to start. What troubles me about this code is that it does not attempt to figure out what is supported, but uses JavaScript exceptions.

As the implementation stands, an exception is generated for a majority of cases. This is because at the time of this writing, Internet Explorer has a market share greater than 80%. This means that attempting to instantiate XMLHttpRequest using the new keyword will not work and will generate an exception.

The alternate way of instantiating XMLHttpRequest is used by the library Jaxson, as outlined in the books *Ajax in Action* (Manning, 2005) and *Professional Ajax* (Wrox, 2006). The technique shown in *Ajax in Action* is perfect[2] and is implemented by Jaxson as follows.

Source: /website/ROOT/scripts/communications.js

```
if( window.ActiveXObject) {
  FactoryXMLHttpRequest = function() {
    return new ActiveXObject( "Microsoft.XMLHTTP");
  }
}
else if( window.XMLHttpRequest) {
  FactoryXMLHttpRequest = function() {
    return new XMLHttpRequest();
  }
}
throw new Error( "Could not instantiate XMLHttpRequest");
```

The FactoryXMLHttpRequest function is different in that it is assigned as the page is being loaded by the browser. The advantage of assigning the FactoryXMLHttpRequest method is that you don't need to make yet another decision via a decision structure. You are defining the

---

2. A variation illustrated in *Professional Ajax* is the technique of checking if the type XMLHttpRequest exists.

behavior of the program during the initialization of the HTML page; you are not constantly asking what the behavior should be. This reasoning is also shown in Recipes 2-4 and 2-7.

Think about the context. If you are loading a page in a browser, do you think you could, for some reason or another, move your executing code to a completely different browser after it's been loaded and executed? The answer is no, because it is physically impossible. The browser you used to load the page will not during the execution decide to run the already processed code elsewhere.

In the initialization, the decision tests for the existence of the `window.ActiveXObject` or `window.XMLHttpRequest` property. The decision is asking the browser if specific types exist, and if they do, then they can be instantiated. This is a better approach than performing an instantiation and waiting for a potential exception, because the code knows what the browser is capable of and asks for the functionality. If the functionality does not exist, then an exception is generated by instantiating the `Error` type. This is a valid use of using an exception; at the time of this writing, you have only two ways to instantiate the `XMLHttpRequest` object. You may be thinking, "But what if the browser does not support Ajax and the `XMLHttpRequest` object?" If the browser does not support Ajax, the `FactoryXMLHttpRequest` function should not be called. The Permutations pattern and recipes in Chapter 3 address these issues.

■**Note** To instantiate the `XMLHttpRequest` object on Internet Explorer, a single line of source code is used. In contrast, other libraries use multiple instantiation attempts. These multiple instantiation attempts are not required because, per the MSDN documentation, it is only necessary to use the `Microsoft.XMLHTTP` string in Internet Explorer version 6 and below.

When instantiating the `XMLHttpRequest` object, keep the following points in mind:

- You will need to use an abstraction, because people will continue to use older versions of Internet Explorer for some time to come. Thus, you'll still have a need to figure out which instantiation technique to use.

- You should not use exceptions to test for expected functionality. Doing so without thinking will cause exceptions to be hidden.

- The better approach is to test for functionality and then instantiate the `XMLHttpRequest` instance.

- All that said, if you use a predefined instantiation that uses exceptions, such as the Yahoo! Design Pattern Library, it's not the end of the world. The point of this recipe is to suggest a better approach to use whenever possible.

2-12. Defining and Extending Classes

Problem

You want an effective strategy for defining and extending classes.

Theory

A function is an object, and as previous recipes illustrate, it is possible to associate properties and methods with a function. So why it is necessary to create classes, since functions can be morphed into classes? The answer relates to the problem of figuring out the instance of the function.

Using JavaScript closures you can define a function within a function, as shown in the following code.

Source: /website/ROOT/ajaxrecipes/javascript/functionsareobjects.html

```
function GetFunctionFixed() {
  var inst = function(cmpval) {
    assertEquals(cmpval, inst.value);
  }
  return inst;
}
```

By using a local variable, the instance of the function can be referenced within the implementation of the function. This works because functions are objects, and thus object referencing is happening.

Solution

Using the principle that functions are objects, it is possible to create a class without using the new keyword, as illustrated by the following example, which builds on the function within function technique.

Source: /website/ROOT/ajaxrecipes/javascript/definingextendingclasses.html

```
function CreateClassInstance() {
  var inst = function() {
    inst.instantiated = 10;
    inst.method = function() {
      inst.instantiated = 20;
    }
  }
  inst();
  return inst;
}
```

In the class example, a "class" is created because calling the function will assign the properties of the function. Thus the function behaves like a "class." The variable inst is referenced throughout the "class," making it possible to reference the properties and methods of the "class." In effect, the "class" is acting like a real class, as evidenced by the following test code.

Source: /website/ROOT/ajaxrecipes/javascript/definingextendingclasses.html

```
function_are_classes : function() {
  var cls1 = CreateClassInstance();
  info( "function_are_classes", cls1);
  cls1.value = 10;
  assertEquals( 10, cls1.instantiated);
  cls1.method();
  assertEquals( 20, cls1.instantiated);
  var cls2 = CreateClassInstance();
  assertEquals( "undefined",  typeof( cls2.value));
},
```

The test code experiments with various facets to demonstrate that the instantiated "object" is behaving like an object. The bold code shows that the "objects" cls1 and cls2 are in fact two separate instances.

Since it seems so easy to create a "class" and an "object," why is there a new keyword? The answer is because figuring out how to cross-reference the function instance with the method is complicated after the "class" has been instantiated, as illustrated by the following source code.

Source: /website/ROOT/ajaxrecipes/javascript/definingextendingclasses.html

```
function_classes_generates_error : function() {
  var cls = CreateClassInstance();
  cls.method2 = function() {
    inst.instantiated = 40;
  }
  try {
    cls.method2();
    testManager.failed();
  }
  catch( e) {
    info( "functions_classes_generates_error", "Expected exception (" +➡
      e.toString() + ")");
  }
},
```

In the additional test, the "class" is instantiated and assigned to the cls variable. The cls variable references an "object" that is extended with the method2 method. In the implementation of method2, the "object" instance is referenced using the inst variable. The inst variable was chosen because it was defined when the "object" was instantiated. Running the code will generate an exception because inst is not defined. To make the example work, the function referenced by method2 would have had to reference cls. In a nutshell, referencing the instance of the "object" within a function is more complicated than it ought to be.

The solution is the new keyword, as it associates the this identifier with the instance of the object from within a function. Rewriting the CreateClassInstance code to use the new keyword, we arrive at the CreateRealClassInstance function, shown in the following code.

Source: /website/ROOT/ajaxrecipes/javascript/definingextendingclasses.html

```
function CreateRealClassInstance() {
  var inst = function() {
    this.instantiated = 10;
    this.method = function() {
      this.instantiated = 20;
    }
  }
  return new inst();
}
```

Comparing CreateClassInstance and CreateRealClassInstance, the only real difference is that the new keyword is used while calling the inst variable as a function, and inst is replaced with this. Using the new keyword in front of a function converts the function into a custom object instance, where the instance of the object can be referenced using the this identifier within the function.

The returned object instance can be extended and the instance referenced using the this keyword, as shown in the following test.

Source: /website/ROOT/ajaxrecipes/javascript/definingextendingclasses.html

```
function_instantiates_real_class : function() {
  var cls = CreateRealClassInstance();
  cls.method2 = function() {
    this.instantiated = 40;
  }
  assertEquals(10, cls.instantiated);
  cls.method2();
  assertEquals(40, cls.instantiated);
},
```

Calling the CreateRealClassInstance function, the returned object instance is assigned to the cls variable. The object is expanded to include the method2 method, and in the implementation of method2 the object instance is referenced using the this variable. This time when method2 is called, there is no exception and the instantiated property has a value of 40.

If you are familiar with JavaScript and have already instantiated a few objects, then the previous instantiation syntax likely looks a bit odd. The classical way of instantiating an object in JavaScript is as follows:

```
function MyObject() { }
var cls = new MyObject();
```

This approach involves defining a function where the function is a constructor for the object of type MyObject. When MyObject is instantiated, the notation is very similar to instantiating a type in Java and C#, and therefore programmers who instantiate types in JavaScript never question what really happens. A more accurate explanation of how an object in JavaScript is defined is when the inst variable was used to instantiate an object. Specifically, an object is constructed by converting a function into an object, and the function associated with the new keyword is the constructor.

When manipulating JavaScript classes, keep the following points in mind:

- It is possible to create JavaScript types without using the new keyword. However, creating raw JavaScript "objects" has the disadvantage of having to cross-reference the "object" instance with the function.

- JavaScript objects are types that you can assign dynamically, making it possible to implement prototype-based programming, where the behavior of the type is determined at runtime.

- Earlier recipes in this chapter showed how to manipulate function objects, a technique that also applies to JavaScript object types.

- The basis of all JavaScript objects is the type Object.

- When using the new keyword to instantiate a type, the prototype property associated with the function object can be used to define behavior that applies to all instances of a particular type.

2-13. Implementing Code Blocks

Problem

You want to implement code blocks in your JavaScript applications, to optimize your code.

Theory

Implementing code blocks is a programming technique that at first glance seems to solve a problem that does not exist. Some might even say that a code block is nothing more than a fancy callback. Code blocks in JavaScript do bear similarities to callbacks. But in languages like Ruby, code blocks are part of the programming language and make for simpler code.

You use code blocks whenever you would iterate a list or a return function where you want to associate multiple pieces of information with a caller.

Solution

Let's first look at a simple example: some code to create a squared series.

Source: /website/ROOT/ajaxrecipes/javascript/codeblocks.html

```
function GenerateSquaredSeries( lastValue) {
  var array = new Array();
  for( var c1 = 0; c1 < lastValue; c1 ++) {
    array.push( c1 * c1);
  }
  return array;
}
```

To generate a series of numbers that are the square, a loop is created that counts from zero to the desired highest value. For each iteration, the value c_1 * c_1 (square of c_1) is pushed onto array. Once the looping has completed, the array is returned.

The example illustrates a problem of looping: the loop, and the initialization of the loop, is generic infrastructure code. The bold code shows the application-specific code, called for each iteration of the loop. The application-specific code is sandwiched between the for loop code. Abstracting the sandwiched code requires a callback, which looks like the following.

Source: /website/ROOT/ajaxrecipes/javascript/codeblocks.html

```
function GenerateSeries( lastValue, callback) {
  var array = new Array();
  for( var c1 = 0; c1 < lastValue; c1 ++) {
    callback( array, c1);
  }
  return array;
}
```

The modified GenerateSeries function has an additional parameter, which is the callback function called for each iteration. The callback function serves the purpose of carrying out the business logic, and thus passes the instantiated array and number to the callback. The callback can then process the passed parameters (array and c1) however it pleases. An example of this follows.

Source: /website/ROOT/ajaxrecipes/javascript/codeblocks.html

```
function ExampleSeriesSquare() {
  var array = GenerateSeries( 10, function( array, value) {
    array.push( c1 * c1);
  });
}
```

The ExampleSeriesSquare function has a single function call that calls GenerateSeries. An anonymous function is passed to GenerateSeries that will process the passed-in array and value. The code in the implementation of the anonymous function is identical to the application logic code in GenerateSquaredSeries, which is rather obvious. The example anonymous function is a code block.

As mentioned previously, a code block is like a callback. What makes a callback different from a code block is that a code block is general in nature and represents a separation of two pieces of code. To convert the code from a callback scenario into a code block scenario, GenerateSeries and ExampleSeriesSquare are rewritten as follows:

```
function GenerateSeriesMod( lastValue, callback) {
  for( var c1 = 0; c1 < lastValue; c1 ++) {
    callback( c1);
  }
}

function ExampleSeriesSquareMod() {
  var array = new Array();
  GenerateSeries( 10, function( value) {
    array.push( c1 * c1);
  });
}
```

In the converted code scenarios are two functions: GenerateSeriesMod and ExampleSeriesSquareMod. The GenerateSeriesMod function still has two parameters: a maximum value and a callback function. The ExampleSeriesSquareMod function still uses an anonymous function. The difference is that the declaration of the array has moved from GenerateSeriesMod to ExampleSeriesSquareMod. This move of the array in this simple scenario is what makes the difference between a plain vanilla callback and a code block.

Look at the details of GenerateSeriesMod and you will see that the implementation of GenerateSeriesMod only relates to requirements asked of it. The requirements are to generate a series of numbers that can be processed by an external functionality. The requirements do not state to create an array or create a buffer. The details of what to do with the generated series are implemented in the code block.

Thus, two code blocks can be independent of each other, but together fulfill the needs of iterating and generating a series. In this example, it might seem like overkill to use a code block, but you will quickly realize that using code blocks is a great way to process data sets. For example, we have all encountered loops embedded within loops. Very quickly in this situation, the code becomes complex and hard to follow. Using code blocks, you can separate the code, and the embedded loops within loops are reduced to smaller, easily understood code chunks.

Code blocks have an advantage in that they can process single results, multiple results, or no results. Looking at the implementation of GenerateSeriesSquared at the beginning of this recipe, an array is returned to the caller regardless of how many numbers are generated. The caller has to query the array and figure out if any numbers have been generated. In contrast, using a code block, the callback will be called only when a number is generated.

The following code shows a more formal way of using a code block.

Source: /website/ROOT/ajaxrecipes/javascript/codeblocks.html

```
function CustomList() {
  this.array = new Array();
}

CustomList.prototype.iterate = function( callback) {
  for( item in this.array) {
    callback( item);
  }
}
CustomList.prototype.addItems = function() {
  for( var c1 = 0; c1 < arguments.length; c1 ++) {
    this.array.push( arguments[ c1]);
  }
}
```

In the example, a CustomList class is being defined. The custom list has two functions: iterate and addItems. The addItems function is used to add an item to a list, and the iterate function iterates each of the elements in the loop and calls a callback. The callback parameter represents a code block. An example of using CustomList is as follows.

Source: /website/ROOT/ajaxrecipes/javascript/codeblocks.html

```
class_list_iterate : function() {
  var list = new CustomList();
  list.addItems( "hello", "world");
  list.iterate( function( item) {
    info( "class_list_iterate", item);
  });
},
```

CustomList is instantiated and assigned to the variable list. An item is added to the list using the addItems function. Notice that addItems is multiple-parameter-aware. Often in programming languages, you need to call the addItem method to add an item to a list as often as there are items. The addItems method is different in that you can specify as many parameters as you like, and each of those parameters represents a single item to add to the list. To iterate the list, a code block is defined, and in the implementation of the code block, the data can be processed however it pleases the caller. In this example, the items are output using the info method.

Code blocks can also be used to generate and process return values. Let's consider an example that creates a function used to find the closing statistics of a stock ticker. Following is the implementation of the code using a traditional non-code-block approach:

```
function StockTracerTraditional( ticker) {
  if( ticker == "YHOO") {
    var obj = new Object();
    this.company = "Yahoo";
    this.close = 23;
    this.change = -1;
    return obj;
  }
  return null;
}

function CallerStockTracer() {
  var obj = StockTracerTraditional( "YHOO");
  if( obj != null) {
    info( "return_value", "Company=" + obj.company + " close=" + obj.close +➡
      " change=" + obj.change);
  }
}
```

The StockTracerTraditional function has a single parameter: the ticker to be found. If the ticker is found, an object is instantiated and the appropriate properties are assigned. Once the properties have been assigned, the instantiated object is returned. The CallerStockTracer function implementation calls StockTracerTraditional with the appropriate ticker, and the returned object instance is assigned to obj. Then a decision is made to verify if obj is null or not. If the ticker has been found, then obj will not be null and the object can be processed. Otherwise, the function returns without doing anything.

The example code can be simplified using code blocks. The following rewritten implementation of StockTracerTraditional uses code blocks results.

Source: /website/ROOT/ajaxrecipes/javascript/codeblocks.html

```
function StockTracker( ticker, callback) {
  if( ticker == "YHOO") {
    callback( "Yahoo", 23, -1);
  }
}
```

The StockTrader function is rewritten, and the same decision block to find the ticker is used. What is new is the use of the callback that is called when a ticker is found. Consider what happens if the YHOO ticker is found: the callback is called with three parameters. If a code block were not used, then an object would have to be instantiated and returned to the caller. Because a code block is used, there is no need to verify if data is returned, as illustrated by the following caller code.

Source: /website/ROOT/ajaxrecipes/javascript/codeblocks.html

```
return_value : function() {
  StockTracker( "YHOO", function( company, close, change) {
    // Do something with the data
    info( "return_value", "Company=" + company + " close=" + close + " change=" +➥
      change);
  });
},
```

Calling StockTracker with the ticker to find as YHOO will result in the anonymous function being called. In the implementation of the anonymous function would be the code that is executed when data has been returned successfully. With code blocks, the caller does not have to implement a decision structure, because the anonymous function will be called only if the ticker exists.

Code blocks are a means to an end, and do not imply that you should never use decision blocks or create loops with application logic. Code blocks provide a mechanism to simplify and decouple code from another. When you use code blocks, remember the following:

- Code blocks are like callbacks, except that code blocks promote the separation of logic, making pieces of code independent of each other.

- The advantage of code blocks is that they can process single results, multiple results, or no results. The calling code does not have to determine if the results worked.

- Using the dynamic nature of JavaScript, a function can process multiple parameters as a set.

- Code blocks can be used as an alternative to the return statement to send more complex data. As mentioned in Recipe 2-17, code blocks are the perfect way to return data to the caller without having to use a return type.

2-14. Turning toSource into a Complete Serialization Solution

Problem

You want a fix to turn toSource into a complete serialization solution.

Theory

Mozilla has developed a very clever method called toSource. Using toSource, it is possible to serialize the state of an object into a buffer. Consider the following type declaration example.

Source: /website/ROOT/ajaxrecipes/javascript/tosource.html

```
function DefinedClass() {
  this.localvalue = 10;
  this.localmethod = function(param) {
    info("DefinedClass.localmethod", "called me");
  }
}
```

The DefinedClass type has defined a localmethod method and a localvalue data member. When the type is instantiated, the instantiated type has a toSource method that can be called, as illustrated in the following source code.

Source: /website/ROOT/ajaxrecipes/javascript/tosource.html

```
var cls = new DefinedClass();
cls.prototypemethod.value = 100;
info("mozilla_tosource", cls.toSource());
```

When toSource is called, the following buffer is generated:

```
{
  localvalue:10,
  localmethod:(function (param) {info("DefinedClass.localmethod", "called me");})
}
```

The generated buffer is a serialized form of an object instance. Missing from the serialization is the type definition. When the object instance is re-created, recreated is the state of the object. Yet this is not completely true, because the following prototype declaration is missed by toSource.

Source: /website/ROOT/ajaxrecipes/javascript/tosource.html

```
DefinedClass.prototype.prototypevalue = new StaticClass();
```

Anything that is declared via the DefinedClass.prototype property is missed by the toSource implementation. Missing the base properties and methods makes sense if the toSource buffer were to contain a reference to the type that created the instance. Yet there is no reference with missing methods and properties, and no support on any browser other than Mozilla/Firefox. So what is the use of toSource?

The toSource method by itself is limited, but the idea behind toSource is good. We want the ability to serialize an object for later consumption, and as will be shown in later recipes, serialization is the key to implementing various object-oriented techniques, such as mixins. As illustrated by Mozilla's implementation of toSource, serialization can have different facets.

Before beginning an implementation of serialization, let's identify the different contexts of serialization:

- *Plain vanilla serialization like* toSource: The default serialization provided by Mozilla is not available on other browsers. For those Web applications that do use toSource, there needs to be an implementation for other browsers. Not serializing the prototype properties is useful when you want to serialize the additional information and not the base information.

- *Full instance declaration serialization*: A complete instance serialization is when all methods, properties, and data members are converted into a buffer that, when executed, will completely re-create the object. When the instance is re-created, its original type information is lost.

- *Instance state serialization*: In contrast to other serializations, state serialization is the generation of a buffer that contains only the state of an object; the function declarations are not generated. The JavaScript Object Notation (JSON) protocol is an example of an instance state–only serialization. When serializing the instance state, data members defined in the prototype property are included.

- *Variable assignment serialization*: A full instance declaration serialization includes all of the state of an object instance, but the function properties are missing because they not used often. If a function property is used, then the serialized state has to be assigned to a variable; otherwise, it is very difficult to assign function properties.

- *Object-oriented serialization*: Object-oriented serialization is an extension of the plain vanilla serialization. The reason for defining an object-oriented serialization is to enable the separation of class-specific data and instance-specific data. Using object-oriented serialization, an object could be serialized and re-created with different default behavior.

Each of the contexts is a specific flavor of serialization. The common feature among all of the contexts is that they serialize the same information and filter out what is not necessary. For example, plain vanilla serialization filters out any property referenced by prototype. State serialization filters out all functions, but iterates properties referenced by prototype.

Solution

As a first step, we'll create a general "serialize everything" implementation. The serialize everything implementation will include filtering capabilities and output generation control capabilities. Using the general serialization requires quite a bit of understanding of the serialization process, so that fine-tuning is possible.

As a second step, we'll implement the specific serialization contexts with the appropriate filtering implementations.

Serializing everything means iterating everything that is stored in the object instance, and then asking the caller if it is OK to serialize the information. From a high level, the serialize everything function is implemented as follows. In the serialize everything functionality, two pieces of functionality have been cut out for clarity purposes and are noted by the comments `// Removed for clarity`.

Source: /website/ROOT/scripts/common.js

```
serialize : function(obj, callbacks) {
  var buffer = "{";
  var comma = function() {
    comma = function() {
      return ",";
    }
    return "";
  }
  var quoteProperties = "";
  var canProcessFilter = function() { return true; }
  var functionPropertyCallback = function() {  }
  var callingStack;
  if (typeof(arguments[ 2]) == "undefined") {
    callingStack = new Array();
    callingStack.push("cls");
  }
  else {
    callingStack = arguments[ 2];
  }
  if (callbacks) {
    // Removed for clarity
  }
  for( property in obj) {
    if (canProcessFilter(obj[property], obj, property)) {
      switch (typeof(obj[property])) {
        // Removed for clarity
      }
    }
  }
  buffer += "}";
  return buffer;
}
```

The serialize function has two parameters, but for certain contexts (explained later) there is a third parameter. The third parameter has been left off so as to not confuse those people who want to use the function. The first parameter, `obj`, represents the object instance that is serialized. The second parameter, `callbacks`, represents the customization methods that are called when the data is serialized.

Until the loop is started using the `for` keyword, variables are initialized. They are defined as follows:

- `buffer`: This variable is used to create the complete text that represents the serialized object.

- `comma`: This variable uses the technique outlined in Recipe 2-7 to determine whether a comma is needed when creating the JavaScript serialized object format. As a reference, each property declaration in a serialized object format (e.g., `{prop1: true;,prop2:false}`) is separated using a comma. The function implements a technique where the first time it is called, no comma is necessary, but for every call thereafter, a comma is necessary. Without using the technique in Recipe 2-7, a decision block and flag would be necessary.

- `quoteProperties`: This variable denotes whether the buffer contains a double quote. The quote is used when serializing the object to JSON format.

- `canProcessFilter`: This variable is a function callback that is called for each property value found. The callback returns either `true` to serialize the property or `false` to ignore the property. The callback has three parameters: `property`, the actual property reference; `obj`, the object being serialized; and `propertyIdentifier`, the string identifier of the property.

- `functionPropertyCallback`: This variable is a function callback that is called when iterating the properties of a function. The properties of the function cannot be stored in the buffer variable because the serialized format does not allow for the definition of function properties. The properties of a function need to be assigned after the definition of the serialized JavaScript object buffer. This is why the complete serialization of a JavaScript object requires a variable definition.

- `callingStack`: To assign a function property embedded within another JavaScript object declaration, you need the serialized object reference (e.g., `variable.embeddedobj.function.value`). To create the reference, a stack is used, where each element in the stack is an object reference.

After the declarations, the properties of the object are iterated (`for(property...)` in a loop. Before explaining the details of the loop, I'll cover the missing callback initialization.

Source: `/website/ROOT/scripts/common.js`

```
if (callbacks) {
  if (callbacks.canProcessFilter) {
    canProcessFilter = callbacks.canProcessFilter;
  }
  if (callbacks.functionPropertyCallback) {
    functionPropertyCallback = callbacks.functionPropertyCallback;
  }
  if (callbacks.variablename) {
    callingStack.pop();
    callingStack.push(callbacks.variablename);
  }
```

```
    if (callbacks.quoteProperties) {
      if (callbacks.quoteProperties == true) {
        quoteProperties = "\"";
      }
    }
  }
}
```

The caller of the serialization does not need to provide a value for `callbacks`. If no value is provided, a default serialization of everything is assumed, except the function properties. The function properties are not serialized because there is no way in the serialized JavaScript object format to associate a function property with the function. More of the code will be explained shortly.

The serialization has four callback functions:

- `canProcessFilter`: Used to determine whether the property can be serialized.

- `functionPropertyCallback`: Called whenever a function property is serialized.

- `variableName`: Represents the variable identifier used when a serialization to a variable is generated.

- `quoteProperties`: Represents a value that when set to `true` generates quotes around the property identifier. This is typically used when generating a serialization format for JSON.

Now that we've looked at the initialization details, let's move on to examine the serialization logic. The loop is responsible for serializing the object instance, and the details of the loop have been abbreviated. At this stage, I'll explain the overall strategy.

In JavaScript, each method and data member can be accessed on an object using the following notation:

```
obj.datamember = ...
```

This notation is the most common way of accessing a method or data member when writing source code. For serialization purposes, the notation is not useful because the programmer is expected to know what the individual methods and data members are. For serialization purposes, reflection is needed. Reflection in JavaScript is a two-step process:

1. The string value property identifiers are available using an enumeration and iterated using a loop (e.g., `for(property in obj)`).

2. The actual property is accessed using an array notation, where the array is the object instance and the index is the string value property identifier (e.g., `obj[property]`).

As each property is iterated, the serialization first queries if the property should be serialized by calling the `canProcessFilter` callback function. If the property can be serialized, then a `switch` statement is called that tests the type of the property. The `typeof` function returns six different identifiers, of which five are of interest (we are not interested in `undefined`, as `undefined` should not be serialized). The details of the `switch` statement are as follows.

Source: /website/ROOT/scripts/common.js

```
switch (typeof(obj[property])) {
  case "boolean":
    buffer += comma() + quoteProperties +
      property + quoteProperties + ":" + object[property];
    break;
    case "function":
    buffer += comma() + quoteProperties +
      property + quoteProperties + ":" + obj[property].toString();
    callingStack.push(property);
    functionPropertyCallback( obj[property], obj, property, callbacks,➥
      callingStack);
    callingStack.pop();
    break;
  case "number":
    buffer += comma() + quoteProperties +
      property + quoteProperties + ":" + obj[property];
    break;
  case "object":
    callingStack.push(property);
    buffer += comma() + quoteProperties +
      property + quoteProperties + ":" +
      ops.serialize(obj[property], callbacks, callingStack);
    callingStack.pop();
    break;
  case "string":
    buffer += comma() + quoteProperties +
      property + quoteProperties + ":" + object[property];
    break;
}
```

In the implementation of the switch statement, the types number, string, and boolean
have a straightforward serialization implementation. The serialization of those types follow
the convention [property identifier] : [property value]. function and object are more
complicated.

When an object is encountered, then an embedded JavaScript object serialization occurs
and the ops.serialization function is called recursively. The result of the serialization is a property value that is added to the buffer to be returned to the caller. The remaining parts of the
serialize function add a curly bracket to close off the serialization and return the generated
buffer to the caller.

The presented serialization is complete, and each of the contexts uses the serialization
function to generate its own generated buffer.

Let's consider the implementation of the Serializer.toSource function, which mimics
the Mozilla toSource serialization. This means that any function or data member defined as
part of the prototype property is not processed. What is being asked is to determine whether
a property should be serialized using a filter. The complete implementation of
Serializer.toSource follows.

Source: /website/ROOT/scripts/jaxson/commons.js

```
Serializer.toSource = function(obj) {
  return ops.serialize(obj,
  {
    currProcessedObject : null,
    iterPrototype : null,
    canProcessFilter: function(property, currObj, propertyIdentifier) {
      if (this.currProcessed != currObj) {
        GetPrototypeObject(currObj, function(prototype) {
          this.iterPrototype = prototype;
        });
        this.currProcessed = currObj;


      }
      if (typeof(iterPrototype) == "object") {
        for( prototypeIdentifier in iterPrototype) {
          if (prototypeIdentifier == propertyIdentifier) {
            return false;
          }
        }
      }
      return true;
    }
  });
}
```

In the implementation of Serialize.toSource is a single method call, and it is to ops.serialize. By default, ops.serialize will serialize everything, and that should be avoided. To be able to distinguish between an instance property and a property defined by the prototype property, the implementation of canProcessFilter has to figure out what properties are associated with the instance. In the canProcessFilter method implementation is a reference to GetPrototypeObject. GetPrototypeObject is a convenience function used to retrieve the prototype property associated with the object. I cover the implementation of GetPrototypeObject shortly.

For the moment, let's focus on what happens in the filter. When ops.serialize is called, it will iterate the properties of the toSerialize object. When a property is retrieved, the user-defined filter canFilterProcess function is called. canFilterProcess has as a second parameter the object to which the soon-to-be-serialized property belongs to.

In the canFilterProcess implementation is a reference to currProcessedObject. The reference is necessary for performance purposes. An object to be serialized can reference other objects that have a prototype property. Because objects can contain objects to be serialized, you cannot retrieve the prototype property for obj and verify every property against obj. The only solution is to retrieve the prototype property for every object that is passed to the canFilterProcess implementation. If an object has five properties, the GetPrototypeObject function is called five times, and that is a waste of resources. Thus, currProcessedObject is used to cache the last used object reference and retrieve the prototype property only when a new object instance is being serialized.

To verify if a property belongs to prototype, a loop is started that iterates the properties of the prototype property reference (iterProperty). If a property from prototype (prototypeIdentifier) matches the property to be serialized, then a value of false is returned, indicating that the property should not be serialized. A returned value of true indicates that the property should be serialized.

Before we move on to look at another context, let's examine the implementation of GetPrototypeObject, which is complicated because it involves the dynamic nature of JavaScript. The problem with JavaScript is that you cannot figure out what the type of an instance is when it has been instantiated. The only reference information you have is the constructor property, which is the function used to instantiate the object. This little piece of information helps us because in JavaScript the constructor function also happens to be the name of the type. So the strategy is to extract the identifier of the constructor function and then reference the prototype property, as shown in the following code.

Source: /website/ROOT/scripts/jaxson/commons.js

```
function GetPrototypeObject(obj, callback) {
  if (typeof(obj.constructor) == "function") {
    var funcMatch = /function\s(.*)\(/;
    var result = obj.constructor.toString().match(funcMatch);
    if (result != null) {
      if (typeof(callback) == "function") {
        var iterobj;
        if (typeof(result[1]) == "string") {
          eval("var prototypePropery = " + result[1] + ".prototype;");
          callback(prototypePropery, result[1]);
        }
      }
    }
  }
}
```

In the implementation of GetPrototypeObject, the first test is the verification that the obj.constructor property actually exists. If the function does not exist, then there is no constructor, and there is no need to continue. If the function does exist, then a regular expression is used to extract the function name. The regular expression in the code example is shown in bold and is recognized as a regular expression because of the slashes.

When using regular expressions in the context of a string, the match function is called and returns the results of the match. If there are results, then an identifier is found that can be used to reference the prototype property. But a text buffer and not an object is found. The text buffer has to be converted into an object, by using the eval statement. The dynamically executed buffer will assign the locally declared prototypeProperty to reference the prototype property. Then using a code block, the object property and identifier are passed to the caller.

Another context is the serialization of an object instance that only includes state and no functions. Without yet seeing the code, you can probably guess what the filter does. The filter code tests if the property to be filtered is a function object. If the property is a function object, then the property should not be filtered. And, in fact, that is how the filter code is written, as shown in the following listing.

Source: /website/ROOT/scripts/jaxson/commons.js

```
Serializer.toSourceState = function(obj) {
  return ops.serialize(obj,
  {
    canProcessFilter: function(property, obj, propertyIdentifier) {
      if (typeof(property) == "function") {
        return false;
      }
      else {
        return true;
      }
    }
  });
}
```

The bold code shows how to test the type of object using the typeof operator.

Another context is the serialization of state to JSON notation. Serializing to JSON is like serializing to a state, except that the property identifiers have quotes around them. The serialization code is identical to the state serialization code, except that the quoteProperties data member is set to true.

Source: /website/ROOT/scripts/jaxson/commons.js

```
Serializer.toSourceJSON = function(obj) {
  return ops.serialize(obj,
  {
    quoteProperties : true,➡
    canProcessFilter: function(property, obj, propertyIdentifier) {
      if (typeof(property) == "function") {
        return false;
      }
      else {
        return true;
      }
    }
  });
}
```

After examining the previous three serialization contexts, you are probably thinking that the code is relatively similar, but the results are very different. This is an example of how code blocks can be used to separate the general iteration from a specific processing.

Another serialization context that you will use that is similar to toSource is serializing with a reference. The context of this serialization is as follows. You are creating a system where a type serves as a basic functionality. After having instantiated the type, customizations are performed. Then you decide to serialize the object, but you want to serialize only the customizations, the reason being that when the object is re-created on another computer or program, you want a different base functionality to be used. Thus, the same class could operate with different base functionalities. The solution is to not serialize the prototype properties and then generate a buffer that instantiates the type.

■**Note** I don't explain the implementation of the other serialization context types because they don't illustrate any new techniques. I cover only how to use `GetPrototypeObject` in a different context and more complicated filter code. If you're interested in learning more, take a look at the test code in the file `/website/ROOT/ajaxrecipes/javascript/tosource.html`, and in particular the test method `jaxson_tosource_oo`.

Serialization in JavaScript seems to be a simple thing, and the `toSource` method looks extremely useful. Yet as discussed in this recipe, `toSource` is incomplete. When you write JavaScript code to serialize, keep the following points in mind:

- Serialization in JavaScript means to generate a buffer that is formatted in the JavaScript Object format.

- In this recipe, we didn't look at how to re-create the serialized object. This is because to do so only requires passing the buffer to the `eval` statement and assigning the results of `eval` to a variable.

- Serialization has many different contexts. The `ops.serialize` function implements a very general serialization that needs to be specialized.

- When serializing, there is no type information. To have type information, you need to extract it and then store it somewhere. Remember that JavaScript is a prototype-based programming language, and JavaScript types are different in concept when compared to types in languages like C# and Java.

- This recipe's serialization techniques show how to define an algorithm that uses code blocks to separate a general iteration code block from a specific context code block.

2-15. Implementing Mixins in JavaScript

Problem

You want to implement Ruby-style mixins in JavaScript to easily extend object functionality.

Theory

In Ruby, *mixins* are a way of extending the functionality of an object by adopting the functionality of another object. When you instantiate a JavaScript type, the methods and properties associated with the type depend on the declaration of the type. To extend the functionality of an instance, a property is assigned with a function or another object.

A mixin, which is an extension of a type using dynamic means, is implemented as illustrated in Figure 2-4.

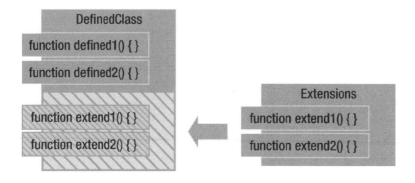

Figure 2-4. *Example of how a mixin is implemented*

In Figure 2-4, the DefinedClass class has two methods: defined1 and defined2. A mixin results when the functionality from another type is copied into DefinedClass. In the case of Figure 2-4, the extend1 and extend2 methods are copied into DefinedClass.

In code terms, consider the following JavaScript type, which represents the DefinedClass.

Source: /website/ROOT/ajaxrecipes/javascript/mixins.html

```
function DefinedClass() {
}
DefinedClass.prototype.defined1 = function() { }
DefinedClass.prototype.defined2 = function() { }
```

The DefinedClass function is used to define a type. Two methods, defined1 and defined2, are associated with the DefinedClass type. Each method is associated with the prototype property, so every time DefinedClass is instantiated, these methods will share the same function instance. Thus, if you assign a property of defined1 or defined2, then all instances of DefinedClass will be able to share the same property instance.

Solution

To extend an instance of DefinedClass, you could individually assign the properties of the instance. Individually copying a property is tedious; a more efficient solution is to copy the properties of one object to another object. Many frameworks, such as Prototype and Dojo Toolkit, provide the ability to copy properties. Following is the mixin implementation for Prototype.

Source: /website/ROOT/prototype/dist/prototype.js

```
Object.extend = function(destination, source) {
  for (property in source) {
    destination[property] = source[property];
  }
  return destination;
}
```

The Object.extend function has two parameters: destination and source. The destination parameter represents an object that will have properties added. The source parameter represents an object that will have its properties copied.

The properties are copied using a for loop because it is not possible to iterate the properties of an object instance in any other way. The property identifier, not the property value, is iterated. To retrieve the property value, you could use the following syntax:

```
source.property
```

The problem with this notation is that the property is defined explicitly, and using it in the context of implementing a mixin function is complicated. The solution is to use the JavaScript array notation and retrieve the property as an array. Going back to the Prototype solution, as each property of the source is iterated, the value is retrieved and assigned to the destination.

Let's apply the extend method using the following object instance declaration.

Source: /website/ROOT/ajaxrecipes/javascript/mixins.html

```
MyExtensions = {
  test : function(tstValue) {
    assertEquals(tstValue, MyExtensions.test.value);
  }
}
```

The MyExtensions class declaration is a static reference to a single embedded property that is an instance of type Object. We want to copy the property to an instance of DefinedClass, as shown in the following test.

Source: /website/ROOT/ajaxrecipes/javascript/mixins.html

```
prototype_mixin : function() {
  var cls = new DefinedClass();
  if( MyExtensions.test.value) {
    testManager.failed();
  }
  Object.extend(cls, MyExtensions);
  cls.test.value = 3;
  cls.test(3);
  cls.test.value = 10;
  cls.test(10);
},
```

The test code goes beyond the simple calling of Object.extend, but reveals that most toolkits implement mixins using duck types based on references. It is not wrong, but because functions are objects they will be shared among multiple class types.

To understand this, look at the implementation of MyExtensions.test. The implementation references the test.value function property and cross-references it with the tstValue parameter. In the implementation of the prototype_mixin function, an instance of DefinedClass is created and then extended with the methods of MyExtensions. The cls.test.value property is assigned a value of 3, and the test method is called.

The implementation of test verifies the value of MyExtensions.test.value as 3. If the test method of cls were a copy of the MyExtension.test method, then the test would fail because MyExtensions.test.value has not been assigned, as evidenced by the if test block. But the test code does not fail, which indicates that cls.test and MyExtensions.test are one and the same method.

Referenced-based duck typing has some odd behaviors, one of which is shown in the following code.

Source: /website/ROOT/ajaxrecipes/javascript/mixins.html

```
function GetExtensionFunctionality() {
  return {
    test : function(tstValue) {
      assertEquals(tstValue, this.test.value);
    }
  }
}
prototype_inconsistent_mixin : function() {
  var cls1 = new DefinedClass();
  var cls2 = new DefinedClass();

  Object.extend( cls1, GetExtensionFunctionality());
  Object.extend( cls2, GetExtensionFunctionality());

  cls1.test.value = 3;
  try {
    cls2.test( 3);
  }
  catch( e) {
    if (e.jsUnitMessage) {
      info("prototype_inconsistent_mixin", "Expected exception➡
        (" + e.jsUnitMessage + ")");
    }
  }
},
```

Here, the extended functionality is defined in the context of a method call. In the previous example, the test method was shared by multiple classes. In the test, cls1 and cls2 should also share the same test method. Running the test code will result in an expected exception stating that cls.test.value does not have the value 3.

In a nutshell, the problem is that you have two ways of calling Object.extend, and you get two completely different behaviors due to the nature of value- and reference-based duck typing. It is something that you need to be aware of, because you might get some odd behavior. This issue goes back to Recipe 2-8, which shows the differences between value and reference duck typing. Sometimes you want value duck typing, and sometimes you want reference duck typing.

Of course, a counterargument could be that if you think about the nature of the `prototype` property, the same sort of behavior results. I agree—that is the case—but also realize that the examples did not use the `prototype` identifier. A JavaScript developer knows what the ramifications of `prototype` are, and thus will know when to use and when not to use the keyword. In this recipe's examples, a prototype behavior was illustrated without using `prototype`.

We know about this situation and have two mixin methods: one that copies references (reference duck typing) and one that does a complete copy (value duck typing). The complete value-based duck-typed mixin implementation follows.

Source: `/website/ROOT/scripts/jaxson/common.js`

```
mixin : function( copyTo, copyFrom, forceCopy) {
  var copiedFrom = eval( ops.singleSerialize( copyFrom));
  for (property in copyFrom) {
    if((copyTo[ property] && force) || !copyTo[ property]) {
      copyTo[ property] = copiedFrom[ property];
    }
  }
}
```

In the implementation of the `mixin` method, the first step is to generate a buffer of the instance to be copied (`ops.singleSerialize`), and then execute the buffer using `eval`. The process of generating a buffer and then executing it has the effect of cloning the object and its properties. Then when the clone is iterated, the object to be extended has references to the cloned object, and not the original object. This fulfills the requirement that the object to be extended has copied the properties of the source object.

In the book's source code, you'll also find a method called `ops.refMixin`, which behaves like the other mixin implementations and assigns references to the object to be extended.

When implementing mixins, keep the following points in mind:

- Mixins are a way of extending the functionality of an object by adopting the functionality of another object. In JavaScript, you can replicate this technique by copying the references or by copying the functionality directly.

- Mixins are a form of prototype-based programming where the behavior of the object is determined at runtime.

- You may not write properties that are part of functions, and thus think that the reference copying is not a problem. But be forewarned: if your source object references properties that reference objects, then the object is not copied, but rather the reference to the object.

- You will use mixins extensively when writing JavaScript code, so be careful with your objects and references.

2-16. Implementing Proxy Methods

Problem

You want an effective strategy for implementing proxy methods.

Theory

The Proxy pattern is defined as an implementation of an interface that acts as a pass-through for the real implementation. Any user of the interface instance will not realize that a particular method call is being rerouted. The full implementation of the Proxy pattern is not the focus of this recipe; rather, this recipe focuses on applying the Proxy pattern for a single method.

As shown in Figure 2-5, the DefinedClass type has two methods: defined1 and defined2. The defined2 method captures the request, and after some processing delegates the call to the original defined2 method.

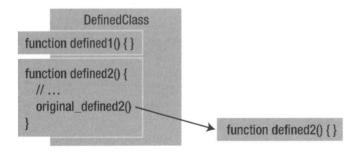

Figure 2-5. *Architecture of a single-method Proxy pattern*

When implementing a single-method Proxy pattern, the outer method that captures the request processes the request and then proxies the information to the inner method. The inner method does not realize that a proxy method has intercepted the request. This may appear to state the obvious, but there is another way to wire together two methods, as illustrated in Figure 2-6.

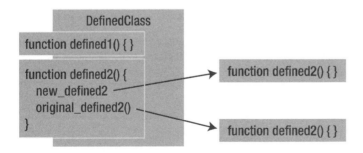

Figure 2-6. *Another way to wire together two methods*

In the alternate way of wiring together two methods, the defined2 method associated with the class instance is wired to first call the new method, and then call the original method. In this form of wiring, you are not implementing the Proxy pattern—you are creating a delegate model. The main difference between a proxy and delegate model is that the proxy model is responsible for calling the original implementation, and the delegate model does not have that restriction.

Solution

Now that you know the difference between the two models and what you want to achieve, let's examine what the source code should look like, and then convert that source into a general method. Consider the following class declaration.

Source: /website/ROOT/ajaxrecipes/javascript/proxy.html

```
function DefinedClass() {
}
DefinedClass.prototype.defined = function(tstvalue) {
  info("DefinedClass.defined", "parameter (" + tstvalue + ") arguments count (" +➥
    arguments.length + ")");
  DefinedClass.prototype.defined.value = 10;
  assertEquals(tstvalue, this.value);
}
```

The DefinedClass class is defined, and it has a single method, defined. The method-level Proxy pattern will be applied to defined. The proxy method that is called before the original method defined is as follows.

Source: /website/ROOT/ajaxrecipes/javascript/proxy.html

```
var proxyfunc = function(tstValue, toCall, args) {
  info("proxyfunction", "parameter (" + tstValue + ") received arg count (" +➥
    arguments.length + ") original arg count (" + args.length + ")");
  toCall.apply(this, args);
}
```

Implementing the proxy can be a challenge, because the current method implementation (defined) has to be moved. Per the Proxy pattern implementation, the function referenced by the proxyfunc variable has to be called before the current method implementation.

The obvious solution is to assign the defined method to the proxyfunc variable reference, as follows:

```
DefinedClass.prototype.defined = proxyfunc
```

This solution is quirky, because the original method is not referenced by proxyfunc. The original method would seem to have disappeared, and when proxyfunc does attempt to call the original method, an error will result. The original method could follow a convention where the method implementation is referenced by another property:

```
DefinedClass.prototype.originalDefined = DefinedClass.prototype.defined;
DefinedClass.prototype.defined = proxyfunc
```

proxyfunc, which is responsible for calling the original implementation using convention, knows that the original method is stored in the originalDefined property.

So this seems OK, but in fact there is another problem. What if you have a proxy method of a proxy method? Since the originalDefined method is already defined, do you overwrite and lose the original method to be called? Another solution is to extend the convention to the following:

```
DefinedClass.prototype.originalOriginalDefined =➥
  DefinedClass.prototype.originalDefined;
DefinedClass.prototype.originalDefined = DefinedClass.prototype.defined;
DefinedClass.prototype.defined = proxyfunc
```

The downside to this solution is that per the convention, the identifier contains a number of original identifiers. The convention requires that a specific proxy method be placed at a specific location; otherwise, the proxy method does not know whether to call originalDefined or orginalOriginalDefined. Another problem is, what if originalDefined referenced a real method?

The solution to the proxy method recipe is not to create new properties, but to create embedded functions. Embedding functions makes it possible to declare a function that is not accessible externally, and the proxy method can be embedded within a proxy method. The generated JavaScript follows:

```
DefinedClass.prototype.defined = function() {
  var origFunc = function (tstvalue) {
    info("DefinedClass.defined", "parameter (" + tstvalue + ") arguments count (" +➥
      arguments.length + ")");
    assertEquals(tstvalue, this.value);
  }
  var proxyFunc = function (tstValue, toCall, args) {
    info("proxyfunction", "parameter (" + tstValue + ") received arg count (" + ➥
      arguments.length + ") original arg count (" + args.length + ")");
    toCall.apply(this, args);
  }
  var args = new Array();
  for (var c1 = 0; c1 < arguments.length; c1 ++) {
    args.push(arguments[c1]);
  }
  args.push(origFunc);
  args.push(arguments);
  proxyFunc.apply(this, args);
}
```

Two variables, origFunc and proxyFunc, reference functions. The origFunc variable represents the original implementation of the defined method. The proxyFunc variable represents the proxy method that is called before the original method. Both functions are embedded in a function that is responsible for calling the proxy method.

Embedding the functions within a function does not require the proxy method to know what the original function is called. For each instance of embedding, there is a proxy method and the original method. The convention is that the method that embeds the two methods keeps track of who calls whom and what parameters are passed around.

The role of the parent method is to manage the references of the embedded methods, manage the this instance, and manage the parameters. The parent method manages the parameters by considering the arguments as an Array type. The JavaScript-defined arguments object is an array of arguments. The parent method will create a new set of arguments so that the proxy method knows which function to call and has the ability to modify the arguments based on the original object instance. The purpose of creating an array of arguments that contains the arguments relates to the declaration of the proxy method, which will always have as its last parameters the method to call and arguments.

Embedding a function within a function has a problem: how do you assign the this reference in the embedded function? JavaScript solves this problem by providing the apply method, which is associated with a function object. The parent method implementation calls proxyFunc.apply and passes as parameters this and the modified arguments array args. Then when the function associated with the proxyFunc variable is executed, whenever this is referenced, the correct object instance is referenced. Using apply is extremely useful and simplifies the proxy method implementation. The downside is that the original method passed to the proxy method must also use apply. If when calling the original method the proxy function does not use apply, then errors might be generated.

When executed, the generated code will work properly. The challenge lies in the generation of the code. One approach is to generate a text buffer that represents the complete implementation of the proxy method. Another approach is to dynamically generate and evaluate some parts of the generated code, and use a dynamic function for the other parts. Each of these solutions is problematic, and the best solution is to use JavaScript generics. Using JavaScript generics, you can define the desired code, and at runtime the behavioral aspects can be expanded. The following code is the complete proxy generation solution.

Source: /website/ROOT/scripts/jaxson/common.js

```
proxy : function(instance, funcIdentifier, newFunc) {
  if (!instance[funcIdentifier]) {
    throw new Error("Method does not exist on this➡
      object (" + funcIdentifier + ")");
  }
  var proxyPrototype = function() {
    var origFunc = __orig;
    var proxyFunc = __proxy;
    var args = new Array();
    for (var c1 = 0; c1 < arguments.length; c1 ++) {
      args.push(arguments[0]);
    }
    args.push(origFunc);
    args.push(arguments);
    return proxyFunc.apply(this, args);
  }
  instance[funcIdentifier]  = Generics.expand(proxyPrototype,
    {
```

```
        __orig: instance[funcIdentifier],
        __proxy: newFunc
    });
},
```

The proxy implementation does not need much explanation, because the code has already been largely explained. Look at the definition of the proxyPrototype variable, and you should notice a similarity to the ideal generated code that was explained throughout the recipe. The only difference with proxyPrototype and the ideal code is that the values for origFunc and proxyFunc have not been defined. The origFunc and proxyFunc variables have been assigned the __orig and __proxy variable values, which are identifiers used in the JavaScript generics expansion. The call to Generics.expand will expand the buffer to resemble the ideal buffer.

The parameters to the proxy method are instance, which represents the object instance to generate a proxy method implementation; funcIdentifier, which represents a string buffer of the method to proxy; and newFunc, which represents the proxy function that is called before the original.

The proxy method can be used as shown in the following example.

Source: /website/ROOT/ajaxrecipes/javascript/proxy.html

```
automated_proxy : function() {
  var cls = new DefinedClass();
  info("automated_proxy{cls.defined|before}", cls.defined.toString());
  ops.proxy(cls, "defined", function(tstValue, toCall, args) {
    info("proxyfunction", "parameter (" + tstValue + ") received arg count (" +➡
      arguments.length + ") original arg count (" + args.length + ")");➡
      toCall.apply(this, args);
  });
  info("automated_proxy{cls.defined|after}", cls.defined.toString());
  cls.value = 10;
  cls.defined(10);
}
```

In the implementation, the DefinedClass type is instantiated and assigned to the cls variable. For purposes of illustration, the implementation of cls.defined is generated (info(..., cls.defined.toString)) to show what the original method implementation is. The call to ops.proxy has three parameters, and the first two parameters (cls and "defined") are obvious. The third parameter is the proxy method, and in the case of the example, it is an inline-defined function. The third parameter does not have to be an inline method; it can be a function reference or another class instance.

After the call to ops.proxy is another call to the info function to illustrate the modified version of the cls.defined method.

■**Tip** To test your own understanding, run the test code from the samples to see how the code works. The last line of code that calls the defined method illustrates that the proxy method is called before the original method.

When implementing the Proxy pattern for a method, keep the following points in mind:

- The Proxy pattern for a method is applied when you want to filter, preprocess, and postprocess parameters before (if) they are passed to the method.

- The implementation of the proxy method is responsible for calling the original method.

- The Proxy pattern for a method is best implemented by embedding functions within functions. The advantage of using an embedded approach is that the function can be referenced by other object instances without corrupting the method implementation.

- The Proxy pattern for a method can be embedded multiple times.

2-17. Implementing Delegates

Problem

You want to use a delegate architecture to streamline how your code runs and avoid code clashes.

Theory

When writing JavaScript, very often code will fight for attention. One example of code fighting for attention is the window.onload event. The window.onload event is called once the HTML page has completely loaded and initialized. When the browser calls window.onload, the browser is giving a script the chance to initialize itself with a complete HTML page. For scripters, this method is very interesting, and if there are two toolkits using window.onload, more likely than not one will overwrite the other. Imagine the following code written by one toolkit:

```
window.onload = function() {  // initialize toolkit 1}
```

In this code example the toolkit is saying that when the onload event is called, use my functionality. The second toolkit interested in the onload event would assign window.onload to the following:

```
window.onload = function() { // initialize toolkit 2 }
```

The second assignment would work, but it begs the question, what happens to the initialization of toolkit 1? The answer is that it is not called. Toolkits 1 and 2 are fighting for the attention of the onload event, and the winner is whichever toolkit assigns the onload event last.

There are three potential solutions to this dilemma:

- Convert the toolkits to use browser-specific tags that will allow them to reference multiple onload functions. The downside of this solution is that you need to write browser-specific code, which increases the maintenance cost of the code.

- Use a function that calls both initializations. The downside is that you need to provide a function that manages both initializations.

- Convert the toolkits to play nicely with each other and not overwrite the other initialization. The downside is that the toolkits have to figure out how to call the other initialization routines.

Solution

As mentioned, the downside of the first solution presented in the previous section is that it's browser specific. For Mozilla, the solution is rather elegant because it implements a delegate architecture. For other browsers, the first solution is not as elegant, and thus the final solution is a mixture of the second and third solutions.

For the moment, though, let's focus on the second solution, which is implemented as follows:

```
window.onload = function() {
  initializeToolkit1();
  initializeToolkit2();
}
```

The `windows.onload` function is assigned a function that calls the initialization routines of toolkits 1 and 2. The solution works, but it has maintenance issues, since a developer has to add or remove initialization routines. This isn't a major problem, however.

If you look at the implementation of the function, it is the conversion of one function call into two function calls. This is the basis of a delegate. The `initializeToolkit1` and `initializeToolkit2` functions have nothing to do with each other, and when called, each could be easily fooled into thinking that it is the only function assigned to the `onload` event. A delegate is not like a proxy, in that a delegate calls all functions, whereas a proxy will call a function first and then expect the called function to call the other functions.

From an implementation perspective, a delegate has a very similar implementation to a proxy. The JavaScript implementation of a delegate does differ from a traditional delegate because there is no single object instance managing all references. Figure 2-7 illustrates the classical delegate implementation.

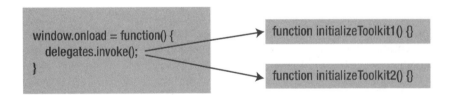

Figure 2-7. *Classical delegate implementation*

In a classical delegate implementation, calling the `window.onload` function will call a delegate object structure, which calls the managed function references. In the case of the example, that means calling the delegate object structure calls `initializeToolkit1` and `initializeToolkit2`.

The classical delegate approach works so long as you are using reference-based duck typing and not planning to serialize the methods. The other solution is to use only serialization and chain the delegates as shown in Recipe 2-16. The architecture resembles Figure 2-8.

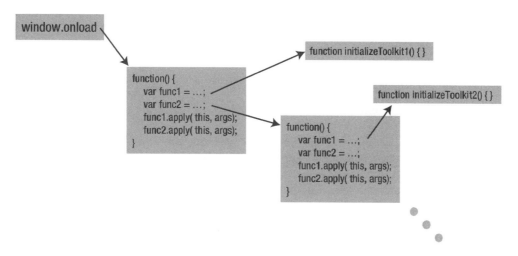

Figure 2-8. *JavaScript delegate implementation*

In the JavaScript delegate implementation, `window.onload` references a parent delegate function that contains two function references: `func1` and `func2`. The parent delegate function calls both `func1` and `func2`. When parent delegate functions are chained together, `func1` (chosen for illustration purposes) references a function to call (`initializeToolkit1`), and `func2` (again chosen for illustration purposes) references the next parent delegation in the chain. In the next parent delegation, one function references the function to call (`initializeFunction2`), and the other function references another parent delegate function.

In terms of complexity, it would seem the architecture shown in Figure 2-8 is more complicated than the architecture shown in Figure 2-7. The architecture of Figure 2-8 excels in its ability to be serialized. This is important, because if you want to serialize the state of an HTML page, you are also serializing the state of the functions. When using references, as in Figure 2-7, serialization is a much more complicated issue and requires intervention on behalf of the function calling the delegates.

To understand the serialization problem, imagine trying to serialize `window.onload` using references:

```
window.onload = function() {
  delegates.invoke( this, arguments);
}
var buffer = ops.serialize( window.onload);
```

In the example, `window.onload` references a function that calls the `delegates.invoke` global variable method, which will call the functions `initializeToolkit1` and `initializeToolkit2`. If we want to save the state of the HTML page, we will serialize `window.onload` because it is a standard reference point. Yet serializing `window.onload` does not serialize delegates. It serializes the reference to delegates, and thus when the page is re-created, the delegates instance will be missing.

You may read the previous paragraph and think I've lost my marbles, because that is not how serialization is done. You might implement the following solution instead:

```
window.unload = function() {
  var buffer = ops.serialize( delegates);
}`
```

In this solution, the unload function will be called, and a stream of data that represents the delegates will be generated. But is this solution actually correct? I argue that the solution is delegating the problem of the delegates variable to another location, and it is not solving anything.

Imagine, for instance, that you are serializing the state of a page. As you iterate the elements, you are generating the associated functions. So you will serialize window.load and window.unload. The state of delegates is still missing. And this is the crux of the problem, as the serialization of delegates is a separate stream from the serialization of the HTML page. With the architecture shown in Figure 2-8, there is only one stream as the HTML page, and its associated functions and objects are the state. This simplifies an HTML page, because the programmer does not need to create separate serialization routines to manage the individual objects created on the HTML page.

The big advantage of this approach is that when coding using a prototype-based language—which JavaScript is—you are not worried about multiple implementations sharing the same references. Using a value-based approach, you can copy a function from one object to another and not worry about the mixin problem described in Recipe 2-15.

Now that you're familiar with the theory behind delegate implementation, let's look at the technical details.

Source: /website/ROOT/scripts/jaxson/common.js

```
delegate : function(instance, funcIdentifier, newFunc) {
  var delegatePrototype = function() {
    var func1 = __replace1;
    var func2 = __replace2;
    func1.apply(this, arguments);
    func2.apply(this, arguments);
  }
  var origFunc;
  if (!instance[funcIdentifier]) {
    origFunc = function() { };
  }
  else {
    origFunc = instance[funcIdentifier];
  }

  instance[funcIdentifier] = Generics.expand(delegatePrototype,
  {
    __replace1 : origFunc,
    __replace2 : newFunc

  });
},
```

As in the function proxy defined in Recipe 2-16, JavaScript generics are used. The delegatePrototype function variable looks very similar to the function declaration of Figure 2-8, because they are the same. Thus, there is no need to explain delegatePrototype, with the exception of the _replace1 and _replace2 identifiers. _replace1 and _replace2 are the placeholder function identifiers that will be expanded using JavaScript generics.

The method delegate can be used as follows.

Source: /website/ROOT/ajaxrecipes/javascript/exceptions.html

```
window.onload = function() {
  window.onerror = function(msg, file, location) {
    info("window.onerror1", "Msg (" + msg + ") file (" + file + ") location (" +➥
    location + ")");
  }
}
ops.delegate(window, "onload", function() {
  window.onerror = function(msg, file, location) {
    info("window.onerror2", "Msg (" + msg + ") file (" + file + ") location➥
      (" + location + ")");
}});
```

In the example, the window.onload function is assigned a function. The next line of source code uses the ops.delegate method call to convert the assigned function into a delegate. Thus, when the window.onload event is called, the two functions are called, both of which assign window.onerror.

A consequence of using delegates is that a programmer might use delegates, but forget the resources they assign using delegates are shared as well. Therefore, a good programmer won't assign window.onerror, but will use a delegate to assign window.onerror.

When writing code where a method or function callback needs to be shared, you can use delegates, but keep the following points in mind:

- Delegates allow programmers to share a method callback, but they should not assume that the resources in their method implementation are exclusive.

- Delegates solve the problem where a single method call can be used to make multiple method calls.

- Delegates cannot return values because multiple methods may return values; thus, delegates should always use code blocks. Code blocks are inherently single, multiple, or no result oriented. Using code blocks does not require the infrastructure to do anything special when data has to be returned.

- Delegates can be implemented using reference or value duck typing, with the main difference between them being the ability to serialize.

2-18. Implementing Overloaded Methods

Problem

You want to implement overloaded methods in your JavaScript code.

Theory

When a method is assigned to any object, there can only be one instance of that property. It is not possible in JavaScript to assign multiple same-named properties. For example, the following code will not work.

Source: /website/ROOT/ajaxrecipes/javascript/overloaded.html

```
var cls = new Object();
cls[ "method"] = function() {
  info( "method1", "hello");
}
cls.method();
cls[ "method"] = function() {
  info( "method2", "hello");
}
cls.method();
```

In the example code, there are two assignments to the method property. The cls.method method is called twice, and for each call the function implementation called is the last assignment value. The code is trivial and is meant to illustrate that you cannot overload a method by assigning it.

Overloading a method is useful in situations where a variable number of parameters are going to be called on a method. Since there are no type declarations, overloaded methods will vary in the number of parameters. The logic used is that if the method is called with five parameters, then an overloaded method that processes five parameters will be called. If the overloaded method does not exist, the default implementation that was initially assigned to the property will be used.

The solution to overloading a method lies in using the same solutions shown in Recipes 2-16 and 2-17. (If you have not yet read those recipes, I advise that you do so before continuing, as I do not repeat the underlying theory of those recipes here.)

To implement an overloaded method architecture, the same architecture of the proxy and delegate implementation will be used, as shown in Figure 2-9.

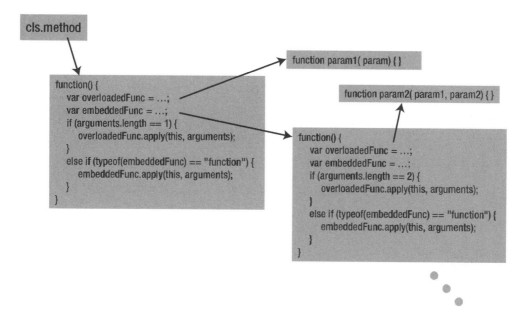

Figure 2-9. *JavaScript overload method implementation*

In Figure 2-9, the `cls.method` function references an implementation that contains two functions, `overloadedFunc` and `embeddedFunc`. The `embeddedFunc` variable is a reference to the overloaded function that will be called if the number of calling arguments equals the number of parameters of the overloaded function. If the parameter counts are not equal, then `embeddedFunc` is called.

Figure 2-9 shows a chaining of overloaded methods, but uses the same architecture as described in Recipes 2-16 and 2-17. For example, it is possible to have a delegate call an over-loaded method, which then calls a proxy.

Solution

The implementation of the overloaded method is as follows.

Source: /website/ROOT/scripts/jaxson/common.js

```
overloaded : function(instance, funcIdentifier, newFunc) {
  var overloadedPrototype = function() {
    var embeddedFunc = __embedded;
    var overloadedFunc = __newFunc;

    if (arguments.length == __paramCount) {
      overloadedFunc.apply(this, arguments);
    }
```

```
      else if (typeof(embeddedFunc) == "function") {
        embeddedFunc.apply(this, arguments);
      }
    }
    var origFunc;
    if (!instance[funcIdentifier]) {
      origFunc = function() { };
    }
    else {
      origFunc = instance[funcIdentifier];
    }

    instance[funcIdentifier] = Generics.expand(overloadedPrototype,
    {
      __embedded : origFunc,
      __newFunc : newFunc,
      __paramCount : ParamCount(newFunc)
    });
  },
```

In the implementation, JavaScript generics are used to expand the overloadedPrototype function. But added to this expansion is a twist not used previously. Look at the __paramCount identifier. If the identifier is cross-referenced with Figure 2-9, then __paramCount when it is expanded will reference a numeric value. This means that the expanded function will be hard-coded, but because JavaScript generics are used, this is not a bad thing. The performance will be faster because there is no need to calculate the number of parameters that the overloadedFunc function has.

To use the overloaded method, the following code is used:

```
function FunctionNoParam() {
}
function FunctionOneParam(param) {
  info("FunctionTwoParam", "param=" + param);
}
function FunctionTwoParam(param1, param2) {
  info("FunctionTwoParam", "param1=" + param1 + " param2=" + param2);
}
var cls = new Object();
cls.value = "original";
cls.example = function() { info( "default", "hello"); }
ops.overloaded(cls, "example", FunctionNoParam);
ops.overloaded(cls, "example", FunctionOneParam);
ops.overloaded(cls, "example", FunctionTwoParam);
cls.example("one param example");
cls.example("first param", "second param");
```

Three functions are defined: FunctionNoParam, FunctionOneParam, and FunctionTwoParam. These functions serve as overloaded functions with a varying number of parameters. The cls variable is a generic JavaScript object with no methods or parameters. The data member value is assigned dynamically to the default method.

After the default has been assigned, the method example is overloaded with the three overloaded functions using the `ops.overloaded` function. Once the methods have been overloaded, they can be called with a varying number of parameters. The overloaded methods, for example, will then sequentially find the correct method to call.

When implementing overloaded methods, keep the following points in mind:

- The overloaded method JavaScript generics expansion was similar to that shown in previous recipes. The only additional twist was the hard-coding of the parameter count. Using traditional programming practices, you would not do that, but using JavaScript generics it is trivial and recommended.

- When overloading methods, you need to provide a default implementation if you want it.

- You need to support not only the number of parameters to determine what you want to call, but also the type. This is a much more common use case, after all. A method that accepts a string could be overloaded by a variant that accepts an array and calls the string version for each element.

- Overloading methods is not possible according to types, but is made according to parameter count.

- You could implement overloaded types that filter on specific types. For example, you could implement an overloaded method filter that queries the presence of a specific object value. To do that, you can combine the proxy with the overloaded recipes.

CHAPTER 3

■ ■ ■

Dynamic Content Recipes

When building Ajax applications, you're creating user interfaces that interact with the data on the server side. Building a user interface includes multiple aspects that could be considered unrelated. For example, it requires a number of elements on a form. You need to place these elements properly and verify them. The placing and verification could be considered unrelated, because verification can proceed regardless of how the elements are placed, and vice versa. This chapter doesn't attempt to dig through the details of how to place elements so that their usability is correct. Instead, this chapter digs through topics that focus on algorithms such as element verification, HTML dialog box generation, and dynamic layout generation.

3-1. Validating Your Data

Due to human error, human incomprehension, or simple ignorance, people sometimes input the incorrect state. Every application needs to implement data validation so you can know if the data is a valid state.

Problem

Validation is not just a data entry problem—it can also be a programmer problem. For example, a human could enter the data correctly, but the code could perform some invalid operations resulting in state corruption. You need to ensure that the validation occurs successfully.

Theory

Validation in an Ajax application means that the client or server can validate the data. Figure 3-1 illustrates a potential architecture of how to validate the data. It shows an HTML page used to add two numbers. Each of the text boxes can reference any type of text, whether that be "fourteen," "14," or "a really big number." Of the three variations, only "14" is a valid state, yet users can enter the other variations.

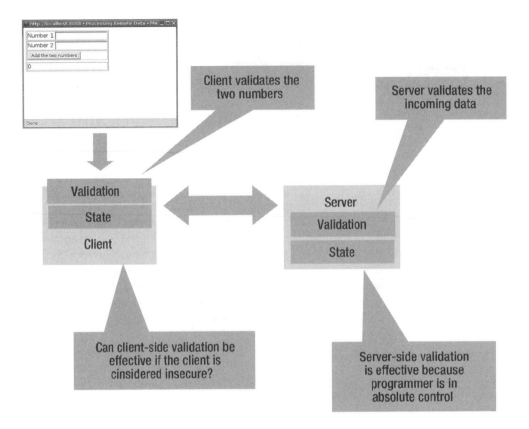

Figure 3-1. *Validation architecture*

The validation to check if a valid number has been entered can be performed on either the client side or the server side. Imagining the validation is performed on the client side, you can define the following points:

- You use JavaScript to implement all validation.

- The client can act and validate before submitting the data to the server, thereby saving a round trip to the server.

- The Web client is considered insecure, so the server could receive invalid data if client-side validation is the only validation.

Client-side validation saves processing power on the server side by doing the validation and using the resources of the client. The downside is that in an HTML application, the client is considered insecure, and hackers can always bypass the security efforts of a Web developer. You can minimize the problems, but you cannot eliminate the problems.

In contrast, let's look at server-side validation, where you can define the following points:

- You can implement all validation in the language of choice, whether that's Java, C#, C++, PHP, or Ruby.

- Server-side validation requires a round trip between the client and the server, which wastes network resources.

- Server-side validation is considered secure, because you can use a firewall to control access to the server-side resource.

Client-side validation is the preferred route from a performance perspective, and server-side validation is the preferred route from a security perspective. However, you want both the best performance and the best security, which seems impossible.

You must choose between performance and security. No magic trick gives you both without any disadvantages. If you were to use a compiled application instead of a Web client, you'd still have the same problems. Even if your compiled client application were to use encryption, you'd still have security problems. And if you have security problems, then you have validation problems, so client-side validation must be considered insecure.

Having established that you cannot ensure the validity of the data from a security perspective, you need to consider whether you need the performance or the partial security. Going back to the calculator application shown in Figure 3-1, you can make the argument that client-side validation is good enough. If a hacker were to present invalid data, then the calculation would not work, and the server would generate an error. If the server is presented with invalid data, under no circumstance should the invalid data cause the server to generate a general protection fault (GPF).

You need to distinguish validation for system correctness from validation for application correctness. When data has been verified for system correctness, it means that the data is correct, but it might not make sense. When data has been verified for application correctness, it means that the data is correct and makes sense. Most developers focus on application data validation and not system data validation, partly because application data validation implies system data validation. However, by mixing the two validations, you can miss many system validation scenarios.

Consider this example, which illustrates the problems of mixing different validations: In a quest to provide the best security, a well-known online Web mail provider implements a server-side validation tool to filter email for malicious JavaScript statements. Without the filter, users could inadvertently display an email that could act as a Trojan or a virus. However, a hacker manages to fool the filter with the following code:

```
<img ➥
    src='http://server/image.gif'➥
    target=""onload="javascript that uses single quotes and just goes on and on">
```

In the example source, the HTML tag `img` has an `src` attribute, but also a `target` and an `onload` attribute. From a system-level perspective, this means there are three attributes. The problem with the server filter is that it treats the `target` and `onload` attributes as one attribute. This probably occurs because an application-level validation filter was created that didn't verify the data at the system level. Had the validation routines performed both a system-level validation and an application-level validation, the error most likely would have been caught.

State and validation are not a simple problem. State and validation involve both a client side and a server side, and involve both system-level validation and application-level validation. With this knowledge, you can now assemble the calculator application into an architecture (see Figure 3-2).

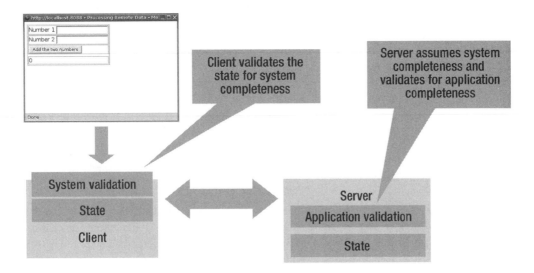

Figure 3-2. *Proposed validation architecture*

Figure 3-2 shows two levels of validation: system-level validation performed by the client, and application-level validation performed by the server. In the calculator example, that means that the client validates the correctness of the number entered by the user, and the server validates that the two numbers can be added together and that no overflow or underflow will happen.

In the proposed validation architecture, one problem remains: The client is considered insecure, but the server expects that the client will send the right data. This could be a recipe for disaster, but not because of how application validation is implemented. With most technical implementations, application validation implies system-level validation.

The architecture of Figure 3-2 proposes an overall plan of action: to let the client do system-level validation only, and to let the server handle the heavy-duty work of validating the data completely. The client fixes up the data so that errors are already removed. The server side assumes that the data is correct, but still has the capability to catch errors if they occur.

Solution

The next step is to convert the architecture illustrated in Figure 3-2 into a usable solution. This recipe focuses on the client side and ignores the server side. It considers the server side to be a black box that receives and sends data.

To start, let's look at the HTML page used to add two numbers together.

Source: /website/ROOT/ajaxrecipes/dhtml/validation/test.html

```html
<html>
    <head>
        <title>Validation Example</title>
        <script language="JavaScript" src="/scripts/jaxson/common.js"></script>
        <script language="JavaScript" src="/scripts/jaxson/converter.js"></script>
    </head>
  <body>
    <form id="calculator">
      <table border="1">
        <tr>
          <td>Number 1</td><td><input type="text" name="Number1" /></td>
        </tr>
        <tr>
          <td>Number 2</td><td><input type="text" name="Number2" /></td>
        </tr>
        <tr>
          <td>Result</td><td><span id="result"></span></td>
        </tr>
        <tr>
          <td colspan="2">
            <center>
                <input type="button" value="Add the two numbers" onclick=""/>
            </center>
          </td>
        </tr>
      </table>
    </form>
  </body></html>
```

Notice that the form HTML element defines only the id attribute and not the method and action attributes. This is done on purpose, as you'll see in the recipe "Don't Submit Your Forms—Ajax Them" presented in Chapter 8. The form uses standard form elements, such as the input button and the input text box. The purpose of the form HTML element is to define a block that contains all of the elements and represents a valid state. In the example, the valid elements include the fields Number1 and Number2. The form block contains a span element that represents the result of the addition.

When submitting forms using the browser-based HTML POST, you're sending all of the form elements (such as Number1 and Number2) to the server. When the POST returns, the result returns. In the example HTML, the result is a span element, which is assigned by JavaScript. Imagine if the result element were an HTML form; using an HTML POST would cause the result to be sent to the server. Sending the state of the result is incorrect, because you're sending output data in an input state. The form example illustrates that there are multiple states and multiple representations of the state. You separate the input state and output state using multiple representations, which is the basis of the Representation Morphing pattern.[1]

---

1. Christian Gross, *Ajax Patterns and Best Practices* (Berkeley, CA: Apress, 2006), p. 197.

In a nutshell, the Representation Morphing pattern says that state can have multiple representations. A representation exposes a way to extract and assign a state. If the representation changes, the state does not. A decoupling of representation and state is possible. In the calculator example, this means that the form has two representations: the numbers and the result. The representation is responsible for how it presents the state. Figure 3-3 illustrates the Representation Morphing pattern.

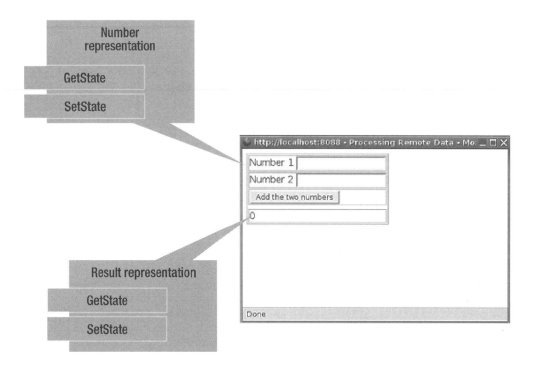

Figure 3-3. *Applying the Representation Morphing pattern when adding two numbers*

Figure 3-3 shows two referenced representations: Number and Result. Each of the representations has associated two methods: GetState and SetState. The purpose of the methods is to extract and assign state to a representation. In programmatic terms, the representations and the associated methods represent a contract. Notice that it has not been mentioned how the data is retrieved from the server. This is important, because it illustrates that the representation is not dependent on how it receives its data.

The architecture cannot be directly implemented as illustrated in Figure 3-3, because HTML considers everything as a single namespace. Thus, if one script defines a function, another script cannot define the same function. In the architecture of Figure 3-3, there are two instances of GetState and SetState. The Representation Morphing pattern solves the problem by associating the state methods with the HTML blocks. In the code example, that means associating state methods to the form and to the span element.

Another solution is to create the global functions GetState and SetState but associate identifiers with the global functions. These global functions are responsible for retrieving or assigning the state with the representation. The advantage of this approach is that you have a centralized location that you can extend or maintain.

Going back to the first code segment of this recipe, adding the global functions GetState and SetState results in the following code.

Source: /website/ROOT/ajaxrecipes/dhtml/validation/test.html

```
<html>
    <head>
        <title>Validation Example</title>
        <script language="JavaScript" src="/scripts/jaxson/common.js"></script>
        <script language="JavaScript" src="/scripts/jaxson/converter.js"></script>
    </head>
<script language="JavaScript" type="text/javascript">

function GetState(identifier, cb) {
}

function SetState(identifier, obj, cb) {
}

</script>
  <body>
    <form id="calculator">
      <table border="1">
        <tr>
          <td>Number 1</td><td><input type="text" name="Number1" /></td>
        </tr>
        <tr>
          <td>Number 2</td><td><input type="text" name="Number2" /></td>
        </tr>
        <tr>
          <td>Result</td><td><span id="result"></span></td>
        </tr>
        <tr>
          <td colspan="2">
            <center>
                <input type="button" value="Add the two numbers" onclick=""/>
            </center>
          </td>
        </tr>
      </table>
    </form>
  </body></html>
```

The modified code, shown in bold in the updated HTML page, illustrates the definition of the functions. The functions `GetState` and `SetState` provide the base infrastructure used to retrieve and assign state to a representation. This means that `GetState` and `SetState` don't include functionality to make Ajax requests.

The function `GetState` has two parameters: `identifier` and `cb`. The `identifier` parameter is the identifier of the representation to extract the state from. Figure 3-3 contains two representations, which results in the parameter `identifier` having two values. The second parameter `cb` is a callback function that is called to indicate an error or retrieved state. The second parameter is a code block, as defined in Chapter 2. The reason for using a code block relates to the multifunctionality of the `GetState` or `SetState` function. More about this will be discussed in a moment.

`SetState` has a similar declaration to `GetState`, except that it includes an additional parameter `obj`. The parameter `obj` is an object that is a state that will be assigned to the representation. It is assumed that the representation knows about the data members defined by the variable `obj`.

In the Representation Morphing pattern, the `GetState` and `SetState` functions are used to assign and extract a state from a representation. The Representation Morphing pattern focuses on the ability to serialize a representation, decouple a state from the representation, and serialize the state when the representation is serialized. For this recipe, there is the additional requirement to perform validation. From a programmatic perspective, adding validation is straightforward. What makes validation more complicated is the additional interaction aspects. For example, what would the application do if a validation failed? Should it display a dialog box or a blinking message? If a validation error occurs, should the application show the first error and stop validating?

Let's focus on the extraction of the state using the function `GetState`. You must implement the following details when using `GetState`:

- When extracting the state for the numbers, you must reference the text box value properties for `Number1` and `Number2`.

- When extracting the state for the result, you must reference the `span` `innerHTML` property.

- You must validate the text box values `Number1` and `Number2` as being numbers.

- If the validation fails, you must generate and display an error so users can take corrective action.

- You must not display errors on a piecemeal basis. The validation routines must go through the entire state and generate errors for everything found.

- When no more validation errors occur, pass the generated state to the caller. Note that multiple state instances might occur.

You should notice the generation of multiple errors or multiple state instances. Whenever an algorithm is confronted with multiple results, the results are stored temporarily in an array that is processed by the caller of the algorithm. As shown in Chapter 2's code block recipe, you could also use code blocks. Code blocks would be the appropriate choice, because there may or may not be errors, and there may or may not be a state instance.

To illustrate the complexities, consider the following code, which illustrates each approach of calling the `GetState` function:

```
function GenerateState() {
    var noErrors = true;
    var result = GetState( "identifier");
    for( int c1 = 0; c1 < result.errors.length; c1 ++) {
        // Do something with error
        noErrors = false;
    }
    if( noErrors == true) {
        for( int c1 = 0; c1 < results.state.length; c1 ++) {
            // Do something with the results
        }
    }
}
```

The first line is an assignment of the variable noErrors. The variable noErrors is used to indicate whether errors occur when extracting the state. If there are errors, then processing the state would be silly since there is no state—or if there is, it is incomplete.

Calling the function GetState returns an object instance, which has two data members: errors and state. The two data members are arrays that contain the errors and generated state instances. After the call to GetState, a loop iterates the validation errors and, if necessary, generates a response. If an error is generated, the variable noErrors is assigned a value of false, indicating an error. If there are no errors, the generated state instances are iterated.

As GetState is coded, the function is called and processes the state. If an error occurs, then the caller of GetState needs to dissect what went wrong and how to indicate the errors to the caller. Another solution is to use code blocks that simplify how the state or errors are processed. Code blocks simplify the code, because they allow you to focus on adding value with respect to code. The following code illustrates how a version of GetState uses code blocks:

```
function GenerateState() {
    GetState( "Identifier", {
        error : function( errorItem) {
            // Do something with error
        }
        state : function( stateInstance) {
            // Do something with results
        }
    });
}
```

In the modified implementation of GenerateState, the GetState function is passed an object instance that has two methods: error and state. Whenever an error occurs, the function error is called. If no errors occur, then the function state is called. The caller of GenerateState has a simplified implementation, because it only needs to take care of the cases when an error or a state instance occur. If the caller doesn't provide an implementation for the function error, then any errors that would occur are ignored, and the caller only waits for a valid state instance. The details of SetState and how to use it are similar to GetState. The difference with SetState is that a state is being assigned to a representation.

Now let's look at the implementation details of the HTML form again, as one additional change has not yet been discussed, and it needs to be covered before discussing the details of GetState or SetState:

```html
<form id="calculator">
  <table border="1">
    <tr>
      <td>Number 1</td><td><input type="text" name="Number1" />
          <br><span id="Number1Error"></span></td>
    </tr>
    <tr>
      <td>Number 2</td><td><input type="text" name="Number2" />
          <br><span id="Number2Error"></span></td>
    </tr>
    <tr>
      <td>Result</td><td><span id="result"></span>
          <br><span id="resulterror"></span></td>
    </tr>
    <tr>
      <td colspan="2">
        <center>
            <input type="button" value="Add the two numbers" onclick=""/>
        </center>
      </td>
    </tr>
  </table>
</form>
```

The bold text shows the addition of HTML span elements, which you use to display any errors associated with the data. In past applications, you might have used a dialog box to indicate errors. The problem with dialog boxes is that they talk about the problematic data but don't pinpoint it. With a fairly complex form, users might be left wondering where the error is. Dynamic HTML (DHTML) gives you the ability to modify the HTML elements, thus making the need to use a dialog box unnecessary.

This recipe uses an HTML span element that contains the error. You can use whatever you want in your applications. Maybe you want to use blinking text, or maybe you want to change fonts—it's your choice. It's important, though, that you associate the error with the local HTML element.

Now let's cover the details of GetState, which can be a bit lengthy:

```javascript
function GetState(identifier, cb) {
    if (identifier == "toadd") {  // 1
        var form = document.getElementById("calculator");
        document.getElementById("Number1Error").innerHTML = "";  // 2
        document.getElementById("Number2Error").innerHTML = "";
        var obj = new Object();  // 3
        var didError = false;  // 4
```

```
        try {
            obj.Number1 = Converter.convertToInteger(form.Number1.value); // 5
        }
        catch( e) {
            didError = true;
            document.getElementById("Number1Error").innerHTML = e.toString();
            if (cb.error) {
                cb.error({ section : "toadd",
                                item: "Number1", error : e.toString()}); // 6
            }
        }
        try {
            obj.Number2 = Converter.convertToInteger(form.Number2.value);
        }
        catch( e) {
            didError = true;
            document.getElementById("Number2Error").innerHTML = e.toString();
            if (cb.error) {
                cb.error({section: "toadd", item: "Number2", error: e.toString()});
            }
        }
        if (cb.state && !didError) {
            cb.state({ section: "toadd", value : obj}); // 7
        }
    }
    else if (identifier == "result") {
        var element = Navigation.findChild("calculator", "result");
        Navigation.findChild("calculator", "resulterror").innerHTML = "";
        var obj = new Object();

        try {
            obj.Result = Converter.convertToInteger(element.innerHTML);
        }
        catch( e) {
            Navigation.findChild("calculator", "resulterror").innerHTML =
                        e.toString();
            if (cb.error) {
                cb.error({section: "Result",
                            item : "Result", error: e.toString()});
            }
            return;
        }
        if (cb.state) {
            cb.state({ section : "result", value : obj});
        }
    }
}
```

```
        else {
            if (cb.error) {
                cb.error({section: identifier,
                    error: "State identifier (" + identifier + "does not exist"}));
            }
        }
    }
}
```

The code is not complicated but lengthy, because the task you need to accomplish is lengthy. The following list explains each of the bold lines of code. The numbers in the list correspond to the numbers in the comments displayed in the highlighted code:

1. GetState makes a decision to determine which representation should be converted into a state.

2. GetState resets the error messages associated with the representation. In this recipe, that means assigning the innerHTML property of the individual HTML span elements to an empty buffer. In your application, that might mean the resetting the blinking text or changing the text font. It's important to reset the error state so that no old errors are displayed as the validation is being executed.

3. GetState instantiates an object using the Object type. The instantiation and use of the Object type has a purpose. You might be tempted to instantiate a type that has predefined data members and methods, but that is not advised. Imagine using DHTML and generating a form dynamically. It could be that one context of the generated form has a data member, and another context does not. From a state perspective, you want to know the state that reflects the context, not what you think the context should be. Thus, when you instantiate an Object that has no data members and you assign the data members dynamically, you're ensuring only that the data associated with the context is present.

4. The variable didError is a flag that indicates whether a validation error occurred. This flag is highlighted here to cross-reference the previous discussion regarding the reason of using callbacks and not loops. The illustration of didError shows that the GetState algorithm needs to track whether an error occurred.

5. Converter converts the HTML data into the requested type, which in the case of the example is an integer value. The conversion is a function call that varies with the application being written. The conversion includes a validation. Note that the conversion is encapsulated within an exception block. The use of an exception block is preferred, because all errors will be caught. The validation routines might miss some errors, but the exception block can capture and display those errors.

6. If an exception is generated, the catch block captures the exception. Once the exception has been captured, the user-defined error callback is called and can process the error further.

7. If no errors are generated, the user-defined callback is called with the state of the form.

The code that is not bold is either a replication of the functionality or support code for one of the seven details. Remember that the GetState and SetState functionalities are self-contained. For example, when a validation fails and an error is generated, you have the option of making the callback display the message. However, this approach isn't desirable, because the state code would have to know about the representation details. As per the Representation Morphing pattern, it is not desirable to have the caller of GetState or SetState know how the representations are implemented. This promotes a decoupling, just as the GetState and SetState functions don't know the origin of the data used to assign a state in a representation.

For illustration purposes, the following code displays the complete SetState functionality and cross-references the details that implement the same functionality as the seven defined details of the GetState function:

```javascript
function SetState(identifier, obj, cb) {
    if (identifier == "toadd") { // 1
        var form = document.getElementById("calculator");
        document.getElementById("Number1Error").innerHTML = ""; // 2
        document.getElementById("Number2Error").innerHTML = "";
        if (typeof(obj.Number1) != "number") { // 5
            var buffer = "obj.Number1 expected a number, but is a " +
                    typeof(obj.Number1);
            document.getElementById("Number1Error").innerHTML = buffer;
            if (typeof(cb) != "undefined" && cb.error) {
                cb.error({ section: "toadd", identifier : "Number1",
                    error : buffer}); // 6
            }
        }
        if (typeof(obj.Number2) != "number") {
            var buffer = "obj.Number2 expected a number, but is a " +
                    typeof(obj.Number2);
            document.getElementById("Number2Error").innerHTML = buffer;
            if (typeof(cb) != "undefined" && cb.error) {
                cb.error({ section: "toadd", identifier : "Number2",
                    error : buffer});
            }
        }
        form.Number1.value = obj.Number1;
        form.Number2.value = obj.Number2;
    }
    else if (identifier == "result") {
        var element = Navigation.findChild("calculator", "result");
        if (typeof(obj.Result) != "number") {
            var buffer = "obj.Result expected a number, but is a " +
                    typeof(obj.Result);
            Navigation.findChild("calculator", "resulterror").innerHTML = buffer;
            if (typeof(cb) != "undefined" && cb.error) {
                cb.error({ section: "result", identifier : "Result",
                    error: buffer});
            }
        }
        element.innerHTML = obj.Result;
```

```
        }
        else {
            if (typeof(cb) != "undefined" && cb.error) {
                cb.error({section: identifier,error: "State identifier (" + identifier +
                        "does not exist"});
            }
        }
    }
}
```

When assigning the representation with a state, the same sort of logic is carried out, with the exception of lines 3 and 7 from the previous code listing. Those numbers are not referenced here, because when assigning a state, you're passed the object instance that contains the state.

The server-side validation is not shown, because this chapter focuses on client-side solutions. To complete the solution, you would use an Ajax request and send or receive the state from the server. It is not necessary to send the state to the server, since you could use the state for other purposes, as Figure 3-4 illustrates.

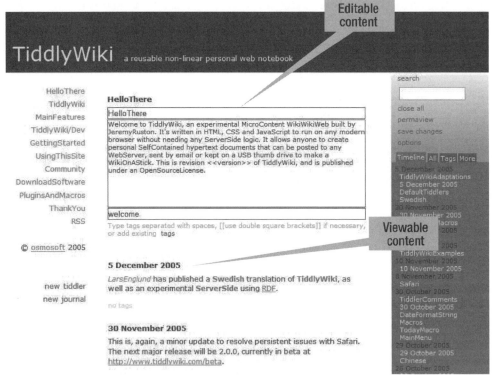

Figure 3-4. *Applying validation to a locally generated state*

Figure 3-4 is not an actual implementation of the recipe, but rather an example of how you can apply this recipe. The example illustrates how to use two representations to display the same state. One representation illustrates the state in editable mode, and the other representation illustrates the state in a read-only mode. Using this recipe, you could retrieve the state remotely, display it in read-only mode, edit it, and then send it back to the server.

Putting all of this together, you need to remember the following things about validation:

- Validation is not about validating some data. Validation first and foremost is about defining a state that is associated with a representation. The purpose of validation is to ensure that when state is transferred, the state is consistent.

- When performing validation, if the state is transferred to the server, then most likely the client cannot be relied upon. The client is considered insecure, and therefore the most you should expect is system-level validation that removes the "dumb" errors. This is not to say that you cannot perform application-level validation—just don't put blind faith into the validation if the application requires high security.

- When the client receives a state from the server, it doesn't need to be validated, because the server is considered secure. Metaphorically speaking, it is like going to a bank: the bank teller doesn't trust you and hence considers you, the individual, insecure. The inverse is not true, as you do trust the teller and won't question what the teller says or the monies that you receive.

- When validating errors, you use DHTML to display an error near the location where it occurred. For example, don't generate a dialog box, because that can lead to cryptic error messages.

- When implementing validation, use get state and set state functionality so that the state, representation, and mechanisms used to transfer state can be decoupled from each other.

- Use code blocks so that user functionality is called when necessary, decoupling the code.

3-2. Creating Dynamic Layouts

This recipe solves an age-old problem, as it looks at creating a dynamic user interface that shifts its layout depending on what resolution or user agent is displaying or viewing the user interface.

Problem

You want to create a dynamic user interface that is laid out as logically and as legibly as possible, is spread across a wide variety of differing user agents (including varying resolutions, browsers, devices, and so on), and makes sensible use of the screen real estate available.

Theory

Think about what happens when you surf to an HTML page such as http://www.eweek.com (see Figure 3-5).

Note I'm not critiquing eWeek specifically, but only as an example, because almost every Web site has the same flaw.

Figure 3-5. *HTML page that doesn't adjust on a large screen*

In Figure 3-5, the HTML page doesn't adjust to the changed width, and instead stubbornly stays as is past a certain maximum width. To see all of the content, you need to scroll up and down the HTML page, which can be tedious. Figure 3-6 shows how a fixed-width page is cut off on an Ultra-Mobile PC (UMPC) device with a resolution of 800×480 pixels.

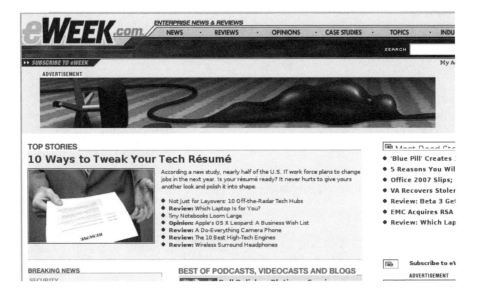

Figure 3-6. *HTML page that doesn't adjust on a small screen*

Figure 3-6 illustrates only the HTML page, with no part of the browser application illustrated. Notice how the HTML page is cut off, requiring users to scroll both horizontally and vertically.

Now let's see how it looks when an HTML page adjusts itself to the size of the browser window. Figure 3-7 illustrates the Slashdot page on a 1920×1200 screen.

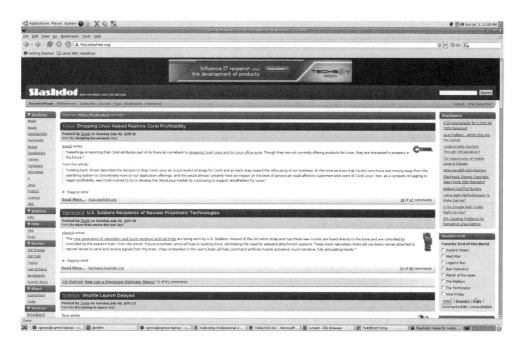

Figure 3-7. *HTML page that does adjust on a large screen*

Notice how the HTML page goes across the entire screen, and the amount of scrolling necessary is lessened. Let's look at the same Slashdot page on the 800×480 UMPC device, which is illustrated in Figure 3-8.

In this example, you can read the document easily, even though a fair bit of scrolling is required. From a usability perspective, the dynamically adjusting HTML page is better than the static page. However, even the dynamically adjusting HTML page has a weakness. Figure 3-7 is a snapshot of what an HTML page on a screen with 1920×1200 resolution looks like in a book. When you're looking at the desktop in the book, it seems OK, if a bit small. However, looking at the full-screen Slashdot page on a desktop in real life is a bit hard to read. The reason is because the screen is too wide, and your eyes keep wandering and losing their place. Because of the way you see, your view is narrower than some screens. Thus, it would seem that the fixed-width strategy of Figure 3-5 is better.

The reality is that neither is better, because each has advantages and disadvantages. Yet neither is optimal. When the Web initially started to become popular, most computing devices had the same screen resolution, and people rarely surfed the Internet on cell-phone devices. Now computing devices are extremely powerful, but vary to an extreme in their screen resolution. Personal computing needs can vary from a low of 800×480 to a high of 4500×1200 for a dual screen. It doesn't make sense to fix the screen resolution.

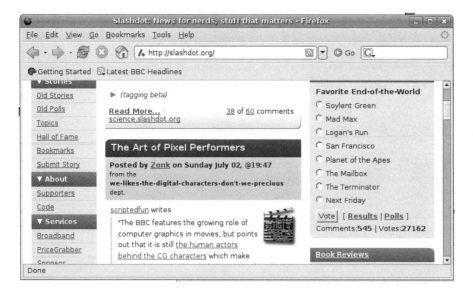

Figure 3-8. *HTML page that does adjust on a small screen*

This recipe proposes a dynamic resize architecture that makes it possible to chunk content into an HTML page. In the simplest case, you can use a table with percentages, which is the solution that Figure 3-7 shows. The problem with a percentage is that it must know the ideal size and then offer some variation for display when the display area is larger or smaller. Figure 3-9 illustrates how a table with percentages behaves when a browser is resized.

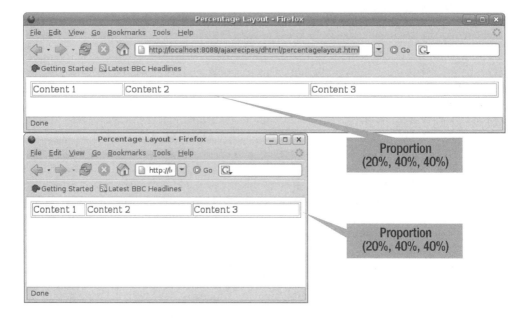

Figure 3-9. *How a percentage-based table resizes itself*

The upper browser window has a proportion of 20%, 40%, and 40%, just like the lower browser window. However, as a ramification of the proportional resize, some table cells become very small, and other cells become too large. To help offset the problem of the cells becoming too large or too small, you could fix the width of some cells and not others. That would result in an HTML page that behaves like those shown in Figures 3-7 and 3-8.

What you want is an algorithm that displays the content proportionally. For example, you could base the algorithm on the proportions of content you want to display, as illustrated in Figure 3-10.

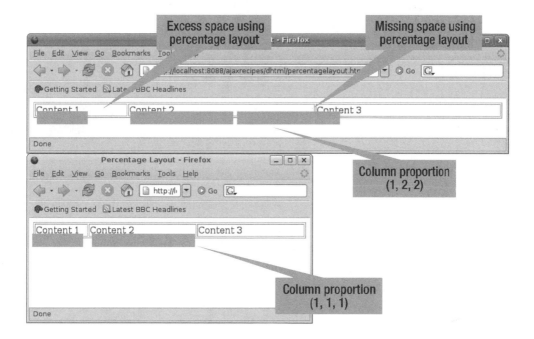

Figure 3-10. *Trying to fit a column-proportional layout on a percentage layout*

The proportions used in the small browser are one column, one column, and one column. However, the bigger browser uses one column, two columns, and two columns. What you are doing is readjusting the space so that in the smaller window, only one column is illustrated. In the bigger window, more columns can be illustrated.

The idea presented in Figure 3-10 is realized in Figure 3-11 as an algorithm that adjusts the number of columns within a table.

Notice how the table cells in the larger and smaller window are allocated. Compare the proportions to Figure 3-9, and notice how the sizing of Figure 3-11 is more pleasing to the eye. From an implementation perspective, the solution to the resizing problem is to use an algorithm that calculates proportions on certain initial parameters.

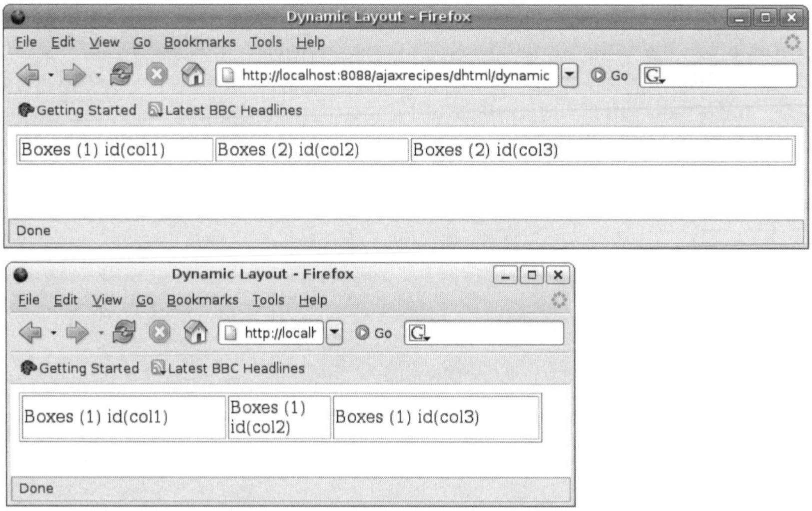

Figure 3-11. *Sizing the cells proportionally within the table using a column width*

Solution

This recipe explains the solution in pieces, starting with the overall calling HTML page that calls the sizing algorithm, and then the sizing algorithm itself. The following code comprises the overall HTML page.

Source: /website/ROOT/ajaxrecipes/dhtml/dynamiclayout.html

```
<html>
  <head>
    <title>Dynamic Layout</title>
    <script language="JavaScript" src="/scripts/jaxson/common.js"></script>
  </head>
<script language="JavaScript" type="text/javascript">

var flexbox;

function updateClientArea() {
    flexbox.update();
}

function InitializePage() {
    flexbox = new FlexBox("content");
    flexbox.setCharacteristics({ col1 : { width : 200, maxCols : 1},
                                 col2 : {width : 100, maxCols : 4},
                                 col3 : { width :200}}); 
```

```
        flexbox.setContentCallback( {
            updateContent : function( cell, childElement, colCount, characteristic) {
                childElement.innerHTML = "Boxes (" + colCount +
                    ") id(" + cell.id + ")"}});
        flexbox.update();
        window.onresize = updateClientArea;
    }
    </script>
      <body onload="InitializePage()">
        <div id="content">
          <div id="col1"></div>
          <div id="col2"></div>
          <div id="col3"></div>
        </div>
      </body>
    </html>
```

Looking at the code for the HTML page, you can see that a type called FlexBox is instantiated and assigned to the global variable flexbox. The type FlexBox is the sizing algorithm. The action of instantiating and calling the FlexBox type is carried out in the function InitializePage, which is called by the body.onload event.[2] You want to instantiate the FlexBox type in the body.onload event, because that is the first safe location for code to operate on a complete DOM model.

When FlexBox is instantiated, it needs a constructor parameter; in the case of the example, that is the buffer "content". The buffer "content" is an ID reference to an HTML element that serves as the basis of the HTML elements that will be resized. In the example, the ID content references a div element, which contains child div elements. In this sizing algorithm, a div element references child div elements. In your implementation of this recipe, you don't need to do that. This sizing algorithm illustrates that an HTML element contains a number of content blocks, which serve as the columns that will be resized.

When you assign an instance of FlexBox to flexbox, FlexBox first initializes itself and reorders the div elements into a table structure. Executing the FlexBox constructor causes it to reorder the div elements to the following HTML:

```
    <div id="content">
      <table>
        <tr>
            <td id="col1"><div id="col1"></div></td>
            <td id="col2"><div id="col2"></div></td>
            <td id="col3"><div id="col3"></div></td>
        <tr>
      <table>
    </div>
```

---

2. body.onload might not be appropriate for all situations, as it might cause the screen to jump around. Please see the following URL for further details: http://dean.edwards.name/weblog/2006/06/again/.

The reordering of the HTML to a table element is a necessity. Two modes proportionally align elements on an HTML page: absolute coordinates and relative coordinates. By default, HTML uses relative coordinates, which the browser calculates. In relative coordinate mode, you only need to define which elements follow the other elements.

Using absolute coordinates solves the problems of aligning the three child `div` elements, but the rest of the HTML page might be oddly aligned, as some elements might not use absolute coordinates. The simple way to align content on an HTML page using relative coordinates is to use a table. Thus, the sizing algorithm looks at the parent `div` element, creates a `table`, and creates a table cell for each child `div` element. Some readers might think that it would have been easier to define `table` rather `div` elements and then have the algorithm work with the `table` elements directly. It is true that using a `table` element would have been easier, but this algorithm illustrates how you can replace HTML elements with new HTML elements.

Getting back to the source code of the calling HTML page, the method `setCharacteristics` is called once `flexbox` has been assigned. You pass an object definition with a number of embedded objects to `setCharacteristics`. The purpose of `setCharacteristics` is to define the proportional column widths of the child `div` elements. Thus, the embedded object has a number of properties that correspond one-to-one with the IDs of the child `div` elements. In the example, the embedded object defines the following restrictions:

- `col1`: Each column should be 200 pixels wide, and there is a maximum of only a single column.

- `col2`: Each column should be 100 pixels wide, and there is a maximum of four columns.

- `col3`: Each column should be 200 pixels wide, and there can be as many columns as there is space.

To understand the restrictions, you need to understand the nature of the sizing algorithm. The idea of the sizing algorithm is to define proportions that allow a client application to order content appropriately. For example, in Figures 3-7 and 3-8, the structure of the content remains identical when the browser window is resized, even though the content is probably easier to read in Figure 3-8. Assuming Figure 3-8 is the ideal reading size, then the middle column that changes in width as the client browser changes in width is a single column width of x pixels. Let's compare Figure 3-8 with Figure 3-7, which has a middle area width of y pixels. A number of columns of x pixels wide in the middle area would be pleasing to the eye. The total number of columns that can be added is y/x.

In terms of alignment, if the smaller browser contains content that can be described as being a box, then the larger browser can place those boxes side by side instead of in a single column, as illustrated in Figure 3-12.

By increasing the width of the browser, you can assemble more blocks of content side by side. The readability of the HTML page is improved, because there is less scrolling, and the HTML page resembles that of a newspaper. The difference with the HTML page is that unlike a newspaper, the number of columns displayed depends on the size of the client window. The advantage is that if you look at the HTML page from the UMPC device or from a wide-screen notebook, you still get a good look and feel.

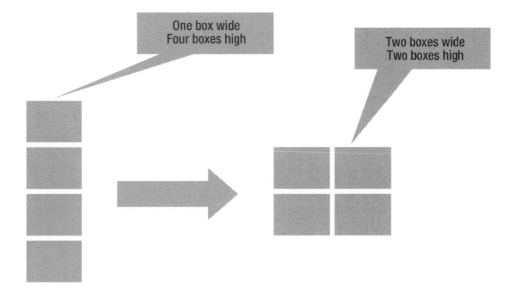

Figure 3-12. *Transformation of content from a single column to a multicolumn design*

The algorithm of Figure 3-12 illustrates the reordering of blocks, but you don't need to do that. It's a user implementation detail. This recipe and the sizing algorithm focus on the awareness of giving the HTML page feedback that a table cell now has room for one, two, or three columns of content. How that content is displayed depends on the HTML page and is beyond the scope of the sizing algorithm.

Getting back to the source code of the calling HTML page, the function setContentCallback is called after calling setCharacteristics. The purpose of the function setContentCallback is to define a user callback that is updated with the new information of how many user-restricted columns can fit in a cell. In the example, the client code displays the parameters in the table cell.

To reproportion the table, you call the method update. The first time update is called, it is from the body onload event. The body onload event is fired only once and won't be called again if the client resizes the client browser. To have the update method called whenever the browser is resized, the window.onresize event is assigned. In the example, you assign window.onresize to the function updateClientArea, which makes a single method call to flexbox.update, which in turn updates the proportions of the table.

Now that the theory of the sizing algorithm has been explained from the abstract level, let's discuss the details of the sizing algorithm. The following code shows the complete implementation of the sizing algorithm. Note that the sizing algorithm is a custom implementation, and you might choose a different strategy in your own situation:

```
function FlexBox(parentIdentifier) {
    if (typeof(parentIdentifier) == "string") {
        this.parentIdentifier = document.getElementById(parentIdentifier);
    }
    else {
```

```javascript
            this.parentIdentifier = parentIdentifier;
        }
        this.table = document.createElement("table");
        this.table.border = 1;
        var tablerow = this.table.insertRow(-1);
        var tempArray = new Array();
        for( var c1 = 0; c1 < this.parentIdentifier.childNodes.length; c1 ++) {
            tempArray[ c1] = this.parentIdentifier.childNodes[c1];
        }
        for (var c1 = 0; c1 < tempArray.length; c1 ++) {
            var child = tempArray[c1];
            if (child.nodeName.toLowerCase() == "div") {
                var cell = tablerow.insertCell(-1);
                cell.appendChild(child);
                if( child.id) {
                    cell.id = child.id;
                }
            }
        }
        this.parentIdentifier.appendChild(this.table);}

FlexBox.prototype.setCharacteristics = function(characteristics) {
    this.characteristics = characteristics;
}

FlexBox.prototype.setContentCallback = function( cbContent) {
    this.cbContent = cbContent;
}

FlexBox.prototype.update = function() {
    var row = this.table.rows[0];
    var totalCells = row.cells.length;
    var availableLength = document.body.clientWidth;
    for( var index in this.characteristics) {
        this.characteristics[ index].cols = 0;
    }
    var Increment;
    if( this.characteristics.updateAlgorithm) {
        Increment = this.characteristics.updateAlgorithm;
    }
    else {
        Increment = function( ref) {
            var takenWidth = 0;
            for( var index in ref.characteristics) {
                takenWidth += ref.characteristics[ index].cols *
                    ref.characteristics[ index].width;
```

```
            }
            var didIncrement = false;
            for( var index in ref.characteristics) {
                var obj = ref.characteristics[ index];
                if((takenWidth + obj.width) < availableLength) {
                    if( obj.maxCols) {
                        if( obj.cols < obj.maxCols) {
                            obj.cols ++;
                            didIncrement = true;
                        }
                    }
                    else {
                        obj.cols ++;
                        didIncrement = true;
                    }
                }
            }
            if( didIncrement) {
                Increment(ref);
            }
        }
    }
    Increment(this);
    for (var c1 = 0; c1 < row.cells.length; c1 ++) {
        if( row.cells[ c1].id) {
            var id = row.cells[ c1].id;
            if (this.characteristics[id] && this.characteristics[id].width) {
                row.cells[ c1].width = this.characteristics[ id].width *
                    this.characteristics[ id].cols;
                if( this.cbContent && this.cbContent.updateContent) {
                    this.cbContent.updateContent(
                        row.cells[ c1], row.cells[ c1].childNodes[ 0],
                        this.characteristics[ id].cols,
                        this.characteristics[ id]);
                }
            }
        }
    }
}
```

For the most part, the code not shown in bold is support code for the bold code. The first bold code section implements the logic used to convert the div and child div elements into a table that contains the child div elements. The second bold code section implements the logic to proportion the table cells.

Let's begin by dissecting the first code block and the manipulation of the table and child div elements. You can manipulate the DOM in one of two ways: You can use the innerHTML property, or you can manipulate objects using methods. This recipe manipulates objects using methods, because that approach is simpler. The child `div` elements could contain some fairly sophisticated HTML code that you don't want to serialize and deserialize. Using objects and moving them in the DOM doesn't corrupt the child `div` elements.

Note the following items from the code:

- *Use the method* `document.createElement` *to instantiate an HTML element*: The returned HTML element instance is instantiated but is not part of the HTML page and needs to be added.

- *If an element represents a specific HTML element such as a table, then associate the methods of the HTML element with that element instance*: In the example, a table is instantiated, and tables reference rows.

- *Use a temporary variable to store elements before they are reordered*: Remember earlier when I said that the sizing algorithm doesn't need to convert `div` elements to `table`? Before looking at the explanation of the sizing algorithm, notice in the first bold code block how elements are saved to a temporary array (`tempArray`) before being added back to the HTML document as child elements of a `table`. This step of saving references temporarily is absolutely crucial when you're manipulating an object document model. If you don't save temporarily, you could experience some very funky side effects. This extra step was added to the recipe to illustrate how to manipulate a document properly.

- *Add an HTML element instance to the HTML page hierarchy using a DOM method such as* `appendChild`: If the instance passed to `appendChild` is an element already located in the HTML page, then call a `removeChild` before calling `appendChild`. The calling of `removeChild` happens transparently.

The second bold code block implements the algorithm to partition the table. The logic is a brute-force technique that distributes the widths among the table cells and sees if the distribution is more or less than the available width. The best way to illustrate the logic is to go through the example HTML page. The restrictions of the example HTML page were outlined in bullet form a couple of pages back.

The logic reads the restrictions and for the first iteration, attempts to place a single column in each table cell. The widths of each column are added together and tested against the width of the client area. If the added width is less than the client area width, then another iteration is executed. In the example, the first table cell can only contain a single column width. Another iteration is carried out, and the second table cell column count is incremented. The pattern of iterations results in a column count pattern that resembles the following:

```
1 1 1
1 2 1
1 2 2
1 3 2
1 3 3
1 4 3
...
```

You use the brute-force technique, because you want to distribute the columns equally among all of the table cells. If you want to use your own distribution algorithm, then the object instance passed to the method `setCharacteristics` needs to have a data member updateAlgorithm. When implementing your own algorithm, keep in mind that you want to distribute the column widths among the table cells.

Remember the following things:

- With today's technology, a wide variety of devices have extreme differences in screen resolution.

- Fixed-width or completely percentage-based HTML pages look good only on specific screen dimensions. If a screen is beyond those dimensions, the HTML page looks bad.

- When accommodating different screen resolutions, consider the page layout dynamically in the horizontal and vertical dimensions. Most pages only consider the HTML page as being dynamic in the vertical dimension.

- Don't use absolute coordinates when using algorithmic proportions, because that requires adjusting all of the elements on the entire HTML page. Use relative coordinates, which imply HTML table elements.

- When moving content in a horizontal and vertical fashion, use a distribution algorithm that distributes the content evenly on the HTML page.

3-3. Manipulating Dynamic Content Blocks

This recipe looks at the best ways to define distinct content blocks in applications—for example, for the purposes of drag and drop.

Problem

When creating distinct content blocks in a Web application, you need to know the best way to define and manipulate them, whether that's through div or span elements, or through iframe elements.

Theory

Many Web sites display content as a single block through the use of an HTML div element. The div element allows content to float on the page, and it supports dragging a block on an HTML page.

The eyeOS[3] Web site makes extensive use of div elements, as illustrated in Figure 3-13.

---

3. http://www.eyeos.org

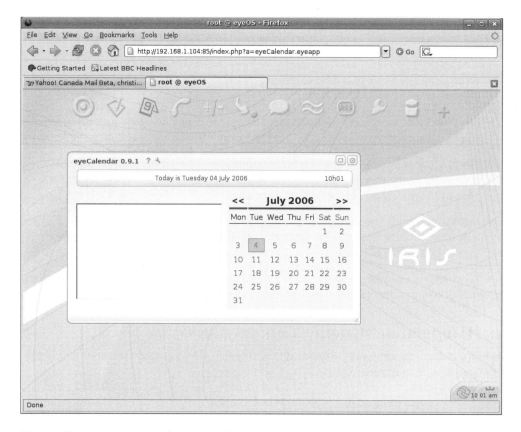

Figure 3-13. *An example desktop created using HTML elements that make extensive use of* div *elements*

The HTML page with the wave image is a desktop that has some icons along the top of the page. The window that resembles a dialog box is an application within the desktop. The dialog box and many other elements are all HTML content blocks defined using div elements.

You could also use an iframe HTML element, which is an embedded frame used as a content block. Figure 3-14 shows an HTML page that uses the iframe.

In both examples, it is not obvious that one HTML page is using div elements and the other is using iframe elements. Why does the Web site in Figure 3-13 use div elements and the Web site in Figure 3-14 use iframe elements? The answer cannot be, "Because one HTML page is coded using modern techniques, and the other is not." There are technical reasons for choosing one technique or the other. This recipe goes through the variations of how to use each element type for defining content blocks.

First, let's define a content block. A content block is an HTML element that serves as a placeholder for HTML content. What distinguishes a content block from, say, a table cell, is that you can move a content block from one location in the HTML hierarchy to another. It is not possible to remove a table cell (a td element) and make it a child of the form element. The HTML elements span and div are the most commonly used elements to define content blocks.

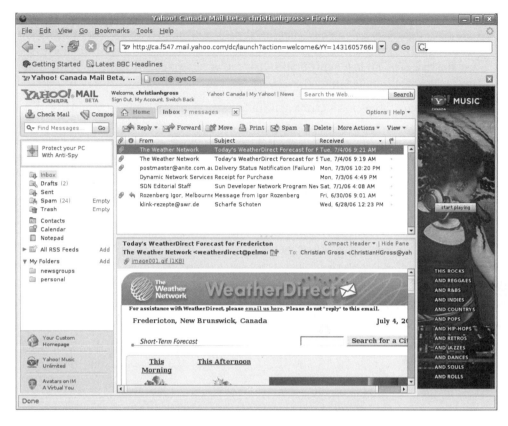

Figure 3-14. *Yahoo! Webmail that makes extensive use of the* iframe *element to display the content*

Solution

The big difference between using a div or span vs. an iframe element to display content is how the content block is populated. A div or span content block cannot populate itself; it requires an external assignment. The assignment could be an XMLHttpRequest or an iframe method call. An iframe can download its own content by assigning the src property. In essence, even though you can use div, span, and iframe as content blocks, each of the three tags has very distinct features. The features of each tag are defined as follows:

- div: Defines an assignable content block that functions as a paragraph separator. This means that when adding a div element to an HTML page in relative coordinate mode, any HTML elements placed afterwards are located on the HTML page underneath the div element. When used in absolute coordinate mode, a div element can behave like a dialog box. A div element is always part of the HTML page.

- iframe: Defines a content block where a script can assign the content, or the iframe can load its own content by assigning the src property. Using an iframe element is like creating an HTML page within an HTML page. For example, if your script messes up the content of iframe, it won't mess up the content of the parent HTML page. The separation of content makes it possible to define identically named variables or functions with different values.

- span: Defines an assignable content block that is nearly identical to a div element, with one exception. A span element is an inline division and places content beside the element. Using a span element, you could define a paragraph of text, and within the text use the span element to identify individually replaceable pieces of text without disrupting the flow of the paragraph.

The remainder of this recipe illustrates the different scenarios where you would use a content block.

Let's start with the simplest scenario: a data placeholder. When a content block is a data placeholder, its role is to define a chunk that you can reference from a script. From the perspective of the user interface, you don't know that a content block exists. Figure 3-15 illustrates an example of a data placeholder content block.

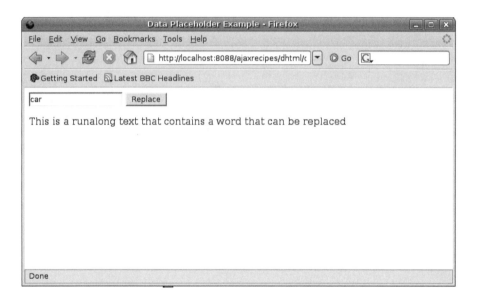

Figure 3-15. *Example HTML page that contains a data placeholder*

Figure 3-15 features a text box, a button, and some text. Users can replace the current text of the data placeholder by entering some text in the text box and clicking the button. The script then replaces the text in the data placeholder, as illustrated in Figure 3-16.

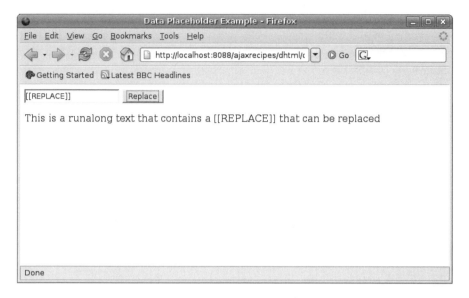

Figure 3-16. *Text that replaces the data placeholder*

In Figure 3-16, the replaced text is [[REPLACE]]. Notice how it is not obvious where the data placeholder resides. This is the intent of the span element. The code for Figure 3-15 is as follows.

Source: /website/ROOT/ajaxrecipes/dhtml/dataplaceholder.html

```
<html>
  <head>
    <title>Data Placeholder Example</title>
  </head>
<script language="JavaScript" type="text/javascript">
function Replace() {
    document.getElementById( "word").innerHTML =
        document.getElementById( "toreplace").value;
}
</script>

  <body>
    <p>
      <input type="text" size="20" id="toreplace" /> 
      <input type="button" value="Replace" onclick="Replace()" />
    </p>
    <p>This is a runalong text that contains a
          <span id="word">word</span> that can be replaced</p>
  </body>
</html>
```

The example code shows a simple wiring of the `onclick` event to a function that uses the `getElementById` method to find, extract, and replace text. For illustration purposes, let's replace `span` with `div` and see what results. Figure 3-17 is the result of using `div` and is the same test as shown in Figure 3-16.

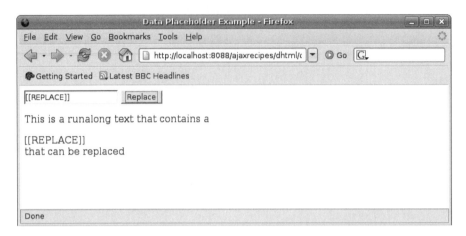

Figure 3-17. *Text using the* `div` *element that replaces the data placeholder*

The difference between Figures 3-16 and 3-17 is that the replaced text is a lone block with its own area. As indicated earlier, it would mean that a `span` element is used for inline text, and `div` is not. While the default case is correct, it is not completely correct. It is possible to make a `span` element behave like a `div` element and vice versa. Figure 3-18 shows an example of how you can switch the behavior of the elements.

In Figure 3-18, the roles of `div` and `span` have been reversed. This is possible because the `style` attribute's subproperty `display` controls how the element is placed. The first italic text in Figure 3-18 is a `div` element with the `display` subproperty set to `inline`. The second italic text is a `span` element with its display subproperty set to `block`. In the context of a content block, it doesn't matter if you choose a `span` or `div` element, since each can be made to look and behave like the other.

The following code illustrates how to define the `div` and `span` elements:

```
    Some text with embedded (
<div style="display:inline"><i>inline div element</i></div>).
    and more text with embedded (
<span style="display:block"><i>block span element</i></span>).
```

You can also use the `span` and `div` elements to display content in an HTML page that can be directly referenced without having to manipulate the referenced elements surrounding HTML. Now suppose you want to create error messages. You should not display error messages before an error occurs, so you should keep the error message hidden. You can use the following HTML code to hide a `span` element:

```
(<span id="hidden" style="visibility:hidden">empty space</span>)
```

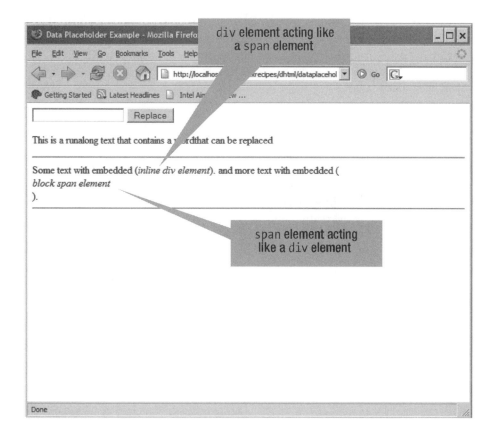

Figure 3-18. *A* span *element behaving like a* div *element, and* div *like a* span

In the example, the `style` attribute and `visibility` subproperty are assigned a value of `hidden`. Figure 3-19 shows how the rendered HTML hides the `span` element.

(   )

Figure 3-19. *A hidden* span *element*

The `span` element is indeed hidden, but it's apparent that some text is being hidden. This is obvious, because the space required by the `span` element is still taken. It is sort of like the ostrich that sticks its head in the ground. Sure, you and it cannot see each other, but you know the ostrich is still there. To hide the `span` element, or any HTML element in particular, you use the `display` property that you used to determine the alignment of the text. To hide the element completely, set the `display` subproperty to `none`, as shown by the following example:

```
(<span id="hidden" style="visibility:none">empty space</span>)
```

You can also hide the HTML element to store reference data, such as the serialization results of a JavaScript object, in the span or div elements.

The downside to using a span or div element and the innerHTML property is HTML content might be escaped or encoded. Consider the following source code, which illustrates the problem of escaped or encoded HTML:

```
document.getElementById( "escaped").innerHTML = "<2 > 1</hello>";
document.getElementById( "valueescaped").value =
        document.getElementById( "escaped").innerHTML;
```

In the example, the method getElementById retrieves a reference to a span or div element with the identifier escaped. The innerHTML property is assigned a string that contains a number of reserved characters (<, >). Then the value of the innerHTML property is assigned to the HTML element valueescaped, which is a textarea. The assignment from the span element to the textarea illustrates that the string is escaped, as Figure 3-20 shows.

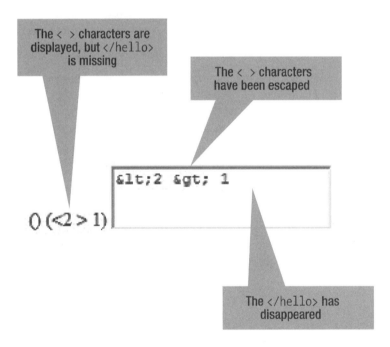

Figure 3-20. span *element with missing content, and* textarea *with missing and encoded content*

Having some of your text encoded or missing is not a good idea; in fact, it's a problem. To avoid this problem, you might tend to favor the use of textareas as content blocks. The problem with using textareas is serialization. When a chunk of HTML is serialized, the textarea is serialized instead of the contents. You need to explicitly serialize the value of the textarea. With a span or div element, that additional step is not necessary. To solve the problem of escaping the text, surround the text with a comment, as illustrated by the following code:

```
document.getElementById( "escaped").innerHTML = "<!--<2 > 1</hello>-->";
```

When the text is surrounded by an HTML comment (`<!-- -->`), the HTML parser doesn't attempt to process the special characters.

Now let's discuss the use of an `iframe` element as a content block. For reference purposes, an `iframe` element is a combination of a `div` or `span` element and the `XMLHttpRequest` object. An `iframe` element is like an HTML frame, except the frame can float on the HTML page. For example, when writing the tests for the pages of this book, the test page would contain an `iframe` that references the page to be tested. With `iframe`, you're delegating the responsibility of retrieving and displaying the content to the frame. In turn, this gives you less control over how the content is retrieved and displayed.

Figure 3-14 illustrates the new Ajax-enabled Yahoo! Web client, which uses `iframes` extensively. This makes sense for Yahoo!, because its Webmail client is designed traditionally, and each of the elements is content that is related to the other elements on the HTML page using links. For example, the navigation contains a list of emails that you can reference and display in the other window. Let's look at a simple example of using the `iframe` element:

```
<iframe width="200" height="200"
    src="/ajaxrecipes/dhtml/otherdisplay.html"></iframe>
```

In the example, the `iframe` element is declared with an initial height and width, and it is set to download the content at the URL defined by the `src` attribute. The URL of the `iframe` can be anything, as the `iframe` will download what is requested. If the URL falls under the same origin policy as the parent HTML page, then a script can reference the DOM within the `iframe`, but if the URL does not fall under same origin policy, then the content will be downloaded by the DOM and cannot be referenced by the script. If the script attempts to reference the content, an access-denied exception will occur.

Figure 3-21 shows the example code in an HTML page.

Figure 3-21. *Illustration of how an* `iframe` *element is rendered*

When rendering, an `iframe` generates a depth-like frame, but otherwise it behaves like a `div` or `span` element and allows users to interact with it as such. The `iframe` obeys the same rules as the `span` and `div` element when hiding or aligning the elements.

You can assign or retrieve the data in the `iframe` window by using a `contentWindow` or `contentDocument` property. The following example illustrates copying the contents from an `iframe` to a `div` element:

```
<script language="JavaScript" type="text/javascript">
function GetSrc() {
    document.getElementById( "gensrc").innerHTML =
        document.getElementById( "newassign").contentDocument.body.innerHTML;
}
</script>
    <p>
        <iframe id="newassign" width="200" height="200"
            src="/ajaxrecipes/dhtml/percentagelayout.html"></iframe>
    </p>
    <div id="gensrc"></div>
```

In the example source code, the `iframe` element preloads the HTML page. Using a button's click event to call the function `GetSrc` transfers the contents of the `iframe` body to the `div` element. This causes the same content to be displayed twice, and as shown in Figure 3-22, illustrates how it is possible to transfer content from one content block to another.

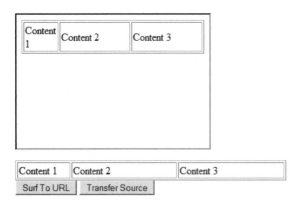

Figure 3-22. *Same content displayed in* `iframe` *and* `div` *elements*

The content in Figure 3-22 is not rendered completely identical, because HTML renders the content with differing element dimensions. The structure of the content is identical and illustrates that a `div` and `iframe` have the same content block programmatic behavior.

Keep the following points in mind when creating and managing content chunks:

- There are three types of content blocks: `span`, `div`, and `iframe`.

- When using a `div` element as a content block, you're responsible for assigning or retrieving the content.

- When using an `iframe` element as a content block, the `iframe` is responsible for retrieving and rendering the content.

- A div element is part of the HTML page. This means that when multiple div elements have the same identifier, getElementById retrieves the first instance. Think of a div element as a shared library that is loaded into the process space of the application.

- When used as a content block, an iframe element is separate from the parent HTML page. An iframe element can have identical identifiers that don't conflict with the parent. Think of an iframe element as another process that can communicate to the parent process.

- When choosing to use either an iframe or div content block, remember they require two different strategies. An iframe uses a delegation model, where the iframe is given a task in the form of a URL. Based on the URL, the iframe and content decide what and how to display the content. A div element doesn't use any delegation, and you're in control of all aspects related to content display and manipulation.

3-4. Implementing "Dialog Boxes"

As the previous recipe hinted at, you can use a div element as a content block that mimics the behavior of a dialog box. This recipe looks more specifically at implementing effective dialog boxes in modern Web applications.

Problem

You want to implement effective dialog boxes in Web applications.

Theory

The title for this recipe shows the words "dialog boxes" in quotes, because the div element is not a true dialog box. Instead, it is restricted to the boundaries of the HTML page. Typically, you can place real dialog boxes anywhere on the computer screen. Real dialog boxes are not of interest in this recipe. What is of interest is how to create an HTML "dialog box." For example, Figure 3-23 shows how you can use a "dialog box" on an HTML page.

In Figure 3-23, the div element indicates which buses are arriving and departing from the station. The dialog box pops up on the HTML page whenever the mouse passes over a hotspot. Once the dialog box appears, users can drag it, move it, and click on it. If users move the mouse away from the dialog box, the dialog box disappears. The disappearance is not a default behavior, but a programmed behavior.

When writing HTML pages, you can use dialog boxes for a whole host of things, such as

- To provide meta information associated with a hotspot on an HTML page

- To ask for extra information when filling in a form or processing a workflow

- Menus

- To behave as a wait icon

Figure 3-23. `div` *element behaving like a dialog box*

You can also use popup windows to indicate failures; popup windows look different from dialog boxes, but the technique used to create them is identical.

The usage of a dialog box to behave as a wait icon is not a common one, but can be tasteful when used properly, as Figure 3-24 illustrates.

In Figure 3-24, the `div` element indicates that users should wait and do nothing. Traditionally, applications use a spinning icon to indicate a busy application. For reference purposes, the Web site captured in Figure 3-24 did originally use a spinning mouse icon, but perhaps they switched because the spinning mouse confused users, and the new solution is more obvious and visually pleasing.

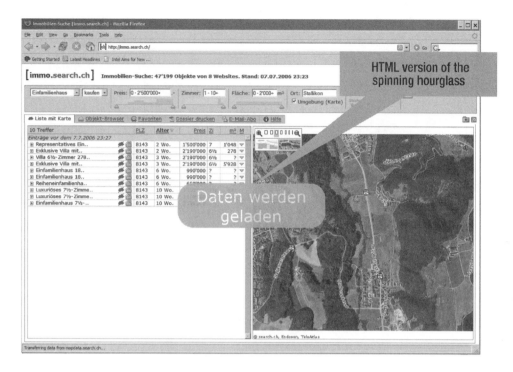

Figure 3-24. `div` *element used to indicate that users should wait until the data has been loaded*

Solution

Two things must happen in order to make a `div` element behave like a dialog box. First, you must place the `div` element on the HTML page using absolute coordinates. Second, you need to make the `div` element aware of mouse movement. The following example places two `div` elements 100 pixels from the left and 100 pixels from the top of the client browser window.

Source: `/website/ROOT/ajaxrecipes/dhtml/divdialogessentials.html`

```html
<html>
    <head>
        <title>DIV dialog essentials</title>
    </head>
<style type="text/css">
.background1 {
    background-color: cyan;
}
.background2 {
    background-color: blue;
}
</style>
<script type="text/javascript">
</script>
```

```
<body onload="Init()">
    <div class="background1" style="left:100px;top:100px;position:absolute">
        Begin
        <div class="background2"
                style="left:100px;top:100px;position:absolute">
            hello
        </div>
        End
    </div>
</body>
</html>
```

The example HTML code contains two div elements, one nested within the other. Ignore the class attribute, as it is used to color the div elements. Instead, look closely at the style attribute, which has three properties: left, top, and position. The position property and the absolute value indicate that the positioning of the element uses absolute coordinates. The absolute coordinates of the top left-hand corner are given by the properties top and left, respectively.

The width and height, which indicate how wide and high the div element will be, are missing. When these properties are missing, the browser dynamically calculates the width and height.

In the HTML code example, one div element is encapsulated within the other. Both of the div elements are placed 100 pixels from the top and 100 pixels from the left. At first glance, the absolute coordinates would indicate that both div elements are located in the same location. However, this is not what the browser displays, as illustrated in Figure 3-25.

The two div elements are not on top of each other, but rather one is relative to the other. That is a bit puzzling; the attribute position is set to absolute, so the coordinates should be absolute. The real question is, "What is absolute?" For example, do you need to calculate all absolute coordinates with respect to the parent element? Imagine if a div element that is not positioned using absolute coordinates contains a div element that *is* positioned using absolute coordinates. Which coordinates would the contained div element use? The answer is that it would use the last element that is either positioned: absolute or position: relative (position: inherit is the default).

This is how you get absolute positioning within relative positioning. Using coordinates makes it possible to have a div element appear and display its information like a dialog box. You could add functionality where a link in the "dialog box" would hide the popup dialog box. To be able to know where to make a dialog appear, you need to capture the onclick message and process it.

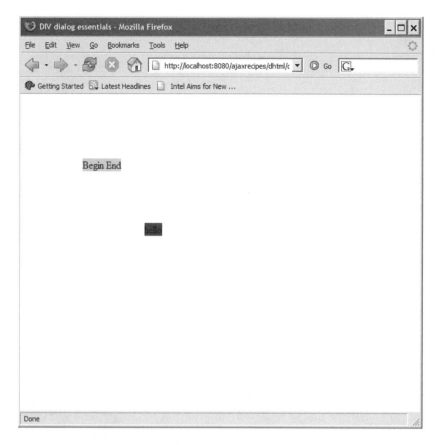

Figure 3-25. *An illustration of how absolute coordinates are calculated for nested elements*

The following source code makes a div element appear where users click on the screen. The div element contains a link that is used to hide the div element.

Source: /website/ROOT/ajaxrecipes/dhtml/clickappeardiv.html

```
<html>
    <head>
        <title>DIV dialog essentials</title>
    </head>
<style type="text/css">
.background {
    background-color: cyan;
}
</style>
```

```
<script type="text/javascript">
function DisplayDiv( evt) {
    evt = (evt) ? evt: ((event) ? event : null);
    x = evt.clientX;
    y = evt.clientY;
    var element = document.getElementById( "display");
    element.style.left = x;
    element.style.top = y;
    element.style.display = "block";
}
function HideDiv() {
    var element = document.getElementById( "display");
    element.style.display = "none";
}
</script>
    <body onclick="DisplayDiv( event)">
        <div id="display" class="background"
            style="width:100px;height:100px;position:absolute;display:none">
            hello some text <a href="" onclick=" HideDiv()">Hide me</a>
        </div>
    </body>
</html>
```

In the example HTML page, the body is a single div element, which is not displayed when the HTML page is loaded. The single div element is the div element that will be placed somewhere in the HTML page when the mouse is clicked. Notice the width, height, and position properties are assigned in the declaration of the div element. These properties are defaults that you can set at design time, thereby reducing the amount of code you need to define when displaying the div element.

The code example contains two functions: DisplayDiv and HideDiv. The function DisplayDiv is used to show the div element. The function HideDiv is used to hide the div element. The body.onclick handler calls the function DisplayDiv. The body element is used because the onclick event bubbles upward from child to parent, and the div element should be placed somewhere on the displayed HTML page. The function HideDiv is called by clicking on the link that is displayed when the div element is displayed.

When the HTML page loads, users are presented with a blank screen. When they click anywhere on the screen, the body element captures the click event and passes the event to the function DisplayDiv. In the implementation of DisplayDiv, the event object evt is tested using a single line. The single line is necessary for cross-browser compatibility. Once the complete event object has been retrieved and assigned to evt, it is assumed that a mouse event is being sent. A browser-sent mouse event has the properties clientX and clientY, which contain the coordinates of the click in the context of the HTML page.

The coordinates position the div element using the style.left and style.top properties. After the div element has been positioned, you display it using the property style.display. Figure 3-26 shows how it looks.

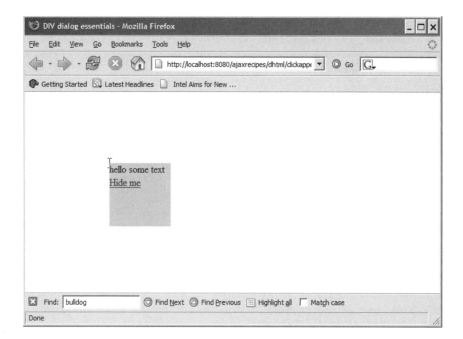

Figure 3-26. *Displaying the* div *element after the mouse is clicked*

You can hide the div element by clicking on the Hide me link, which then results in a blank HTML page. The displaying and hiding of the div element is fairly elementary, but there is a hidden gotcha. If a div element uses absolute coordinates and is encapsulated within another div element that uses absolute coordinates, then setting the coordinates will result in an incorrectly positioned element. This happens because the click event uses coordinates relative to the browser, and the encapsulated div element uses coordinates relative to the parent element. To remedy this problem, you need to reference different properties, as the following rewritten DisplayDiv function illustrates:

```
function DisplayDiv ( evt) {
    evt = (evt) ? evt: ((event) ? event : null);
    if( evt.layerX) {
        x = evt.layerX;
        y = evt.layerY;
    }
    else if( evt.offsetX) {
        x = evt.offsetX;
        y = evt.offsetY;
    }
    var element = document.getElementById( "display");
    element.style.left = x;
    element.style.top = y;
    element.style.display = "block";
}
```

The bold code represents the code used to find the coordinates of the click event relative to the element being clicked. The code has two tests for the existence of either layerX or offsetX. If layerX exists, then you're using a Mozilla-compatible browser, and if offsetX exists, then you're using Microsoft Internet Explorer.

This modified code will work in simple situations, but it is not reliable, because the coordinates are relative to the element being clicked. For example, if you have a div element encapsulated within a div element encapsulated within a div element, and you click on the middle div element, the relative coordinates will be wrong.

In a nutshell, once you begin using absolute coordinates within elements that are positioned using absolute coordinates, you're going to have problems figuring out the real position. Instead, use clientX and clientY, and calculate the absolute coordinates of the HTML elements using a recursive iteration.

The ability to display div elements wherever users click allows you to implement menu-type functionality. You can implement error-display handlers and other informational messages that need to be positioned. The only thing you cannot do is display a message or functionality that you can drag to another position on the HTML page. To do that, the simplest solution is to implement the mouse-down, mouse-move, and mouse-up events. This sounds simple, but it requires quite a bit of extra work to do it robustly.

For starters, you can't use the onclick event, because this event is sent when the mouse button is released. To implement a dragging operation, you must capture the onmousedown, onmousemove, and onmouseup events. The remainder of this recipe uses a precanned solution, because quite a few details are involved, and you can apply this base solution in multiple contexts. The solution is to use a file from a Web site called Dynamic Drive (or, dom-drag.js),[4] which only requires users to specify which HTML element should be draggable. The dom-drag.js implementation handles all of the lower-level mouse click event details. Figure 3-27 illustrates an example that uses dom-drag.js.

In Figure 3-27, the div element has two child div elements, where one represents a toolbar and the other represents the content window. The toolbar is recognized as a hotspot used to drag the div element around the HTML page. It isn't necessary to define a div element using the traditional dialog box notation. The following HTML code, used in Figure 3-27, shows how you can define a div element as a hotspot:

---

4. http://www.dynamicdrive.com

Figure 3-27. *Example implementation of a draggable* div *element*

```
<html>
    <head>
        <title>Drag DIV</title>
    </head>
    <script type="text/javascript" src="/scripts/jaxson/dom-drag.js"></script>
<style type="text/css">
.dialogbox {
    background-color: cyan;
    border: 1px solid black;
    color: black;
    padding: 0px;
    position: absolute;
}

.dialogtitle {
    background-color: blue;
    color: white;
    font-weight: bold;
    padding: 2px 2px 2px 2px;
}

.dialogcontent {
    padding: 2px;
}
</style>
```

```
<script type="text/javascript">
function Init() {
    Drag.init(document.getElementById("example"));
}
</script>
    <body onload="Init()">
        <div id="example" class="dialogbox" style="left:100px;top:100px;">
            <div class="dialogtitle" style="width:200px;">
                <center>Drag Me</center>
            </div>
            <div class="dialogcontent" style="width:200px;">
                <a href="">link</a> any content</div>
        </div>
    </body>
</html>
```

Notice how much layout code and script code exists. The layout code outnumbers the script code, which is what will most likely happen in your dialog box implementations. With the dom-drag.js solution, your primary focus is on adding value in terms of look and feel. The dom-drag.js solution doesn't require using a div element, as you could have created a draggable table element.

Remember the following things when implementing dialog boxes:

- To implement a dialog box in HTML, use absolute coordinates; the properties top, left, and display; and onclick or onmousedown, onmousemove, and onmouseup mouse events.

- When implementing dialog boxes, you're going to be confronted with two major problems: getting the right coordinates, and making sure the element that fires the event has some relation to the element that will be manipulated. For example, you don't want a menu to appear in the top right-hand corner when the bottom left-hand corner is clicked. This behavior can confuse users.

- Always delegate drag-and-drop functionality to another library. This recipe used the dom-drag.js solution, but plenty of other solutions abound, and you're advised to try them out.

3-5. Serializing HTML

Now let's turn attention to serializing HTML properly in modern Web applications, working around some of the constraints you're faced with.

Problem

Some of the DOM properties exhibit inconsistent behavior—in particular, the innerHTML property. The purpose of innerHTML is to extract the child elements of an HTML element in a string form. The problem is that the innerHTML property doesn't generate the correct text. You need to work around this.

Theory

To understand where the innerHTML property fails, let's work through some examples and incrementally show where the problem lies. The example that will be illustrated is the dynamic addition of a button and text field. The source code for the example is as follows.

Source: /website/ROOT/ajaxrecipes/dhtml/inconsistent.html

```html
<html>
  <head>
    <title>Inconsistent .innerHTML</title>
  </head>
    <script language="JavaScript" src="/scripts/jaxson/common.js"></script>

<script language="JavaScript" type="text/javascript">
function DOMInserted() {
    var element = document.createElement( "input");
    element.type = "button";
    element.value = "dynamically inserted";
    element.onclick = function() {
        document.getElementById( "generated").innerHTML = "hello";
    }
    document.getElementById( "dynamicallyinserted").appendChild( element);
    element = document.createElement( "input");
    element.type = "text";
    element.value = "dynamically inserted";
    document.getElementById( "dynamicallyinserted").appendChild( element);
    document.getElementById( "output").value =
        document.getElementById( "dynamicallyinserted").innerHTML;
}
</script>
  <body>
      <div id="dynamicallyinserted">
          <input type="button" value="hello" onclick="callme()" />
      </div>
      <div id="generated"></div>
      <textarea id="output" cols="40" rows="10"></textarea><br />
      <input type="button" value="Dynamically Insert" onclick="DOMInserted()" />
  </body>
</html>
```

The function DOMInserted adds the button and text to the div element with the ID dynamicallyinserted. The div element with the ID dynamicallyinserted has no child elements. Thus, if innerHTML were called, the returned string would contain no text.

When users press the button Dynamically Insert, the function DOMInserted is called. Use the same HTML element input to create either a button or text box. What distinguishes a button from a text box is the value of the property type. To create an input element instance, use the method `document.createElement`. Once the element instance has been instantiated and assigned, you add it to the `div` element using the `appendChild` method.

After both input instances have been added to the `div` element, you can use `innerHTML` to retrieve the value of its child elements in HTML. The value of `innerHTML` is assigned to the `textarea` element to illustrate the raw HTML value.

Running the code in a Mozilla Firefox browser results in an image similar to Figure 3-28.

Figure 3-28. *Investigation of the* innerHTML *property using Firefox*

In Figure 3-28, the value of the retrieved `innerHTML` property has an error. The error is that no `value` attribute exists. In fact, the `value` attribute does exist, because you assigned it in the script and displayed it in the HTML, but with respect to the `innerHTML` property, the `value` attribute does not exist.

In contrast, look at what Internet Explorer generates, as illustrated in Figure 3-29.

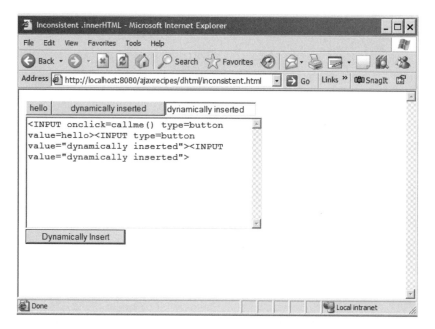

Figure 3-29. *Investigation of the* innerHTML *property using Internet Explorer*

Internet Explorer generates the correct output. Running the same code in Opera generates the same error as in Mozilla. A DHTML user interface is completely dynamic, so any changes made by users or the script need to be reflected in the property.

Solution

The remainder of this recipe focuses on how to solve the serialization problem of the HTML elements. The solution is simple in that to generate the buffer, you need to iterate all of the elements individually and generate a long buffer. The following code illustrates the complete solution.

Source: /website/ROOT/scripts/jaxson/common.js

```
htmlSerialize : function( element) {
    var Recursive = function( element) {
        var buffer = "";
        if( element.nodeType == 1) {
            buffer +="<" + element.nodeName + " ";
            var didGenerateValue = false;
            for( var i = 0; i < element.attributes.length; i ++) {
                var attr = element.attributes[ i];
                var name = attr.name.toLowerCase();
```

```
                    if(!(name.charAt( 0) == 'o' && name.charAt( 1) == 'n') &&
                        attr.value != null && !(typeof(attr.value) == "string" &&
                          attr.value.length == 0)) {
                        if( new String( element[ attr.name]).toLowerCase() ==
                            "undefined") {
                            buffer += attr.name + "=\"" + attr.value + "\" ";
                        }
                        else {
                            buffer += attr.name + "=\"" + element[ attr.name] + "\" ";
                        }
                    }
                    if( attr.name.toLowerCase() == "value") {
                        didGenerateValue = true;
                    }
                }
                if( element.nodeName.toLowerCase() == "input" && !didGenerateValue) {
                    buffer += "value=\"" + element.value + "\" ";
                }
                buffer += ">";
                // If this is a textarea node, then inject the value directly
                if( element.nodeName.toLowerCase() == "textarea") {
                    buffer += element.value;
                }
                else {
                    for( var i = 0; i < element.childNodes.length; i ++) {
                        buffer += Recursive( element.childNodes[ i]);
                    }
                }
                buffer += "</" + element.nodeName + ">";
            }
            else if( element.nodeType == 3) {
                buffer += element.nodeValue;
            }
            return buffer;
        }
    var buffer = ""
    for( var i = 0; i < element.childNodes.length; i ++) {
        buffer += Recursive( element.childNodes[ i]);
    }
    return buffer;
}
```

The function Recursive is used to iterate the individual elements and can be used with all browsers. The Recursive function has a single parameter that represents an object instance that will be introspected for properties and methods. The serialization only supports two types of nodes (element.nodeType): 1 and 3. If you don't know what the various node types are, then the numbers 1 and 3 aren't going to help you. Node type 1 represents a plain vanilla HTML element, and node type 3 represents a piece of text. The serialization ignores comments, page directives, and the like, because generally speaking, they're not important to the serialization.

If the node type is 1, then a buffer is generated for the element identifier and all of its associated attributes. You would think that iterating all of the attributes would include the value attribute. For any browser other than Internet Explorer, the attributes that are present in the element.attributes array depend on the type of attribute. Depending on the type of input element, the value attribute might not be part of the list, meaning it isn't accessible. It also means that you need to reference it directly using the notation element.value.

The fact that some elements are displayed and others are not is a bit worrisome, because you're left wondering what the browser is hiding. If you look closely at source code and the generated output of the inconsistent HTML page, you'll notice that the browsers are handling one attribute inconsistently: They're missing the onclick handler for the dynamically generated button element. The onclick attribute is generated for the statically defined button, but not for the dynamically generated button.

You need to ask yourself if you want to generate the event handlers when the HTML is serialized. If you answer no, the htmlSerialize function will check for events by testing if the attribute starts with the letters *o* and *n*. But is it correct not to serialize the events? One can argue that if you're going to serialize HTML, you need to serialize everything. However, serializing everything is difficult, because you must somehow store function references. You cannot store the implementation of a function in an attribute, because attributes cannot contain line feeds. Your decision should be based on what you most likely want to do with HTML serialization, and that is extracting state.

The proposed solution is by no means complete, but it solves a specific context, and that is what you need to realize. When solving the problem of serializing the function reference, there is the question of how to serialize the function that has been assigned dynamically, as illustrated in the example HTML page. For illustration purposes, let's try an initial serialization of functions, though you'll quickly see that serialization of functions is rather complicated. To serialize functions, you'd rewrite the htmlSerialize function as follows:

```
htmlSerialize : function(element) {
    var scriptBuffer = "";
    var Recursive = function(element) {
        var buffer = "";
        if (element.nodeType == 1) {
            buffer += "<" + element.nodeName + " ";
            var didGenerateValue = false;
            for (var i = 0; i < element.attributes.length; i ++) {
                var attr = element.attributes[i];
                var name = attr.name.toLowerCase();
                if( name.charAt( 0) == 'o' && name.charAt( 1) == 'n') {
                    if( typeof( attr.value) == "string") {
                        buffer += attr.name + "=\"" + attr.value + "\" ";
                    }
                }
```

```
            else if ( attr.value != null && !(typeof(attr.value) == "string" &&
                attr.value.length == 0)) {
                if (new String(element[attr.name]).toLowerCase() ==
                    "undefined") {
                    buffer += attr.name + "=\"" + attr.value + "\" ";
                }
                else {
                    buffer += attr.name + "=\"" + element[attr.name] + "\" ";
                }
            }
            if (attr.name.toLowerCase() == "value") {
                didGenerateValue = true;
            }
        }
        if (element.nodeName.toLowerCase() == "input" && !didGenerateValue) {
            buffer += "value=\"" + element.value + "\" ";
        }
        if( element.onclick) {
            scriptBuffer += "var " + element.id + "_onclick = " +
                element.onclick;
            buffer += "value=\"" + element.id + "_onclick()\"";
        }
        buffer += ">";
        if (element.nodeName.toLowerCase() == "textarea") {
            buffer += element.value;
        }
        else {
            for (var i = 0; i < element.childNodes.length; i ++) {
                buffer += Recursive(element.childNodes[i]);
            }
        }
        buffer += "</" + element.nodeName + ">";
    }
    else if (element.nodeType == 3) {
        buffer += element.nodeValue;
    }
    return buffer;

}
var buffer = ""
for (var i = 0; i < element.childNodes.length; i ++) {
    buffer += Recursive(element.childNodes[i]);
}
return buffer;
}
```

The bold code in the modified implementation relates to the serialization of the event handlers. The first piece of bold code is the declaration of a script buffer. The script buffer is the script code that you saved with the serialized HTML. You need both pieces, as the script code will dynamically attach itself when you assign the serialized HTML using the `innerHTML` property.

The second bold code is the serialization of the events that you declared at design time. If the element is attached dynamically, then any associated event is not serialized.

The last and third piece of bold code is the problematic and touchy code. In the example HTML page, the `onclick` event was assigned dynamically where a button was injected dynamically. The `onclick` event was not a string that referenced another call. The `onclick` event referenced an anonymous JavaScript function. Because serialized attributes cannot contain complete function implementations, you must serialize the function and create a reference to the function resembling the serialization to the design-time HTML element declaration.

The dynamically associated `onclick` event is an anonymous function, and therefore has no identifier. The bold code defines a function that is a concatenation of the element `id` and the `onclick` event. Though the dynamic example has no `id`, multiple identical `onclick` events will be generated. You could also generate a random identifier and then reference that random identifier in the serialized HTML.

The random identifier solves the problem of the function identifier. But now there are two buffers. One buffer contains the serialized HTML code, and another buffer contains the script that you need to execute so that the function references won't generate errors. As you can see, the code is now starting to become very complicated and rickety. This is why I recommend not serializing the events unless absolutely necessary.

Remember the following points regarding this HTML serialization recipe:

- HTML serialization is fraught with details, exceptions, and little problems. For example, when serializing using `htmlSerialize`, IE generates oodles of attributes that you didn't define. This is due to defaults and makes it more difficult to extract some HTML. You should assume that the style sheet is managing defaults.

- When implementing HTML serialization, don't trust general solutions. Trust specific solutions that solve specific problems in a given context.

- Properties that you assign with the method `setAttribute` are visible for both browsers when using the `innerHTML` property.

- Modified HTML content that you save from the browser by using Save As is not stored consistently across all browsers.

- Chapter 2 showed how to serialize a JavaScript object, and this chapter showed how to serialize DHTML. Each type of serialization is a specific serialization for a unique purpose. You need to be aware of these details and choose the appropriate serialization.

3-6. Dealing with Formatted Data and Forms

The first recipe of this chapter dealt with the topic of validating your form data. This recipe takes a step back and deals with the topic of how to interact with the data that is being manipulated on the server. The focus in this recipe is not code, but rather an illustration of how to think differently, in preparation for the rest of the chapters in this book.

Let's look at how to make forms more intelligent, so, for example, they can adjust their data setup automatically if you move to a different country, or they can look up data in order to save users work when filling them in.

Problem

There must be a better way of dealing with form data in modern Web applications. You need to know the best way to go about it.

Theory

Filling in forms can be painful. They require you to enter the data in a piecemeal manner. The way you enter the data is a direct reflection of how the data is stored in the database. The advantage of doing a one-to-one mapping is that it simplifies the work for you. It's easier for you to write a database statement such as "Search for this city" rather than "Search for this thing, which could be a city, address, or country." Yet, the seemingly vague input is the better approach from the perspective of the user.

Figure 3-30 illustrates a Web site that uses the traditional approach of creating one field for each part of the address.

Figure 3-30. *Traditional approach to searching for an address*

The Web site asks you to enter the address or intersection, city, state, or zip code. This can be confusing, as an address can mean the street, city, state, zip code, *and* country. If you enter a complete address into the address text field, you get an error saying that you need to enter a city, state/province, and so on. What if you don't live in North America? A link is provided, but you must click on the link. Following the link takes you to a combo box that allows you to select the country, but this seems clunky.

Solution

You might think I'm being overly harsh, but there is a better way, and it is illustrated in Figure 3-31.

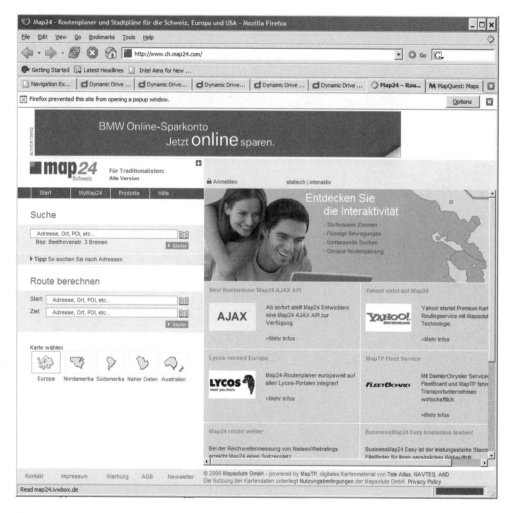

Figure 3-31. *Another approach to searching for an address*

The featured Web site, http://www.map24.com, is a worldwide map service. In Figure 3-31, the user is living in Switzerland, and Map24 realizes this and adjusts the settings to Switzerland. In contrast, the Web site in Figure 3-30 always assumes a North American address. With Map24, even though your settings might be Switzerland, it offers a search across Europe. This is a logical assumption, because Map24 is intended to help you find directions, and your car travels might be further than your own country but they aren't likely to be across continents.

It's a good idea to provide good defaults when greeting new visitors. When you do make assumptions, make sure users can switch to different content easily. In the case of Map24, users can switch continents easily by simply clicking on a link in the lower left-hand corner. The Web sites Google and MSN use localization techniques to tailor their content.

Assuming you've selected the right continent, now you need to find the correct route between two points. The approach used by Map24 is more akin to a search engine in that you enter the address and let Map24 figure out the details. Figure 3-32 shows two example addresses, where one is defined in German and the other in English.

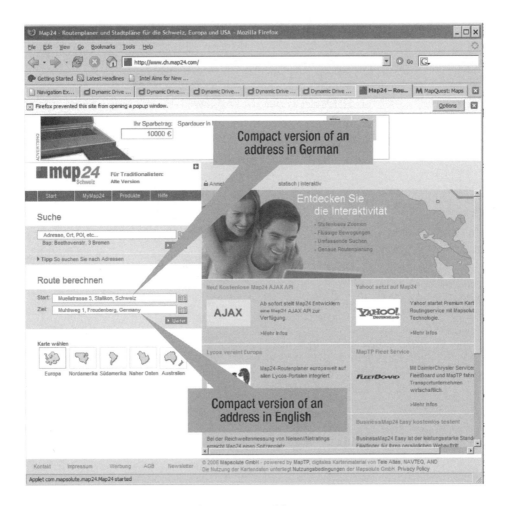

Figure 3-32. *Searching for a route between two addresses*

The address in Figure 3-32 is defined using the following notation in a particular language: street, town, and country. If you think about it, you don't need more information than that. You can also define an address using zip code and country. Regardless of how you define the address, Map24 attempts to figure out what the address is referencing. If Map24 cannot figure it out, then an error will be generated.

This sort of input is interesting, because you need to create a generic format preprocessor. Let's compare what this means in terms of the validation recipe illustrated at the beginning of this chapter. Figure 3-33 shows the modified validation architecture that adds two numbers together.

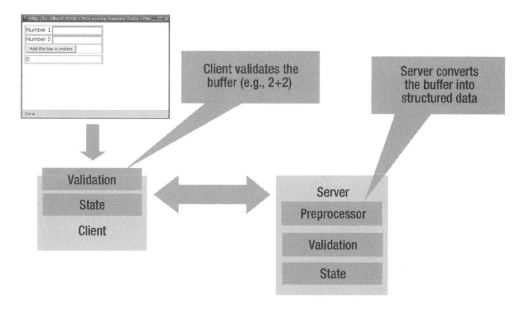

Figure 3-33. *Modified validation architecture*

The validation architecture has changed from two fields to a single-field form. The single-field form has a single text box that accepts a buffer in the form [number]+[number]. The buffer is validated on the client side to contain the numbers and operator. On the server side, the data would be preprocessed and the individual numbers and operator would be extracted and assigned to a state. The state is then validated and passed to the underlying business logic.

The advantage of using a search-engine-type approach is that users can define a buffer as [number] + [number] + [number] wiithout having to change the user interface. You would need to make some minor changes to the client-side validation logic and some minor changes to the server-side preprocessor.

Going back to Figure 3-32, entering the validation information and clicking the Next button results in something similar to Figure 3-34.

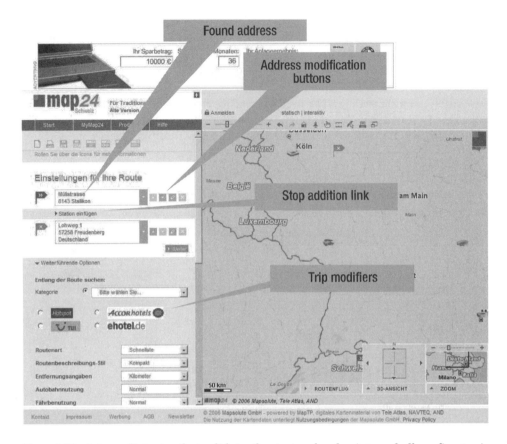

Figure 3-34. *Intermediate step that validates the start and end points and allows fine-tuning modifications before the route is finalized*

Notice the location of the start and end locations of the route. In between the start and end locations is a link that allows you to stop along the route. This link is in between the two end points, which gives users an immediate understanding of the link's purpose. Below the route destinations are a number of options that serve as trip modifiers, allowing user to fine-tune the route being calculated. Notice that all of the fine-tuning elements are logical and don't require additional instruction to use.

You can also format your data by cross-referencing the information with common items that people use today. For example, both http://map.search.ch and http://immo.search.ch represent information that you can find elsewhere, such as in the telephone book, classified ads, and so on. However, the information is cross-referenced and assembled in such a way that users find the information in a very short time.

The Web site http://immo.search.ch is an extension of http://map.search.ch and represents a way of finding real estate in Switzerland, whether you're looking to buy or rent. Users determine the parameters of the search. The results are presented in two panes, where one pane lists all of the found properties, and the other pane shows those found properties on a map. Figure 3-35 illustrates the Web site.

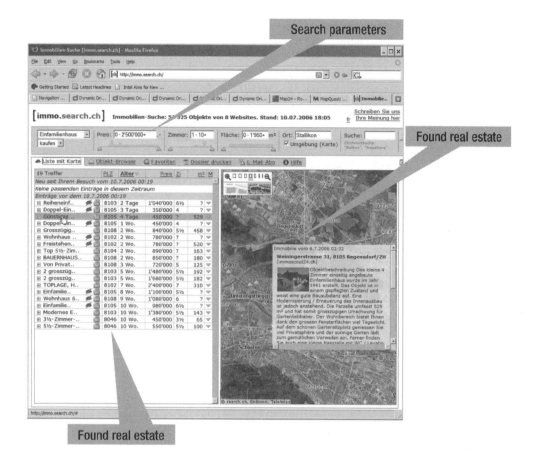

Figure 3-35. *Tweaking the parameters for a search that is user-friendly*

The top of the Web page represents the controls used to define the criteria used to select the properties. The criterion is not just a bunch of numbers that users can select. The criterion is detailed using a histogram and numbers that allows users to create brackets to see which properties are available. When some criteria have been selected, the properties that are available in the region shown in the right-hand pane are selected in the left-hand pane.

The right-hand pane not only shows the properties and the associated details, but also shows the public transportation, shopping, and topographic information. When investigating a property, users can instantly figure out what is nearby, thus making it easier to narrow down which properties they want to visit.

This recipe did not illustrate a single line of code, and that was done on purpose. This recipe is a lead-in to the next chapter, because it illustrates that the user interface is directly coupled to the data being presented. Think of the presented user interfaces as data-mining user interfaces. The next chapter will dissect the architectures behind the user interface. When developing the user interface to your data, keep the following things in mind:

- User interfaces in an Ajax context are tightly coupled to the data that they're managing.

- There is absolutely no reason why user interfaces to the data have to be bad.

- When searching and narrowing down data, think of the technology that search engines use and the criteria they use to fine-tune the results.

4-1. Implementing an SOA Architecture

In Chapter 1, I touched on the topic of using a service-oriented architecture (SOA), Web services, and Ajax to build a client from a theoretical perspective, but I didn't delve into the practical details of how to implement the SOA architecture. In this feast of a recipe, I cover how to implement an SOA architecture using Web services and Ajax. The solution also addresses the issue of how to upgrade an already existing architecture to an SOA architecture.

This recipe covers the following topics:

- Designing Representational State Transfer (REST)–based URLs to content that is described as a set

- Creating a new SOA architecture without throwing out all of the original architecture

- Validating and testing a Web service

- Picking apart the data

- Implementing a REST-based Web service

Problem

Your blog software uses fixed-width columns for the articles, but you want the content to adjust itself to the window size, so you'd like to add a feature to handle this.

Figure 4-1 shows an example of a layout that contains fixed-width columns.

In Figure 4-1, the content does not attempt to adjust itself to the size of the window. This may be by design, but it is not ideal for our purposes. Figure 4-2 shows an example of a layout with content that adjusts to the window width.

Figure 4-2 is a screen shot from a Microsoft Origami UMPC device that has a screen resolution of 800×600 pixels. The content in the Web browser adjusts itself to whatever maximum width can be used. For example, if a device's screen size is 1920×1200 pixels, four or five columns of content will appear onscreen. In effect, the content displays its information like a dynamic newspaper article.

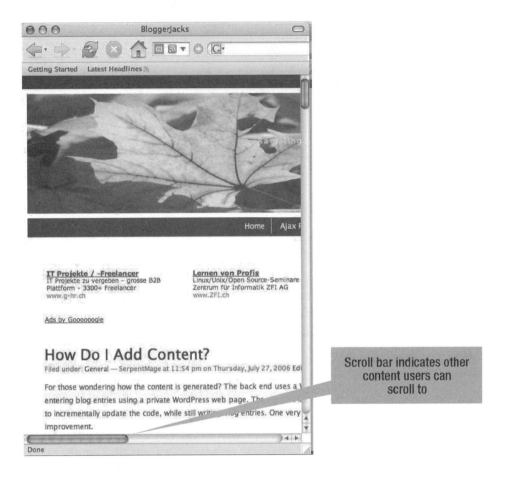

Figure 4-1. *A fixed-width layout*

The way the content adjusts itself in Figure 4-2 highlights the ability of the client to act separately from the server. The server is only responsible for serving content and does not care how that content is displayed. The display and processing of the content has been delegated to the client, and in the case of Figure 4-2, the client has digested the data and created a layout of columns and rows.

Visual discrepancies aside, the major differences between Figures 4-1 and 4-2 are architectural. When a traditional Web application builds its content to generate an image like Figure 4-1, a single application manages access to the database and generates the different content types. Figure 4-3 illustrates this type of architecture, which is not unique by any means—this is the general approach used by Web applications. If you use the traditional Web application approach, then making a change could have potentially large ramifications. You could even say that Web applications are similar to mainframe applications, where the mainframe or Web application server is in complete control.

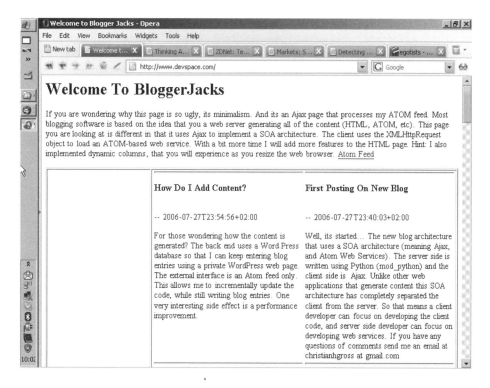

Figure 4-2. *Content adjusted for size of the Web browser window*

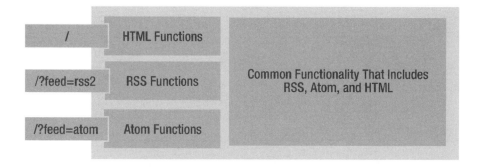

Figure 4-3. *Architecture for a traditional Web application*

Figure 4-3 has three exposed URLs. Each URL represents a unique data format:

- HTML

- Really Simple Syndication (RSS)

- Atom

Each of the formats is unique, but the content structure within the formats is the same. From a programming perspective, the solution would involve a Model-View-Controller

(MVC)–type architecture. MVC is implemented by many Web frameworks. As time has passed, these Web application architectures have become very complicated, as people attempt to solve every problem using this one design pattern.

The MVC architecture has its problems. In the case of blog software, the problem is that the user has to implement the same loops and same method calls three times (once for each format). If the underlying subsystem changes, the code may have to change in three different places. Not considered in Figure 4-3 is the situation where the HTML code has to support different screen-size factors.

We can summarize the problem as being the creation of an application that is in control of what the client sees, what is stored on the server, and how the client and server are connected. There is a single point of failure for both the client and the server, and that is a bad programming practice. An n-tier application has the client, business objects, and the database. At best, a Web application has two tiers: client/server/business objects and database.

Solution: Re-architecting the Application

Let's re-architect the application so that it supports different screen sizes, like the example in Figure 4-2. The re-architected application is not as complicated as you may think at first. It just requires that you think in a different way, moving from a Web application architecture to a traditional architecture. This is the irony of using Ajax: we are moving back to how we used to build applications. The difference is in the use of open protocols and technologies.

The re-architected application is a combination of client/server, n-tier, and Web application architecture styles. You could say that the re-architected application picks and chooses what works best from each architectural style. Figure 4-4 shows the re-architected application.

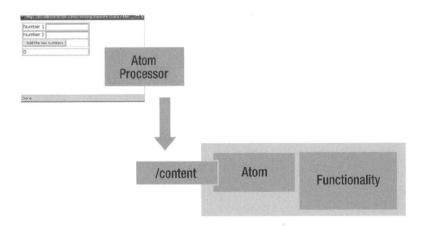

Figure 4-4. *Re-architected application*

The re-architected application has only one URL and one data format, Atom, so the code behind the URL needs to generate content just for that format. In the case of the re-architected application, the Atom format is considered a Web service, the idea behind which is to present a universal format understood by a wide audience. And if the end device does not understand the format, then it is up to the browsing device to figure it out. Of course, asking the end device to figure out the format might sound harsh, but it isn't really—whenever you are generating HTML using the HTTP protocol, you are asking the end device to figure out how to display the data.

If HTML and HTTP are nearly universal, why not just generate well-structured HTML and let the Atom end device figure it out? The answer is that it doesn't work quite as smoothly as that. HTML is a user interface technology that is not universally understood across all devices. An Atom end device could probably guesstimate the format structure, but you probably know the sweat and pain associated with writing HTML code that can display on all devices.

With a Web service based on the Atom format, you have a clear understanding of what the data is and represents. For a start, a Web service says to the server, "Here's the data—figure out how to display it." If the end device is an Atom reader, it's easy to figure out what to do with the data, but if the end device is a Web browser, you have a challenge. Most new browsers do understand Atom Web services, but another option is to have Ajax at hand to help—and specifically the XMLHttpRequest object, which can generate a request to call the Web service. The Web service delivers the data, which is then processed by the XMLHttpRequest object, and because the vast majority of Web services are XML based, figuring out the format of the data delivered by the Web service is trivial.

By delegating the work of creating a GUI away from the server, there is a clear separation between the roles the client and server play. This separation is absolutely critical, as it allows the server developers to focus on performance, scalability, robustness, and storage, while the client can focus on usability, visual aesthetics, and understandability. The designer and the programmer have two very different skill sets, and they should not interfere with each other.

Implementing the Server

The example application is a blog whose architecture will be kept plain vanilla for ease of understanding. For the blog architecture, only database support is going to be required and discussed in any depth.

The legacy portion of the blog example is not code; rather, it is data generated by the previous blog software. It is not beyond the realm of possibility to write a piece of software to convert the old data into a new format, but that act itself causes more problems than it solves.

Let's put the act of converting the data from one format to another into a bigger context. Imagine writing an application that serves as an incremental version of a working application. The chances of any corporation switching from one application to another with the flick of a switch is virtually zero. Thus, for a period of time, you will have two applications running and concurrently processing data. If during that period of time your data becomes inconsistent, you will have major problems reconciling the changes and you will potentially lose data—this makes it not worth the effort.

Returning to the blog architecture, you could implement one of two solutions. The first solution is to use the existing database; the second is to create an adapter using a Web service. For the blog architecture, let's choose the first solution, which uses the existing database as shown in Figure 4-5.

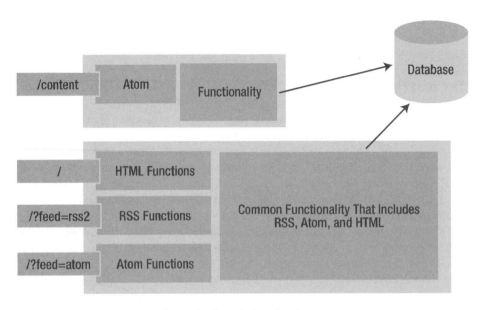

Figure 4-5. *Blog architecture that uses the existing database*

In the blog architecture shown in Figure 4-5, two Web applications run concurrently, and they access, process, and manipulate the same data. This does not mean that the two applications use the same physical database. With most modern databases, you have the ability to couple two database processes and synchronize the two physical databases. This has the advantage that data consistency is managed by the database. If you plan on writing synchronization software, ask yourself if you think you could do a better job than a database when it comes to managing consistency.

Letting the database manage consistency is patently a good idea, so let's update the architecture to use two separate databases (see Figure 4-6).

The modified architecture has two database processes, and the two processes are connected using the synchronization mechanism of the database. From the perspective of the user, developer, and administrator, each application uses its own database.

The two database processes manage the exact same tables, views, and stored procedures. It is assumed that this new architecture will use the same tables, views, and stored procedures, but in reality this is not always the case because a new application typically involves the addition of tables, columns, and data. The solution to this issue is to use database encapsulation, which is possible with views and stored procedures. The blog architecture therefore requires further changes, which are implemented as shown in Figure 4-7.

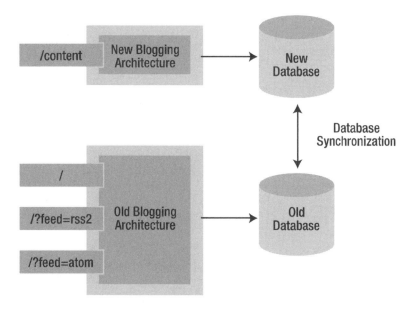

Figure 4-6. *Updated architecture that uses two separate databases*

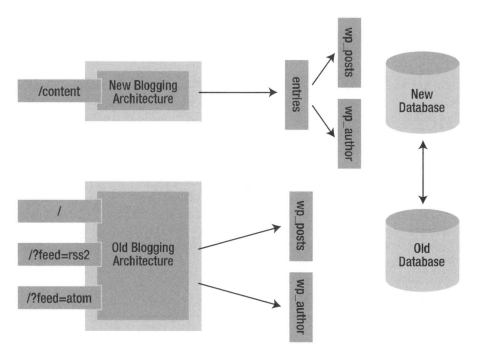

Figure 4-7. *Updated new and old architecture*

The updated architecture accesses the existing data using the `entries` table. The `entries` table is a view that joins the `wp_authors` and `wp_users` tables. The old application can continue executing, and the new application can use its own tables, views, and stored procedures.

So are you in the clear yet? Not quite—there is a problem in that if you make extensive use of views, it is often not possible to update a view. The solution to this is to use stored procedures that will update the appropriate tables (see Figure 4-8).

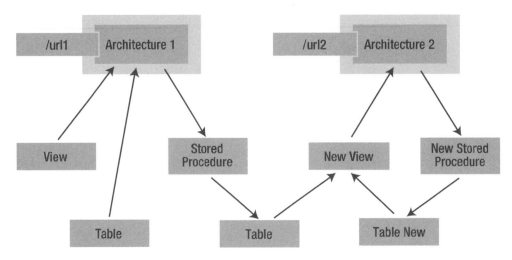

Figure 4-8. *Database architecture with stored procedures, views, and tables from the old and new architectures*

Figure 4-8 shows two architectures that access a common set of tables, views, and stored procedures. As you can see, the diagram is a mess of tables, views, and stored procedures. If multiple versions of the database were involved, it would be truly difficult to manage the database.

Database synchronization reduces the complexity to an absolute minimum. The reason for using database synchronization is to begin the process of separating two applications without losing data integrity. For example, in Figure 4-7, the new database uses the view `entries`, which is dependent on the `wp_authors` and `wp_users` tables. As the new architecture stands, the `wp_authors` and `wp_users` tables are the only dependencies of the original database. Thus, when a database synchronization is defined, only the `wp_authors` and `wp_users` tables are synchronized. Any other table used by the original blog architecture is not synchronized and thus does not affect the architecture of the new application.

Reorganizing Figure 4-8 to account for this, we arrive at Figure 4-9.

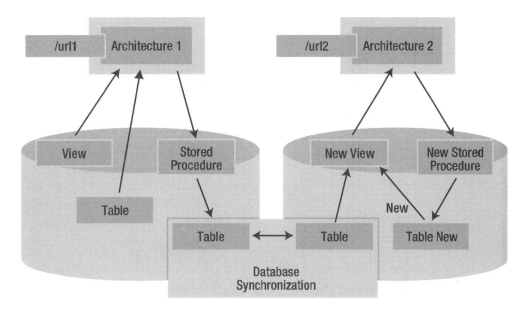

Figure 4-9. *A precise database architecture with stored procedures, views, and tables from the old and new architectures*

The architecture of Figure 4-9 is a precise way of defining the new and old architectures. In Figure 4-9, only one table needs to be synchronized between the new and old architectures. The developer can go ahead and create his or her own database design without having to worry about corrupting the old database design. It goes without saying that the old database design is not modified, but this design does not stop the creation of stored procedures that could potentially corrupt the data in the original database design. To prevent or at least minimize the potential of data corruption, it is absolutely vital that the database design use constraints and validations. Most SQL databases allow the definition of constraints.

Stepping back and looking at this architecture, you should notice that it relies on the capabilities of the relational database. There could be situations where a developer is not using a relational database. For those situations, I have no solution, as for the most part I have to deal with relational databases, and I am tempted to believe most readers have the same problem.

Relying on the capabilities of the relational database requires that you understand the database. With the introduction of object-relational mapping (ORM) tools, the need to know SQL is reduced. For example, using ORM tools such as Hibernate does not require knowledge of views or stored procedures. ORM tools create "views" in the form of object hierarchies. Using an ORM tool allows you to implement the same architecture as in Figure 4-9; however, it means that you will probably not be using stored procedures and views.

The real difference between using an ORM and the relational database stored procedure and view solution is the shifting of the coupling between the code and the persistence of the data. Figure 4-10 compares the two approaches from a decoupling perspective.

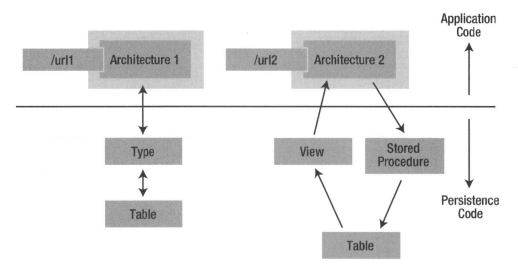

Figure 4-10. *A precise database architecture with stored procedures, views, and tables from the old and new architectures*

In Figure 4-10, the architecture on the left side represents the ORM approach, and the architecture on the right side represents the relational database approach. In terms of application code and persistence code, the relational database is in both approaches on the persistence code side. In the ORM approach, the application code interacts with a type that looks, feels, and behaves like a type used to write the application code. If the application code were coded in Java, then the type is a Java class with data members that resemble the columns of the relational database. The messy details of moving the state from the Java type to the relational database are managed by the ORM layer.

By contrast, the relational database layer uses views and stored procedures to interact with the data. The coder needs to know about the columns and types of the relational database and has to provide a mapping between his or her programming language and the SQL programming language. Using classical programming languages such Java and C# involves quite a bit of legwork in terms of preparing commands and retrieving data. Using a programming language such as Ruby, Python, or PHP, interacting with a relational database is trivial since the aforementioned languages do not have to declare the data types.

Using an ORM, the coder washes his or her hands of the problem and puts the focus on the ORM layer. For Java and C# programmers, an ORM removes the drudgery of interacting with a database, with the only cost being the programmers' lack of control of the transactions and manipulations of the database—although in most cases that lack of control is acceptable when weighed against the drudgery of writing the relational database code.

The question is, which architecture should you use? Personally, I use whatever is easiest in the programming language I am developing in at the time. So when I am writing code in Java and C#, I tend to use ORMs, and when I'm writing Python code, I access the relational database directly. You need to ensure that the ORM layer does not dictate the design of the database, under any circumstances. The database design is determined by the database and the data being persisted, so it means you need to understand table, view, constraint, and trigger design. This could become tricky if the ORM dictates the database design, and it could result in an inefficient database as well. Remember that in any application, the slowest part will be the database. The database has to pore through millions of records, manage transactions, and send that data across a network. If you design an application to be efficient at the expense of database design, then there is no way you can magically speed up the performance of the database.

Implementing the Application Logic Layer

In the entire solution, the simplest part is the implementation of the application logic layer. It is trivial and is illustrated by the following Python code:

```
def current( req, cache, urlComponents) :
    req.content_type = configuration.Atom.mimeType
    conn = MySQLdb.connect (host = configuration.Database.server,
                                user = configuration.Database.user,
                                passwd = configuration.Database.password,
                                db = configuration.Database.db)
    cursor = conn.cursor ()
    cursor.execute ("SELECT * from entries order by post_date desc")
    row = cursor.fetchone()
    generateHeader( req, row)
    generateEntry( req, row)

    row = cursor.fetchmany( configuration.Blog.entryCount - 1)
    for entry in row :
        generateEntry( req, entry)
    generateFooter( req)
```

Don't get too excited by the code's simplicity, as the code provides an infrastructure of methods that are called. The method illustrates what a Web service does for the most part, which is accept data, process it, and persist it. You will at times implement algorithms that perform some type of calculation. During the processing, business rules are applied that process the sent and received data. For the scope of this solution, the data is pushed and pulled with very little in-between processing.

An external process drives the application logic, which in the case of the solution is a browser. The application logic is triggered by a number of requests that are defined using URLs. There are other ways of creating Web services using other technologies, but this book's focus is on using Representational State Transfer (REST). Using REST implies designing URLs and using the HTTP protocol. From the perspective of the Ajax client, REST is a perfect protocol.

Let's start the application design process by correlating what the sample source code is referencing. The name of the function in the sample source code is current, and the last n blog entries are returned. When using a blog reader or an Ajax client, you will want to see the current blog entries, therefore the simplest approach is to associate the URL http://myserver.com/ to the function current.

Ignoring the correctness of the URL for now (I discuss that in the next section), a valid question is, how does the server know to cross-reference the URL with a specific functionality?

The answer is that all Web application infrastructures have a cross-referencing algorithm, as presented in Figure 4-11.

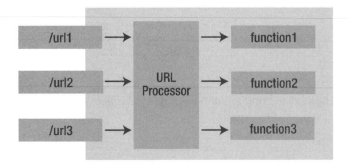

Figure 4-11. *URL cross-referencing to functionality*

In Figure 4-11, the HTTP server receives a request that starts a series of steps on the HTTP server. The HTTP server has a notion of executing filters and a handler. The filters are responsible for manipulating the request so that the called handler has the proper context. Which handler is called is determined by some algorithm, which we will call the *URL processor*.

By default, when an HTTP server executes the URL processor, the URL is mapped to a file. If the request was [http://myserver.com]/dir/file.html, then the HTTP server attempts to find the file [base directory]/dir/file.html. If the file is found, the file extension processor is loaded, which in the case of .html happens to be a static file processor. (If the extension is .php or .aspx, then the PHP or ASP.NET processors are executed and generate content based on the instructions in the file.) From a REST perspective, this is the wrong URL processor algorithm. It is an easy algorithm, but it is the wrong algorithm, at least from the perspective of REST.

Understanding Why We Want REST

From the perspective of REST, all URLs represent resources on the server side; however, while a file *is* a resource, it is not a resource from the perspective of the application. This is very a big distinction that must be understood: REST URLs are application-specific resources. Using an application-specific resource means that you are exposing functionality based on the business logic, not technology. Using REST, you can separate the resource from the implementation, much like interface- or contract-driven development.

To illustrate the separation of the resource from the implementation, consider the following C# code:

```csharp
interface IBase {
    void Method();
}

class Implementation1 : IBase {
    public void Method() { }
}
```

```
class Implementation2 : IBase {
    public void Method() { }
}
```

The IBase interface defines a method and is implemented by two classes, Implementation1 and Implementation2. This process is referred to as *interface-driven development*, because when the client uses either implementation, the client doesn't use the actual implementation but the interface of the implementation, as illustrated by the following source code:

```
class Factory {
    public static IBase Instantiate() {
        return new Implementation1();
    }
}

class UseIt {
    public void Method() {
        IBase obj = Factory.Instantiate();
        // ...
    }
}
```

In the example source code, the Factory class has a static method, Instantiate, that creates an instance of IBase by instantiating Implementation1. In the UseIt.Method class, an instance of IBase is instantiated by calling the Factory.Instantiate method. The UseIt class has no idea whether Implementation1 or Implementation2 is instantiated, and it uses the interface as defined by IBase, expecting the interface methods to be implemented correctly. When using dynamic languages, you use duck typing, and the defined contracts result in implied functionality.

Let's relate interface-driven development to URLs and separate the resource from the representation. The resource is the interface, and the representation is the implementation. Currently, most Web technologies bind together the resource and representation or use implementations directly, as the URLs http://mydomain.com/item.aspx and http://mydomain.com/item.jsp illustrate. The direct bindings are the .aspx and .jsp extensions, and the proper interface-defined URL would have been http://mydomain.com/item.

Ironically, all Web technologies implement the separation of resource from representation for the root URL /, as illustrated by the following HTTP conversation. (Note that the conversation has been abbreviated for explanation purposes.)

Request

```
GET / HTTP/1.1
Host: 192.168.1.242:8100
User-Agent: Mozilla/5.0 (Macintosh; U; PPC Mac OS X Mach-O;➥
    en-US; rv:1.7.8) Gecko/20050511
```

Response

```
HTTP/1.1 200 OK
Server: Apache/2.0.53 (Ubuntu) PHP/4.3.10-10ubuntu4
```

The requested URL is /, and it is returned by the server as `index.html`, `index.jsp`, `index.php`, or even `default.aspx`. If Web technologies are capable of separating the resource from the representation for the root URL, why can't they carry this throughout the entire Web application?

Implementing a REST URL Processor

Implementing a REST URL processor is similar to implementing a standard URL processor found in most Web servers today. The difference is that a REST URL processor uses a different mapping technique. Figure 4-12 outlines the request processing.

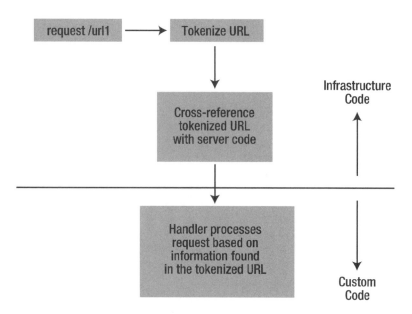

Figure 4-12. *Execution flow of a REST URL processor*

The execution flow of a REST URL processor is simple in that, to determine which user code to execute, we simply dissect the URL. Based on the structure of the URL, the appropriate server-side code handler is called. If the client calls the URL `/blog/entries/current`, the tokenized URL is `blog`, `entries`, and `current`. In case of the blog software, the Python handler requires at least three pieces of the URL that are translated into the Python call `[module namespace].[module].[function]`. The URL called from the client is then translated to `blog.enteries.current()`. Any URL pieces after the first three pieces are passed to the called function to fine-tune the required information.

The rule of requiring at least three URL pieces is purely specific to my Python handler framework. Your framework might need two, or five, or whatever number of URL pieces—it is an arbitrary number. In the example blog software, the algorithm used to cross-reference the URL to the custom code used convention over configuration techniques. Yet there is nothing wrong with using a lookup table to cross-reference certain pieces of the URL with a piece of custom functionality. Again, how you cross-reference the URL pieces to the custom functionality is up to you.

When implementing your own REST URL processor, the actual implementation will vary according to the technology used. There is no common theme, but there are two ways to implement a REST URL processor:

- Find a way to associate a base URL with a specific handler. For example, I tend to use `/services` as a base for all my Web services. The server needs to support the notion that whenever the requested URL starts with `/services`, a specific handler is called. The specific handler called is the REST URL processor that then makes the handler call.

- If you cannot associate a base handler for a base URL, then you need to write an HTTP filter. The difference between an HTTP filter and an HTTP handler is that a filter is called before a handler. The idea of HTTP filters is to enable user code to perform certain common steps on all requests. A common example is authentication. Using an HTTP filter, you have the ability to define which handler is called. In the context of the REST URL processor, the processor would be embedded as a last step after all of the other filters have executed. It is the last step because you want steps such as authentication to execute on the requested URL, and not the redirected execution URL.

When implementing your REST URL processor, you must remember that only the URL determines which functionality is called. You must not use an HTTP cookie as part of your decision. As outlined later in this chapter, using HTTP cookies to decide which functionality to execute is very bad design. For the scope of this solution, this is all I'll discuss regarding the REST URL processor.

Implementing the URLs

Assuming you have implemented your own REST URL processor, the next step is to define the URLs used. In this section, I outline the URLs used in the blog application and explain them in such a way that the explanation can be used in a general nature. For all of my URLs, there are a minimum of three pieces, and that is particular to the REST URL processor I'm using—don't think you must use the same number of pieces.

The design of the URLs depends on the design of the application data, and that includes the HTML pages. Remember, you are creating an SOA application where the client is an Ajax client that makes Web service calls. In the case of the blog application, the high-level URL view is shown in Figure 4-13.

The two base URLs are `/blog` and `/services/blog`. You need these two base URLs because you are serving two different types of content: static HTML files and Web service content. In theory, you could use only one base URL and have the Web service generate everything, but I am wary of doing that because it complicates the implementation.

Let's step back and think about why having a single URL complicates the implementation. When implementing an Ajax SOA application, you have a client coder and a server coder. The client coder does not do any server programming and does not want to; it wants to focus on the client side of things. Thus the client-side programmer has to be able to do everything he or she wants with static files served by an HTTP server. If the programmer needs a Web service to serve static files, then he or she would be dependent on the server programmer, and that dependency is not desired. By having two base URLs, the client programmer can do what he or she deems appropriate, and the server programmer can do what he or she deems appropriate, independent of one another.

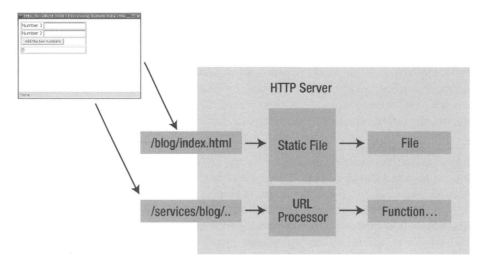

Figure 4-13. *High-level URL view of the blog architecture*

■**Note** There is no reason you could not have a base URL such as /blog and then subdivide that base namespace to /blog/static and /blog/services. The point to remember is that you have two URL namespaces: one for the client side and one for the server side.

Because I use mod_python for the server side and Apache HTTPD for static content, it makes sense for my Web services to all be Python based. Thus, I have a base Web service handler and specific Web services, such as the blog software, all implemented as a Python namespace. The base client-side URL for all applications is /, and the base server-side URL for all applications is /services. With other architectures such as ASP.NET, the base URL would be /blog, and then that URL could be further subdivided.

I am not going to focus on the client-side URLs, because they are driven by the Web service URLs for the scope of the blog application. For example, if you had the entry URL /services/blog/entries/archive/2006, there would be an appropriate static file URL /blog/entries/archive/2006.

Before I explain the nature of the URLs, let's review the four common HTTP verbs. Usually you use two HTTP verbs, GET and POST, often for the same purpose. For example, an HTML form can post its data using either GET or POST. From a REST perspective, it is bad practice to use GET to send data to the server.

I explain how to use each HTTP verb in the following list. The best way to understand the individual verbs is to think of them as instructions much like SQL commands. The difference between the HTTP verbs and SQL commands is that SQL manipulates tables and rows, and HTTP manipulates resources associated with URLs.

- DELETE *(SQL equivalent* delete from*)*: A rarely used verb that is used to delete a resource on the server side. For example, if the DELETE verb is used for the URL /services/blog/archive/entries, the result is that all blog entries on the server are deleted. If the URL has query parameters associated with it (e.g., ticker=DELL&value=23), then all entries that match the query parameters are deleted. In SQL-speak (and in terms of the delete command), the query parameters are the SQL where parameters.

- GET *(SQL equivalent* select*)*: A commonly used verb that is used to retrieve content from the server. The specified URL retrieves the resources associated with the URL. If there are any query parameters, a selection of items associated with the URL that match the query parameters is performed. In SQL-speak the query parameters are the where parameters associated with the select statement.

- POST *(SQL equivalent stored procedures)*: A commonly used verb that is used to send data to the server. It is important to consider an HTTP POST as a stored procedure. Things get funny with an HTTP POST in interpreting the role of the URL. You could say that the URL defines the resource that is manipulated, and the parameters define how to manipulate the resource, but that is not the nature of a SQL stored procedure. The name of the stored procedure does not impact which tables are manipulated. So another view of POST could be to define a resource that manipulates other resources, and which resources are manipulated depends on the implementation of an HTTP POST. Choose whichever definition makes sense to you. I find an HTTP POST to be both too general and too specific to nail down to a single idea. I personally choose the first solution, where the URL defines the resource to manipulate, and which algorithm used to manipulate the resource depends on the parameters. An HTTP POST can generate data even though it is not generally used. In SQL-speak, stored procedures can generate results, even though for the most part you would use the select command.

- PUT *(SQL equivalent* insert*)*: A rarely used verb that is used to replace the content of a resource. If the resource associated with URL does not exist, then it is created.

The URLs used by the application are described in the sections that follow.

/services/blog/entries/current

Specifically, this URL represents the last *n* entries of a blog. With the passing of time, the last *n* entries change, and you can use a single URL to reference the latest and greatest information. In an abstract sense, the URL represents a view on some data. The problem you will have in your application is that people want a single URL they can use until the end of time. For instance, going back to the blog example, if the month is 06, the day is 07, and the year is 2006, then to get the latest and greatest blog entries, you only have to reference the appropriate year, month, and day URLs. The problem is that nobody would do this, as it is too complicated and requires knowledge of how data is organized. Another way to organize blog entries is to use incremental numbers or long values that count the seconds since 1970.

By having a "view" URL, you create a reference to data organized by an embedded server-side algorithm. The server-side algorithm is not obvious to the user, and it does not need to be. Be very careful of allowing query parameters to select data from the view. The aim of the view URL is to provide an easy-to-remember and -use URL. Allowing query parameters with a view URL is silly because the same effect can be achieved using a resource URL, as you will see shortly.

View URLs for the most part only accept HTTP GET. View URLs should not accept an HTTP PUT or an HTTP DELETE because the data retrieved is a reference to another URL. If you want to support an HTTP PUT or an HTTP DELETE on a view URL, you need to delete or replace the logic associated with the URL, and not the data. It's more difficult to determine whether a view URL should accept an HTTP POST. It could be argued that an HTTP POST of view URLs does not make sense because for the most part you cannot update data generated by a SQL view. I counter that since a view URL contains some logic to extract the appropriate data, and an HTTP POST contains logic, an HTTP POST could be used to insert data.

With regard to the blog application, POSTing to the URL /services/blog/entries/current would have the effect of adding a blog entry at the time that it was posted. If you had to HTTP PUT a new blog entry, the client would have to know how the server organizes the underlying blog data. The blog application discussed in this recipe is organized by date, but it need not be.

/services/blog/entries/archive

This URL specifies the base root URL for all blog entries stored on the HTTP server. In an abstract sense, all Web services have a notion of root resource URL. The purpose of the root resource URL is to define a main entry point to all of the resources in the Web service. Think of this URL as the index.html of your Web service. This is not to say that some URLs are disconnected from the base root URL hierarchy (e.g., view URLs), but it does mean that an end device can iterate all of the resources using the root URL.

The root URL is also an example of a collection URL. Collection URLs behave a bit differently than regular URLs. For example, consider the following two responses for the root URL. Note that the URL must not return XML, but XML is used for simplicity.

```
<root>
    <item href="/root/item1" id="item1" />
</root>
```

```
<root>
    <item id="item1" url="/root/item1">
        <data>embedded data</data>
    </item>
</root>
```

There are two responses in the example code. The first response is a root element that has as a child a single item element. The item element contains no child elements and has two attributes, href and id. The second response is like the first, except that item has a data child element, and there is no href attribute. Instead, in the second response, there is a url reference. The difference between the two responses is the translation of what should be returned when a collection URL is referenced.

A collection URL is a URL that itself does not contain any data, but serves as a reference to a collection of data pieces. When the collection URL is referenced, the client can return a set of URL references to the actual data or the actual data itself. Taking as an example the blog application, the Atom format referencing the collection URL means to return all of the data pieces. However, it is often impractical to return all of the data pieces, as the returned data stream could be gigantic. To reduce traffic, link references are returned. But chasing our tail again, various formats do not allow links. As a rule of thumb, return what is best suited for your application. Regardless of how you return the data, be consistent. This means if all of your collection URLs return data, then return data, and vice versa.

A root or collection URL for the most part will be called using the HTTP `GET` verb. There will probably be query parameters to select specific entries, which when applied to URLs with a large number of entries reduces the document length. For example, the view URL `/services/blog/entries/current` could also be expressed as `/services/blog/entries/archive?last=35`. The query parameter `last` is used to select the last *n* entries.

The HTTP verbs `PUT` and `DELETE` can apply if valid collection entries are added. While it is possible to convert a collection URL to a data-resource URL, it makes sense to do so only if the server does not dynamically generate the collection. For example, in the case of the blog software, the collection is generated from a database. Executing `PUT` or `DELETE` does not make sense unless there is logic that processes the data sent by the commands. And finally, it is possible to process an HTTP `POST` if there is associated server-side logic.

/services/blog/entries/archive/2006/07/06

This URL specifies a data-resource URL that when referenced contains the data a user is interested in. The data that is sent is determined by the client in the `Accept` HTTP headers (this is discussed further in Chapter 5). A data-resource URL is capable of processing all of the HTTP verbs (`GET`, `PUT`, `POST`, and `DELETE`), as explained in the previous sections.

When the URL is referenced, a piece of data is returned, but you have to ask yourself what the format of the data is. Using the blog application as an example, the piece of data returned must make it seem that the URL is referencing a collection URL, because the Atom format is a single format that assumes every URL is a collection of blog entries, even though there might be only a single entry.

So when you create data-resource URLs, keep in mind that although logically they are a single piece of data, the format of the data could make the URL seem like a collection URL. When the client executes an HTTP `GET`, the server will have no problem generating the data. The server can get confused, however, if the client executes an HTTP `PUT` or an HTTP `POST`. The data sent to the server might contain multiple pieces of data, even though the server expected only a single piece of data. Thus, the logical solution is to generate an error saying that users cannot post multiple entries. Another solution might involve looking through the list of entries and posting the first entry. The problem with that strategy is that it is inconsistent with the intent of the client. When the client sends data that contains multiple pieces of information, they expect those multiple pieces of information to be saved. If the server saves only one piece, the client is left wondering what went wrong. When an error is generated, the client is not left wondering what went wrong.

Data-resource URLs need to be as specific as possible. You do not want any ambiguity arising at some later point in time. For example, if today your blog application allows only a single user, but at some point in the future it could allow multiple users, then add that functionality. In the case of the blog application, that would mean `/user/services`. For the initial release of the application, `/user/services` might be hard-coded and not relevant when processing the URL. However, you have created a placeholder for the case when you have multiple users. I am not saying you should compensate for every potential change in the future, because after all you can use server redirection (e.g., `http://user.server/services`).

What you want to remember is that data-resource URLs will outlive your server, your technology, and even your company. URLs are like pieces of real estate and are part of your brand recognition, so you must choose them carefully. Once people know and associate a certain

URL with a Web site or company, it is very difficult for those people to switch to using another URL. For example, imagine if tomorrow Google decided to call itself ReallyCoolServer. The company ReallyCoolServer would not immediately have the same impact or brand recognition as Google has today.

`/services/blog/entries/archive?delete=35` **and**
`/services/blog/entries/archive/2005?past=35`

The examples in this chapter show that URLs can have query parameters. However, both of the URLs presented in this section's heading are not examples of logic that has the same intention—only the second one is an acceptable URL. The first URL is not acceptable because it implies changing the data.

You've previously used query parameters to perform a filtering operation of an HTTP `GET`. Using query parameters in that context is acceptable because it does not change the underlying nature of the data; you are specifying a filter. The filter could be used to convert the result set from one language to another, and it may contain complex algorithms. But regardless of the algorithm, there is no change to the data that is being filtered.

The first URL, `/services/blog/entries/archive?delete=35`, is different in that it uses the word "delete," and "delete" means to delete a record(s). Thus the query parameter will change the underlying data and is not acceptable. Of course, there is an exception if the word "delete" doesn't mean delete in the sense of "delete from the data source," but instead means delete from the generated result set. Then the `delete` keyword becomes a filtering operation and is acceptable. Changes to the underlying data are the result of executing the HTTP `POST`, `PUT`, or `DELETE` verb.

The URLs used by the blog application are relatively generic and illustrate most of the variations that you will encounter when building REST-based Web services. Overall, you should remember that building REST-based Web services is like interacting with a database that supports SQL. You have a number of HTTP verbs that can be used to add, manipulate, delete, and retrieve data. How that data is managed is the responsibility of the REST Web service designer.

I am not going to walk through the server implementation because it is an application issue. In the case of the blog application, you are manipulating blog entries, which have very little business logic. For example, if you contrast a blog application with a mortgage application, you can see that a mortgage application has quite a bit of logic, and it also has a type of URL that does not contain data and is defined as follows.

`/services/mortgage/calculate/payments`

The defined URL is not a data-resource URL, but a "question in, answer out" URL. There is no server-side data, or view of data, or collection of data. There is only a calculation; hence, the only HTTP verb that can be used is HTTP `POST`. The other HTTP verbs do not make sense and should not be used in this context.

Testing the Web Service

With the Web service created and running, you could go ahead and start coding the client. But that would be the incorrect approach. One of the things that has changed with Web services and SOA is that the client and server communicate using a contract. Previously, client/server applications communicated using a protocol that the developers decided upon. If the developers needed a new method or piece of information, that alteration would be made. It was not a big deal to make changes on the fly. With Web services and SOA, that is no longer the case.

With the advent of Web services and SOA, we have the ability to define a contract that can be reused and shared by other parties. If there is one major advantage to SOA, it is its ability to seamlessly share data.

Let's put this into another context. Imagine you own a pizza restaurant, with take-out orders, online orders, and wait staff to take orders from onsite customers. So customers can order a pizza in a few different ways, and each way probably has a completely different ordering system. In fact, it's questionable that you even need wait staff to take an order in the first place. In this day and age, you could put a touch screen on each table and let the customers order their pizza directly. Then as the order is fulfilled, somebody brings it to the table. Or how about enabling customers to order a pizza online, and then indicate that they want to eat it in the restaurant at a certain time? The system could reserve a table for the customers, making it possible for them to take a seat at their reserved table when they enter the restaurant and have their meal served immediately. But wouldn't that ruin the experience of going to restaurant? In my opinion, it wouldn't—going to restaurant can be a pretty hectic experience.

This pizza restaurant example illustrates the client/server architectures of days past, with wait staff taking the customers' orders. SOA, on the other hand, represents a uniform pizza ordering system regardless of the entry device being used (in person, online, by cell phone, etc.). After all, is a pizza ordered through the wait staff any different from a pizza ordered online? The answer is no.

Having your Web service used in multiple contexts poses a challenge in that the contract must be extensively tested. If you do not extensively test the Web service, you could cause problems. For example, imagine you created a blog Web service feed that had a minor bug. End developers who use your feed encounter the bug and see that it's minor. To save hassle, they do a quick little workaround. Workarounds are dangerous because they assume things will happen a certain way. You give your feed to other third parties who don't encounter the minor bug for one reason or another. As time passes, a client receives the feed, and they encounter the bug. Unlike everybody else, they send an email about the bug and ask it to be fixed.

So what do you do when you receive the bug notification? Do you fix the bug or not? The answer should be that you fix the bug, but the reality is that if the bug is minor, the bug fix could cause working code to stop working.

This is why testing a Web service is so critical: by testing, you minimize the chance of future problems. Web service testing has to be exhaustive and extensive; it is not a minor undertaking. In the case of the blog application, an online testing service can make your life easier.

Figure 4-14 is a snapshot of the excellent Web site `www.feedvalidator.org`, which you can use to validate the correctness of an Atom or RSS feed.

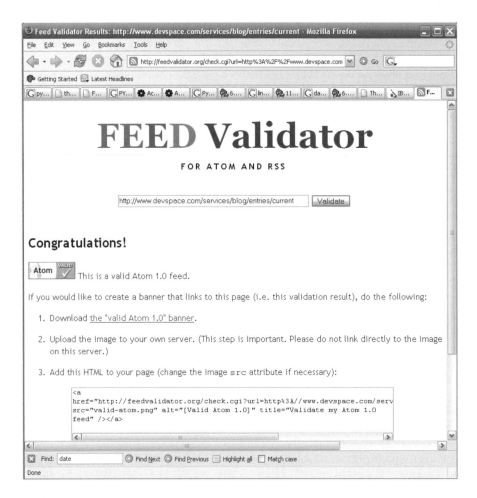

Figure 4-14. *The Feed Validator Web site, which you can use to validate the correctness of an Atom Web service*

Figure 4-14 shows the correctness of the blog feed. Had there been a problem, the feed validator would have marked the problem and illustrated how to fix it. The feed validator is an application on its own, but it serves an important purpose. If your Atom feed works correctly, then your feed can be consumed by any feed reader. And if your (soon-to-be-explained) client consumes the feed, then that client can also be used to consume any other Atom feed.

The feed validator makes sure that the Atom feed is correct, but the feed validator does not validate if the contents of the feed are correct. That is another level of testing and validation that would be necessary.

The feed validator makes it possible to decouple the client from the server. Having the client and server decoupled makes it simpler to introduce changes in the overall architecture because you can make the changes gradually. Going back to the original architecture of the blog architecture, imagine changing the structure of how blog entries are displayed. Because the client and server code are intertwined, the developer might be tempted to tweak the server code. However, the server generates three different formats, and you have to wonder if the tweaks will have to be added to the other two formats.

Using a single feed that is validated, client programmers have no choice but to tweak their own code. Client programmers cannot touch the code of the server and hence cannot introduce unintended bugs.

I mentioned that testing an interface requires an exhaustive and extensive set of tests—the feed validator provides just that. But not all Web services fit into the category of a blog application, and you have to implement your own testing infrastructure. Ideally, you want an architecture like a feed validator, because it makes testing a snap. But a feed validator is a big application, and you probably don't have enough time to write such a complicated piece of code.

Experience has taught me that the easiest way to write tests quickly and cleanly is to use a programming language that has support for test-driven development techniques (e.g., NUnit or JUnit). You can also use a dynamic language such as Python or Ruby.

Something else experience has taught me is to not reinvent the wheel. If a protocol, XML grammar, or implementation already exists, then use that. Don't try to come up with new ways of doing the same old thing—you will only complicate your life. It might be a bit more complex initially to adhere to the standard, but in the long run you'll have fewer concerns. For example, by sticking to the Atom feed in the blog architecture, you can use a publicly available tool to test the application. It doesn't require writing any test code; you just have to write a few test scripts to call the Feed Validator Web site.

Implementing the Client

Implementing a client in an Ajax context always involves two steps: loading the document and executing the document. These steps are shown in Figure 4-15.

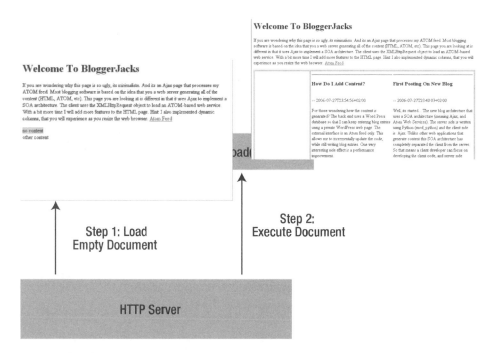

Figure 4-15. *Two-step loading process*

As shown in Figure 4-15, the first step is loading an empty document. The empty document contains no data, and it serves as a framework. The framework may have some text, buttons, forms, and a look and feel. And as in Figure 4-15, the empty document will look bare.

After the document has been loaded, the client needs to execute the document. Depending on the application, there are various ways of executing the document. Some clients may require that the user enter some data and then click a button. Other clients might load the content using a periodic interval, and yet others might load the content once the document has been loaded.

In the case of the blog application, there is no need for the client to intervene, so the document should be executed once it has been loaded. In JavaScript, the body.onload event is fired once the document has been completely loaded. It is very important that you use the body.onload event and not some script that is executed while the document is being loaded. While the document is being loaded, it is considered incomplete, so referencing HTML elements on the document might be successful, but it might not. When using the body.onload event, you can be sure that the document has been completely loaded and every element that needs referencing is available.

When the body.onload event is fired and the content is loaded, the content can be processed and injected into the HTML document. To the user, this two-step process seems like a single page load rather than a two-step process (if both the client and server have enough bandwidth). If the two-step loading does not execute fast enough, you will notice a slight flicker, indicating that some content has been loaded and arranged. The end result is the same, and the client is presented with a single document that presents itself as a single application.

In a nutshell, this process is no different than building a traditional client/server or n-tier application, except open standards and a dynamic programming language environment are used.

With the overall client-side architecture covered, let's dig a bit deeper into each of the steps.

Loading the Document

As mentioned previously, the first step is loading the document. If we compare loading the document with loading a traditional application, what is happening is that the browser is like an operating system preparing the memory, modules, and foundation for the program to execute.

So, for example, if we are loading the document, the following code will instantiate the XMLHttpRequest object:

```
getTransport: function() {
  return Try.these(
    function() {return new ActiveXObject('Msxml2.XMLHTTP')},
    function() {return new ActiveXObject('Microsoft.XMLHTTP')},
    function() {return new XMLHttpRequest()}
  ) || false;
},
```

The source of the code is not important because many Ajax libraries do the same thing. Essentially, when the code is executed, it tries to figure out which browser it's dealing with so it can return at runtime the correct way to instantiate the XMLHttpRequest object. I contend this is the wrong approach, and it uses the traditional executable loading and running mentality.

When an operating system loads a traditional program, the variables, modules, and so forth are initialized before program execution. While a browser loads source code, the browser has the ability to execute JavaScript code. With this in mind, you could write the following code:

```
if (window.ActiveXObject) {
    FactoryXMLHttpRequest = function() {
        return new ActiveXObject("Microsoft.XMLHTTP");
    }
}
else if (window.XMLHttpRequest) {
    FactoryXMLHttpRequest = function() {
        return new XMLHttpRequest();
    }
}
```

In the example, there is no function, just a decision. The decision is if the browser loading the document is Internet Explorer, then define the FactoryXMLHttpRequest function to instantiate ActiveXObject. If the browser is not Internet Explorer, then define the FactoryXMLHttpRequest function to instantiate the XMLHttpRequest object directly. The second source code initialization example is not as flexible during the runtime because the defined FactoryXMLHttpRequest function can only instantiate the XMLHttpRequest object as it was defined when the document was loaded. Even though this seems like a drawback, you have to ask yourself what the chances are that the loaded document will be moved byte by byte to another browser type. The answer is that there is no chance this will happen, as it is not possible.

The advantage of the second source code example is that functionality can be tuned to the browser it is executing on while the document is being loaded. In the example, the tuning was based on the browser. There are other ways to tune and reasons for tuning your application, such as figuring out the language or dimensions of the browser. Tuning has the advantage that you don't need to carry around the executable baggage that is associated with decisions made at runtime. This is an important factor to remember, as you can reduce the runtime footprint of your code by preconfiguring the application during document loading.

But there's one big disadvantage to using a document loading–generated configuration having to do with serialization. Previous chapters demonstrated how to use JavaScript serialization to generate proxies or mixins. If a document-loaded configuration is serialized and stored on an HTTP server, and then it's loaded at a later point in time using a different browser, an error will be generated.

The rule of thumb is that when there is an advantage in terms of performance or resources, use the document-loaded configuration. Use the general runtime approach, which includes a runtime decision-making process, if there's a slight chance that the code will be serialized. And for those situations where it really does not matter one way or the other, use whatever makes sense for you.

Executing the Document

After the document has been loaded, the body.onload event is triggered and the associated code is executed. In HTML terms, the code looks as follows. Note that the code has been abbreviated for clarity.

Source: /client/index.html

```
function LoadAtomFeed() {
    var asynchronous = new Asynchronous();
    asynchronous.settings = {
        onComplete : function(xmlhttp) {
            parseAtom( xmlhttp.responseXML);
            flexbox.update();
        }
    }
    asynchronous.get("/services/blog/entries/current");
}


function InitializePage() {
    // Extra initialization code cut out relating to
    LoadAtomFeed();
}
</script>
    </head>

    <body onload="InitializePage()">
        <h1>Welcome To BloggerJacks</h1>
        <!-- Document section -->
    </body>
</html>
```

Consider the bold code. When the document is loaded, the body.onload event is fired. That calls the InitializePage function, which in turn calls the LoadAtomFeed function. In the implementation of LoadAtomFeed, the Asynchronous class is instantiated, which in turn instantiates the XMLHttpRequest object.

XMLHttpRequest **Details**

Regardless of how the XMLHttpRequest type is instantiated, and regardless of the browser or platform, XMLHttpRequest has the same set of methods and properties. Table 4-1 defines the properties and methods.

Table 4-1. XMLHttpRequest *Methods*

Method	Description
abort()	Stops a request that is being processed.
getAllResponseHeaders()	Returns the complete set of HTTP headers from the HTTP request as a string.
getResponseHeader(label)	Returns the associated HTTP header identified by the label variable.
open(method, URL, asyncFlag, username, password)method	Opens and prepares an HTTP request identified by the HTTP and URL. The asyncFlag variable can be either true or false, where true means to make an asynchronous HTTP request. The username and password variables are used to access a protected HTTP resource.
send(content)	Executes the HTTP request, where the variable content represents data that is posted if applicable.
setRequestHeader(label, value)	Assigns an HTTP header before the HTTP request is made.

I don't provide any more details of the methods, as they are used throughout the book. However, I do want to give special attention to the properties, because they are used extensively. When a request has retrieved data, four properties are used to indicate how the request fared. Consider the following HTML code, which references the four properties and is called after the send method has completed:

```
document.getElementById( 'httpcode').innerHTML = xmlhttp.status;
document.getElementById( 'httpstatus').innerHTML = xmlhttp.statusText;
document.getElementById( 'result').innerHTML = xmlhttp.responseText;
document.getElementById( 'xmlresult').innerHTML = xmlhttp.responseXML;
```

The four properties can be subdivided into two subcategories: result and HTTP status. The status and statusText properties retrieve the HTTP result codes. The status property contains an integer value, such as 200 for success. The statusText property contains a textual representation of the HTTP result code, such as OK. The responseText and responseXML properties contain the result of the HTTP request. The difference between the two properties is that responseText contains a string buffer of the results, and responseXML references an XML DOM representation of the results.

Making Asynchronous Requests

It is possible to use the XMLHttpRequest object in a synchronous manner, meaning that the moment send is called, the browser stops processing other messages and waits for an answer. But it is a bad idea to use the XMLHttpRequest object in a synchronous manner, as it locks the browser.

For the moment, ignoring the LoadAtomFeed code and focusing on XMLHttpRequest, let's look at how the browser can be locked. The following example is an ASP.NET page that hangs for ten seconds, and it will be referenced by the XMLHttpRequest object:

```
<%@ Page Language = "C#" %>
<html>
<head>
<title>Hanging page</title>
</head>
<body>
    <%
      System.Threading.Thread.Sleep( 10000);
     %>
    Hello, after a ten-second sleep!
</body>
</html>
```

The ASP.NET sample is written using the C# programming language, and there is a single statement, System.Threading.Thread.Sleep. The single statement causes the current thread to sleep for ten seconds.

Modifying the previous Ajax application to retrieve the hanging page and pushing the button to retrieve the hanging page causes the browser to appear similar to Figure 4-16.

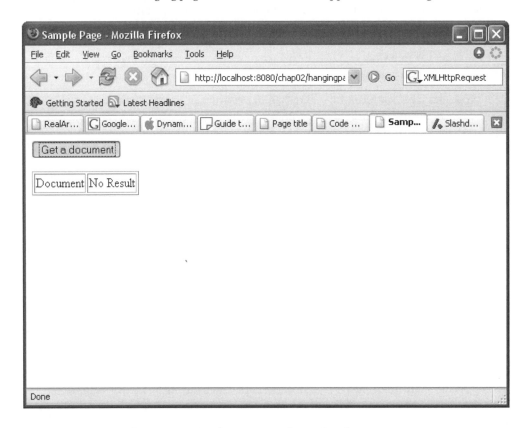

Figure 4-16. *Hanging browser waiting for content to be retrieved*

In Figure 4-16, the pressed button remains pressed because it is waiting for the content to be returned. While the browser is waiting, it is not possible to switch to another tab to process other HTTP requests. A hanging browser is a problem, and it can make the Ajax experience painful for users.

The solution is to use an asynchronous Ajax XMLHttpRequest. An asynchronous request will not block the browser, and the user could continue clicking or using other tabs of the browser. The following source code is the properly written Ajax application to use an asynchronous request:

```
<html>
<head>
<title>Sample Page</title>
</head>
<script language="JavaScript" src="/lib/factory.js"></script>
<script language="JavaScript" type="text/javascript">
var xmlhttp = FactoryXMLHttpRequest();

function AsyncUpdateEvent() {
    switch( xmlhttp.readyState) {
    case 0:
        document.getElementById( 'status').innerHTML = "uninitialized";
        break;
    case 1:
        document.getElementById( 'status').innerHTML = "loading";
        break;
    case 2:
        document.getElementById( 'status').innerHTML = "loaded";
        break;
    case 3:
        document.getElementById( 'status').innerHTML = "interactive";
        break;
    case 4:
        document.getElementById( 'status').innerHTML = "complete";
        document.getElementById( 'result').innerHTML = xmlhttp.responseText;
        break;
    }
}

function GetIt( url) {
    if( xmlhttp) {
        xmlhttp.open( 'GET', url, true);
        xmlhttp.onreadystatechange = AsyncUpdateEvent;
        xmlhttp.send( null);
    }
}
</script>
</head>
```

```
<body>
<button onclick="GetIt('/chap02/serverhang.aspx')">Get a document</button>
<p><table border="1">
    <tr><td>Document</td><td><span id="status">No Result</span></td>
    <td><span id="result">No Result</span></td></tr>
</table></p>
</body>
</html>
```

There are several new additions to the rewritten Ajax application, and they deal with the technical issues of loading content asynchronously. Let's start by focusing on the GetIt function. The implementation of GetIt is similar to previous Ajax application examples, except that the third parameter of the open method is true to indicate that the request will be asynchronous. This means that when the send method is called, it will return immediately.

Whenever XMLHttpRequest operates in asynchronous modes, feedback is given to the caller on the state of the request. The onreadystatechange property is a function that receives the feedback. It is important to note that the feedback function must be assigned before each send, because upon request completion the onreadystatechange property is reset. This is evident in the Mozilla and Firefox source.

The onreadstatechange property is assigned the AsyncUpdateEvent function. In the implementation of AsyncUpdateEvent is a switch statement that tests the current state of the request. When an asynchronous request is made, the script is free to continue executing other code. This could cause problems if the script attempts to read the request results before the request has been completed. Using the readyState property, it is possible to know the stage of the HTTP request. The readyState property can contain one of five values, where each value represents a request state:

- 0: The XMLHttpRequest instance is in an inconsistent state, and the result data should not be referencing.

- 1: A request is in progress, and the result data should not be retrieved.

- 2: The request has downloaded the result data and is preparing it for reference.

- 3: The script can interact with the XMLHttpRequest instance, even though the data is not completely loaded.

- 4: The request and result data are complete and have been finished.

The request states would seem to indicate that it is possible to manipulate various properties at different states. The problem is that not all browsers support the same property states at the same state codes. The only cross-platform solution is to reference the XMLHttpRequest result properties (status, statusText, responseText, and responseXML) when the request state is equal to 4. When the request state is 4, you can be sure that the result properties contain a valid value.

Executing the asynchronous Ajax application results in a call being made, and the browser is not locked. You can click the button, open a new browser, and surf to another Web site.

Implementing the Asynchronous **Class**

Having determined asynchronous XMLHttpRequests are the way to go, the Asynchronous encapsulation class is defined. An encapsulation class is not necessary, but it makes it simpler to work with the XMLHttpRequest object. The main advantage of using an encapsulation class is the association of the XMLHttpRequest object with a code block.

For a refresher, let's look at the code to load an Atom feed again:

```
function LoadAtomFeed() {
    var asynchronous = new Asynchronous();
    asynchronous.settings = {
        onComplete : function(xmlhttp) {
            parseAtom( xmlhttp.responseXML);
            flexbox.update();
        }
    }
    asynchronous.get("/services/blog/entries/current");
}
```

To make the Asynchronous class work, the user needs to do two things: associate the settings data member with some information and call an appropriate method (e.g., get) to make an HTTP request. The purpose of the settings data member is to provide the callbacks and extra information associated with a request. In the example, the onComplete method is called once the HTTP request has completed.

The code as it stands is fairly easy to understand, but remember that the code is asynchronous. As a result, when the asynchronous.get method is called, the LoadAtomFeed function will exit before calling onComplete and returning control to the user. In a worst-case scenario, if a user goes click-crazy, there could be dozens of requests being made. The alternative is to use synchronous calls, which lock the browser, and that itself is not an option. On the positive side, asynchronous behavior allows a user to launch tasks and wait for the results. The programmer has to remain vigilant and make sure that the user does not get ahead of him- or herself.

Now that you have a basic understanding of how to use the Asynchronous class, let's look at the details of the Asynchronous implementation. The class exposes a method for each HTTP verb, and in the example the get method corresponds to the HTTP verb GET. The implementation of get is as follows:

```
function HttpRequest_get(strurl) {
    this.call({ action : "GET", url: strurl});
}
```

In the implementation of HttpRequest_get, which is mapped to Asynchronous.get, a reference to the function call is made. The get function is a convenience method to the call method. The call method accepts a single parameter: an object with specific data members. In the case of the get method, the action and url data members are defined. So why create an object, when you could have used two parameters, action and url, for the method call? The answer is flexibility. JavaScript does not understand overloaded functions, and there can be only a single function with a single set of parameters. So that the developer does not have to play the permutations and combinations game with the parameters (e.g., which parameters, what order, etc.), an object with data members is created.

The most important method of Asynchronous is call, because regardless of which HTTP verb is used, the method is executed. The following code is the complete implementation of call.

Source: /client/scripts/jaxson/communications.js

```
function Asynchronous_call(request) {
    var instance = this;
    if (! this.settings) {
        throw new Error("Settings is not defined ");
    }
    if (this.xmlhttp.readyState != 4 && this.xmlhttp.readyState != 0) {
        throw new Error("Currently active request cannot continue");
    }
    this.xmlhttp.open(request.action, request.url, true,
        this.settings.username, this.settings.password);
    if (request.headers) {
        for( defHeader in request.headers) {
            this.xmlhttp.setRequestHeader(defHeader, request.headers[defHeader]);
        }
    }
    if (this.settings.headers) {
        for( defHeader in this.settings.headers) {
            this.xmlhttp.setRequestHeader(defHeader,
                    this.settings.headers[defHeader]);
        }
    }
    this.xmlhttp.onreadystatechange = function() {
        switch (instance.xmlhttp.readyState) {
            case 1:
                if (instance.settings.onLoading) {
                    instance.settings.onLoading(instance.xmlhttp);
                }
                break;
            case 2:
                if (instance.settings.onLoaded) {
                    instance.settings.onLoaded(instance.xmlhttp);
                }
                break;
            case 3:
                if (instance.settings.onInteractive) {
                    instance.settings.onInteractive(instance.xmlhttp);
                }
                break;
            case 4:
                if (instance.settings.onComplete) {
                    try {
                        instance.settings.onComplete(instance.xmlhttp);
```

```
                }
                catch (e) {
                    globals.errorHandler(e);
                }
            }
            break;
        }
    }
    try {
        this.xmlhttp.send(request.data);
    }
    catch( e) {
        globals.errorHandler(e);
    }
}
```

I'll now explain the `call` method from beginning to end, and I'll reiterate the individual code pieces, with some reiterations abbreviated. I show the code again where appropriate for ease of understanding, as the implementation of `call` is relatively long and does many different things.

Starting at the top, the `instance` variable is assigned to the `this` value:

```
var instance = this;
```

This assignment is necessary because a code block will be assigned to the `onreadystatechange` data member, and the code block has to remember which `Asynchronous` instance is being referenced.

After the assignment, we validate that the `settings` data member has been populated:

```
if (! this.settings) {
    throw new Error("Settings is not defined ");
}
```

The `settings` data member has to exist because it contains information about which methods to call when the request has completed and which HTTP headers to add to the request.

At this point, you should notice that two objects are required to make the `call` method work. The first object is `settings`, and the second object is the `request` parameter. As a shortcut, a developer could combine the two objects into one, and either pass it to the `call` method or assign it to the `settings` data member. This shortcut would be misguided, because each object has a different purpose. The `request` object is used to define the settings for the specific URL request being made. The `settings` object is used to define settings that transcend all calls and could be a considered a global callback for the `Asynchronous` object instance. The idea is that you allocate an instance of `Asynchronous`, define how it should behave, and then start making requests with the possibility of calling different URLs.

Then the next step is to verify that the current `XMLHttpRequest` instance is not already preoccupied:

```
if (this.xmlhttp.readyState != 4 && this.xmlhttp.readyState != 0) {
    throw new Error("Currently active request cannot continue");
}
```

When using XMLHttpRequest in asynchronous mode, it is possible to make a new HTTP request on an executing XMLHttpRequest instance. The problem is that XMLHttpRequest cannot serve two requests, and it will stop the already executing request to make a new request. The readyState property is used to indicate the state of the XMLHttpRequest object. If readyState is 0, then no request has been made and an HTTP request can be made. If readyState is 4, then a request has been made, the request has completed, and the object is ready to make another request. If readyState has any other value, a request is being executed, and thus executing another request does not make sense.

After the initialization and checking has completed, it is possible to make a request:

```
this.xmlhttp.open(request.action, request.url, true,
    this.settings.username, this.settings.password);
```

Calling the open method, you need to specify at a minimum the HTTP verb (e.g., GET, POST) via the request.action data member and the URL via the request.url data member. Whenever you make any XMLHttpRequest request, make sure that the first action is the open method. If you assign the onreadystatechange function before calling open, your request will not work properly. If you attempt to assign request headers before calling open, your request will not work properly. The open method is used to initialize and create a new request; open will not call the server, as that is the responsibility of send.

In the open method example, a username and password (this.settings.username and this.settings.password, respectively) are always sent to the server, even if there is no username and password. It does no harm to send null values, and it will not affect the operation of an HTTP request. The username and password are used only when the HTTP server performs a challenge and asks for a username and password. In the context of the XMLHttpRequest object, the username and password are used only if the underlying implementation of XMLHttpRequest needs the information.

After you've opened the request, you can add custom HTTP headers using the setRequestHeaders method:

```
if (request.headers) {
    for( defHeader in request.headers) {
        this.xmlhttp.setRequestHeader(defHeader, request.headers[defHeader]);
    }
}
if (this.settings.headers) {
    for( defHeader in this.settings.headers) {
        this.xmlhttp.setRequestHeader(defHeader,
            this.settings.headers[defHeader]);
    }
}
```

The headers are assigned two times: once for the settings associated with the request (request.headers) and once for the global settings (this.settings.headers). The headers that you assign can be standard HTTP headers or custom headers. If you plan on using custom HTTP headers, it is always a good idea to prefix them with X-. That way, your headers will not be confused with standard HTTP headers.

After you've assigned the headers, the onreadystatechange callback function is assigned:

```
    this.xmlhttp.onreadystatechange = function() {
      switch (instance.xmlhttp.readyState) {
        case 1:
            if (instance.settings.onLoading) {
                instance.settings.onLoading(instance.xmlhttp);
            }
            break;
        case 2:
            if (instance.settings.onLoaded) {
                instance.settings.onLoaded(instance.xmlhttp);
            }
            break;
        case 3:
            if (instance.settings.onInteractive) {
                instance.settings.onInteractive(instance.xmlhttp);
            }
            break;
        case 4:
            if (instance.settings.onComplete) {
                try {
                    instance.settings.onComplete(instance.xmlhttp);
                }
                catch (e) {
                    globals.errorHandler(e);
                }
            }
            break;
      }
    }
```

In the Asynchronous implementation of onreadystatechange, a switch statement executes
one of the four valid ready states. From the source, you can associate each number with a specific state. The most important ready state is 4, indicating that the content has been retrieved,
loaded, and processed. The 4 ready state calls the method defined by the client in the settings
property. Notice in the implementation of the assigned onreadystatechange function that the
instance variable has replaced a reference to this. The variable is necessary, as illustrated in
Recipe 2-13.

The implementation of the onreadystatechange function is overkill, as 98% of the time
you use Asynchronous you will only care about the ready state of 4. For all of the other ready
states, depending on the browser, certain functionality is possible. Because of this inconsis-
tency and the incompleteness of the XMLHttpRequest object state, there is no real need to
process the other ready states.

The remaining call function code involves sending the request to the server using the
send function:

```
try {
    this.xmlhttp.send(request.data);
}
```

```
    catch( e) {
        globals.errorHandler(e);
    }
```

The send function is used to make the physical request to the server. The function is also used to send any data associated with the request. If there is no data, then calling send with a null value will not generate an error.

When the send method has made its request, it returns immediately, and the JavaScript Asynchronous_call function will return control to the browser. At this time, the client should add some code to not allow multiple calls. For example, if the request was activated using a button, then until the request has returned, the button could be disabled. Of course, this introduces a potential problem if the request never returns and the button remains disabled. To solve that problem, you can introduce a timer that gives the request a maximum amount of time. If during that time, the request still has not returned, the XMLHttpRequest.abort method is called and the button is enabled again.

Implementing the Synchronous Class

Another potential solution is to use the synchronous version of XMLHttpRequest. For the most part, I use asynchronous mode, but there are times when synchronous mode is more appropriate. Recipe 1-3 presents an example in which the test cannot continue until the Ajax page has finished loading its content. To implement a Synchronous version of Asynchronous, only the call method needs to be adapted—everything else can remain as is.

For example, to convert the initial client code to use synchronous mode, you could use the following code:

```
function LoadAtomFeed() {
    var synchronous = new Synchronous();
    synchronous.settings = {
        onComplete : function(xmlhttp) {
            parseAtom( xmlhttp.responseXML);
            flexbox.update();
        }
    }
    synchronous.get("/services/blog/entries/current");
}
```

The bold code shows the only major change: instead of instantiating Asynchronous, it instantiates Synchronous. You still provide a settings code block, and you still call the get function. The reason this approach works is due to the way that Asynchronous and Synchronous are wired together, as illustrated by the following code:

```
function Asynchronous(userSettings) {
    this.xmlhttp = new FactoryXMLHttpRequest();
    this.isBusy = false;
    this.userSettings = userSettings;
}

Asynchronous.prototype.get = HttpRequest_get;
```

```
Asynchronous.prototype.put = HttpRequest_put;
Asynchronous.prototype.del = HttpRequest_delete;
Asynchronous.prototype.post = HttpRequest_post;
Asynchronous.prototype.call = Asynchronous_call;

function Synchronous(userSettings) {
    this.xmlhttp = new FactoryXMLHttpRequest();
    this.isBusy = false;
    this.userSettings = userSettings;
}

Synchronous.prototype.get = HttpRequest_get;
Synchronous.prototype.put = HttpRequest_put;
Synchronous.prototype.del = HttpRequest_delete;
Synchronous.prototype.post = HttpRequest_post;
Synchronous.prototype.call = Synchronous_call;
```

The bold code shows the single change in each class. Notice that this way of defining a class uses a contract. Each type has five functions: get, put, del, post, and call. The four functions get, put, del, and post could be considered a module and thought of as a mixin. Each of the four functions adds value in some way, but relies on a contract where the type contains a call method. The call method is what varies on the Asynchronous and Synchronous types, as each has a unique implementation.

The synchronous call implementation is as follows.

Source: /client/scripts/jaxson/communications.js

```
function Synchronous_call(request) {
    var instance = this;
    this.xmlhttp.open(request.action, request.url, false,
    this.settings.username, this.settings.password);
    if (request.headers) {
        for( defHeader in request.headers) {
            this.xmlhttp.setRequestHeader(defHeader, request.headers[defHeader]);
        }
    }
    if (this.settings.headers) {
        for( defHeader in this.settings.headers) {
            this.xmlhttp.setRequestHeader(defHeader,
             this.settings.headers[defHeader]);
        }
    }
    try {
        this.xmlhttp.send(request.data);
        if (instance.settings.onComplete) {
            instance.settings.onComplete(instance.xmlhttp);
        }
    }
```

```
    catch( e) {
        globals.errorHandler(e);
    }
}
```

Without going into too much detail, you can see that the implementations are very similar. The only real difference is that calling onComplete after calling the send method mimics the asynchronous calling of the onComplete code block. In synchronous mode, after the send method returns, the state of XMLHttpRequest is valid and calling onComplete is correct.

Handling Errors

In both implementations of the call method, try-catch blocks surrounded critical operations, such as retrieving the HTTP request data and processing the HTTP request data. Revisiting the code reveals the following generalized approach:

```
    try {
        // Critical operations
    }
    catch( e) {
        globals.errorHandler(e);
    }
```

The exception block will surround critical operations so that the script can continue. Depending on the nature of the exception and the browser, an exception can cause the page to stop functioning properly. Then the user can only reload the HTML page and hope for the best. If the page generates an exception while reloading the page, the user has no chance of figuring out how to fix the problem.

Using an exception block, you can manage these issues and then attempt to fix the problem. A problem fix could require loading other content or intervention from the user. Without the exception blocks, an error will cause the browser to stop processing the code and display the error. The error display is where the problems begin, because most browsers display errors as little icons, or in an invisible JavaScript console. For developers, it is easy to figure out the source of the error, but users are often bewildered.

The generalized approach is effective because of the way the error is routed. In the exception block, there is a general reference to the globals.errorHandler method. globals.errorHandler is defined in a JavaScript file that is loaded right at the beginning of loading an HTML page.

```
var globals = {
    state : new Object(),
    errorHandler : function(e) {
    },
    info : function() {}
}
```

The globals variable has three data members, but only errorHandler interests us. The default implementation of errorHandler is to do nothing. Of course, you might consider doing nothing a very bad solution. And I agree, it is a bad solution. However, it is necessary to define a default handler; otherwise, the exception handler will generate an exception. Therefore, it is up to the developer to add into every page an error handler that could look as follows:

```
globals.errorHandler = function( e) {
    document.getElementById( "error").innerHTML = e.toString();
}
```

In this implementation of the error handler, the error is displayed in a span element with an ID of error. The solution is simple, but it's effective because the user will immediately see what went wrong.

Processing the Atom Feed

When it receives the Atom feed, the LoadAtomFeed function will call the parseAtom function. The following parseAtom function is responsible for picking apart the Atom feed and assigning the pieces to variables. The variables are used by the user interface routines to assemble an HTML page.

```
items = null;
items_count = 0;
title = null;
link = null;
author = null;
dates = null;
content = null;

function parseAtom( xmldoc) {
    items = xmldoc;
    items_count=items.getElementsByTagName('entry').length;
    title = new Array();
    link = new Array()
    author = new Array()
    dates = new Array();
    content = new Array();

    for (var i=0; i < items_count; i++) {
        title[i] = items.getElementsByTagName('entry
                    ')[i].getElementsByTagName('title')[0];
        link[i] = items.getElementsByTagName('entry
                    ')[i].getElementsByTagName('link')[0].getAttribute('href');
        dates[i] = items.getElementsByTagName('entry
                    ')[i].getElementsByTagName('updated')[0];
        author[i] = items.getElementsByTagName('entry'
                    )[i].getElementsByTagName('author').firstChild;
        content[ i] = items.getElementsByTagName('entry'
                    )[i].getElementsByTagName('content'
                    )[0].getElementsByTagName( 'div')[ 0];;
    }
}
```

The way that the Atom feed is parsed is very simple. The XML DOM `getElementsByTagName` method is used to iterate the elements of the tree. The `getElementsByTagName` function is chained together so that individual elements can be picked out. The advantage of chaining is that parts of the XML hierarchy can be filtered out to serve as the basis for another filter.

Recipe Summary

This chapter focused on a new way of building Web applications using SOA. You looked at an example application and learned how to shift into the new architecture based on Ajax and Web services.

In your Web application development efforts, keep the following points in mind:

- Don't try to do everything at once. This recipe showed an approach where you continue using the old database and old data, and incrementally build a new architecture using abstraction and modularization.

- The aim of this recipe is to help you modularize and granularize your Web applications so that there is a client developer, server developer, and database developer. This is not to say you need three developers—but when each developer implements a contract, he or she only needs to worry about the contract and not the other pieces. Ideally, all the pieces will be assembled like a jigsaw puzzle.

- The server will expose itself as a general Web service adhering to a standard. The standard might be an already developed standard or a standard created within a closed circle. The idea behind developing a standard is to permit the creation of tests that can be used to verify that everything functions correctly.

- When using a SQL relational database, you should at all times attempt to stick to the SQL standard so that it is possible to move the data from one database to another.

- One of the main reasons for keeping the old architecture side by side with the new is to make it possible to not have to implement all functionality right away. In the example of the blog software, you do not have to implement the functionality to add entries; you can continue using the old software. This allows you to bring your software to market quickly.

- You can develop your Web service using standards like SOAP/WSDL, but the example demonstrated the use of REST. REST treats the server-side data as resources that can be manipulated using HTTP verbs (`GET`, `PUT`, `POST`, and `DELETE`). Think of REST and the HTTP verbs like a SQL database and the manipulation of the data. Remember the purpose of each HTTP verb, so you don't confuse the end user of your REST Web service.

- REST can expose URLs that fit into the following categories: view URLs, root URLs, collection URLs, and data-resource URLs. Make sure in your architecture to clearly define the purpose of each URL and what HTTP verbs it will accept. Failing to do so will confuse the end user of your REST-based Web service.

- The Ajax SOA-based client has two distinct phases. The first phase is loading the document. When loading the document, the client is being initialized. During initialization, the client is preparing the code to be executed. The second phase is executing the document, which means the loading and processing of data that is loaded, using Ajax techniques to call a Web service. This separation of loading and execution is very similar to the loading and execution of a traditional program.

- When using `XMLHttpRequest`, remember to use it for the most part in asynchronous mode. You do not want to lock your browser while waiting for content. Note, however, that asynchronous mode means writing more checking code, as you do not want the client to start clicking buttons while waiting for a request to complete.

- The implementation of the `Asynchronous` and `Synchronous` classes illustrates the use of mixins to create similar types that have some specialized functionalities. Additionally, the `Asynchronous` and `Synchronous` classes show how to implement contracts in JavaScript.

- You will want to implement a global error handler in your Ajax application so that any errors that may happen will be displayed in a user-friendly manner. Failing to do so might cause the client to click buttons wildly, and the subsequent reloading of pages will cause even more errors to occur.

- When you are processing an XML data stream, take a look at the XML DOM methods to help you pick apart the data. You should not need to iterate each individual node, as XML DOM has great facilities to filter nodes.

- The overall message to take away from this recipe is that by using the approach outlined here, you are moving back to a traditional form of developing client/server applications. The difference is that you are using open standards, which makes it easier to modularize your applications. By using open standards, you make it easier to deploy your application worldwide and easier for third parties to interact with you. In general, this approach to building Web applications is a win-win-win scenario.

CHAPTER 5

■ ■ ■

5-1. Implementing a Universal Web Service Architecture

This recipe focuses on building a Web service architecture. In the previous recipe, you learned how to create an overall architecture that included the basics of how to construct a Web service and its appropriate URLs. However, it didn't explain the details of what a Web service does and why a Web service should do what it does.

This recipe outlines the guidelines of how to develop a Representational State Transfer (REST)-based Web service. Specifically, it covers the following points:

- Structuring a Web service to solve a specific task

- Combining Web services to filter and modify data

- Combining Web services to create mashups

Problem

Let's look at a problem within a stock-trading application as an example of a problem in building Web services. The problem is that a number of clients need access to real-time historical and order information. Figure 5-1 illustrates the original architecture.

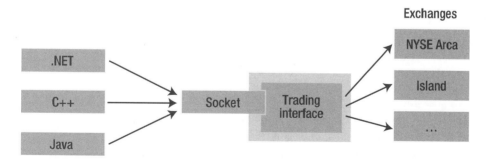

Figure 5-1. *Original trading architecture*

The trading application is a piece of middleware that connects to a number of exchanges and the local database. If users want to access the historical data, they need to connect to the middleware via a socket connection and query the local database. If users want to buy and sell stocks, they need to connect to the middleware, which relays the quotes to the exchanges.

Regardless of the technology used, the client connects to the middleware using a socket connection, across which historical data, order information, or real-time market information is transmitted. The problem with the socket connection is that the same code has to be implemented for various flavors of technology (.NET, Java, and C++). Clients that don't implement the socket code have to either bridge via another technology or switch to another technology.

This application needs a way to modernize the architecture without getting rid of the legacy code. You cannot replace the original middleware socket server, because it's a working piece of code and many transactions flow across the software. Put yourself in the place of the developer who would advocate a complete conversion. Any sign of problems would mean potential liabilities. The solution is to put a Web service front end onto the socket connection, as illustrated in Figure 5-2.

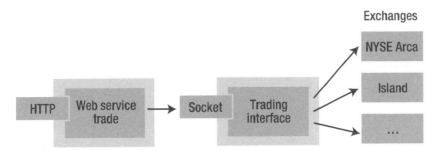

Figure 5-2. *Web service front end to trading middleware*

Adding a Web service front end allows you to leverage the middleware socket server without making any changes to it. While it may seem like a waste of resources to add a front end to a service in an overall Web service context, it makes sense here. This recipe will explore why.

Solution Part 1

The implementation of the solution involves taking one of the already existing socket technologies and using that technology to build a Web service. For illustration purposes, this recipe uses a single technology—Java. You could choose .NET or C++—the actual technology is not important, because the exposed Web service can be consumed by any technology that is Web service–aware. The initial approach to building the Web service is to define the general operations and then implement those general operations using some technology. Figure 5-3 illustrates a high-level view of the architecture.

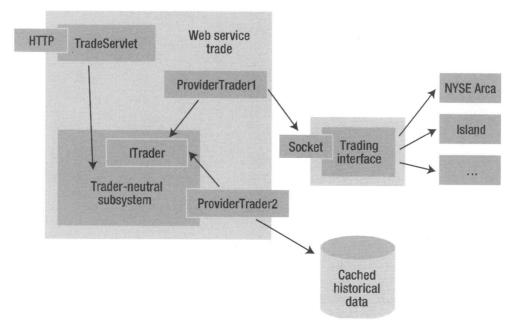

Figure 5-3. *High-level view of initial Web service architecture*

In the high-level view of the trading architecture, a class type called TradeServlet that implements a Java servlet provides the Web service. For those not versed in Java technologies, a Java servlet is a way of implementing an HTTP handler. TradeServlet executes the historical requests, real-time data requests, and order requests using an interface named ITrader.

From a programming perspective, using an interface is the correct approach because it allows you to use the Bridge pattern. The Bridge pattern lets you decouple the intention of trading from the implementation of trading. In the high-level view of the Web services architecture, the type ProviderTrader1 implements the calling of the appropriate functionality via the socket layer. The Bridge pattern theory allows you to use a socket call today as a stopgap solution, but tomorrow replace ProviderTrader1 with a new implementation (such as replacing the middleware with the Web service) without having to change the implementation of TradeServlet or the interface ITrader.

Implementing the Bridge pattern results in an architecture similar to Figure 5-4.

Figure 5-4 looks similar to Figure 5-3, but there is a world of difference. In Figure 5-3, the abstraction only involves a single interface. Figure 5-4 implements a trading-neutral subsystem where data source implementations could be plugged in. The class ProviderTrader1 implements the ITrader interface and provides a bridge from the trader-neutral subsystem to the socket-based trading system. Another provider could be used to access a legacy database. Regardless of the number of providers, the Web service interacts with the trader-neutral subsystem. And the trader-neutral subsystem interacts with the socket-based trading system.

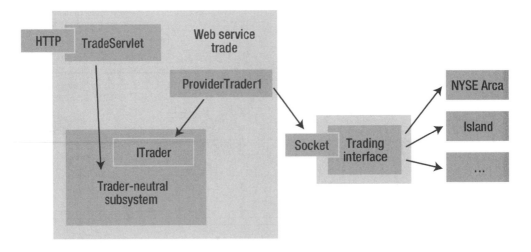

Figure 5-4. *Resulting architecture that doesn't work*

In theory, this approach is sound, but it suffers from being too complex. The problem of the approach is a question of focus. In the example of the trader subsystem, the focus is the subsystem, and the Web service layer is an add-on to the trader subsystem. In theory, the Web service add-on is not even needed, because the trader subsystem manages everything. In the context of an Ajax Web service application, this is the wrong approach because the focus is the Web service, and it should not be an add-on.

Solution Part 2

The solution to the trader subsystem is to neither define nor implement a trader-neutral subsystem using a specific technology, as Figure 5-4 showed. The trader subsystem is converted into a series of Web services that you can assemble into a subsystem. A Web service–based trader subsystem still requires an interface, but the interface is defined at the HTTP Web service level. In architectural terms, the ITrader implementations converted into Web services appear as Figure 5-5.

The architecture shown in Figure 5-5 relies on reusing the already existing implementations of ProviderTrader1 and ProviderTrader2 directly from the class TradeServlet. Each implementation provides a set of methods, properties, and result sets that the trader-neutral subsystem defines. Using a Web service, the methods, properties, and result sets are converted into something that is Web service–compatible. Then at a higher level, another technology assembles the Web services into a trader subsystem.

Taking a step back and thinking about the overall architecture, you get an architecture similar to Figure 5-6.

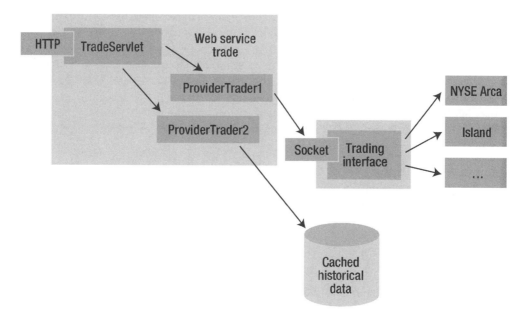

Figure 5-5. *Modified trading system architecture*

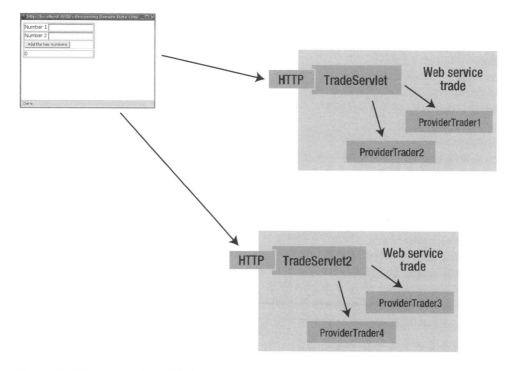

Figure 5-6. *Big picture of modified trading system architecture*

Figure 5-6 shows an Ajax client referencing two separate instances of the trading application. `TradeServlet` implements version 1.0 of the trading application, and `TradeServlet2` implements version 2.0 of the trading application. To switch the Ajax client from version 1.0 to version 2.0 is trivial and only requires specifying a new server. Of course, this assumes that the data formats of version 1.0 and version 2.0 are compatible. On the server side, `TradeServlet` could be using a socket connection to access the trading information, and `TradeServlet2` could be the middleware replacement. The Web service has become the abstraction, and the code behind the Web service is irrelevant from the perspective of the Web service consumer.

Implementing the Trader-Universal Web Service

The trading Web service is an example of what to expect when implementing a complete Web service solution. This recipe covers these remaining pieces:

- Defining the URLs

- Identifying the formats that can be sent and received

- How to support relative URLs

Defining the URLs for the Trader Application

Let's continue with the evolution of the trader Web service and outline the important pieces, namely the URLs and supported data formats. The trader application exposes the following base URLs:

- `/services/controller`

- `/services/realtime`

- `/services/orders`

- `/services/orders/trader123/order345`

- `/services/historical`

`/services/controller` is the base URL used to manage the engine on the server side. The controller URL lets you reset the code behind the Web service manually. For example, in the case of the trader application, `/services/controller` would connect the Web service implementation to the socket that provides the trading interface.

You could use the URL `/services/controller/start` to start the server code, and you could use the URL `/services/controller/stop` to stop the server code. However, this approach wouldn't be usable, because it would seem that the identifiers `start` and `stop` are resources, which they are not. Compare it to a light switch. A light switch is a single resource that has two states: on and off. It does *not* have two resources, one for each state.

You use query parameters to start and stop the server code. To start the server code, you execute the verb `POST` on the URL `/services/controller` with the computer graphics interface (CGI) parameters `action=start`. To stop the server code, the URL remains the same, as does the verb, but the CGI parameters change to `action=stop`. The verb `POST` is appropriate, because you're executing some server-side process, and what the process should do depends on the data sent. Calling the verb `GET` on the URL `/services/controller` returns the status of the server code.

If you'd like to control multiple pieces of server code in your application, then create child URLs such as the following: `/services/controller/code1` and `/services/controller/code2`. The guidelines for starting, stopping, and retrieving the status of the individual server code pieces remain the same.

Often, server-side code pieces require configuration directives, such as the location of the base directory, how many threads to start, and so on. These configuration directives are typically stored in a configuration file. You should be able to specify these directives when the server code starts or stops. For example, if you want to specify a thread count, then you could use the CGI parameter `action=start&threadcount=12` for starting the server code.

If you have the ability to define configuration directives, then they can be queried and retrieved when the status of the server is requested. If you want to query the individual value of a server variable, you could filter it using query parameters such as `/services/controller?status=threadcount+uptime`.

You use the base URL `/services/realtime` to manage the real-time stock-ticker data. For example, if you're interested in the ticker GM, you'd use the URL `/services/realtime/GM` to retrieve the real-time information. It would seem that this base URL is the simplest, but the simplicity is misleading.

For example, if users execute `GET` on the URL `/services/realtime`, what is returned? This is a tricky question, because you're approaching the limits of a piece of software. From a theoretical perspective, calling `GET` results in the return of real-time data for all tickers. This sounds good in theory, but it's completely impractical. There are literally thousands of stocks on multiple exchanges. Getting all tickers in one request in real time using a `GET` request is practically unfeasible.

This is an example of a URL where the theory and practice are in conflict. The solution doesn't support the root URL as a reference to real-time data. The root URL is used to return a list of all available real-time links. The root URL is not used to indicate what the real-time information is because doing so would require following thousands of tickers. The root URL will return links to where you can retrieve real-time data. This could mean returning links to thousands of stock tickers. You could also use the root URL to return both the link to the ticker and an abbreviated corporate description. This would help in building a search engine, as most people don't know the ticker but do know the name of the corporation.

Delegating the root URL to individual URLs creates a problem in that the Web service cannot manage the real-time feeds for all stock tickers on all exchanges. To put it simply, you cannot track all stocks on a single computer. Tracking all stocks requires massive amounts of horsepower that this recipe won't get into. The only solution is to use a track-if-asked solution.

In a track-if-asked solution, no stocks are tracked initially for real-time data. Real-time data will be tracked only if an HTTP `GET` is executed on a particular stock. An HTTP `POST` or `DELETE` or `PUT` makes no sense on the real-time feed, because a real-time feed comprises data that goes from the server to the client. The server is not interested in any information from the client other than which ticker to generate real-time data for. If a verb other than `GET` is executed, the server will generate an HTTP 500 error.

`/services/orders` specifies the root URL for order processing. In the context of stocks, order processing makes use of all HTTP verbs. You use HTTP `POST` to submit an order, HTTP `PUT` to modify an order, HTTP `GET` to retrieve the status of an order, and HTTP `DELETE` to delete an order.

Each order will be represented as a unique identifier—for example, `/services/orders/1232445`. The unique identifier doesn't have to be numeric, but it can be alphanumeric or even a more complicated Globally Unique Identifier (GUID).

The root URL can be the host of many orders, which could literally mean millions of orders. For the order URL, it's important that you have the ability to filter orders according to a specific status. You might be tempted to organize orders according to a date, but I would advise against that. Whenever you're creating a root URL, the data in the collection should be accessible in its natural form. In a blog application, it's natural to organize by date. However, the natural order of a stock application is not by date but rather by order ID. Thus, the root orders URL will literally have millions of orders associated with it. If an application happens to ask for all orders, the server will need to give all of those orders. In the case of a SQL database, if a table has millions upon millions of records, and somebody executes the query `select * from table`, the database won't ask, "Are you sure about this?" The database will go ahead and select all of the records, even though it might not be efficient.

You create filters to optimize access to the orders. For example, if you want to find all orders in 2006, you could execute the URL `/services/orders/?year=2006`. You could also convert the query parameters into a view URL, such as `/services/orders/2006`. Whether you use the query parameter or the view URL approach depends on your preference.

There is one filter that will prove problematic, and it relates to users. In any order system, you have multiple users. A stock-trading application is no different. What makes a stock-trading order application more complicated is that an order is not fulfilled automatically. It might not ever be fulfilled, and it might even be canceled. If an order system doesn't have the ability to filter per trader, you could potentially run into a situation where one trader might open a position and another trader closes a position.

In theory, you could buy and sell a future stock at the same time (called *wash trading*). By buying and selling at the same time, you are neither gaining nor losing, at least other than your brokerage fee. This technique of buying and selling at the same time through two different brokers is illegal, because it makes it seem like there is action on a position when in fact there is not. Therefore, traders are tied to their orders, and the orders are tied to their traders. A logical refinement of the orders URL would be `/services/orders/[trader]`. This refined URL illustrates that sometimes you have to create URLs that fulfill other needs, like, in this case, the legal department's needs.

With this refinement of the URL, does the root URL `/services/orders` become obsolete? Everything, including the query parameters and the view URLs, still applies. The difference is that the URL to access the order information will contain the unique identifier of the trader.

Assuming that you're going to use the refinement to the URL, let's go through what the individual verbs will do at the different URL levels. At the root URL level (`/services/orders`), only the HTTP GET applies. At this level, you can only filter out the orders you want to see. You cannot POST, because the root URL is missing the trader ID, and you cannot PUT, because the root URL is a collection URL. Finally, you cannot DELETE, because that would cause the deletion of all the orders and the traders.

One level down, you would have the root URL for an individual trader (`/services/orders/trader-abc`). At the root URL for an individual trader, only the HTTP GET and POST apply. You would use GET to retrieve and potentially filter all trades that a trader has made. For example, you could filter for trades made in a particular month, year, or day. You could use the URLs `/services/orders/trader-abc/2006` or `/services/orders/trader-abc?year=2006`. The HTTP POST verb applies, because it allows the users to submit an order without an order ID. The submission of the order returns the URL where you can retrieve the status of an order. If an HTTP `POST` to the URL `/services/orders/trader-abc` is sent, the URL `/services/orders/trader-abc/123456` could be returned.

Applying the verb `DELETE` at the root URL is a bit tricky because of what the verb means. If you were to apply the `DELETE` verb, it would delete all of the orders at the root URL. Practically speaking, this is very ill-advised. One reason to support the `DELETE` verb is to be able to delete items selectively via a query parameter that acts as a filter. For example, to delete all orders in a year, you could use the URL `/services/orders/trader-abc?year=2006`. Notice the URL used to selectively delete is the same as the URL used to selectively select. The difference is the verb (`DELETE` vs. `GET`). It is a common occurrence that URLs will match but exhibit different behavior depending on the verb. In the context of the trading system, deleting orders would have restrictions. If an order is executing, you cannot delete the order.

The remaining verb `PUT` is for the most part not applicable at the root URL level. You use the verb `PUT` to send a complete representation of the resource to the server. In the case of the root URL, this means sending all orders to the server. The problem with sending orders to the server is that you cannot send complete orders. The order is complete, but the order identifier (calculated at the time an order is posted) is missing. Thus, you cannot use `PUT` to send a new order to the server.

Another reason for using `PUT` would be to modify an existing order. In general, this is a legitimate use, but it is incorrect in the context of the trading system. What happens if you attempt to modify an order that is executing currently? There is no simple recourse, and thus in the context of the order system, modifying an order can cause more problems than solutions. The appropriate trading solution is to delete the order and create a new one.

`/services/orders/trader123/order345` represents a URL referencing the order resource. In general, you can apply all HTTP verbs, but you would have to create limits to reflect business processes. In the case of the trader application, you could not use the `PUT` verb on a new order, because the order application does not allow you to determine an order ID ahead of time. You also cannot `PUT` an existing order, because that would mean modifying the order, and in the context of a trading system, an order can either execute or be canceled. You could apply and use the `DELETE` verb to define a cancellation of the order. A `POST` to an order would only make sense if the `POST` represents an order that is a cancellation. A `GET` would be used to retrieve the execution status of an order.

`/services/historical` represents a root URL used to retrieve the historical data from the middleware. Getting a historical feed is unique in that there is only one applicable verb—namely, `GET`. The word *historical* implies something that already happened, and you cannot rewrite history. Rewriting history would occur if you attempt to use the `PUT` or `DELETE` verb. A `POST` would apply if you use the `POST` to create a sophisticated query. For example, you can use a `POST` to scan and filter historical data according to a set of criteria.

To make the historical Web service as effective as possible, you need the ability to define sophisticated queries. REST is not equipped to do that, because REST relies on the HTTP protocol. This is not to say that you cannot use REST to query the data, but that you need to write the plumbing. For example, say you want to find all stocks that traded in a specific range for five days out of 10. You would need to code this sort of query in the form of a REST call that delegates to a relational query, assuming that the data is stored in a relational database.

Another approach is to use an XML-based database, though you'd need to decide this ahead of time. The advantage of storing your data in an XML-based database is that you can easily map the HTTP queries to the XML hierarchy. Using XML Query Language (XQL) and

XPath on the XML database, you can easily execute sophisticated queries without having to write the plumbing. You need to remember that the power of a historical Web service lies in how you implement the queries.

What Format of Data to Send?

Thus far, all of the example Web services have been explained in terms of URLs, but not in terms of the content that is accepted and generated. In the case of the blogging application introduced in Chapter 4, the Web service generated Atom data using the MIME type `application/atom+xml`. When building REST Web services, the MIME type is important, because it determines how the data is received and sent.

In the case of the blogging application, if the Atom URL is called, it will generate an XML stream. In theory, the REST development strategy is to create a Web service that is technology-neutral and will generate the right content for the right query.

Identifying the Resource and Representation

REST promotes the separation of the resource from the representation. For illustration purposes, let's work through the historical stock-ticker example. The URL used to retrieve the historical ticker information is `/services/historical/AMZN/2006`. The default format generated by the Web service is CSV, but the default could just as easily have been XML or JavaScript Object Notation (JSON). If a client can only accept JSON, then the conversion from CSV to JSON requires an extra step and extra resources.

To optimize this application, you can let the server decide which content to generate based on the needs of the client. If the client wants JSON, then the server will generate JSON. The data that is generated as JSON, XML, and CSV is all the same. Thus, it can be said that the data is the resource, and JSON, XML, and CSV are the representation. Separating the resource from the representation means that a single URL will have separate representations. The representation that is sent depends on the value of the HTTP `Accept-*` header, but doesn't need to be the only one. Let's focus on the `Accept` HTTP header and consider the following HTTP conversation that returns some content.

Request

```
GET /services/historical/AMZN/2006 HTTP/1.1
Host: 192.168.1.242:8100
User-Agent: Mozilla/5.0 (Macintosh; U; PPC Mac OS X
  Mach-O; en-US; rv:1.7.8) Gecko/20050511
Accept: text/xml,application/xml,application/xhtml+xml,text/html;
  q=0.9,text/plain;q=0.8,image/png,*/*;q=0.5
Accept-Language: en-us,en;q=0.5
Accept-Encoding: gzip,deflate
Accept-Charset: ISO-8859-1,utf-8;q=0.7,*;q=0.7
Keep-Alive: 300
Connection: keep-alive
```

Response

```
HTTP/1.1 200 OK
Date: Mon, 21 Aug 2006 14:51:40 GMT
```

```
Server: Apache/2.0.53 (Ubuntu)
Last-Modified: Thurs, 11 May 2006 17:43:45 GMT
ETag: "41419c-45-438fd340"
Accept-Ranges: bytes
Content-Length: 69
Keep-Alive: timeout=15, max=100
Connection: Keep-Alive
Content-Type: text/html; charset=UTF-8
```

The request is an HTTP GET, which means the HTTP server needs to retrieve the data associated with the resource. The operation becomes specific when the request provides the HTTP headers Accept, Accept-Language, Accept-Encoding, and Accept-Charset. These HTTP headers are accepted by the HTTP server and serve as an indication of what content to send.

Focusing on the HTTP header Accept, the values are a series of MIME-encoded identifiers that the client will accept. The order and type of the identifier are important, because they specify the priority of the content that the client wants to receive from the server. The logic is to send the content available with the priority defined by the client that, for example, forces the server to send HTML content before plain-text content. The priority of content is the priority of the MIME types as defined in the HTTP specification. The following list is generated when you reorder the example request:

```
1.    application/xhtml+xml
2.    text/xml
3.    application/xml
4.    image/png
5.    text/html;q=0.9
6.    text/plain;q=0.8
7.    */*;q=0.5
```

The ordering of the identifiers depends on the identifier specialization and its q value. A MIME type identifier that has no q value indicates a default value of 1.0. When a q value exists, you must lower the priority of the MIME type identifier to the value specified by the q value. Identifier specialization is when one identifier is a higher priority because the specified content is more specific than the other identifier. In the list of priorities, the identifier text/xml is more specific than */* because */* means everything. Additionally, text/xml is more specific than text/*, and hence text/xml is a higher priority.

Note that the first MIME identifier from the HTTP conversation is text/xml, and the second is application/xml. Yet, in the priority order, the first MIME identifier is application/xhtml+xml. I made this assumption after having read the HTTP and MIME specifications, but I feel it's a bug that just happened to work.

Let's dissect the example request to understand why this bug happened to work. The MIME type identifiers application/xml, text/xml, and application/xhtml-xml are considered specific, and each has a q value of 1. If the server follows the ordering of the MIME types, it means that the browser prefers receiving XML content to HTML or XHTML content. The application/xml and text/xml MIME types are XML content, albeit the XML content could be XHTML content.

Reading the specification solves the problem with the phrase regarding the priority ordering of the MIME types, which generically says that a more specific MIME type is ordered before a less specific MIME type. This means application/xhtml-xml is ordered before application/xml and text/xml, because application/xhtml-xml is specifically formatted XML.

The example HTTP conversation illustrated that the browser was explicit in what it wanted. There are browsers though that do not explicitly indicate what they want, as illustrated by the following HTTP conversation.

Request

```
GET /services/historical/AMZN/2006
Accept: */*
Accept-Language: en-ca
Accept-Encoding: gzip, deflate
User-Agent: Mozilla/4.0 (compatible; MSIE 6.0; Windows NT 5.1; SV1;
  .NET CLR 2.0.50215; .NET CLR 1.1.4322)
Connection: Keep-Alive
```

Some browsers send the Accept type identifier */*, which essentially means, "Send me whatever you've got; I will accept it." Such a request is extremely unhelpful and makes it difficult to implement the separation of the resource from the representation. The solution to this problem is to define a default representation for the identifier */*. It's not an ideal solution, but a solution begot out of the necessity to send something. Most likely, those clients that send */* are HTML-based Web browsers.

Reality of Representations and Resources

Let's take a look back at Figure 4-3 and the blogging architecture. Using the architecture that separates the resources from the representation, you could define a single URL (instead of three) for the three possible representations (RSS, Atom, and HTML).

Figure 4-3 showed how not to build a Web application that generated the three different formats. Is the separation of resource and representation in conflict with the discussion we've been having thus far? For the most part, the answer is yes. The separation of resource from representation is a solution when you know that the client is not an Ajax client. The difference between an Ajax client and a non-Ajax client is that the Ajax client knows how to reference and process a Web service, and the non-Ajax client doesn't. Thus for a non-Ajax client, you must send the content and formatting to the client in a single step.

Now let's see whether the separation of resource from representation makes sense in an Ajax/Web service combination. Generally speaking, the separation doesn't matter. It matters only when the client is interested in receiving different Web service formats, such as CSV or JSON.

This introduces the next problem, which has to do with the fact that the Internet is not based solely on Ajax clients. The Internet has oodles of different client types, so you need to be able to support all of those formats. The solution is to split the tasks into separate applications, as illustrated in Figure 5-7.

The architecture contains two HTTP servers, both of which can expose themselves using the same URL. Because there are multiple HTTP servers, there will be multiple server name entries or multiple HTTP server ports. Figure 5-7 can be made more specific in terms of naming, as Figure 5-8 shows.

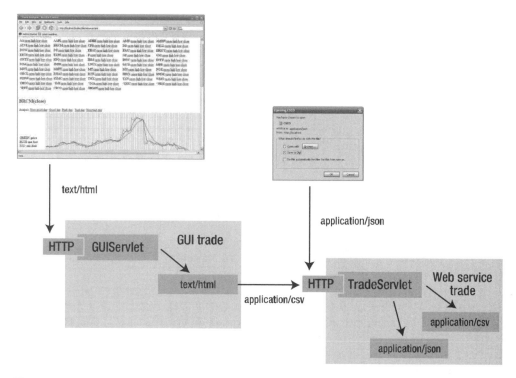

Figure 5-7. *A complete application architecture that implements the separation of resource from representation*

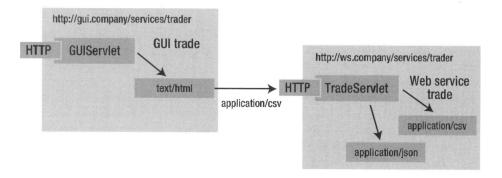

Figure 5-8. *URLs and DNS entries of the complete architecture*

The DNS entry level shows a clear distinction between the individual servers, even though the URLs are completely identical. When you reference URLs, you generally don't use absolute addressing but relative referencing, as the following HTML illustrates:

```
<a href="/services/historical/DELL/2004">Dell 2004 Historical</a>
```

Notice in the HTML that the `href` attribute doesn't specify the server `gui.company.com` or `ws.company.com`. Only the end client knows what the original server identifier is and will call the right server when resolving a URL. This gives you the flexibility to move functionality from one server to another without having to update the URLs in the application.

Looking back at Figure 5-7, the browser client references the server `gui.company.com` and sends a request `/services/trader` asking for `text/html`. The server supporting that format generates the content automatically. While generating the content, however, the `GUIServlet` is acting like a mashup. A mashup is when you generate content based on content defined elsewhere. The `GUIServlet` consumes a data Web service to generate the GUI. Ajax and the GUI Web service consume the same data Web service, making the application data consistent. Going back to the blogger application, when the data Web service is updated internally, there is no need to update Ajax or the GUI Web service.

This illustrates the next advantage of having multiple applications and HTTP servers. When generating the HTML content, you'll likely not only be pulling data from a single Web service, but you'll be generating content based on multiple Web services. Thus, you don't want a single Web service to support all representations, as the resulting Web service would be too complex and inefficient.

In Figure 5-7, the mashup server `gui.company.com` doesn't need to generate GUI content. The mashup server could have been another Web service that generated more complex content. The idea behind using multiple Web services is to modularize the application using Web services as the contract.

Going back to resources and representations, the Web service server `ws.company.com` can generate three types of content:

- JSON (`application/json`)

- XML (`application/xml`)

- CSV (`application/csv`)

The three types of content represent the same data in three different formats. The rule of thumb for separation of resource from representation is: same data, different formats. If the representation `text/html` were supported on the server `ws.company.com`, then the Web service would have to get data from other sources and break the rule.

The rule of thumb is the result of building many Web applications that make use of Web services. It's difficult and complex to build a universal Web service that can support all representations. Therefore, even though the theory says you should, it is simply not possible in practice. What is possible is the support of formats that are similar in purpose. The formats JSON, XML, and CSV are similar in that they represent data. The formats HTML, XHTML, and SWF are similar in that they represent GUI elements. In a nutshell, the separation of resource from representation makes sense when the representations have similar purposes.

Supporting HTML Pages with Relative URLs

Looking closely at Figure 5-8, you'll see that the idea of having GUI URLs identical to the service URLs sounds like a good idea, but it's questionable from an implementation perspective. Referencing the blog application and Figure 4-13 in particular, notice how the GUI component is referenced using the URL `/blog/index.html`, and the services component is referenced using the URL `/services/blog/entries/current`. In that particular example, the GUI URL doesn't match the Web service URL. The Web service URL is hard-coded into the `index.html` page and cannot be adapted.

Imagine creating a generic HTML page that is used to display the individual Atom entries that use the page `/blog/index.html`. It's not possible, because the URL is hard-coded into the page. If you want to see the blog entries accessible by the service URL `/services/blog/entries/2006`, you would need to create the GUI URL `/blog/2006/index.html` and the page `index.html`. Now imagine if your Web service can reference more than 100 entries. It would mean creating more than 100 `index.html` pages, because you would need to hard-code the different URLs into the HTML page.

At this point, you would question the efficiency of using an SOA architecture in the context of a Web application. The original blogging architecture, illustrated in Figure 4-3, solved this problem by generating the pages dynamically based on the query parameters.

One solution would be to convert the GUI service to use a technology such as the one illustrated in Figure 5-7, but to use a Web service instead of communicating to a database. However, that would not be an effective solution, because you haven't solved anything other than replacing a database technology with a Web service technology.

You want to define a solution where you can use a single HTML page to service multiple GUI HTML requests. If you call the URLs `/services/historical/2006` or `/services/historical/2005`, a single HTML page will be loaded that then references the appropriate Web service URL. Without the help of a server-side technology to get a general static HTML page to load, context-specific information would seem complicated.

The solution of converting a specific request into a request for a general HTML page that knows the specific request URL is trivial if you were to use the Apache Web server HTTPD:

```
RewriteEngine On
RewriteRule ^/services/historical(.*)$ /gui/historical.html
```

The example configuration directive uses an Apache module called mod_rewrite.[1] You can use mod_rewrite to rewrite one URL into another without indicating to the client that a redirect has occurred. The configuration directive used to start mod_rewrite, `RewriteEngine`, has two arguments: a URL to match, and a URL to be written. Both parts can use regular expressions, and to use mod_rewrite in an effective manner, you do need to understand regular expressions. In the example, the first part of the rule says that whatever URL is requested and starts with `/services/historical` should be redirected to the URL `/gui/historical/index.html`. If the client calls `/services/historical/2006` or `/services/historical/2005`, then the content at the URL `/gui/historical/index.html` will be returned.

For those of you who know mod_rewrite, you might look at the rewrite rule and think that the original URL will be lost. From the perspective of the server, the original URL will be lost, but that doesn't matter since the server will not be generating content. However, from the perspective of the client side, no information has been lost, as Figure 5-9 illustrates.

---

1. If you plan on making extensive use of mod_rewrite, I highly advise that you purchase Rich Bowen's book, *The Definitive Guide to Apache mod_rewrite* (Berkeley, CA: Apress, 2006).

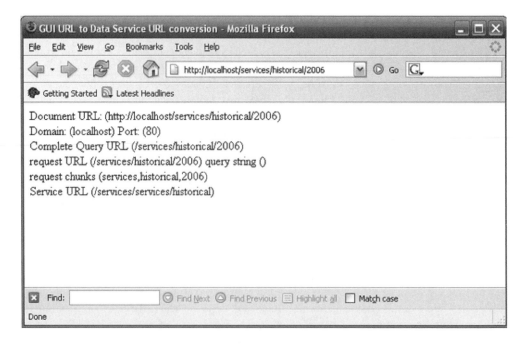

Figure 5-9. *The content* /gui/historical.html *being displayed for the URL* /services/
historical/2006

Notice how the browser thinks that the content is associated with the URL /services/
historical/2006. If you were to use the URL /services/historical/2005, then the same content would be generated. What is clever about this is that you've mimicked a Web application
architecture where the server generates the content dynamically with static pages that make
Web service requests.

The last missing piece is the client calling the appropriate server-side URL. To make this
work, you need to make sure you never hard-code URLs into the HTML page. Whenever you
need to reference a URL in the HTML page, you need to use an algorithm. The algorithm will
figure out what the calling URL is and will give you a mechanism to create the appropriate
Web service URL dynamically.

To explain this algorithm, first let's examine the HTML page that uses the algorithm, and
then the algorithm itself. The following HTML page uses the algorithm:

```html
<html>
  <head>
    <title>Historical Data</title>
    <script language="JavaScript" src="/scripts/jaxson/common.js"></script>
  </head>
<script language="JavaScript" type="text/javascript">
URLEngine.serviceURL = function() {
    return "/" + this.requestChunks.slice( 0,
        this.requestChunks.length - 1).join( "/");
}
```

```
function Initialize() {
    document.getElementById( "serviceurl").innerHTML =
        URLEngine.serviceURL();
}
</script>
  <body onload="Initialize()">
    Service URL (<span id="serviceurl">service url</span>)
  </body>
</html>
```

The HTML page shows the bare essentials that are used to determine the Web service URL in the context of a static HTML page. The bold code represents the algorithm that is used to translate the GUI URL into a Web services URL. In the bold code, a function is assigned to the method URLEngine.serviceURL. The object URLEngine is instantiated when common.js is loaded. When instantiated, URLEngine dissects the URL used to load the page. The array requestChunks represents an individual piece of the URL. For example, if the URL were /services/historical/ 2006, then the array would contain services, historical, and 2006.

In the implementation of the serviceURL function, the logic is to recombine the URL pieces. This is the simplest of all possible implementations, but it can be more complicated. The serviceURL function illustrates the ability to algorithmically determine a URL based on the URL used to call the content of the static HTML page. As explained earlier, the GUI and data URLs don't need to match 100%, but you need to have a mapping that you can express algorithmically.

The following code shows the complete implementation of URLEngine:

```
var URLEngine = {
    splitApart : function() {
        this.docURL = location.href;
        var leadSlashes = this.docURL.indexOf("//");
        var delResource = this.docURL.substring(leadSlashes + 2,
            this.docURL.length);

        var nextSlash = delResource.indexOf("/");

        this.domain = delResource.substring(0, nextSlash);
        var portOffset = this.domain.indexOf( ":");
        if( portOffset != -1) {
            this.domain = this.domain.substring( 0, portOffset);
            this.port = this.domain.substring( portOffset + 1,
                this.domain.length).valueOf();
        }
        else {
            this.port = 80;
        }
        this.completeQueryURL = delResource.substring(
            nextSlash, delResource.length);
        var questionMarkOffset = this.completeQueryURL.indexOf( "?");
```

```
        if( questionMarkOffset == -1) {
            this.request = this.completeQueryURL;
            this.queryString = "";
        }
        else {
            this.request = this.completeQueryURL.substring(
                0, questionMarkOffset);
            this.queryString = this.completeQueryURL.substring(➥
                questionMarkOffset + 1, this.completeQueryURL.length);
        }
        this.requestChunks = this.request.split( "/");
        this.requestChunks = this.requestChunks.slice(
            1, this.requestChunks.length);
    }
};
```

`URLEngine.splitApart();`

The essence of the `URLEngine.splitApart` is to take apart the URL referenced by the property `location.href`. The purpose of the property `location.href` is to identify the URL loaded by the browser window or frame. The property value contains a complete URL—for example, `http://localhost/services/historical/2006`. The details of the `URLEngine` implementation dissect the complete URL into individual pieces: `domain`, `port`, `queryString`, and `request`. The function `splitApart` is called when `common.js` is called. Thus, the `URLEngine` is ready for URL processing when the `body.onload` event is executed.

Closed Access Web Services

With the creation of REST-based Web services and their ability to store and retrieve data comes the question of how to store data. In a SQL database, you can use the SQL `SELECT` to query the database and generate a result set. That's what you're doing for 90% or so of the database operations and the Web.

However, to be able to query a database or Web site, you have to have data to query or browse. This raises the question of how to put the data into the Web. In the case of the database, the answer is easy: you execute SQL statements, and data is stored in the database. However, it is possible to use C and some file operations to add entries into the database. Well, at least that is theoretically possible. The problem is that companies such as Oracle, Microsoft, and IBM aren't going to tell you how their files are structured.

That lack of documentation is the decision maker of whether you use REST to store data, or whether you use background processes. The database vendors aren't going to allow you to add data to their database using C file operations, because you would corrupt the database. Whenever you execute a SQL `insert` statement, a whole host of things happen (such as indexing and optimization) that wouldn't occur if you accessed the database directly.

Let's go back to the original question: Should REST-based Web services be closed access? The answer is yes, whenever possible. For example, it might not be possible when you're dealing with legacy applications such as the blogging application.

You want a REST-based Web service to have closed access, because it is your next-generation data source. Relational databases are wonderful persistence tools, but they have their limits, especially in the context of Internet-based applications. You could use object-oriented databases, but they haven't caught on for one reason or another—the reality is that most data is stored in relational databases. With REST-based Web services, you want to encapsulate the logic on the server and expose a set of URLs that represent Web service operations.

Recipe Summary

This recipe illustrated how to build universal Web services using REST-based techniques. Remember the following points:

- You should treat Web services as components and only implement the functionality necessary.

- As the example illustrates, you don't need to componentize the Web service. That doesn't mean that componentization is not necessary, nor does it mean that you should ignore good object-oriented design principles. It does mean that you don't always need to componentize, and you should consider the Web service boundary as part of your componentization.

- Only create code components when it makes sense. The aim is to componentize your application using Web services.

- Your Web service will be a success based on its interface and the usability of the interface, not on the code behind the interface. For example, if you need a fast response time, write code that is fast, even if that means using arrays instead of linked lists and so on.

- Using classes instead of components doesn't mean that you cannot configure the behavior of your Web service. For example, you don't have to hard-code the URLs used to define the Web service. Configurability and componentization are two orthogonal issues.

- When defining the Web service, focus on the URLs and the data that the URLs accept and generate.

6-1. Implementing Web Services for Large or Slow Data Sets

In the context of an Ajax and REST application, Web services that expose large data sets or slow data sets deserve special attention because of the requirement that the resulting solution be as efficient as possible.

This recipe covers the following aspects of implementing a Web service that exposes large data sets or slow data sets:

- Understanding the context of what a large or slow data set application is

- Outlining the overall architecture of the solution

- Determining how an application should be architected in coding terms

Problem

You want to create Web services that expose large data sets or data sets that take a long time to generate.

Theory

Many developers experience the need to show a huge number of records to end users. The first reaction of most developers to this issue is, "No, it can't be done." Yet when you look at the Google and Yahoo! search engines, you see that it can be done. This recipe sets out to solve such a problem—specifically, how to display 64,000 records in a Web browser.

Please note that the solution for a large data set or slow data set Web service is very specialized and should not be used as a general solution. The added complexity of the solution makes it impractical for use in every application. Web services that are a single request and response are simple and require no management of state or callbacks. In this recipe's solution, state and callbacks are required. Efficiency is one of the requirements of this solution, but remember that efficiency is relative, and the solution will be as efficient as possible for the context.

The simplest illustration of the problem of large data sets that take a long time to generate is a search, as shown in Figure 6-1.

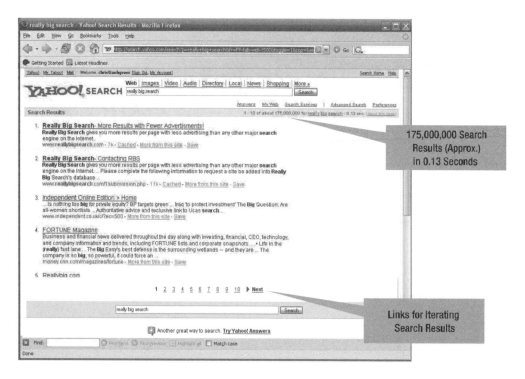

Figure 6-1. *Yahoo! search results for the phrase "really big search"*

As you know, in any search engine, you enter a term or phrase in a text box, click the Search button, and the relevant HTML pages are returned for the term or phrase you typed in. Whether the search engine presents useful results is not the point of this solution. What is relevant is the fact that a search was executed that resulted in an HTML page displaying 10 results per page of the roughly 175,000,000 available results.

The HTML search result page looks good, and the search took only 0.13 seconds. The search speed should amaze users, but I tend to be cynical. I am sure that the 0.13 seconds is not a lie, but the question is, what does the 0.13 seconds measure? Is the 0.13 seconds a measure of having found the search terms in 175,000,000 pages? I doubt it, because if this were the case, it would mean each page was found in 0.00000000074286 seconds, or each page was found in two clock cycles of a 3GHz CPU. These statistics should make anybody wary of the results found, even if parallel processes were involved.

So if the statistics are very approximate to the point of being irrelevant, what is actually going on? The search engine is solving the problem of large or slow data sets using an illusion. The illusion is that the search engine is presenting you with the information in a fast manner, even though you are seeing only an extremely small sliver of the total information.

It is not difficult for a search engine to search its indices and return 10 results of a huge data set. As the 10 results are generated and returned as a single HTML page, the second and third batches of results are being generated. I would even hazard a guess that Yahoo! generates a result list of 100 found links. I guess that it is probably a result set of 100 elements because at the bottom of the page there are 10 page links of search results. Multiply 10 and 10, and you get 100 links.

What is very interesting is how Yahoo! allows you to retrieve the result set. Consider the URL generated by the query:

```
http://search.yahoo.com/search?p=really+big+search& ➥
fr=FP-tab-web-t500&toggle=1&cop=&ei=UTF-8
```

Based on your experience with the REST URLs discussed in the previous recipes, you should be able to guess what the individual query parameters do. Before I explain what I think the query parameters do, let's look at the URL that appears after clicking the second page link (indicated by "2" at the bottom of the results):

```
http://search.yahoo.com/search?p=really+big+search& ➥
toggle=1&ei=UTF-8&fr=FP-tab-web-t500&b=11
```

From this URL, it seems that /search is a root URL from a REST perspective. So does this mean that executing the URL /search would return all search results? In theory, yes, but I doubt it actually would, because this would mean returning an alphabetical listing of all HTML pages indexed in Yahoo!, which is completely impractical from an implementation perspective.

I think Yahoo! is using a REST-ful approach, because if you click the Images link at the top of the results page, the following URL is generated:

```
http://images.search.yahoo.com/search/images?p=really+big+search& ➥
toggle=1&ei=UTF-8&fr=FP-tab-web-t500&fr2=tab-web
```

Notice that the Images URL is /search/images, meaning that images belong to the search URL, but they represent a more specific type of search. In a REST Web service approach, this represents the ideal naming strategy. Also notice how the query parameters for a general and image-based search are identical. This again illustrates a well-engineered REST Web service. The parameters of the URL represent a way of filtering the huge amount of search results. The first method involves filtering on the query itself, which is defined by the p query parameter. This is a very clever way of defining a result set, because it means that multiple people searching for the same terms will see the same view. From a search perspective, Yahoo! does not distinguish between users.

Since multiple people can see the same results, a way of identifying which results are to be returned needs to be identified. The b query parameter serves that purpose in that it defines the start index of the search results. If you were doubtful that Yahoo! keeps a server-side result set, then the b query parameter should convince you of this. The b query parameter is a numerical value that in effect says, "Please return the links available at the list indices 11, 12, 13, 14, 15, 16, 17, 18, 19, and 20 of the search result set really big search."

The Yahoo! example illustrates that a key component to presenting large data sets is creating an illusion. The illusion in this case is presenting a subset of the results, with the remainder of the results presented when they are requested. So if a SQL query results in 64,000 records, the illusion is to present the top 100 or so results, while in the background preparing another batch of 100 or so results.

The following list presents the attributes of a situation in which you would apply the techniques defined in this recipe:

- The data set could be construed as infinite. Even though there are theoretical limits, from a practical perspective the data set seems infinite. For example, any mathematical algorithm that generates a series of data, such as all squares of the numbers 1 to 1 million, could be construed as infinite. Another example is a search engine linked to an enormous database that generates a huge result set when the database is queried.

- The data set is not available at the time of the request. In this context, you make a request that triggers a sequence of events. Because the events require some computing time, the results are not available immediately. For example, in the case of a search engine mashup, delivery of the results from the individual search engines requires a small amount of time. Another example is the profit and loss calculation for an investment portfolio.

- The data is a single block of many elements, and the block must be considered as a single contiguous piece of data.

Solution

The architecture for large or slow data sets requires a server component that supports multithreading or multiprocesses, and a client component that includes a two-channel communication mechanism. The architecture is laid out in Figure 6-2.

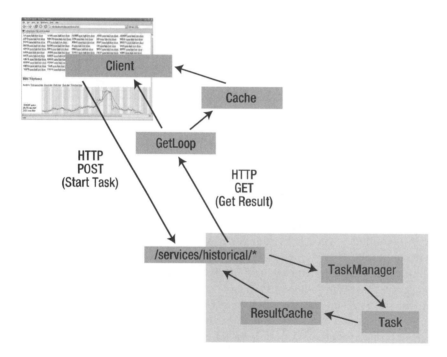

Figure 6-2. *Large and slow data set architecture*

The architecture shown in Figure 6-2 is an example historical ticker application. The client has two interactions: HTTP POST and HTTP GET to the same URL, /services/historical/*. At a technical level, the two interactions are separate, but they often work together. The POST interaction is used to send data, and the GET interaction is used to retrieve data. Technically, a REST Web service implies such an interaction: to start a task, a POST request is sent, and the answers for the task are retrieved using a GET.

Two channels are used so that the client can receive multiple answers to an executing task. This ability is a necessity when you are working with large or slow data sets. You cannot execute a task and wait for the complete answer, even though using XMLHttpRequest in asynchronous mode would not stop the browser from functioning. You want to retrieve data on a piecemeal basis because you want to display the results as soon as they are available.

On the server side, two components implement the interactions: TaskManager and ResultCache. TaskManager responds to all POST requests and executes the appropriate task. The individual tasks then generate their results and add them to ResultCache. When the client executes a GET, the data from ResultCache is retrieved.

TaskManager is only responsible for executing the tasks and managing the reference to ResultCache. TaskManager is not responsible for knowing the details of the results generated or the nature of the task that is executed.

Managing the Client Request/Response Cycle

For the moment, let's ignore the URLs and the server side, and focus on the client side. We can define the most amazing URLs and the most interesting server side, but if the client side functions inefficiently, everything else does not matter. Defining what the client can and cannot do goes a long way toward defining the server URLs and server-side code.

First, let's look at a mapping example along the lines of http://map.search.ch or http://maps.google.com. You will see the logic to make the scrolling of the map smooth, as the map is composed of a number of image pieces (see Figure 6-3).

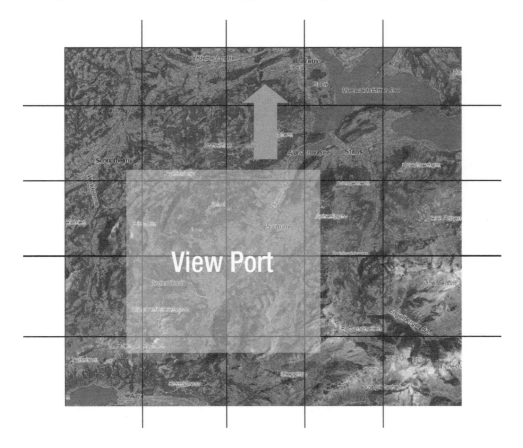

Figure 6-3. *Mapping logic*

Figure 6-3 shows a square that represents the view port. The *view port* is the visible map pieces as viewed by an HTML page. Each view port can display four complete map pieces, and it provides four ways to navigate. In Figure 6-3, an arrow pointing north is shown, indicating that the user wants to move the view port north.

Based on this configuration, let's walk through how the architecture in Figure 6-2 can be implemented as a series of steps:

1. The client surfs to the URL and loads the HTML page that contains the view port.

2. The HTML page sends a POST asking to load four map pieces.

3. TaskManager begins a task that retrieves the requested map pieces. The task adds the map pieces to ResultCache.

4. The HTML page executes a periodic loop that asks if the requested map pieces have been added to ResultCache. If the pieces have been added, then they are retrieved and displayed.

At this moment, there is a disconnect, as the identifier of the map pieces has not been defined. When the HTML page loads, which map pieces are loaded? Do you load the default? And if you do load the default, what exactly *is* the default? When loading the map pieces, you need to first determine how to identify a map piece. The best strategy is to use a coordinate system, as shown in Figure 6-4.

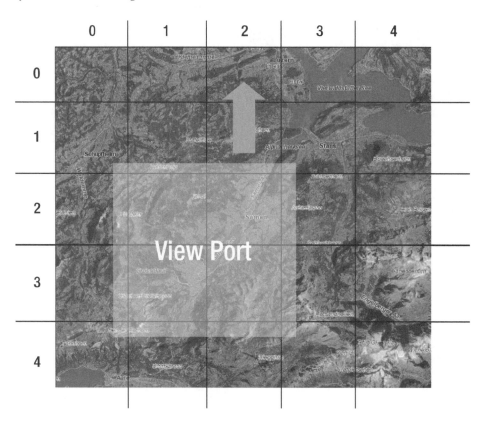

Figure 6-4. *Mapping logic with coordinates*

Adding coordinates as shown in Figure 6-4 is not an original idea by any means, as any point on this planet can be expressed in terms of longitude and latitude. What is different about the coordinates in Figure 6-4 is that they do not apply to the lines; they apply to the map pieces. In this example, the view port would be loaded with the map pieces with the coordinates (2,1), (2,2), (3,1), and (3,2).

Identifying and loading the individual map pieces does not make a complete Web application. If you have ever used `http://map.search.ch` or `http://maps.google.com`, you know that scrolling a map results in very little lag time. Scrolling a map through the view port is smooth, not jerky. To optimize and make the scrolling look smooth, a look-ahead has to be executed. In the case of the images, the look-ahead uses the `img` tag.

The look-ahead of Figure 6-4 would preload the map pieces (1,0), (1,1), (1,2), (1,3), (2,0), (3,0), (4,0), (4,1), (4,2), (4,3), (3,3), and (2,3). Loading all of these pieces might take some time, and by preloading the map pieces, a cache is created that speeds up the application. You need to define what the look-ahead algorithm will be, and then load those pieces. Using a look-ahead algorithm is a good idea, because the time taken for someone to view the pieces and then react involves a slight delay, giving the application time to look ahead and see what should be loaded.

Defining the Constraints of the Client

The mapping example shows what you need to do to manage large or infinite data sets, although all applications that work with large or infinite data sets have the following common attributes on the client side:

- The referencing of all data can be defined. In the case of the mapping application, this means assigning coordinates to all map pieces. You want the data to be prefixed with a reference so that the client can jump to the data using a calculated URL approach. This does not mean that data available is at the URL, as the server side might not yet have generated that data. The references can be timestamps, coordinates, or an incremental counter, but they must possess the ability to be determined before the data is loaded.

- The client will directly reference the view port data and the data that will probably be viewed. The data that will probably be viewed is the look-ahead data that is preloaded. The algorithm to determine the data that is probably going to be viewed is completely dependent on the application and the user interface of the application. For example, most mapping applications have an arrow to move the map up and down by one map piece. If a user interface were to offer an arrow called "Jump 100 Units," then the selection that is probably going to be viewed would include the immediate as well as the "Jump 100 Units" map pieces. The idea behind the data that is probably going to be viewed is to let the client or server preload the information, which makes the iteration of the data seem like one smooth process.

In our case, we are building a stock ticker viewing application. The client will have the capability to navigate a list of stock tickers and then view the history of those tickers. In the snapshots, the historical data is not illustrated, because the focus is on the navigation and data manipulations.

Figure 6-5 shows the HTML page that has loaded the references for the data.

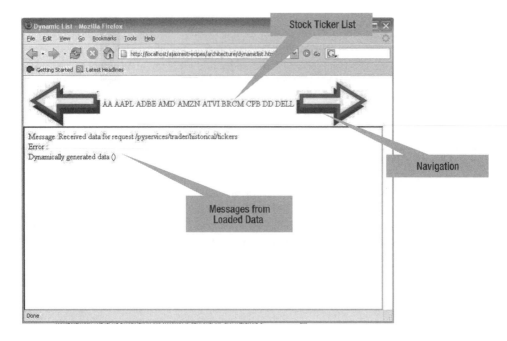

Figure 6-5. *HTML page loading index for large or slow data sets*

At the top of Figure 6-5 are a number of stock ticker identifiers, with a big arrow on either side. The stock ticker identifiers represent the data that can be loaded into the big empty space of the HTML page. The arrows on the sides of the ticker list are used to navigate the ticker list.

List navigation makes or breaks the functionality or performance of the client. In the case of the mapping application, users navigate by using the mouse to select and drag map pieces. In the case of the ticker example, users navigate using the arrows by moving the mouse over a ticker. Under no circumstances should you use a list box or a combo box for navigation—these elements cannot hold a large amount of data, so navigating with them can be an unpleasant experience.

Slashdot (www.slashdot.org) has managed to solve the problem of data sets being too large by using personal preference techniques, as shown in Figures 6-6 and 6-7.

Something people like about Slashdot is the fact that they can read a story and then post their opinion on the topic—sort of like a book club for Internet geeks. Controversial Slashdot stories can garner over 300 postings, some of which are garbage but others of which are interesting.

Slashdot was the first Web site to successfully employ a technique called *metamoderation*. Metamoderation is when the readers are their own referees and determine whether a posting is interesting. Good postings that are funny or interesting have a higher ranking than those that are drivel. Using their personal preferences, readers can choose at what level they want to read messages—in other words, they can select to read only the most interesting postings if they like. It is a system that works.

Figure 6-6. *Personal preferences used to filter Slashdot stories*

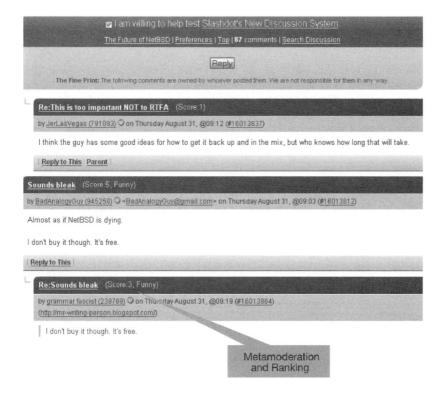

Figure 6-7. *Metamoderation and rankings used to filter Slashdot postings*

The Slashdot preferences and filtering mechanism is a navigation mechanism. Traditionally, a filtering system is like a SQL SELECT statement that has an associated WHERE clause. The WHERE clause acts like a filter and selects only those entries that fulfill the WHERE clause. If you want to view the entries that did not fulfill the WHERE clause, you need to execute another SELECT statement, and that is not a good navigation mechanism. The Slashdot filtering mechanism, however, allows you to view items that are not part of your preferences. Granted, the unviewed items are less conspicuous, as Figure 6-8 shows.

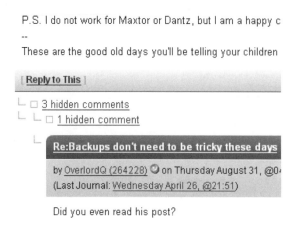

Figure 6-8. *Slashdot navigation driven by a filtering mechanism*

Figure 6-8 shows two links with the text and three hidden comments followed by another hidden comment. The data associated with the links is not shown because it doesn't meet the criteria of the preferences. But if there was a comment that you found interesting, you could look at the hidden comments to see the complete conversation.

I detoured from the stock ticker navigation (see Figure 6-5) to the Slashdot navigation to illustrate the fact that navigation comes in many different forms. When designing a navigation mechanism, you need to figure out what your data is and then separate it into two blocks: metadata and data (see Figure 6-9).

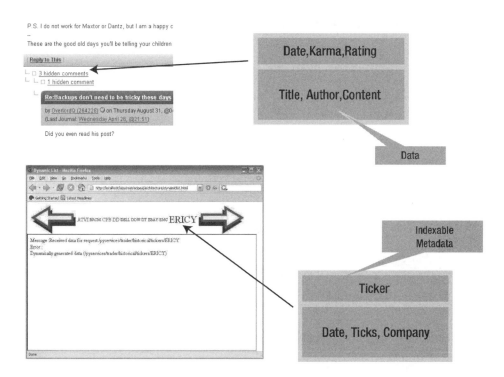

Figure 6-9. *Two examples of how data is split into metadata and data for use in a navigation scheme*

In the two examples of data in Figure 6-9, each piece of data is split into two parts: metadata that describes the data and the data itself. The metadata of Slashdot is Date, Karma, and Rating. Using these pieces of metadata, the data can be organized and displayed at the right moment. The metadata can be used to create an index in a relational database, but it need not be the only information used to create an index. The metadata is an index for the navigation that is created on the HTML page.

Implementing the HTML Client

For the remainder of this section, we'll examine the HTML page in Figure 6-5. As displayed in Figure 6-9, the metadata for the stocks are the tickers. Ticker information is loaded based on the tickers clicked by the user. We want to achieve fluid behavior, so that the user does not have to wait while content is being downloaded.

I explain the code in chunks. First, I illustrate the overall architecture and then I fill in the individual pieces. The following is the source code for the entire HTML page.

Source: /client/ajaxrestrecipes/architecture/dynamiclist.html

```
<html>
  <head>
    <title>Dynamic List</title>
    <script language="JavaScript"
     src="/scripts/jaxson/common.js"></script>
    <script language="JavaScript"
     src="/scripts/jaxson/cachecommunications.js">
    </script>
    <script language="JavaScript" src="/scripts/jaxson/uimorphing.js"></script>
    <script language="JavaScript" src="/scripts/json.js"></script>
  </head>
<script type="text/javascript">

function Initialize() {
    DynamicIterator.initialize("display", "listElements");
}
 // Removed for clarity
</script>

  <body onload="Initialize()">
    <table>
      <tr id="listElements">
        <td onmouseover="DynamicIterator.startIteration( -1)"➥
            onmouseout="DynamicIterator.stopIteration()">➥
             <img src="/images/left.jpg"/></td>
        <td onmouseover="DynamicIterator.highlightItem(this)" id="1"></td>
        <td onmouseover="DynamicIterator.highlightItem(this)" id="2"></td>
        <td onmouseover="DynamicIterator.highlightItem(this)" id="3"></td>
        <td onmouseover="DynamicIterator.highlightItem(this)" id="4"></td>
        <td onmouseover="DynamicIterator.highlightItem(this)" id="5"></td>
        <td onmouseover="DynamicIterator.highlightItem(this)" id="6"></td>
        <td onmouseover="DynamicIterator.highlightItem(this)" id="7"></td>
        <td onmouseover="DynamicIterator.highlightItem(this)" id="8"></td>
        <td onmouseover="DynamicIterator.highlightItem(this)" id="9"></td>
        <td onmouseover="DynamicIterator.highlightItem(this)" id="10"></td>
        <td onmouseover="DynamicIterator.startIteration( 1)"➥
            onmouseout="DynamicIterator.stopIteration()">➥
             <img src="/images/right.jpg"/></td>
      </tr>
    </table>
    <iframe id="display"➥
      style="top:100px;left:0px;width:400px;height:500px;position:absolute"➥
      src="hello.html"></iframe>
  </body>
</html>
```

In the source code at the top of the HTML page are a number of `script` tags that reference a number of JavaScript files. The JavaScript files contain the reusable logic that has been used previously and can be used in different contexts for manipulating large or slow data sets.

Our main interest right now is the bold HTML code, which represents the base structure of the large and slow data sets. There is a `table` tag and an `iframe` tag. The `table` tag, in an abstract sense, represents the navigation of the data set, and how you structure the navigation depends on your personal preferences. The `iframe` represents the content of that data set. An `iframe` is used so that the navigation is separate from the display of the data. Separating these two actions using a physical HTML barrier makes it simpler to manage the generated output of each.

Our ticker example's navigation includes the facility to dynamically increase and decrease a ticker, making the navigation appear like the OS X navigation bar. Figure 6-10 shows the increasing font size of the text and the updating of the current selection in the `iframe`.

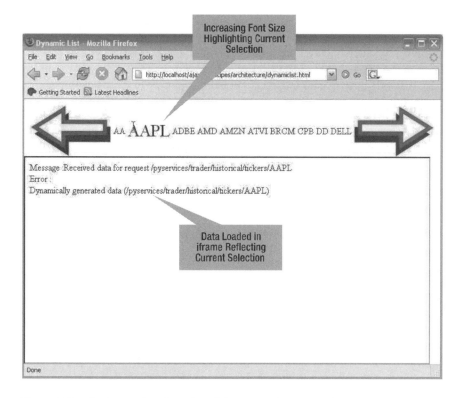

Figure 6-10. *The increasing font size of the text indicates a selection that updates the content of the* `iframe` *window.*

In Figure 6-10, `AAPL` is the currently selected ticker, and the data URL of `AAPL` (`/pyservices/trader/historical/tickers/AAPL`) is displayed in the output window. When the ticker increases in size, it causes an automatic alteration of the position of the HTML related to the table. If the navigation and content are displayed in a single HTML page, the browser will automatically reposition the data. And if the data is not repositioned, at least the browser will calculate whether or not a repositioning is necessary. In either of the calculations, the browser wastes resources and time. By using a floating `iframe`, the browser does not bother to recalculate the positioning of the content in the `iframe`, which increases performance and makes the navigation fluid. Keep in mind that the data will be loaded asynchronously, and JavaScript is not multithreaded. If your navigation is very resource intensive, whenever data arrives it will cause your navigation to appear choppy.

Getting back to the HTML, and in particular to the `table`, each of the cell elements (`td`) represents the output of a single element of the navigation data. Going back to Figure 6-9, the cell elements will contain a human-understandable form of the metadata.

The cell elements are split into two types: those that allow users to navigate metadata and those that link metadata to data. The following is the navigation of metadata code:

```
<td onmouseover="DynamicIterator.startIteration( -1)"
    onmouseout="DynamicIterator.stopIteration()">
<img src="/images/left.jpg"/></td>
```

The navigation of the metadata is unique in that the `onclick` event has not been implemented, but `onmouseout` and `onmouseover` have. `onclick` is not supported because clicking is overrated when navigating large or slow data sets. Removing the need to click reduces the particular problem of overclicking that most Web sites seem to promote.

If your users constantly need to click to navigate the data, they are likely to become mentally and digitally fatigued and give up after a number of clicks. For example, if you've ever visited an image Web site and clicked through hundreds of pictures, trying to find the one you're interested in, then you know how tedious this type of navigation experience can be. When creating your own navigation, it is important to make sure that you do not lose users' attention. One way to keep their attention is to avoid using click-based navigation.

Bound like bookends by the navigation elements are the data elements—here's an example:

```
<td onmouseover="DynamicIterator.highlightItem(this)" id="10"></td>
```

Again, this element has not implemented the `onclick` event to avoid click fatigue. When hovering their mouse over the element, users will expect to see the data associated with it. One exception to this rule is if users pass their mouse quickly over the HTML element—we'll examine that situation shortly. Each of the data elements has an ID with a number, with the idea being to create an array of HTML elements that can be addressed and manipulated directly. You do not need to do this, and you could create an array of elements when the navigation HTML content is loaded.

Clickless Navigation

In my opinion, we rely too much on clicking to navigate. This was not always the case: originally, the default for Unix operating systems was to assign focus to the window that the mouse was hovering over. It was the Windows world that promoted its own brand of clicking to accomplish tasks and activate items. Very quickly it became apparent that too many clicks were needed to accomplish even the most basic tasks. For example, to activate items in an application you usually have to click or double-click them.

■**Tip** Windows XP has a setting that enables you to single-click instead of double-click to activate items. You can find more information here: `http://www.microsoft.com/windowsxp/using/setup/learnmore/singleclick.mspx`.

HTML pages suffer because users are forced to use clicks to navigate results. In Figure 6-1, to view the results of the next page, you have to click. To view the results of the current page, you have to click. In the case of search results, when you're typically looking at only four or five pages, it's OK to click. It becomes unacceptable when you need to sift through hundreds of results.

The Windows world has understood this problem of viewing hundreds of items and cleanly solved it using sliders. *Sliders* allow you to examine data using a sliding operation, as shown in Figure 6-11.

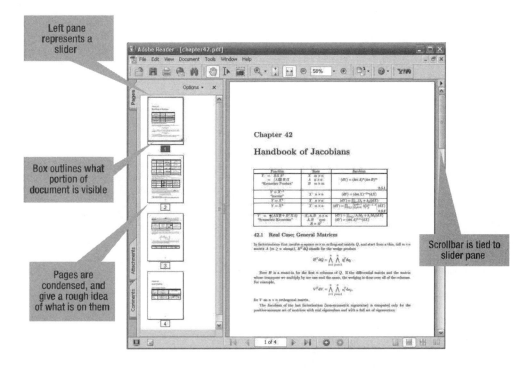

Figure 6-11. *Adobe Reader illustrates how sliders can be used to navigate very large data sets.*

Adobe Reader is not an HTML application, but I am referencing it here because I consider it an ideal illustration of how navigation can be customized to fit to the type of data you are iterating. By default when you open a PDF document in Adobe Reader, the application displays the document. To navigate the various pieces of the document, you use the tabs in the left pane. In Figure 6-11, the Pages tab was clicked, causing the page navigation slider to appear.

The page navigation slider has the appearance of a lengthy list box of images, which is exactly what it is. Each image is a condensed view of a page, which gives you a general idea of what is on the page. Using the slider gives you the ability to select with a click which page should be displayed in the right pane. Also present in the slider pane is an outlined box indicating which part of the page(s) is being displayed.

The Adobe Reader slider is a great way to sift through the data and find the page you want. However, what if the document you're looking at has thousands of pages? It would seem that the Adobe Reader slider pane has the same problem as all other sliders have—it's easy to iterate 10, or maybe 100 pages, but beyond that the navigation gets tedious.

The solution Adobe Reader implements is a *dual slider*. On the right side is a scroll bar, which has a much coarser iteration and allows you to quickly jump from page 1 to page 300. For larger documents, Adobe Reader will even tell you which page you are scrolling to.

The dual scrolling method, where one slider is a "coarse" slider and the other is a "fine" slider, is extremely effective, because moving the coarse slider also moves the fine slider. An effective strategy is to use the coarse slider to get you in the neighborhood of the content you're interested in, and then use the fine slider to hone in on the exact content.

Another approach of using a clickless navigation is http://www.dontclick.it, which is shown in Figure 6-12.

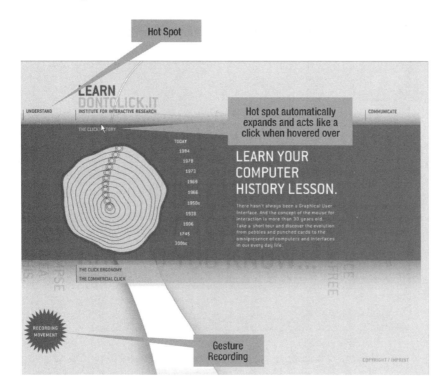

Figure 6-12. *Clickless navigation example*

The http://www.dontclick.it site is a great example of how you can navigate without clicking. To understand its sophistication, it is best if you actually experience it yourself. The site implements the following types of clickless navigation:

- Gesture history remembers where you navigated so that questions about your navigation can be asked in the future. The example question relates to whether you enjoy navigation without clicking.

- Navigation to an external Web site does not need a click. In the clickless navigation paradigm, the act of hovering for a specific period of time activates a new navigation.

- Moving around the Web site activates and deactivates pieces of functionality. This aspect is particularly useful for tablet-style computers.

The `http://www.dontclick.it` site illustrates how effective clickless navigation can be, without losing any functionality. All that is necessary is a change of perspective in how you navigate content.

Implementing this type of navigation using HTML is a challenge because JavaScript is not multithreaded. In a multithreaded scenario, you would have a thread watching what the mouse is doing and then acting. What you need to do in JavaScript is mimic multithreaded behavior. But even with mimicking, your success will be limited. The strategy that needs to be implemented is akin to throwing a ball and having a dog bring it back.

As an analogy, I have a good friend who has had dogs all of his life. One time when I visited him, he had an Australian shepherd. Anyone familiar with this breed knows that Australian shepherds have boundless energy, so my friend needed to find a way to release his dog's energy. His solution was golf. My friend was a budding golfer and he had problems with shorter shots, so he would practice his golf shots and let his dog bring the golf ball back. To finish the story, the dog loved the game, consistently brought the ball back, and my friend's golf game improved dramatically.

Now let's relate this story to the strategy of mimicking threads in JavaScript. When real multitasking isn't available, you need to use events. In the case of my friend, his events were hitting the golf ball and the dog bringing back the ball. Between taking the shot and waiting for the ball to come back, my friend could do other things (because initially he kept hitting the ball into the bushes); admittedly, his time to do other things was limited, but he could still have a conversation with someone else and so forth. Thus, when mimicking multithreading in JavaScript, you are not really implementing multithreading, but you are implementing a proactive event-driven architecture.

Mimicking Multithreading in JavaScript

A proactive event-driven architecture is like the dog asking (if it could), "When are you going to throw the ball, when, huh, when?" The pseudo-thread architecture is implemented using timeouts. The pseudo-thread is the result of a periodic function or object call, and the complete implementation is shown in the following source code.

Source: `/client/scripts/jaxson/common.js`

```
function ThreadObject() {
    this.obj = null;
    this.data = null;
    this.intervalId = null;
    this.isUsed = false;
}
```

```
ThreadObject.prototype.makeCall = function() {
    if( typeof( this.obj) == "function") {
        this.obj( this.data);
    }
    else if( typeof( this.obj) == "object") {
        this.obj.run( this.data);
    }
}

var Thread = {
    threadObjects : new Array(),
    startThread : function( obj, data, time) {
        for( var c1 = 0; c1 < this.threadObjects.length; c1 ++) {
            if( !this.threadObjects[ c1].isUsed) {
                this.threadObjects[ c1].isUsed = true;
                this.threadObjects[ c1].data = data;
                this.threadObjects[ c1].obj = obj;
                this.threadObjects[ c1].intervalId =➥
                    window.setInterval( "Thread.threadObjects[ " + c1 + "].➥
                    makeCall()", time);
                return this.threadObjects[ c1].intervalId;
            }
        }
        throw new Error( "Could not start a thread");
    },
    endThread : function( intervalId) {
        for( var c1 = 0; c1 < this.threadObjects.length; c1 ++) {
            if( this.threadObjects[ c1].intervalId == intervalId) {
                window.clearInterval( intervalId);
                this.threadObjects[ c1].isUsed = false;
            }
        }
    }
}

function InitializeThreads( maxThreads) {
    for( var c1 = 0; c1 < maxThreads; c1 ++) {
        Thread.threadObjects.push( new ThreadObject());
    }
}

InitializeThreads( 30);
```

In the source, two object types are defined: ThreadObject and Thread. The ThreadObject type is used to manage the mock thread, and Thread manages the mock threads. The InitializeThreads function is used to set up the pseudo-threading environment. To explain this source code, a top-down approach is used.

When the JavaScript file containing the pseudo-thread architecture is loaded, the InitializeThreads function is called with a parameter value of 30. InitializeThreads is used to initialize the array of pseudo-threads that will be called. Hard-coding to a limit of 30 threads may seem like a bad programming practice, but there is a reason for it.

To create a pseudo-thread, you create a periodic event, which means you need to use either the window.setInterval or window.setTimeout method. Calling either of these methods requires a function reference or a piece of JavaScript code. The problem with both approaches is that you need to serialize the source code. For example, imagine that you want to call either of the periodic event methods with a local object reference inst, as illustrated by the following source code:

```
window.setInterval( "CallFunction( inst)", 300);
```

The reference to inst in the string buffer will have no meaning, because when the periodic timer executes, local variables are not in context. The execution will result in an error. Another way to call the function is to serialize inst to a buffer, but that has the disadvantage that the state being used in the periodic event will not be the same object instance, thus if any changes are made between the calling of the function setInterval and expiration of the timer, they will not be present.

The only time when inst is valid is if inst is a global variable. As a general rule of thumb, the safest way to make a context-specific method call using the methods setInterval or setTimeout is to use a global reference. A global reference can be created by dynamically instantiating random variables or by using an array index reference. The approach chosen by Thread is the array index.

The InitializeThreads function will initialize 30 global references of ThreadObject. Each ThreadObject has four data members:

- obj: References the object to execute. The ThreadObject.makeCall method can distinguish between a function and object. If obj is a function, then obj will be called using a function notation. If obj is an object instance, then the obj.run method is called.

- data: References the data used as a context when obj is executed.

- intervalId: References the value returned by the window.setInterval method. This value is used to stop the periodic event.

- isUsed: Used by Thread to determine whether an array index is currently used. When a new thread wants to start, the startThread method searches for an empty index, where isUsed equals a value of false. Once a thread has been started, the isUsed data member is assigned a value of true. And when the thread has finished executing, the isUsed data member is assigned a value of false again.

The pseudo-thread architecture is used in the declaration of DynamicIterator referenced by the metadata navigational onmouseover and onmouseout events. When you move the mouse from one region of the HTML page to another, and the other region has the onmouseover event implemented, the event is triggered. The onmouseover event is triggered only the first time the mouse moves over the event, and that causes the startIteration method to be called, calling Thread.startThread. When the mouse moves out of the metadata navigation region, the stopIteration method is called, calling Thread.endThread. The implementation of startIteration and stopIteration is defined as follows.

Source: /client/scripts/jaxson/uimorphing.js *(DynamicIterator)*

```
    intervalId : 0,
    startIteration : function(direction) {
        this.intervalId = Thread.startThread( function( direc) {
                            DynamicIterator.shiftArrayElements( direc);
                        }, direction, 500);
    },
    stopIteration : function() {
        Thread.endThread( this.intervalId);
    },
```

Putting the Remaining Pieces of the Client Together

Several times I've referenced the DynamicIterator implementation, which is used to navigate the metadata of the result set. The main role of DynamicIterator is to load the metadata navigational elements, and when the individual elements are referenced, the main data is loaded.

I explain the implementation of DynamicIterator in pieces, with the following representation of the initialization of the navigation elements.

Source: /client/scripts/jaxson/uimorphing.js

```
var DynamicIterator = {
    lastElem : null,
    floatingIframe : null,
    parentRow : null,
    initialize : function(floatingIframeID, parentRowID) {
        this.floatingIframe = document.getElementById(floatingIframeID);
        this.parentRow = document.getElementById(parentRowID);
        this.doLayout();
        this.getMoreRootElements( 0);
    },
    doLayout : function() {
        this.floatingIframe.style.width = document.body.clientWidth - 4;
        this.floatingIframe.style.height = document.body.clientHeight - 104;
    },
    // Other declarations...
};
```

Going back to the beginning of the "Implementing the HTML Client" section, recall the piece of HTML code that implemented the body.onload event, which called the local Initialize function. In the implementation of Initialize, the DynamicIterator.initialize method is called. Calling DynamicIterator.initialize will cross-reference the HTML user interface elements with the DynamicIterator instance.

DynamicIterator.initialize expects two HTML user interface elements: the floating iframe (this.floatingIframe) and the table row (this.parentRow) that contains the navigational elements. DynamicIterator needs these two user interface elements because it loads the data highlighted in the navigational area. After the user interface elements have been assigned to the data members, the doLayout method is called. The purpose of doLayout is to resize the iframe so that it covers the appropriate client area. And the last method call in DynamicIterator.initialize is the calling of the getMoreRootElements method, which is responsible for loading the metadata navigational elements.

In the context of DynamicIterator, the getMoreRootElements method is declared as an empty function similar to the following:

```
getMoreRootElements : function( direction) { }
```

The empty function is a placeholder, and it is expected that the HTML code will declare an implementation. In the case of the HTML code, getMoreRootElements is defined as follows.

Source: /client/ajaxrestrecipes/architecture/dynamiclist.html

```
DynamicIterator.getMoreRootElements = function( direction) {
    if( direction == 0) {
        var asynchronous = FactoryHttp.getCachedAsynchronous();
        asynchronous.settings = {
            onComplete : function(xmlhttp) {
                var arrTickers = new Array();
                var tickers = JSON.parse( xmlhttp.responseText);
                for( var c1 = 0; c1 < tickers.length; c1 ++) {
                    arrTickers.push( { text : tickers[ c1],➡
                        url : "/pyservices/trader/historical/tickers/" +➡
                        tickers[ c1]});
                }
                DynamicIterator.associateElements( arrTickers);
            }
        }
        asynchronous.get("/pyservices/trader/historical/tickers");
    }
}
```

In the case of the HTML code, the tickers that represent the metadata used to navigate through the application (as shown in Figure 6-10) are loaded once. Metadata might be unlimited, but often it can be limited to a fixed set size, even if that set size is very large. Looking at the example, each piece of metadata is a ticker that can have one to four letters (on average). If you multiply that number by 1,000 tickers, then you have to download about 4KB–5KB of data (in this era of broadband, downloading 4KB–5KB is trivial). The stock application will allow at most 50 tickers due to technical limitations, so all of the tickers can be downloaded in one request.

In the case of our example, getMoreRootElements with a direction of 0 means to download an initial set of metadata elements. How that data is downloaded is the responsibility of the getMoreRootElements implementation. This example uses the Asynchronous class, and the response is encoded as a JSON array. For every ticker found, an object is created where the ticker is combined with a URL and added to the arrTickers array.

Once the arrTickers array has been filled with elements, the DynamicIterator. associateElements method is called as follows.

Source: /client/scripts/jaxson/uimorphing.js *(DynamicIterator)*

```
associateElements : function( arrElements) {
    this.arrElements = arrElements;
    this.shiftArrayElements( 0);
},
```

The `associateElements` method does two things: assigns the `arrElements` reference array and refreshes the data in the HTML page using the `shiftArrayElements` method.

If the user hovers the mouse over either the left or right arrow, the list of tickers shifts to the left or right. The implementation of `shiftArrayElements` is shown in Figure 6-13.

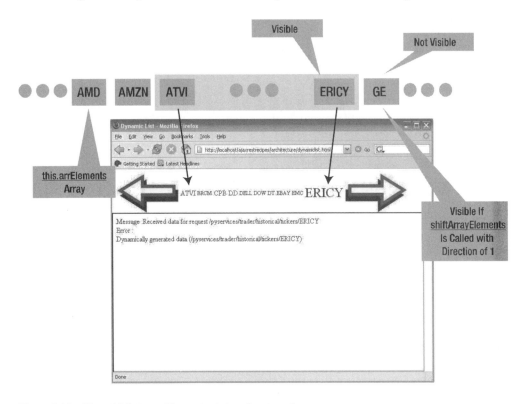

Figure 6-13. *How* `shiftArrayElements` *is implemented*

Figure 6-13 shows an array of metadata elements represented by tickers. The array of tickers can go on as long as you desire. In the HTML navigation window there is only a view port of the data. The view port is reflected in the array, and the leftmost visible array has an index identifier. If the user hovers the mouse over the left arrow, the index to the array of tickers will move to the left; if the user hovers the mouse over the right arrow, the index to the array of tickers will move to the right.

The index movement is contained within the `shiftArrayElements` method. The caller of the method provides the direction of the shift using a positive or negative value. Based on the directional value, the index will be shifted. If the shifted index goes beyond the boundaries of the array, then more metadata elements need to be retrieved.

The full implementation of shiftArrayElements is as follows.

Source: /client/scripts/jaxson/uimorphing.js *(DynamicIterator)*

```
shiftArrayElements : function( offset) {
     this.currOffset = this.currOffset + offset;
     if( this.currOffset < 0) {
         this.getMoreRootElements( -1);
         this.currOffset = 0;
     }
     else if((this.currOffset + this.parentRow.cells.length) >=
         this.arrElements.length) {
         this.getMoreRootElements( 1);
         this.currOffset =
             this.arrElements.length - this.parentRow.cells.length;
     }
     for( var counter = 1; counter <
         (this.parentRow.cells.length - 1); counter ++) {
         this.parentRow.cells[ counter].innerHTML =
             this.arrElements[ this.currOffset + counter - 1].text;
         this.parentRow.cells[ counter].refElemInfo =
             this.arrElements[ this.currOffset + counter - 1];
     }
},
```

In the implementation of shiftArrayElements, a calculation of the shift requires a test to determine if the shift will cause a jump beyond the boundaries of the array. If a jump to the left or the right of the array boundaries happens, then the getMoreRootElements method is called, where the direction value –1 or 1 specifies to prefix metadata to the beginning of the array or append data to the end of the array, respectively.

If the shift does not cause a jump beyond the boundaries of the array, then the individual HTML user elements are redrawn with new reference information attached to the refElemInfo property. It is not customary to attach your own data to an individual HTML user interface element, but in this case it is absolutely necessary for reasons to do with a user hovering the mouse over the element.

If the user hovers the mouse over a ticker, you want the ticker information to be loaded into the floating iframe window. This is accomplished by the DynamicIterator.HightlightItem method, which is defined as follows.

Source: /client/scripts/jaxson/uimorphing.js *(DynamicIterator)*

```
highlightItem : function (elem) {
     if (this.lastElem != null) {
         this.shrinkElement( this.lastElem);
     }
     this.expandElement( elem);
     this.lastElem = elem;
     this.fetch( elem.refElemInfo);
},
```

highlightItem does nothing more than delegate the actions to the shrinkElement, expandElement, and fetch methods. All of these methods are by default empty functions that the HTML page needs to implement. The idea of highlightItem is to provide a clickless navigation scheme. How you make the navigation function is the responsibility of the HTML page. DynamicIterator's responsibility is the coordination.

So, the first step is to resize back to normal the last element that was highlighted using the shrinkElement method. In the case of the ticker example, it is implemented as follows.

Source: /client/ajaxrestrecipes/architecture/dynamiclist.html

```
DynamicIterator.shrinkElement = function( elem) {
    elem.style.fontSize = 12;
}
```

The ticker implementation is simple in that it shrinks the font of the table cell back to 12. For a more sophisticated user interface, shrinking the element might have meant closing a menu or a pop-up div element.

The next step of highlightItem is to highlight the current element using the expandElement function, which is implemented as follows.

Source: /client/ajaxrestrecipes/architecture/dynamiclist.html

```
DynamicIterator.expandElement = function( elem) {
    elem.style.fontSize = 30;
    var asynchronous = FactoryHttp.getCachedAsynchronous();
    asynchronous.settings = {
        onComplete : function(xmlhttp) {
        }
    }
    asynchronous.get(elem.refElemInfo.url);
}
```

The expandElement implementation does two things: increases the size of the font and downloads the data associated with the metadata element. However, in the implementation of onComplete, there is no action, because when you highlight the metadata element, you are probably not interested in displaying the data, but you are interested in caching the data for quick future reference. At this point, you need to make a decision about the mechanism of displaying the data in the iframe.

If you want to display the data using a click, then you need to implement onclick for the individual table cells. If you want to use the act of highlighting as the trigger to display the data, then you need to implement the onComplete method that I just said did not need to be implemented. My point is that the way you display the data is up to you, and DynamicIterator defines no framework. DynamicIterator is only responsible for preloading the data.

Some readers may think that retrieving data every time a metadata element is highlighted is very expensive, but the cost depends on how you implemented your cache. Looking back at Figure 6-2, you can see that the client references a cache. This means that whenever Asynchronous is referenced, the first thing it does is check the cache for the information. If the information is already available, the onComplete method is called directly. The magic lies in the cache, and if there is no cache, then every time the metadata element is highlighted, the data associated with the resource will be loaded.

Let's step back and think about the implementation of the client-side architecture and how it solves our problem of large or slow data sets. If we were working with an email application, then the metadata would be the individual email titles, and we would iterate over the titles and highlight them. To check for new emails, we could spin off a thread that would automatically add metadata elements to the end of the arrElements array. As we iterate over the email titles, their content would be downloaded and displayed in the iframe window.

Now let's say that we were calculating all of the prime numbers and wanted to see the results. In this case, the metadata is the data, and like the email application, a thread would be spun off to keep adding results to the arrElements array.

I mentioned these two examples of threads being spun off, because thus far the example illustrates only the expansion and loading of data when the user asks for it. Using JavaScript threads, the data is automatically loaded without having the user ask for it.

Managing the Data Using a Client Cache

The application performance depends on the caches that are implemented on the client and server sides. If the caches perform poorly, the application will perform poorly. If the caches are effective, the application will be effective. To a large degree, what I just said is obvious, but I want to stress that no matter how well written the other parts of your code are, if you have a bad caching strategy, the application will perform poorly.

Four types of caching strategy can be implemented:

- *HTTP validation*: A form of caching where the client and browser share information about a URL using a handshaking protocol. This form of caching does not reduce the conversation counter, but it does reduce how much data is sent in the conversation. Use this approach if you have data that changes regularly and your network connection between the client and server is of broadband quality.

- *Client-side only*: A form of caching where only the client side caches the information. Typically, you use this approach when the server does not support caching, or if the round-trip between the client and server requires too much time.

- *Server-side only*: A form of caching where only the server side caches the information. The client will constantly query the server for the appropriate information. This form of cache is generally inefficient, and it should be used only if the physical network distance between the client and server is minimal (e.g., the browser and server are on the same computer).

- *Client and server side*: A generalized ideal way of caching where both the server and the client cache information.

In each of these caching strategies, you need to think about the available bandwidth, what kind of data you are receiving, and how far apart the client is from the server. An additional worry is the proxies sitting between the client and server that could cache the information. However, if you are using REST URL principles, that additional worry is minimal. One of the most important rules to follow when implementing a caching strategy is to use unique REST URLs, as discussed in Chapters 4 and 5.

Implementing a Single Request Client Cache

An effective and efficient cache would not change the programming model of the client. Therefore, a client-side cache is best implemented by modifying the Asynchronous class. Then whenever some code uses Asynchronous, the cache is checked and verified to see if the response is already available. If the response is available, then the code receives the response immediately. The following example has hooks to make use of a cache.

Source: /client/scripts/jaxson/common.js

```
function Asynchronous_call(request) {
    var instance = this;
    if (! this.settings) {
        throw new Error("Settings is not defined ");
    }
    if (this.xmlhttp.readyState != 4 && this.xmlhttp.readyState != 0) {
        throw new Error("Currently active request cannot continue");
    }
    this.xmlhttp.open(request.action, request.url, true,
        this.settings.username, this.settings.password);
    globals.info("Opening request " + request.url);
    if (request.headers) {
        for( defHeader in request.headers) {
            this.xmlhttp.setRequestHeader(defHeader, request.headers[defHeader]);
        }
    }
    if (this.settings.headers) {
        for( defHeader in this.settings.headers) {
          this.xmlhttp.setRequestHeader(defHeader,
              this.settings.headers[defHeader]);
        }
    }
    this.settings.url = request.url;
    if (this.cache.processAndBreakBeforeRequest(this.xmlhttp,
      request, this.settings) == true) {
      globals.info("Retrieved data from cache for request " +
        instance.settings.url);
      return;
    }
    this.xmlhttp.onreadystatechange = function() {
        if (instance.xmlhttp.readyState == 4) {
            globals.info("Received data for request " + instance.settings.url);
            if (instance.cache.processAndBreakAfterRequest(instance.xmlhttp,
                request, instance.settings) == true) {
                return;
            }
```

```
            try {
                instance.settings.onComplete(instance.xmlhttp);
            }
            catch (e) {
                globals.errorHandler(e);
            }
        }
    }
    try {
        this.xmlhttp.send(request.data);
    }
    catch( e) {
        globals.errorHandler(e);
    }
}
```

The `Asynchronous` code is very similar to what was presented in Chapter 4. The new parts are in bold. Hooking a cache into `Asynchronous` is easy: you need to capture the request before it is sent, and then capture the response when it arrives. `Asynchronous` does not implement a cache, because there are many ways to code a cache. The smartest strategy, and the one chosen by `Asynchronous`, is to delegate the calls to another method.

In the case of capturing a request, the `this.cache.processAndBreakBeforeRequest` method is called. The `XMLHttpRequest`, `request`, and `settings` of the `Asynchronous` instance are passed to the method. If the method returns `true`, then `Asynchronous_call` returns immediately. The immediate return usually indicates that data is in the cache, but it can also be used to stop a request.

In the case of capturing a response, within the implementation of `onreadystatechange` is a request to the `instance.cache.processAndBreakAfterRequest` method. Three parameters are passed to the method: an `XMLHttpRequest` instance, `request`, and `settings`. Based on those three parameters, the cache can store the response data to be retrieved at a later point. If the `processAndBreakAfterRequest` method returns `true`, then the response data is not sent to the `onComplete` method. Generally speaking, you would not do this, but it is necessary if you are implementing an HTTP validation cache.

The type of cache that you want to implement depends on your needs. It can be either a client-side cache or an HTTP validation cache. In the context of the stock ticker application, a single request client cache is created. The single request client cache will cache every request once and never make a second physical HTTP request. This is fine for the case of the stock ticker example, because the historical ticker data never changes. If the data were to change, you would need to have a way of indicating stale data. In such a case, an HTTP validation cache would be more appropriate.

The following code is the implementation of a single request client cache.

Source: `/client/scripts/jaxson/common.js`

```
var CacheController = {
    _cache : new Array(),
}
```

```
function CachedProcessAndBreakBeforeRequest(request, settings) {
    if (request.action == "GET") {
        var obj = CacheController._cache[settings.url];
        if (obj != null) {
            var fakeXMLHttp = {
                status : 200,
                statusText : obj.StatusText,
                responseText : obj.ResponseText,
                responseXML : obj.ResponseXML
            }
            try {
                settings.onComplete(fakeXMLHttp);
            }
            catch (e) {
                globals.errorHandler(e);
                return false
            }
            return true;
        }
    }
    return false;
}

function CachedProcessAndBreakAfterRequest(xmlhttp, request, settings) {
    if (xmlhttp.status == 200 && request.action == "GET") {
        CacheController._cache[settings.url] = {
            Status : xmlhttp.status,
            StatusText : xmlhttp.statusText,
            ResponseText : xmlhttp.responseText,
            ResponseXML : xmlhttp.responseXML
        };
    }
    return false;
}
```

The single request client-side cache operates only when the HTTP GET is called, which is completely logical but does beg the question of whether a POST, DELETE, or PUT can be cached. The answer is, yes they can, if the cache is intelligent. For example, if you were to cache a PUT, then when the same URL is called using GET, you don't need to query the server. This strategy can get you into trouble if there is a chance that multiple users will be executing a PUT. But there is an optimization in that you can spin off a JavaScript thread and query the status of the data sent by the PUT using HTTP validation. It's important to realize that you can tune the cache to suit your preferences. You could even tune the cache such that it can preload URLs when certain URLs have been requested.

The single request client-side cache is not that intelligent and returns an object if it exists in the cache; otherwise, it queries the HTTP server. The CachedProcessAndBreakBeforeRequest function is called before Asynchronous makes a physical request. When the function is called, the existence of the URL is tested in the CacheController._cache object. If the URL does not exist, then `false` is returned, indicating that the URL should be executed. If the URL does exist, then a cached object exists. The existence of a cached object means that it is not necessary to call the server, and the code's `onComplete` method can be called directly.

The only problem with the cached object is that there is no available `XMLHttpRequest` instance. The solution to this problem is to create a fake instance of `XMLHttpRequest`. Using JavaScript, it's easy to create a fake object. Where things get tricky is that the methods have not been defined, thus they are not available. The headers are not available because they have not been stored in the object when the cached object was created. Again, the fact that the headers have not been stored in the cache highlights that this is a simple implementation of `XMLHttpRequest`. The `fakeXMLHttp` variable represents the fake `XMLHttpRequest` object and is used to call the code's `settings.onComplete` method. Because `settings.onComplete` is called, the cache returns a `false` value, indicating that `Asynchronous` should not make an HTTP request.

The other part to the cache code is the `CacheProcessAndBreakAfterRequest` function, which is used to add a cached object entry. The addition of the object to cache is constrained to an HTTP status code of 200 and an HTTP `GET`. If the object is added to the cache, then the `XMLHttpRequest` property, `status`, `statusText`, `responseText`, and `responseXML` are saved. If you wanted to create a complete implementation of the fake `XMLHttpRequest` object and save the HTTP headers, you would put that code in the `CacheProcessAndBreakAfterRequest` function.

As an alternative, you might be tempted to save a reference to the `XMLHttpRequest` instance. The problem is that the cache is not in control of the `XMLHttpRequest` instance, so by saving a reference, you are not saving the data, as the `Asynchronous` instance could reuse the `XMLHttpRequest` instance for another request. Therefore, whenever implementing your cache, you need to copy the information that should be saved in the cache.

Implementing an HTTP Validation Client Cache

The cache implementation is simple in that once a request has been executed and saved, it will never be executed again. For URLs where the data never changes, this is acceptable. However, there are URLs where the data changes, such as is the case with a real-time stock ticker, and the single request client cache is completely unacceptable. In those situations, the single request client cache needs to be extended to use HTTP validation.

HTTP Expiration Caching Is a Bad Idea (Generally) When you are using HTTP validation, you are letting the Internet infrastructure manage the caching. There are two models: HTTP expiration and HTTP validation. When using *HTTP expiration*, you are saying that content is valid for a certain period of time. The period of time for which the data is valid depends on what the HTTP headers say. It is generally not a good idea to use the HTTP expiration model; rather, it's better to use *HTTP validation* and write code to help the Internet infrastructure do its work.

To understand why the HTTP expiration model is problematic, consider the following scenario. Say you are running a Web site that hosts news feeds. To reduce repetitive traffic on the Web site, you enable HTTP caching and assign an expiration time of 30 minutes. (The expiration time is an arbitrary value used for illustrative purposes.) This means that when a browser downloads some content, the next version of the content will be available in 30 minutes. Indicating a wait period of 30 minutes is a bad idea—in that 30 minutes, news can dramatically change. A client who has downloaded some content is then restricted to retrieving news in 30-minute cycles. Of course, the client could ignore or empty the cache, resulting in downloads of the latest information. If the client always empties the cache, the client will always get the latest news, but at a cost of downloading content that may not have changed. The resource cost should not surprise anyone, because always getting the latest content means using no caching whatsoever. Scripts such as Java servlets/JSP or ASP.NET pages often use this strategy, and the administrator managing the Web site wonders why there are performance problems.

A Better Approach: Using HTTP Validation   The better approach is to use the HTTP validation model. This model sends each response with a ticket that references the uniqueness of the data. If the client wants to download the content again, the client sends the server a ticket from the last download. The server compares the sent ticket with the ticket that it has, and if the server notices the tickets are identical, it sends an HTTP 304 to indicate no changes have occurred. At that point, the client can retrieve the old content from the cache and present it to the user as the latest and greatest. The HTTP validation model still requires an HTTP request, but it does not include the cost of generating and sending the content again.

In terms of an HTTP conversation, the HTTP validation model is implemented as follows. This example illustrates a request from a client and the response from the server.

Request 1

```
GET /ajax/chap04/cachedpage.html HTTP/1.1
Accept: */*
Accept-Language: en-ca
Accept-Encoding: gzip, deflate
User-Agent: Mozilla/4.0 (compatible; MSIE 6.0; ➥
Windows NT 5.1; SV1; .NET CLR 2.0.50215)
Host: 127.0.0.1:8081
Connection: Keep-Alive
```

Response 1

```
HTTP/1.1 200 OK
ETag: W/"45-1123668584000"
Last-Modified: Wed, 10 Aug 2005 10:09:44 GMT
Content-Type: text/html
Content-Length: 45
Date: Wed, 10 Aug 2005 10:11:54 GMT
Server: Apache-Coyote/1.1

<html>
<body>
Cached content
</body>
</html>
```

The client makes a request for the document /ajax/chap04/cachedpage.html. The server responds with the content, but there is no Cache-Control or Expires identifier. This seems to indicate that the returned content is not cached, but that is not true. The server has indicated that it is using the HTTP validation model, and not the HTTP expiration model. The page that is returned has become part of a cache identified by the unique ETag identifier. The ETag identifier, called an *entity tag*, could be compared to a unique hash code for an HTML page. The letter W that is prefixed to the entity tag identifier means that the page is a weak reference and the HTTP server may not immediately reflect updates to the page on the server side.

The next step is to refresh the browser and ask for the same page again. The HTTP conversation is as follows.

Request 2

```
GET /ajax/chap04/cachedpage.html HTTP/1.1
Accept: */*
Accept-Language: en-ca
Accept-Encoding: gzip, deflate
If-Modified-Since: Wed, 10 Aug 2005 10:09:44 GMT
If-None-Match: W/"45-1123668584000"
User-Agent: Mozilla/4.0 (compatible; MSIE 6.0;
   Windows NT 5.1; SV1; .NET CLR 2.0.50215)
Host: 192.168.1.100:8081
Connection: Keep-Alive
```

Response 2

```
HTTP/1.1 304 Not Modified
Date: Wed, 10 Aug 2005 10:11:58 GMT
Server: Apache-Coyote/1.1
```

When the client makes the second request, the additional identifiers If-Modified-Since and If-None-Match are sent in the request. Notice how the If-None-Match identifier references the identifier of the previously sent ETag value. The server queries the URL and generates an entity tag. If the entity tag is identical to the value being sent, the server returns an HTTP 304 code to indicate that the content has not changed.

When using entity tags, the client can send an If-Match or an If-None-Match. If the client sends an If-Match, and the data on the server is out of date, the server returns a cache miss error, and not the new data. If the client sends an If-None-Match identifier when the server data is unchanged, the server sends an HTTP 304 return code. If the data is out of date, new data is sent.

The advantage of using the HTTP validation model of caching is that you are always guaranteed to get the latest version at the time of the request. The clients can make the request every couple of seconds, hours, weeks, or whatever period they choose. It is up to the client to decide when to get a fresh copy of the data. Granted, there is still some HTTP traffic due to the requests, but it has been reduced to a minimum.

Having said all that, there are situations when using the HTTP expiration model does make sense—for example, when the HTML content is static and changes rarely. The HTTP expiration model could be used in the single request model to prune entries from the cache controller when they become stale.

Implementing a Client Cache Using HTTP Validation The single request client cache can be extended to use HTTP validation. What changes in the HTTP validation model is that a physical request will always be made. From the perspective of the metadata navigation, this might cause a small delay due to the necessity to make a request to verify that the data is current. However, the request response cycle is fairly quick, as most cases result in a "not changed" response.

The complete implementation of the two required functions for Asynchronous is as follows.

Source: /client/scripts/jaxson/common.js

```
var HttpValidationCacheController = {
    _cache : new Array(),
    didNotFindETagError : function( url) { }
}

function HTTPValProcessAndBreakBeforeRequest(xmlhttp, request, settings) {
    if (request.action == "GET") {
        var obj = HttpValidationCacheController._cache[url];
        if (obj != null) {
            this.xmlhttp.setRequestHeader( "If-None-Match", obj.ETag);
            this.xmlhttp.setRequestHeader( "Pragma", "no-cache");
            this.xmlhttp.setRequestHeader( "Cache-Control", "no-cache");
        }
    }
    return false;
}

function HTTPValProcessAndBreakAfterRequest(xmlhttp, request, settings) {
    if (xmlhttp.status == 200 && request.action == "GET") {
        if (xmlhttp.status == 200) {
            try {
                var foundetag = xmlhttp.getResponseHeader("ETag");
                if (foundetag != null) {
                    HttpValidationCacheController._cache[url] = {
                        ETag : foundetag,
                        Status : xmlhttp.status,
                        StatusText : xmlhttp.statusText,
                        ResponseText : xmlhttp.responseText,
                        ResponseXML : xmlhttp.responseXML
                    };
                }
                else {
                    HttpValidationCacheController.didNotFindETagError(url);
                }
            }
            catch( exception) {
                HttpValidationCacheController.didNotFindETagError(url);
            }
        }
```

```
        else if (status == 304) {
            var obj = HttpValidationCacheController._cache[url];
            if (obj != null) {
                var fakeXMLHttp = {
                    status : 200,
                    statusText : obj.StatusText,
                    responseText : obj.ResponseText,
                    responseXML : obj.ResponseXML,
                }
                try {
                    settings.onComplete(fakeXMLHttp);
                    return true;
                }
                catch (e) {
                    globals.errorHandler(e);
                }
            }
            else {
                throw new Error("Server indicated that this data is in ➡
the cache ");
            }
        }
    }
    return false;
}
```

Take a moment to examine the code. You should see many similarities to the single request client cache code. The major differences have been highlighted in bold. A big difference in the HTTPValProcessAndBreakBeforeRequest request is the addition of the HTTP validation headers identifying the ETag for a previously executed request. Because using HTTP validation means executing a request, HTTPValProcessAndBreakBeforeRequest has to return false in all situations.

The HTTPValProcessAndBreakAfterRequest function is more complicated because its logic is more sophisticated. If HTTP validation is used and the server supports HTTP validation, then the server can respond with two HTTP status codes for every request: 200 and 304. If the status code is 200, either the data has changed or the data has never been changed. Regardless of the reason for the status code of 200, the data needs to be added to the HttpValidationCacheController cache instance. The one big difference with respect to the single request client cache is the additional storing of the ETag. If the status code is 304, then a fake XMLHttpRequest instance is created and the settings.onComplete method is called, as shown in the single request client cache implementation.

Defining and Implementing the REST URLs

The architecture and implementation of the client from a general "what to do" perspective is complete. We still need to cover the details of the URLs and the architecture of the server.

At this point, I want to show Figure 6-2 again (now Figure 6-14) to refresh your memory.

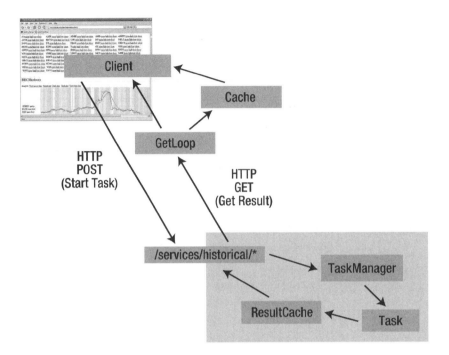

Figure 6-14. *Large and slow data set architecture*

Let's now focus on how to structure the server side for the different situations of when large or slow data is being generated. In the stock ticker example, the complete server architecture as defined by Figure 6-14 was not implemented. Only the code that queried the result cache was implemented. The HTTP POST used to start the task was missing.

A more accurate representation of the architecture of Figure 6-14 is shown in Figure 6-15.

The big difference between Figures 6-14 and 6-15 is that two separate browsers are being used. One browser is used to start a task, and another browser is used to retrieve the results associated with the task. You might look at this architecture and wonder what the difference is between this and regular Web architecture. From an abstract perspective, this architecture mimics a form-entry Web application, where one user enters the data, and another user can view the entered data. To a degree, this interpretation is correct, but a fundamental difference is that an HTTP POST does not generate data. To find out what the data is, you must explicitly make another request using the HTTP GET.

The separation between sending and receiving data is very important because it is what makes it possible for a client to make a request today and ask for the answer tomorrow. If the question and answer had to be in the context of a single request, then the client might have to wait for a very long time.

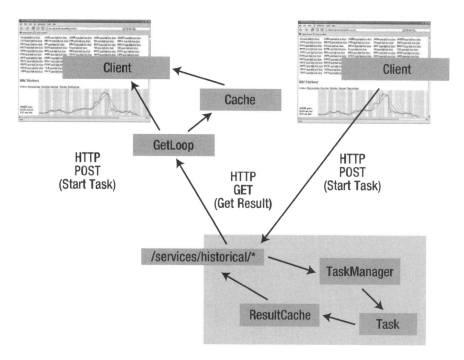

Figure 6-15. *A more accurate representation of the large and slow data architecture*

To put this in another context, you can think of the separation of request and response as the difference between standing in line for assistance at a store and selecting a number for assistance. Imagine shopping and buying some specially sized pieces of lumber. Each lumber store has its own strategy of serving its customers. One strategy is to have the customers line up (queue) and wait their turn. But what if the line is long? Will you be tempted to get in line? What if you decide to get in line and realize that you have to go to the washroom, or you need to put some money into the parking meter? The moment you step out of the line, you lose your position and have to start the waiting game from the start. From an architectural perspective queues are annoying for the server because the server needs to manage the request and keep the attention of the client connection.

Another approach, and one that is fairer, is that each customer who wants a special piece of lumber selects a number and fills in an order. The order is submitted to a salesperson, and he or she will tell you roughly when the lumber will be available. During the wait time, you can go to the washroom, have lunch, or shop for other things. The order and token approach makes it possible to decouple the waiting customer from the store to optimize the time it takes to prepare the special pieces of lumber. For example, based on a set of orders, the store can queue the orders based on priority, ability, and complexity.

This architecture is unique because you use an HTTP POST to submit the order, and in return you receive an indication of where the code can find the answer. You don't have to provide the indication, as that might be programmatically determined. In the case of the ticker application, the location is programmatically determined.

The following sections describe the URLs for the ticker application.

/pyservices/trader/historical/tickers

This represents a root URL that accepts HTTP POST and GET. Executing a GET will return a list of links to all available results. The results might be results in the pure calculation sense or, in the case of the ticker application, a listing of tickers being watched.

Getting a listing of all available results is useless when you don't know what the listing means. The ticker application with its listing is easy to decipher because each result represents a watched ticker. But what if the root URL represents a calculation? The potential listing of results URLs might include random numbers used to index the individual results. This illustrates the fact that it is extremely important to be able to distinguish results based on some metadata, as shown in Figure 6-9. If you cannot do so, you are going to run into major problems.

Sometimes, however, you do not want any metadata descriptors. If the POST executes a calculation where the result is meaningful only in a specific context, then it is the responsibility of the client to keep track of the links. Relating this concept to a shopping cart, most stores have them, and there is no metadata descriptor. When you're in a store, you know which cart belongs to you based on the items in the cart. There is no identifier for the cart, and in the words of a great British comedian, "Until you buy the contents in your shopping cart, it is a great way of rearranging the food in a store." I want to point out that yes, you can generate results without metadata, but those situations are specialized (and will be covered in Chapter 7).

When executing a POST to the root URL, you are starting a task on the server side. Starting tasks on an HTTP server can be challenging because HTTP servers expect all processing to be completed when the request ends. However, because of the nature of the data, this is not possible; therefore, you need to extend your server.

Extending your server can be as simple as executing a thread to run the task, or it can mean making an interprocess call to start off a process to run the task. Regardless of how you will be running the task, the important aspect is to not run the task in the context of the request. The role of the POST is to combine the data for a task, and then execute a task. After the request has been submitted, the server should return an identifier that represents the task. The identifier could be the metadata, some random number, or some arbitrary link. The returned information should provide enough data for the client to algorithmically create a complete link to the data and metadata.

If the POST does not provide any order information, then the assumption is that the client knows how to compose the metadata and link from the submitted data. The downside to this strategy is that if the server-side metadata changes, the client-side code will need to be updated.

/pyservices/trader/historical/tickers/DELL

This URL represents the root URL of a result. Only the HTTP verbs GET and DELETE are supported. The verb POST may be supported if you wish to recalculate the result of a request. The concern with performing a recalculation is that in a multiuser situation, other users will see the new data and not be aware that some parts of the data have changed. Generally speaking, it is better to consider a result as immutable.

The GET verb is supported to allow retrieval of the results. The DELETE verb is supported to prune a result from the list. A pruning is necessary so that the cache does not become cluttered with old results that have no meaning. In the case of the ticker application, DELETE would not be appropriate because ticker history is a time series, and you can turn back the clock. Pruning a time series is only appropriate when you have some data that is considered old and not appropriate for the context.

`/pyservices/trader/historical/tickers/DELL/2006`

This URL represents a specific part of a result and, if appropriate, should always be supported. Supporting child URLs in a result allows the client code to fine-tune the result.

`/pyservices/trader/historical/tickers/DELL?filter=now`

This URL represents another way of fine-tuning the results. For example, if a result generates too much data, using the filter with a value of `now` could fine-tune the result to the last 15.

Fine-tuning does run the risk of missing results. For example, say you are waiting for all of the results from a calculation, and therefore periodically call to retrieve the last 15 results. What if the check period is an hour, and during one hour, 30 results are generated? Using a filter to retrieve the last 15 means you will have missed 15 results.

You should not use a task-based approach when retrieving the last 15 deletes[1] to maintain stability and the ability to reread results that might be lost if a browser stopped downloading the data. You want a way to execute a backfill where the only reliable cache or storage mechanism is the server.

The best way to fine-tune the returned data is to use a cursor on the result set. For example, if there are 15 results to a calculation, in addition to the mentioned URLs each result should be referenced using a unique URL identifying the result number. Think of the result number as being part of a time series. In a time series, you can retrieve all ticks in an hour, but also all ticks in a minute and all ticks in a second.

Solution Variation: (Nearly) Real-Time Data

When trading equities or fixed-income products on a market, you will also want to retrieve real-time data sets. By "real-time" data sets, I mean *nearly* real-time data sets, as people building truly real-time applications might take offense at how loosely I define "real-time." From a personal perspective, I believe that real-time data is not possible with Ajax, as there are simply too many layers of software. What is possible is nearly real-time data, with about half a second or so of lag (of course, this is based on my own experiences—it's by no means definitive). In terms of most trading applications, not including scalping, nearly real-time is good enough.

Real-time data is a variation of the recipe we've already seen, where a real-time task is similar to a long-running task. A long-running task that generates data is like a real-time task, in that both generate data whenever they can. The difference between a long-running task

---

1. In my book *Ajax Patterns and Best Practices* (Berkeley, CA: Apress, 2006), I present an example where getting the last result will delete the last result. At the time of the book's writing, it seemed like the best solution. From the feedback provided by my readers, and for the stability and robustness purposes, KISS was implemented. Using KISS, the server would generate a complete result set where a client would keep a cursor to the latest result. In the next version of *Ajax Patterns and Best Practices*, the Infinite Data pattern will be updated. Please note that the approach outlined in the Infinite Data pattern works. The problem is the nature of the XMLHttpRequest client and Web browser being insecure and unreliable (there is no way to validate who is using the Web browser nor what data that person has received).

and a real-time task is that the data generated by a real-time task has a source beyond the task (e.g., the stock market, a machine running process, etc.). Another difference is that usually a long-running task will have an answer, whereas a real-time task has no answer—just data that keeps being generated.

On the client, the difference between a long-running task and a real-time task is virtually nonexistent. The one major difference with respect to a client is that a long-running task has a beginning and a maximum generated size, whereas a real-time task has no beginning and no end. The difference in cached data sets is shown in Figures 6-16 and 6-17.

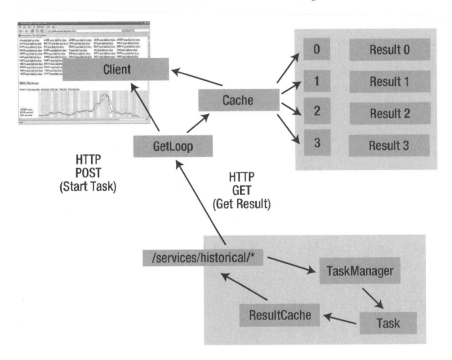

Figure 6-16. *How data is cached by a long-running task*

In Figure 6-16, the cached data set of a long-running task has a direct correlation between when it was generated and the index in the cache. The first generated result will be stored in the first index, and the second result in the second index. In Figure 6-17, which represents the cached data for a real-time task, there is no such correlation, because real-time data is a window of the complete data set. It can also mean that for one client, the data pointed to by the first index may not be the same as the data set for another client.

The mismatch of what each client sees as data can be desired or it can be a problem. For example, say that you are controlling a machine process that creates foam car seats. Each seat takes about 5 minutes to create, and so your Ajax application will store about 7 minutes of data. The window of time for your application is big enough to include one cycle of the item being watched.

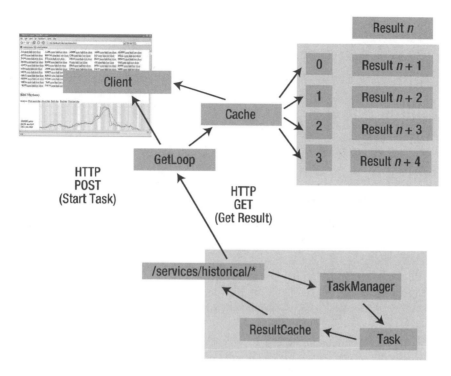

Figure 6-17. *How data is cached using a real-time task*

Now let's turn our attention to the stock market. What would be an adequate window of time for watching a stock ticker? Would it be 1 minute, 10 minutes, a few hours, days, weeks, or years? And depending on the window, what is the length of each individual graph marker? Is it 1 second, 5 seconds, hours, days? Again, we don't know, and we have a problem in that a user could ask for a graph for each second for the past year. The data for such a graph is enormous. In real time on the client side, you can only reasonably expect to keep track of data within a certain window of time.

Keeping track of a window of time is acceptable if you are only interested in the window being presented. The reality is that you will want to know what happened in the past. Looking at the past data for a real-time task is called *backfilling* the data. In the case of the equity example, you need to include a backfill because the calculations performed on the stocks might not be accurate otherwise.

This then introduces a further complication: how do you manage a backfill and real-time task at the same time on the client? The answer is you don't. An Ajax client is not capable of such complicated logic. The backfill and the real-time process need to be managed by the server. The client sees only a view of the data as if it were an infinite data source. Figure 6-18 shows the structure of a backfilled data set.

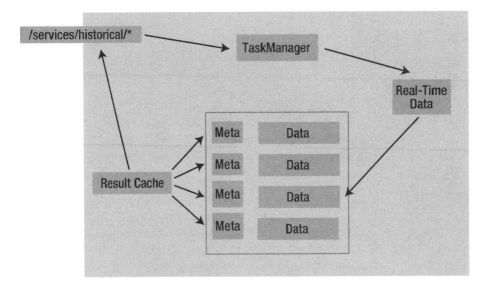

Figure 6-18. *Architecture of real-time task and backfilled data*

In Figure 6-18, the server-side architecture has a `TaskManager` as illustrated in Figure 6-14. The role of `TaskManager` is not to start a task that will end at some later point in time, but to start a task that generates real-time data. If in your implementation of `TaskManager` you had a thread or process wait for the child task to finish, in the case of the real-time task the `TaskManager` should not wait for the child task to finish.

When the real-time task starts, the time series data needs to have its metadata extracted from it. The metadata would then be used to determine where the real-time task adds data to the result set. So, for example, if you are tracking a real-time stock, the metadata would be the stock ticker and the time of the stock tick. If you started the real-time task at 10:00 a.m., then the first tick would be 10:00 a.m. If you are tracking stocks on the New York Stock Exchange, then your complete result set would span the times from 9:30 a.m. to 4:00 p.m., at least the official trading hours. For our example, that means the missing data are the ticks from 9:30 a.m. up to and including 9:59:59 a.m. The missing data is added to the result by executing a task that loads the historical data from an alternate data source. When the historical data has been added, the combination of the two data sets results in a complete and consistent data result set. Regardless of when or how end users see the data, all end users see the same data.

You could come to the conclusion that when data is presented in a consistent format, you have switched the problem from a real-time data generator to a problem of generating a data set that just happens to require a complete day to calculate the results.

In implementation terms, the following rules of thumb are applied:

- You need to define what constitutes a complete result set. You need to define a complete result set in terms of days, hours, or some other quantifiable unit of measure. For example, you could use as the unit of measure an empty barrel that is filled.

- The data generated by the real-time task must be describable by its metadata, which can be used to create an index.

- When the real-time task is started, the data is added to the result set using an index.

- For situations where the real-time task is started at a later point in time, the missing data in the index is provided by a task that executes a backfill.

- A backfill task is executed whenever the real-time task misses data due for one reason or another. The backfill task also serves the purpose of ensuring that the data generated by the real-time task is consistent and accurate.

From the perspective of the client, we see a complete result set with a large number of elements. The client decides at which index they want to start tracking the real-time generated data.

Recipe Summary

This recipe's focus was on building a Web application that manipulates large or slow data sets. Keep the following points in mind:

- Large and slow data sets are dealt with using the same solution. The solution might have implementation variations, but there will always be a task-based approach and the use of a cache on the client or server.

- All results are composed of sets of data, where each individual result has a metadata element.

- The metadata element is used to uniquely identify an individual result. Based on the metadata, it is possible to algorithmically determine a URL to the data. There should be no metadata elements that can be confused with each other; however, a single metadata element descriptor can contain multiple individual results.

- Think of the metadata element as supporting your ability to implement set theory to select, display, or navigate data.

- Navigating large or slow data sets requires specialized navigation.

- The specialized navigation is based on users being able to quickly navigate the metadata, allowing users to get a quick and rough idea of what is contained in the data.

- The specialized navigation should involve the use of clickless navigation techniques as much as possible.

- The performance of the application is dependent on the implementation of the cache on the client and server.

- For most implementations of this recipe, you will need to tune the cache so that the cache can algorithmically determine what the end user needs to see next.

- The simplest cache for read-only type applications would be a single request client cache. For applications where the data changes regularly, an HTTP validation-based cache is needed. For any other application, the cache would be a combination of single request and HTTP validation.

- How long data is kept in the server and client caches depends on the nature of the application, and is a tunable parameter.

- A slow and large data set application distinguishes itself from a regular Web application in that the answer to a POST is retrieved using a separate GET.

- The POST will spawn a task where the task could be executing in another thread or in another process. The POST, having spawned the task, will in most cases return enough metadata information to uniquely identify the URL of the results.

- The results are stored in their own URL that may reference a cache. The results are generally only accessible using the GET and DELETE verbs. There may be ways to fine-tune the result set using subdirectories or query parameters.

- Do not delete results using a stack-based approach. The client in general would keep a cursor on the latest results or constantly download all of the results. This approach is preferred for stability and robustness.

- Real-time data is a variation of the slow and large data set recipe. The big difference with respect to a long-running task is that a real-time task will execute for as long as the monitored information is being tracked.

- Real-time data needs to be combined with a bigger picture of what a result set is. You want to convert the real-time data set into a bigger data set that includes a backfill, making it seem that the real-time data task is in fact a slow data task that happens to need a complete day or unit of time to complete its calculations.

■ ■ ■

7-1. Implementing an Ajax Shopping Cart

The focus of this recipe is to explain how to create a Web application that implements a shopping cart. A shopping cart is a personal thing, yet it is available to everyone. This recipe goes through the problems of handling both personal and public data.

This recipe discusses the following topics:

- Understanding the differences between a personal URL and a general URL

- Controlling access to a personal URL

- Knowing which HTTP verbs to use with a personal URL

- Using Asynchronous JavaScript and XML (Ajax) to retrieve a personal URL

Problem

You want to implement a robust shopping cart in your Web application so that access of the data, which may be public or private, is consistent and straightforward.

■**Note** This recipe discusses two examples: a shopping cart and a bank-account information display. Both examples illustrate the common problem of identity and personalization.

Theory

When you go to a grocery store, you grab a shopping cart. The shopping cart is one of thousands of identical-looking shopping carts. No identifier on the shopping cart makes it distinguishable from another shopping cart. A shopping cart is not like a key, because a key is unique from another key due to its shape. The uniqueness of the shopping cart is defined not by the actual cart, but by the items that you place in the cart and plan to purchase.

In Europe, this uniqueness is critical because Europeans tend to shop in sections. They find a spot to park their shopping cart and then find what they need, carry those items back to the cart, and place them into the cart. They take a hunter-and-gatherer approach, where the prey is the food in the grocery store. There are literally hundreds of carts without owners, yet people don't take the wrong cart, nor do they start taking things out of other people's carts,[1] nor do they walk away with somebody else's cart on purpose. I say "on purpose" because people do occasionally walk 10 feet with somebody else's cart before realizing, "Oops, these aren't my items."

Looking at this from an abstract perspective, the shopping cart has become personalized, even though it becomes generic again when the person is done shopping. Web shopping carts are not implemented like shopping carts in real life. On a Web site, you can have only one shopping cart. In real life, you could walk around with multiple shopping carts (which, in fact, I've done). On a Web site, you cannot hand off your shopping cart to another user. In real life, you can give your shopping cart to anybody. From a programmer's perspective, a shopping cart on a Web site is associated with a user and requires managing the details of an individual. In real life, from the perspective of a cashier, no personal information is exchanged. The reality of Web-based shopping carts is that they associate general data, such as which item is being purchased, with a specific user.

Part of the problem with the current implementation of shopping carts is that Web applications cannot distinguish URLs from one other. Shopping carts are implemented using technologies that make shopping carts difficult to manage.

Let's look at another situation that is similar to a shopping cart. A bank account is similar to a shopping cart in that everybody can have an account, and the bank account can be manipulated the same way as a shopping cart. The big difference between a shopping cart and a bank account is that a bank account requires authorization.

Let's say that a bank creates a Web application that allows users to access their bank accounts from the Internet. Using current technologies, the application allows users to access their account using the same URL and then asks them to authenticate themselves. Based on the authentication, the users see whatever bank account information is associated with them.

A cookie is used to distinguish one user from another (cgross from maryjane, in this case), as illustrated in Figure 7-1.

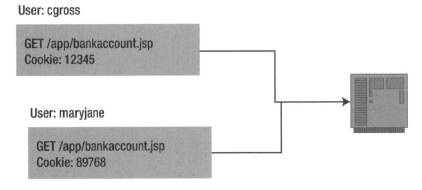

Figure 7-1. *Associating a bank account with a user*

---

1. One of the Europe-based editors of this book commented to me that people *have* grabbed items out of his cart—oh well, the exception to the rule, I suppose.

Figure 7-1 shows the JavaServer Pages (JSP) page /app/bankaccount.jsp. If either maryjane or cgross wants to access their bank account, each would need to perform a login, and an HTTP cookie would be associated with each login. Then both cgross and maryjane would access their bank account information from the same URL. This is a bad way of designing a URL for the following reasons:

- *A user can use only one data set, because there is no way for an administrator to exist*: For example, a user with multiple accounts would not be able to access all the accounts, unless you write code that aggregates the controlled accounts. Using a unique URL with a Web service, users can aggregate the accounts themselves.

- *Security is put into the hands of the Web application developer*: The Web application developer must add barriers to ensure that only authorized people are allowed access to certain pieces of information. All too often, however, the barriers can result in security problems. HTTP security is well known, well defined, and stable, and those who manage it—administrators—are well aware of any security holes. Programmers, although capable and intelligent, are not security specialists.

Solution

The solution to both the shopping cart and bank account problems is to use unique URLs. For example, the shopping cart URL might be /shoppingcart/12324, and the bank account might be /bankaccount/maryjane.

Many people might balk at this solution, because it means each and every user will have a unique URL, and managing unique URLs adds complexity. For example, imagine sending out an email that says, "Hey, buy this, and you'll get credited with 1,000 points in your bank account." You're probably asking, "What URL will be sent in the email?" The answer is a general URL that becomes specific after a login, as Figure 7-2 illustrates.

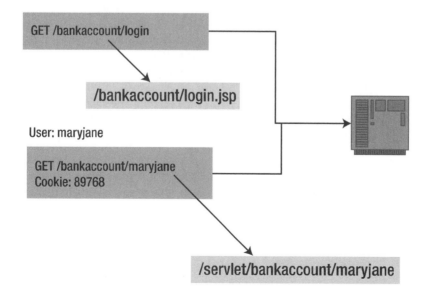

Figure 7-2. *URLs used to access a bank account*

In Figure 7-2, the user that reads the email is sent to the URL /bankaccount/login. If maryjane were to log in and provide her password, then she would be redirected to the URL /bank/maryjane. The redirection would be authenticated, and she would be given an HTTP cookie that allows her to access the content at the URL /bankaccount/maryjane. What is unique about this approach is that HTTP cookies are still used. However, they're not used to define what information is generated, as the architecture in Figure 7-1 showed. The HTTP cookies are used to grant access to a particular URL. Going back to the requirement of allowing a single user access to multiple accounts, the administrator would need to allow the cookie access to the other URLs. The unique URL approach is used in shopping carts, with the exception being that there is no need to authenticate.

Implementing Unique URLs

Unique URLs can be determined ahead of time, or they can be generated dynamically. Generally speaking, you will be managing three URL types, defined as follows:

- *Root URL:* The purpose of the root URL is to provide a context for the action and unique URLs. The root cannot be the action URL. Imagine a situation where you want to get a listing of all available shopping carts. If the root URL is the action URL, a unique URL would be returned whenever the root URL is queried.

- *Action URL:* An action URL, such as /cart/retrieve, is the URL referenced by the client. Depending on the verbs supported, a reference to a unique URL is returned. In the case of the shopping cart, the only verb supported by the server is GET, which generates a unique URL when called. In the case of the bank account, the action URL supports the POST verb, which generates the unique URL when called. The verbs DELETE and PUT are not supported, because they have no meaning.

- *Unique URL:* In the case of the shopping cart, an identifier URL such as /cart/12345 has a numeric identifier appended after the root URL of the shopping cart application. A unique URL does not need to have a numeric identifier appended, but it can be alphanumeric or some other identifier. A unique URL can support all HTTP verbs and depends entirely on the context. Each generated unique URL does not have to be identical in structure. For example, one application could use both URLs /cart/12234 and /big/cart/12/first. The uniquely generated URLs do not need to be tracked by the server, and often are the responsibility of the client. The server only needs to keep track of the unique URL for deletion purposes. For example, if the shopping cart has not been used for a certain period of time, the server deletes it.

Algorithmically, the challenge lies in converting the action URL into a unique URL. One way of solving the problem is to create an HTTP request and then define the unique URL in the response. The HTTP 1.1 protocol provides the means to redirect the action URL to the unique URL. In HTTP protocol speak, this is called *performing a redirection.*

Understanding HTTP Redirection

HTTP redirection is a handshaking protocol. The client makes a request, and the server receives and processes the request. If the server indicates a redirection is in order, then an HTTP status code in the 300 range is returned. Upon receiving the 300-range status code, the client inspects the response and can take action by loading the redirected URL.

The following is an example HTTP conversation that performs an HTTP redirection. As usual, a client makes an HTTP request:

```
GET /resource/ HTTP/1.1
Accept: */*
Accept-Language: en
Accept-Encoding: gzip, deflate
User-Agent: Mozilla/5.0 (Macintosh; U; PPC Mac OS X; en) ➡
AppleWebKit/412.6.2 (KHTML, like Gecko) Safari/412.2.2
Connection: keep-alive
Host: 192.168.1.242:8100
```

The URL /resource is recognized by the HTTP server as a generic URL that will redirect to a specific URL when called. The HTTP server responds with an HTTP 302 to indicate a redirection, as illustrated by the following HTTP response:

```
HTTP/1.1 302 Found
Date: Tues, 05 Sep 2005 16:29:04 GMT
Server: Apache/2.0.53 (Ubuntu) PHP/4.3.10-10ubuntu4
Location: /resource/joesmith
Content-Length: 346
Keep-Alive: timeout=15, max=100
Connection: Keep-Alive
Content-Type: text/html; charset=iso-8859-1
```

In the example, the specific URL sent to the client is defined as /resource/joesmith. When either a Web browser or an XMLHttpRequest object receives a redirect, the client will recognize the redirect and attempt to retrieve the contents of the redirected URL, as illustrated by the following final request:

```
GET /resource/joesmith HTTP/1.1
Accept: */*
Accept-Language: en
Accept-Encoding: gzip, deflate
User-Agent: Mozilla/5.0 (Macintosh; U; PPC Mac OS X; en) ➡
AppleWebKit/412.6.2 (KHTML, like Gecko) Safari/412.2.2
Connection: keep-alive
Host: 192.168.1.242:8100
```

An HTTP redirection, whether executed by the Web browser or XMLHttpRequest, can be executed only if the redirection follows the same origin policy. If a redirection to another domain is attempted with XMLHttpRequest, the results vary. For example, Microsoft Internet Explorer returns a status code of 0 and no further data. Mozilla-based browsers return the status code 302 and the redirected URL.

Although using HTTP redirection can be effective, it can also be problematic from an Ajax perspective. When using the XMLHttpRequest object and calling a URL that generates a redirection, the redirected URL will be loaded automatically. This is bad because the script needs to know what the redirected URL is, but the XMLHttpRequest object doesn't give that URL. Therefore, in the context of this recipe, you cannot use a 300-range HTTP status code.

Creating HTTP Resources

It would seem that the original idea of retrieving the unique URL in the body of the action URL response is the only solution, but never fear. Another solution does exist, and it's compliant with the HTTP protocol. The HTTP status code 201 corresponds to a response where the server has created another URL that can be found in the Location HTTP header. This logic corresponds closely to what the role of the action URL is with respect to the unique URL.

When the server responds with an HTTP status 201, the browser or XMLHttpRequest instance doesn't perform a redirect automatically. It's up to the code or browser to take action on the response. You can use the following JavaScript class to retrieve the unique URL from the action URL.

Source: /client/scripts/jaxson/communications.js

```
function UniqueURL( url) {
    this.asynchronous = null;
    this.baseURL = url;
    this.uniqueURL = null;
    this.haveIt = function() { }
}

UniqueURL.prototype.getIt = function() {
    var instance = this;
    this.asynchronous = FactoryHttp.getAsynchronous();
    this.asynchronous.settings = {
        onComplete : function(xmlhttp) {
            if( xmlhttp.status == 201) {
                instance.uniqueURL = xmlhttp.getResponseHeader( "Location");
                instance.haveIt();
            }
        }
    }
    this.asynchronous.get(this.baseURL);
}

UniqueURL.prototype.postIt = function( inpData) {
    var instance = this;
    this.asynchronous = FactoryHttp.getAsynchronous();
    this.asynchronous.settings = {
        onComplete : function(xmlhttp) {
            if( xmlhttp.status == 201) {
                instance.uniqueURL = xmlhttp.getResponseHeader( "Location");
                instance.haveIt();
            }
        }
    }
    this.asynchronous.post(this.baseURL, inpData);
}
```

The class UniqueURL is a single-purpose class, only in that you use it to retrieve the unique URL based on what is defined as the action URL. UniqueURL is instantiated, and the constructor requires you to define the action URL that is then assigned to the data member baseURL.

You could call two methods to retrieve the unique URL: getIt and postIt. Both methods serve the same purpose, except getIt uses the HTTP GET verb, and postIt uses the HTTP POST verb.

Internally, the Asynchronous methods are used to make the GET or POST requests. The methods would execute the action URL using either get or post methods and then await a response in the onComplete method. Because UniqueURL is only interested in a redirection, the onComplete method only processes HTTP status code 201. Every other status code is ignored. When the 201 status code is received, the method getResponseHeader retrieves the HTTP header location, as it contains the unique URL. Once the unique URL has been retrieved, the user-implemented method haveIt is called, indicating that a unique URL has been generated.

The implementation of UniqueURL is simple and only does one thing, which is convert an action URL into a unique URL. How the server generates the unique URL depends on how the consumer of UniqueURL called the server. In the case of the shopping cart example, all that is required is calling the method getIt. In the case of the bank account, the postIt method with appropriate data is called.

Implementing a Shopping Cart

The shopping cart example will be implemented in abbreviated form for explanation purposes. The solution will focus on the generation of the unique URL and using that unique URL when buying something.

The Initial Solution

The following illustrates the shopping example source code.

Source: /client/ajaxrestrecipes/architecture/shoppingcart.html

```
<html>
  <head>
    <title>Shopping cart</title>
    <script language="JavaScript" src="/scripts/jaxson/common.js"></script>
    <script language="JavaScript" src="/scripts/jaxson/communications.js"></script>
  </head>
<script type="text/javascript">

var unique = new UniqueURL( "/pyservices/shopping/cart/getone");
unique.haveIt = function() {
    document.getElementById( "status").innerHTML = "Have shopping cart";
}

function Initialize() {
    unique.getIt();
}
```

```
function CustomerDetails() {
    var obj = new Object();
    obj.data = "address=...";
    obj.length = obj.data.length;
    obj.mimetype = "application/x-www-form-urlencoded";
    return obj;
}

function BuyItems() {
    if( unique.uniqueURL != null) {
        var asynchronous = FactoryHttp.getAsynchronous();
        asynchronous.settings = {
            onComplete : function(xmlhttp) {
                // Process the data ...
                unique.uniqueURL = null;
                unique.getIt();
            }
        }
        asynchronous.post( unique.uniqueURL + "/checkout", CustomerDetails());
    }
}
</script>
  <body onload="Initialize()">
    <input type="button" value="Buy it" onclick="BuyItems()" />
    <div id="status"></div>
    <div id="error"></div>
  </body>
</html>
```

In the source code example, the bold code represents the pieces of functionality that relate to a specific use of UniqueURL. The HTML page in an overall context represents the parent page that everyone uses to get a shopping cart and buy some items. When the page is loaded, the body.onload event is triggered, causing the Initialize function to be called. In the implementation of Initialize, unique.getIt is called, which results in a unique URL that represents a shopping cart.

By adding the unique URL code to the body.onload event, you're assured that whoever visits the HTML page will have a shopping cart at their disposal. The generated URL is used whenever users click on the Buy It button, triggering the function called BuyItems. The general implementation of BuyIt is not important, because what you're doing is posting the last remaining details to buy whatever users have added to the shopping cart. In the asynchronous.post method call, the URL used is unique.uniqueURL. When the purchase has cleared in the onComplete implementation, the uniqueURL data member is cleared and a new, unique shopping-cart URL is retrieved.

The code provides an understanding of how to use the unique URL, but you must understand the following considerations:

- When a unique URL, such as `/pyservices/shopping/cart/122343`, is returned, the client appends the identifier `/checkout`. Using a nonappended URL would require the URL to accept `POST` and `GET` requests for multiple data structures, and that would be non-REST compliant. On the client side, appending an identifier is not a big deal, but on the server, it does become a big deal, as will be discussed shortly.

- The example HTML page doesn't include the code to search, browse, and add items to the HTML page. You could use two solutions: content injection or an `iframe`. Using content injection, the catalog items would be pieces of HTML code that would be added to the current HTML page using the `innerHTML` property. The other approach is to use a floating `iframe`, which allows you to separate the display of the catalog items from the manipulation.

- In the case of the shopping cart, the owner of the unique URL is the client. This raises the question, "If the users press the page refresh, how will they remember what they were referencing?" The server won't tell the clients what the unique URL is. The clients can manage this using client-side cookies, as will be illustrated shortly.

Keeping Track of Unique URLs

Typically, Web application frameworks use cookies to keep server-side session objects. While it might seem that server-side session objects solve many problems, they in fact can cause many problems. Let's say you're writing a service-oriented architecture (SOA) client that uses Web services—nowhere in the Web service documentation will you ever find instructions on how to keep session, because that's how code is written. Remove the term *Web service* and use a remote procedure call. By default, a remote procedure call won't remember who called it. Remote procedure calls expect the caller to remember that, as that is the right approach.

To give you a real-life example of why it's bad to use server-side sessions, let's say you're shopping on Amazon.com, and you decide to purchase some things. You're not going to pay for the contents in your shopping cart, because your mother has decided to purchase everything as a birthday present. In a real-life grocery store, having your mother purchase the contents of your shopping cart is as easy as handing her the shopping cart. Yet at Amazon.com, it is not possible, because the shopping cart is associated with the user as a session object on the server side, as Figure 7-3 illustrates.

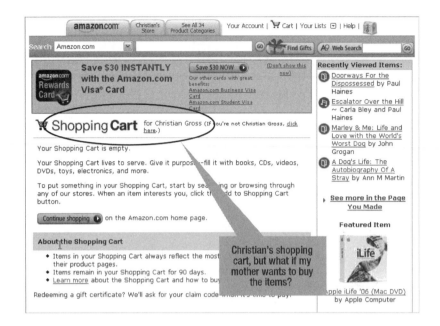

Figure 7-3. *Amazon.com's association of a user and his shopping cart*

At Amazon.com, each and every user gets a single shopping cart. Therefore, to have your mother pay for the contents, you must manually create a list that you email to your mother. Or you could ask your mother for her credit card details. The first option is easy to do, but it is time consuming and "lame," as it requires you to write out the contents of your shopping cart and then have her add the items to her shopping cart. It's as if you go into a store, fill the cart, and then create a list of items in the cart and hand that list to your mother. Your mother then has to race around the grocery store and fill up her cart with the same items so that she can pay.

The second option does not require any such extra effort, but it does require your mother trusting you with her credit card details. I'm sure your mother would trust you, but she would probably be uneasy, as would anybody. As you can see, there is no viable option involving server-side, session-based URLs.

The only viable option is to stop using server-side, session-based URLs and start using unique URLs with the client managing the references to the URL. Using client-managed unique URLs opens new possibilities. For example, let's say that you create a TV, radio, and sound system and add those items to a shopping cart. Then as an added value service, you promote your shopping cart, and whenever anybody wants to purchase your super sound system, they only pay for the shopping cart and don't have to go around the site finding the individual items. In theory, you could create thousands of different shopping carts with different configurations. However, you can't do that type of added value today with server-side, session-based URLs.

Many say HTTP cookies are bad, but it depends on how cookies are used. I consider cookies as a supporting role for any type of implementation. Now let's talk about client-side cookies and delay a more in-depth cookie discussion until later in this chapter.

There's no real difference between a client-side or server-side cookie, because a cookie is a token held by the client and sent to the server. The client or server can assign the token, and in the case of the shopping cart, the client will assign the cookie. The cookie that is assigned is the unique URL, and the modified shopping cart code is as follows (note that only the code has been abbreviated for clarity purposes):

```
<script type="text/javascript">
var unique = new UniqueURL( "/pyservices/shopping/cart/getone");
unique.haveIt = function() {
    document.getElementById( "status").innerHTML = "Have shopping cart";
    createCookie( "shoppingcart", unique.uniqueURL, 2);
}

function Initialize() {
    var url = readCookie( "shoppingcart");
    if( url == null || url.length == 0) {
        unique.getIt();
    }
    else {
        document.getElementById( "status").innerHTML =
            "already have a shopping cart";
        unique.uniqueURL = url;
    }
}

function CustomerDetails() {
    var obj = new Object();
    obj.data = "address=...";
    obj.length = obj.data.length;
    obj.mimetype = "application/x-www-form-urlencoded";
    return obj;
}

function BuyItems() {
    if( unique.uniqueURL != null) {
        var asynchronous = FactoryHttp.getAsynchronous();
        asynchronous.settings = {
            onComplete : function(xmlhttp) {
                // Process the data ...
                unique.uniqueURL = null;
                eraseCookie( "shoppingcart");
                unique.getIt();
            }
        }
        asynchronous.post( unique.uniqueURL, CustomerDetails());
    }
}
</script>
```

The bold code represents the code related to managing a cookie. In particular, three as-of-yet still undefined functions are used: createCookie, readCookie, and eraseCookie. These three functions are used to write, read, and delete a cookie. The functions have been geared toward ease of use, making it as simple as possible to read and write key-value pairs. The key is a cookie name, and the value is a cookie value.

The logic of the cookie functionality is as follows:

- When the page is loaded, the `Initialize` function checks using the function `readCookie` to see if a cookie with a name `shoppingcart` exists. If the cookie exists, then it is not necessary to create a new cookie, but the cookie value has to be assigned to the data member `unique.uniqueURL`. If the cookie does not exist, it means that there is no associated shopping cart, and thus the function `unique.getIt` needs to be called.

- If a cookie has to be retrieved using the method `unique.getIt`, then when the unique URL is generated, the method `unique.haveIt` is called. In the implementation of `unique.haveIt`, the cookie `shoppingcart` is assigned the value of the data member `unique.uniqueURL` with an expiry of two days.

- When the shopping cart has been paid and a new unique URL is generated, the existing cookie is erased using the function `eraseCookie`.

The implementation of the cookie routines manipulates the `document.cookie` object. The `document.cookie` object returns all cookies applicable to the current domain. The following code shows the implementation of the cookie[2] functions:

```
function createCookie(name,value,days) {
    if (days) {
        var date = new Date();
        date.setTime(date.getTime()+(days*24*60*60*1000));
        var expires = "; expires="+date.toGMTString();
    }
    else var expires = "";
    document.cookie = name+"="+value+expires+"; path=/";
}

function readCookie(name) {
    var nameEQ = name + "=";
    var ca = document.cookie.split(';');
    for(var i=0;i < ca.length;i++) {
        var c = ca[i];
        while (c.charAt(0)==' ') c = c.substring(1,c.length);
        if (c.indexOf(nameEQ) == 0) return c.substring(nameEQ.length,c.length);
    }
    return null;
}

function eraseCookie(name) {
    createCookie(name,"",-1);
}
```

---

2. You can find the original source of the cookie functions at `http://www.quirksmode.org/js/cookies.html`.

The bold code illustrates how the `document.cookie` object is manipulated. The manipulation is rather peculiar and completely unorthodox. In the implementation of `createCookie`, a buffer is created and then assigned to `document.cookie`. Usually an assignment to a data member resets the value of the data member. Not so with the `document.cookie` data member. Assigning the data member either creates a new cookie or reassigns the value of an existing cookie.

In the implementation of `createCookie`, the parameter days assign a time to the cookie being created, indicating that the cookie will expire. If the cookie and the function `createCookie` are not associated with a date time, then the cookie would expire the moment the browser is closed.

When reading the data member `document.cookie`, the cookies applicable to the currently loaded domain and document are retrieved. The following could be an example value of `document.cookie`:

```
cc=value1;shoppingcart=/pyservices/shopping/cart/toRedirected
```

The value of `document.cookie` is problematic, because it is a string that contains multiple cookies. To find a single cookie, the string has to be parsed. The implementation of `readCookie` automatically manages the parsing and retrieves the value for a particular cookie identifier.

The function `eraseCookie` uses the `createCookie` function to delete a cookie. Again, this is unorthodox, but it uses the functionality where assigning an expired date to a cookie will automatically delete the cookie.

Having the Server Process Unique URLs

With respect to the server side, the conversion of the action URL to a unique URL requires the ability to define an HTTP header. Based on the requirement, the algorithm to determine what the `Location` HTTP header should be is dependent on the context of the application.

Once the unique URL has been determined and sent to the client, the client will add what are called *specializations*. For example, let's say that you're managing a shopping cart and have to process the URLs `/shopping/cart/1224/additem`, `/shopping/cart/2344/additem`, `/shopping/cart/56743/checkout`, and `/shopping/cart/8853/checkout`. Current Web application infrastructures such as JSP, ASP.NET, or PHP have a difficult time processing these URLs because each URL is unique from the other, despite there being only two types of URLs from a pattern perspective: `additem` and `checkout`.

There are two ways to solve this problem. The first is to use Apache, and the second is to create a filter. In either solution, you're taking the URL and converting it into a request that you can process using a standard HTTP handler.

The first solution is to use Apache, because Apache contains an extremely useful handler called mod_rewrite.[3] Using mod_rewrite, you have the ability to accept any URL request and convert the URL into something else. While I do like the fact that Apache has such a powerful tool to rewrite a URL, using it to process unique URLs, in my opinion, is a stopgap measure so that REST-based URLs can be used in the context of existing infrastructure.

To rewrite the shopping cart examples, you would add the Apache mod_rewrite rules to the Apache configuration file and use them in combination with a reverse proxy. A reverse proxy enables Apache to call Microsoft Internet Information Services (IIS), Tomcat, or any other HTTP server as if the request were calling IIS, Tomcat, or any other HTTP server directly:

---

3. If you plan on creating more complicated mod_rewrite rules, you would be well served to read Rich Bowen's book *The Definitive Guide to Apache mod_rewrite* (Berkeley, CA: Apress, 2006).

```
RewriteEngine on
RewriteRule ^/shopping/cart/(.*)/additem/(.*)$ /additem.php?id=$1&additional=$2
RewriteRule ^/shopping/cart/(.*)/checkout/(.*)$ /checkout.php?id=$1&additional=$2
```

In the rules, the first line is used to start up the mod_rewrite module. The second and third lines are the important rules. The first block of text is an identifier `RewriteRule` indicating that a URL rewrite example is being created. The second block of text that starts with a ^ character and ends with a $ character is a regular expression. The regular expression is used to test if the incoming URL matches one of the rules. If the regular expression maps successfully, then the rewritten URL is the third block of text.

The overall intent of the mod_rewrite rules is to convert a REST-based URL into a traditional URL. The unique pieces of the URL are converted into query parameters. If you don't happen to use the Apache server, then you'll need to implement either a handler or filter with an architecture similar to Figure 7-4.

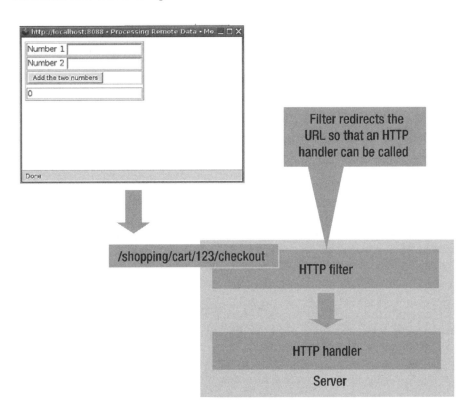

Figure 7-4. *Using a filter to redirect the request to a specific handler*

In Figure 7-4, the HTTP server receives the URL. Depending on the technology used, the first step is to call a filter. For example, IIS has Internet Server Application Programming Interface (ISAPI) filters or ASP.NET modules, Java has filters, and Apache has filters. The filter is responsible for being able to process the unique URL and converting the request into a specific handler. You should not have to jump through hoops to be able to process unique URLs.

The handler that is called as a result of the decisions made by the filter needs to be able to decipher the URL. Ideally, the handler retrieves the URL and breaks the URL into individual pieces. For example, the URL /shopping/cart/1224/additem would be broken up into the individual arrays [shopping], [cart], [1224], and [additem].

Implementing a Bank Account

Implementing a bank account is similar to implementing a shopping cart. The only real difference is that you need security. For example, if maryjane logs into her account and she references the URL /account/maryjane, then you only want maryjane or an appropriate person to view the data. Anybody else should get an invalid security credentials error.

The remainder of this recipe will focus on how to use cookies and HTTP authentication to authenticate users:

- HTTP *cookies*: HTTP cookies are identifiers sent in the HTTP header between the client and the server. The server is responsible for generating a cookie, and the client is responsible for sending the cookie to the server for a given URL and its descendents.

- *HTTP authentication*: By using HTTP authentication, it is possible to authenticate users. Then, whenever the users request content for a given URL realm, the client sends the authorization information. HTTP authentication is similar to a cookie, except that users must authenticate themselves.

Whether you use cookies or HTTP authentication, the clients send a token whenever they wish to access a given URL. The server will validate if the token has permission to access the URL.

Using Cookies to Authorize Access

HTTP cookies[4] have a bad reputation, partially undeserved, and therefore many will argue that you should not use cookies. The problem with cookies doesn't have to do with their theory, but rather with their implementation and ramifications.

As a real-life analogy, consider entering a shopping mall where somebody gives you a token at the entrance, which you can take or refuse. If you refuse the token and enter the mall, all of the store doors suddenly close. You can wander the mall, but you can only look at the merchandise through the windows. You can still view the content and everything that the store offers, but it is behind glass.

On the other hand, if you accept the token, the store doors remain open, and you can browse all the products. To be helpful, the store clerks offer recommendations on the best offers in the mall. Yet there is a dark undertone to the experience: the shopping mall is watching every step you make, and everything you look at is being tracked. Of course, the shopping mall assures you that the information will not be used for other purposes, but the question is, where do those recommendations or best offers come from? The tokens—or cookies—are being used to track people.

I'm split regarding the use of cookies—I find nothing extremely disturbing about them, nor am I enthused about them. HTTP cookies are a means to an end.

---

4. http://en.wikipedia.org/wiki/HTTP_cookie

Generating the Cookie It is possible to generate an HTTP cookie[5] without using any help from a library. Because of the prevalence of cookies, most server-side libraries have classes or functions to generate cookies based on a few parameters. Using the available server-side libraries is highly recommended.

Generating the cookie by using the server-side libraries is not difficult. When using ASP.NET, you would use the following source code:

```
HttpCookie mycookie = new HttpCookie("Sample", "myvalue");
mycookie.Path = "/ajax/chap07";
Page.Response.Cookies.Add(mycookie);
```

You instantiate a cookie (HttpCookie), and at a minimum, you specify the key (Sample) and value (myvalue). The combination key-value pair is sent between the client and server. The cookie property mycookie.Path specifies for which URL and its descendents the cookie is valid. Comparing this to HTTP authentication, the cookie path is equal to the HTTP authentication realm. You add the newly created cookie to the response by using the method Page.Response.Cookies.Add. When a cookie is added, the HTTP response will generate a cookie using the Set-Cookie HTTP header, as illustrated by the following HTTP server response:

```
HTTP/1.0 200 OK
Server: Mono-XSP Server/1.1.13.0 Unix
X-Powered-By: Mono
Date: Mon, 28 Aug 2006 17:31:14 GMT
Content-Type: text/html; charset=utf-8
Set-Cookie: Sample=myvalue; path=/ajax/chap05
Content-Length: 388
Keep-Alive: timeout=15, max=99
Connection: Keep-Alive
```

The cookie Sample has a value of myvalue and is valid for the path /ajax/chap05. Because there is no expires value, the cookie is valid only for the lifetime of the browser. If the browser is closed, the cookie is deleted, thus behaving like an HTTP authentication-based user identifier.

Understanding How the Client Manages the Cookie When the client receives the cookie, the cookie will be saved automatically if the client is a browser or the XMLHttpRequest object of the browser. In fact, the JavaScript on the client side has absolutely nothing to do with the assigned cookie, because everything occurs transparently. For example, if a browser loads a page and a cookie is assigned for the entire domain, the cookie will be sent when the XMLHttpRequest object calls a page within the domain.

Storing sensitive information, such as passwords or any kind of personal information, within the cookie is not recommended. A cookie is a reference to information, not a repository for information. When users have been authenticated by using other means, a cookie should be used only as a token to identify the user.

Identifying a User with a Cookie When the server generates a cookie, it means nothing, because a cookie is just a token. The cookie needs to be cross-referenced with a specific user. To cross-reference the token, you must apply an authentication mechanism. You could use one of two

---

5. http://www.ietf.org/rfc/rfc2965.txt

authentication mechanisms. First, you could tie the cookie with HTTP authentication. Second, you could create an HTML page that associates the cookie with a user.

Using HTTP authentication to associate a user with a cookie would involve protecting a file that requires an explicit authentication. When the user is authenticated by using HTTP authentication, the protected file is responsible for associating the cookie and authentication information.

The user does not have to be authenticated using HTTP authentication. An HTML form could be used instead. Using the HTML form, you're responsible for providing code that manages a user. Because of this added code, the HTTP authentication mechanism is preferred, because it is the basis of the HTTP protocol.

Using HTTP Authentication

HTTP authentication is probably one of the most underused techniques of creating a user identifier. Most Web applications tend to prefer HTTP cookies, but HTTP authentication offers some yet-to-be-discussed options that HTTP cookies do not.

In the early nineties, HTTP authentication was not well known and was considered generally insecure, because the client would constantly be sending the username and password to the server whenever an authorization was performed. To get around the security issue, a more secure form of HTTP authentication was created, called *HTTP digest authentication*. HTTP digest authentication was not widely distributed in the early Web days. Of course, today that is not the case, as every browser, or at least most browsers, support HTTP digest authentication.

Understanding How HTTP Authentication Functions at a Practical Level HTTP authentication is a great way of creating a user identifier, because the authentication mechanism is formal and requires participation by the user. If the user declines, authentication will not occur, and no information is sent to the server. The user can remain anonymous. Granted, the user might not be able to access all of the content, but there is anonymity, and some people treasure their anonymity. Figure 7-5 illustrates how HTTP authentication is presented to the user via current browsers.

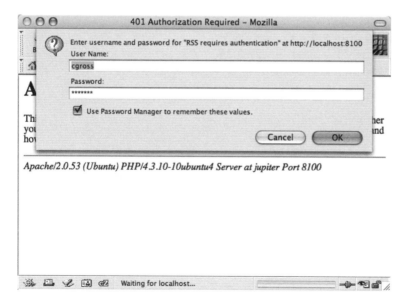

Figure 7-5. *HTTP authentication dialog box prefilled with authentication information*

Also illustrated in Figure 7-5 is the ability of current browsers to remember past HTTP authentication sessions. HTTP authentication is both a blessing and a curse, in that users must authenticate themselves whenever they exit and restart the browser. The blessing is that authentication information is not sent automatically, and the curse is that users must authenticate themselves before starting a session at a Web site. Some may consider requiring to be authenticated a downside, but when security is important, using HTTP authentication ensures giving the correct rights to the identified user.

At a technical level, HTTP authentication is a mechanism whereby a user requests the contents of a resource, and the server issues a challenge, asking for identification. The browser converts the challenge into something similar to Figure 7-5. After the user enters the appropriate information, the server will authenticate the user. If the authentication works, the browser downloads the representation of the resource.

A typical HTTP digest authentication conversation is described in the following steps. The process starts with the client requesting a resource:

```
GET /test/ HTTP/1.1
Host: jupiter:8100
User-Agent: Mozilla/5.0 (Macintosh; U; PPC Mac OS X Mach-O;➡
    en-US; rv:1.7.8) Gecko/20050511
Accept: text/xml,application/xml,application/xhtml+xml,text/html;q=0.9,➡
    text/plain;q=0.8,image/png,*/*;q=0.5
Accept-Language: en-us,en;q=0.5
Accept-Encoding: gzip,deflate
Accept-Charset: ISO-8859-1,utf-8;q=0.7,*;q=0.7
Keep-Alive: 300
Connection: keep-alive
```

The resource is protected, and therefore the server will challenge for an authentication:

```
HTTP/1.1 401 Authorization Required
Date: Sun, 27 Aug 2006 14:00:05 GMT
Server: Apache/2.0.53 (Ubuntu) PHP/4.3.10-10ubuntu4
WWW-Authenticate: Digest realm="Private Domain", ➡
nonce="OhvlrVH/AwA=8225d4804076a334d81181695204fee405adaaee", ➡
algorithm=MD5, domain="/test", qop="auth"
Content-Length: 497
Keep-Alive: timeout=15, max=100
Connection: Keep-Alive
Content-Type: text/html; charset=iso-8859-1
```

The client receives the HTTP error code 401 and looks for the HTTP header WWW-Authenticate. The value of HTTP WWW-Authenticate contains which authentication mechanism is being requested. In this example, HTTP digest authentication is requested. As a side note, it is possible to use basic authentication, but because it is not considered secure, it is avoided. As a response to the challenge, the browser generates a dialog box similar to Figure 7-5, asking for a username and password. The user types in the username and password, which causes the browser to reissue the original request with the added user authentication information, as shown here:

```
GET /test/ HTTP/1.1
Host: localhost:8100
User-Agent: Mozilla/5.0 (Macintosh; U; PPC Mac OS X Mach-O; ➥
    en-US; rv:1.7.8) Gecko/20050511
Accept: text/xml,application/xml,application/xhtml+xml,➥
    text/html;q=0.9,text/plain;q=0.8,image/png,*/*;q=0.5
Accept-Language: en-us,en;q=0.5
Accept-Encoding: gzip,deflate
Accept-Charset: ISO-8859-1,utf-8;q=0.7,*;q=0.7
Keep-Alive: 300
Connection: keep-alive
Authorization: Digest username="cgross", realm="Private Domain",➥
nonce="0hvlrVH/AwA=8225d4804076a334d81181695204fee405adaaee",➥
uri="/test/", algorithm=MD5,➥
response="fc4ec419438f87a540d8898a537ea401", qop=auth,➥
nc=00000001, cnonce="01b6730aae57c007"
```

The resulting request is similar to the initial request, except that there is an additional HTTP header, Authorization. When confronted with the same URL request, the server searches for the Authorization HTTP header. If the server finds the header, the server will verify the information and then, depending on the verification, either return another HTTP 401 error, causing the browser to generate a dialog box that asks the user to authenticate himself, or consider the user authenticated. If the provided authentication information is correct, the associated representation is downloaded.

When using HTTP authentication, the Authorization HTTP header is sent for all URLs and their dependents that were specified by the WWW-Authenticate header sent by the server. In this example, the value domain="/test" refers to the single URL /test and its dependencies.

Implementing HTTP Authentication You shouldn't write any code that manages HTTP authentication. All Web servers are capable of managing HTTP authentication, and you should leave this as an administrative exercise. This doesn't mean that you don't use HTTP authentication. You still need to know whether a user is authenticated, and you need to associate that user to the user identifier information. From a programmatic perspective, the authentication information is available by the server-provided request structure.

Authenticating When It Is Not Necessary One of the side effects of HTTP authentication is that content usually is either protected or not protected. Traditionally—and this is why cookies are used—HTTP authentication cannot be turned off for a resource and then turned back on again for the same resource. That would confuse users, because as it stands right now, HTTP authentication is a global setting and not an individual setting. In other words, if authentication is required for one, then it is required for all. That could pose a problem. Let's say a user is browsing a site and wants to purchase something; that user will need a shopping cart. However, a user identifier is needed to implement a shopping cart. To create a shopping cart, unprotected resources need to be protected, but the protection is global, so everybody would need to get a shopping cart after browsing the first page of a shopping site and start buying something. Nice idea to jump-start an economy, but it is not going to happen. To get around this issue of sometimes protection, you can use an HTTP authentication technique, as follows:

1. Let the user browse the site as usual (for example, `http://mydomain.com/browse`).

2. On each browsed page, add a protected link to indicate that the user wants to be authenticated (`http://mydomain.com/browse/authenticate`).

3. When the user clicks on the authentication link after the authorization, the HTTP realms (domains) that include the unprotected content are assigned in the response (`http://mydomain.com/browse`).

4. When the user browses the URL `http://mydomain.com/browse`, user identification information is sent, even though it is not required.

This trick works extremely well if you use HTTP digest authentication. The following Apache HTTPD configuration example uses this technique:

```
<Directory "/var/www/browse/authenticate">
        AllowOverride AuthConfig
        AuthType Digest
        AuthDigestDomain /browse /browse/authenticate
        AuthDigestFile "/etc/apache2/digestpasswd"
        AuthName "Private Domain"
        Require valid-user
</Directory>
```

The technique is implemented by the configuration item `AuthDigestDomain`, where both the URLs `/browse` and `/browse/authenticate` are referenced. Because the configuration item `Directory` references the URL `/browse/authenticate`, only the URL `/browse/authenticate` will be challenged for an authentication. To illustrate that the technique actually works, consider the following HTTP conversation. First, a request is made for an unprotected resource:

```
GET /browse/ HTTP/1.1
Host: jupiter:8100
User-Agent: Mozilla/5.0 (Windows; U; Windows NT 5.0; en-US;➡
    rv:1.7.5) Gecko/20041220 K-Meleon/0.9
Accept: text/xml,application/xml,application/xhtml+xml,text/html;q=0.9,➡
    text/plain;q=0.8,image/png,*/*;q=0.5
```

The server responds as usual with an HTTP 200 return code, which causes the client to load the resulting page. Then the client makes another request to the protected link, because the user wants to shop and needs to be authenticated. The client makes the following request for the protected content:

```
GET /browse/authenticate HTTP/1.1
Host: 192.168.1.103:8100
User-Agent: Mozilla/5.0 (Windows; U; Windows NT 5.0; en-US;➡
    rv:1.7.5) Gecko/20041220 K-Meleon/0.9
Accept: text/xml,application/xml,application/xhtml+xml,text/html;q=0.9,➡
    text/plain;q=0.8,image/png,*/*;q=0.5
```

The server responds with an authentication challenge:

```
HTTP/1.1 401 Authorization Required
Date: Mon, 28 Aug 2006 16:08:28 GMT
Server: Apache/2.0.53 (Ubuntu) PHP/4.3.10-10ubuntu4
WWW-Authenticate: Digest realm="Private Domain", ➥
nonce="yiLhlmf/AwA=e1bafc57a6151c77e1155729300132415fc8ad0c",➥
    algorithm=MD5, domain="/browse /browse/authenticate",➥
    qop="auth"
Content-Length: 503
Content-Type: text/html; charset=iso-8859-1
```

In the server response for the domain identifier, an unprotected resource is defined. This is the technique used to send authorization information for unprotected content. The client responds with user authentication, as follows:

```
GET /browse/authenticate HTTP/1.1
Host: 192.168.1.103:8100
User-Agent: Mozilla/5.0 (Windows; U; Windows NT 5.0; en-US;➥
    rv:1.7.5) Gecko/20041220 K-Meleon/0.9
Accept: text/xml,application/xml,application/xhtml+xml,text/html;q=0.9,➥
    text/plain;q=0.8,image/png,*/*;q=0.5
Authorization: Digest username="cgross", realm="Private Domain",➥
nonce="yiLhlmf/AwA=e1bafc57a6151c77e1155729300132415fc8ad0c",➥
    uri="/browse/authenticate", algorithm=MD5,➥
    response="c9b5662c034344a06103ca745eb5ebba", qop=auth,➥
    nc=00000001, cnonce="082c875dcb2ca740"
```

After the authentication, the server allows the downloading of the protected content. Now if the client browses the unprotected URLs again, the authorization information is passed to the server, as illustrated by the following request:

```
GET /browse/morecontent / HTTP/1.1
Host: jupiter:8100
User-Agent: Mozilla/5.0 (Windows; U; Windows NT 5.0; en-US;➥
    rv:1.7.5) Gecko/20041220 K-Meleon/0.9
Accept: text/xml,application/xml,application/xhtml+xml,text/html;q=0.9,➥
    text/plain;q=0.8,image/png,*/*;q=0.5
Authorization: Digest username="cgross", realm="Private Domain", ➥
nonce="yiLhlmf/AwA=e1bafc57a6151c77e1155729300132415fc8ad0c",➥
    uri="/browse/morecontent/", algorithm=MD5,➥
    response="18ccd32175ce7a3480d5fbbc24de8889", qop=auth,➥
    nc=00000005, cnonce="0d448aca73b76eb1"
```

For this request, the client has sent authorization information for a URL that doesn't require authentication. Simply put, the authentication mechanism has become an "HTTP cookie" mechanism that is controlled by the client. The client is in full control of when to become authenticated and when to remain anonymous.

Recipe Summary

This recipe illustrated how to build a shopping cart application, but the solution could be considered as a general approach used to personalize content. You should remember the following points:

- The recipe of implementing a shopping cart or bank account involves defining an action URL and a unique URL.

- The action URL is responsible for generating a unique URL.

- You can consider the unique URL to be a personalized URL that replaces the need to keep a server-side session object.

- Server-side session objects are not useful when you want to write flexible Web services. The shopping cart examples illustrated that you can use predefined shopping carts to add value to an online store.

- You can implement the redirection from the action URL to the unique URL using the HTTP 300 series of status codes. However, using this series of status codes results in the XMLHttpRequest caller not knowing what the unique URL is.

- The preferred mechanism when using XMLHttpRequest to redirect is to use the HTTP status code 201. This code means that a new resource has been created that, from a theoretical perspective, matches the intent of the unique URL principle.

- The server generally does not track unique URLs. It is the responsibility of the client to associate a particular user with a particular unique URL. If the unique URL is anonymous, like a shopping cart, then you should use client-side cookies. If the unique URL has security restrictions, then you should use server-side cookies or HTTP authentication.

- When implementing security, you can use cookies as long as the cookies are not used to generate content. Cookies are used to authorize access to a resource.

- Cookies and HTTP authentication mechanisms are the preferred means used to implement user identification.

- When implementing the redirection functionality, you cannot cache the response from the action URL, because it will lead to data consistency problems.

- Unique URLs are processed on the server side using one of two mechanism: a predefined URL rewriting mechanism, such as Apache mod_rewrite, or the implementation of a filter that targets a specific handler. The preferred mechanism is a filter that targets a specific handler, but for legacy purposes, it is completely acceptable to use a predefined URL rewriting mechanism.

CHAPTER 8

■ ■ ■

8-1. Don't Submit Your Forms— Ajax Them

This recipe focuses both on solving the problem of sending data using HTTP POST, and on the definition of a state that is associated with an HTML page.

This recipe covers the following topics:

- Explanation of the problems associated with HTTP POSTs

- How to fix the problems related to HTTP POSTs

- Illustration of a workflow architecture

- Association of state with a handler

Problem

You want to use Ajax to solve some of the problems associated with submitting forms the traditional way with POST.

Theory

When implementing a workflow such as buying an airplane ticket, you use HTML forms. An HTML form has a number of UI elements, such as a text box, a list box, or a combo box, that users can use to enter information. When they're content with the information entered, they press a button to submit the data to the server. The server receives the data and generates some kind of result.

Figures 8-1 and 8-2 illustrate the process.

Figure 8-1. *Filling in the contents of an HTML form*

Figure 8-2. *Server-side–generated results based on the data sent by the HTML form*

Figure 8-1 features a single text box and a single button. The text box is used to enter some data that will be sent to the server. The button is used to HTTP POST the form to the server.

In previous recipes, an HTTP POST was used when data was sent to the server. None of the examples used the HTTP POST in the context of an HTML form. When an HTTP POST is used in the context of an HTML form, the server processes the form and generates some data that then becomes the next HTML page, as Figure 8-2 shows.

From a content-processing perspective, the difference in processing between an HTTP GET and POST is dramatic. In Figure 8-1, the content was retrieved using an HTTP GET, where the server does not expect any state from the client. The client could call the URL multiple times, and the content would be generated each time. An HTTP POST is different in that the client has to send state. Based on that state, the server does some processing and generates some content, as illustrated in Figure 8-2. The state that the client has to send is not optional. A browser helps the client by caching the state sent previously, and when requested, sends the state again with an appropriate dialog box, as illustrated in Figure 8-3. The problem with sending the state again is that you might execute the process to buy a plane ticket again, thus buying two.

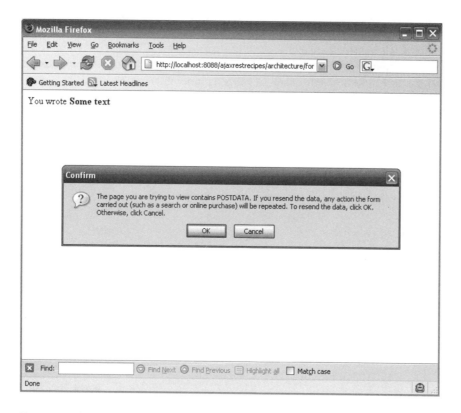

Figure 8-3. *Message box indicating a reposting of the data*

In Figure 8-3, the message box indicates that the action will cause the data to be sent to the server as a POST. A warning is necessary, because the data has already been sent previously, and if you were purchasing a ticket, then you might end up purchasing another ticket unintentionally.

In Figure 8-3, you would obviously press Cancel, but doing so would cause the page to not be generated, resulting in a blank screen or a screen with an error. Not being able to navigate to some previous page is wrong, because most traditional clients allow you to navigate to previous screens without causing an automatic posting to the server.

Imagine a situation in which you're buying a plane ticket and you want to experiment with different times and airports. To search for a particular ticket, you would use an HTTP POST. Each tweaking of the parameters could cause the dialog box of Figure 8-3 to appear. Yet you would probably reply that in fact, this is an incorrect assertion, as the dialog box rarely appears. The reason why the dialog box rarely appears is because you're guided and told which buttons you can and cannot press. To go back a step in the workflow process, you would not press the Browser Back button. Next time, look closely at a typical HTML-based workflow, and you'll notice how information is repeated on multiple screens and how the workflow guides the user. It is very clever, and users are typically not aware of being manipulated into thinking in certain directions.

Solution

Web application frameworks have gone to great extents to solve the HTTP POST problem. You need to look no further than the ASP.NET framework to see the complexity involved in making sure that the Browser Back or Refresh buttons don't cause a mountain of problems with respect to the server-side state. ASP.NET is not to be blamed, because its creators were trying to fit a dynamic architecture into an old static Web infrastructure.

You can solve the HTTP POST problem elegantly using the XMLHttpRequest object. The idea behind using XMLHttpRequest is to POST the data before the next page is loaded, as Figure 8-4 illustrates.

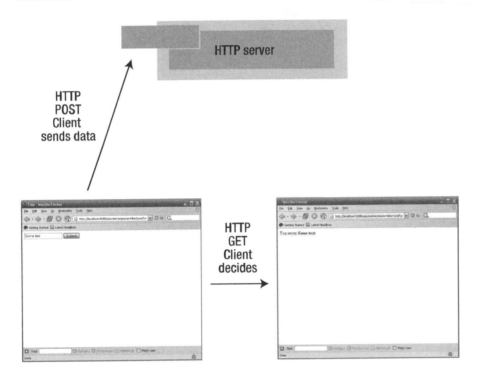

Figure 8-4. *Client posts and navigates to the next HTML page.*

In Figure 8-4, the client posts the data to the server and then navigates to the next HTML page. Notice that this way of sending data to the server is similar to how a traditional application is built, in that you send data to the server and then decide which user interface to load next.

The following points sum up the advantage to using this approach:

- The data is sent to the server only once, and only if the user presses the Form Submit button.

- The server side stores an application state that you can use HTTP GET to call whenever a particular HTML page is called. Therefore, you can use the Browser Back and Browser Forth buttons to move between pages without corrupting the server-side state or the client-side HTML page.

Converting the POST to Use the XMLHttpRequest Object

The solution to the HTTP POST problem is simple, but it requires the ability to use the XMLHttpRequest object. In this section, you'll learn how to convert the original application to use the new architecture. The original and new HTML pages will be illustrated at a code level. The idea of this section is to illustrate the conversion.

The Original HTML Form

The original HTML form used an HTTP POST, and is illustrated as follows:

```
<html>
  <head>
    <title>Title</title>
  </head>
  <body>
    <form action="/ajaxrestrecipes/architecture/forms/Posted.ashx"
         method="POST">
      <input type="text" name="example" />
      <input type="submit" value="Submit" />
    </form>
  </body>
</html>
```

The bold form attributes show that when the Submit button is pressed, the URL /ajaxrestrecipes/architecture/forms/Posted.ashx is called using a POST. From a Representational State Transfer (REST) perspective, the URL only accepts a single verb, POST. This is the heart of the problem in that you cannot retrieve the page using a GET, which is the default HTTP verb used by a browser.

The Converted HTML Form

The converted HTML form uses the same HTML constructs, but it delegates the POST to an XMLHttpRequest and retrieves the next page using a GET. The following code shows the converted HTML form:

```
<html>
  <head>
    <title>Title</title>
  </head>
  <script language="JavaScript" src="/scripts/jaxson/common.js"></script>
  <script language="JavaScript" src="/scripts/jaxson/communications.js"></script>
  <script language="JavaScript" src="/scripts/jaxson/commonmorphing.js"></script>
<script language="JavaScript" type="text/javascript">
var representations = { };

function OnSubmit() {
    var obj = RepresentationManager.iterateHtml.get( representations,
        document.getElementById( "form"));
    var stringToSend = Ops.serializeCGI( obj);
```

```
        var asynchronous = FactoryHttp.getAsynchronous();
        asynchronous.settings = {
            onComplete : function(xmlhttp) {
                location.href = document.getElementById( "form").action;
            }
        }
        var obj = new Object();
        obj.data = stringToSend;
        obj.length = obj.data.length;
        obj.mimetype = "application/x-www-form-urlencoded";
        asynchronous.post( document.getElementById( "form").action, obj);
}

</script>
  <body>
    <form id="form"
      action="/ajaxrestrecipes/architecture/forms/AjaxPosted.ashx"
     method="POST">
      <input type="text" name="example" />
      <input type="button" value="Submit" onclick="OnSubmit()"/>
    </form>
    <div id="output"></div>
    <div id="error"></div>
  </body>
</html>
```

The important modified parts of the HTML page are shown in bold. The overall change has been to convert the input type of submit to button, and have the button implement the click event. The click event calls OnSubmit and is responsible for doing a POST and GET.

When OnSubmit is called, the function RepresentationManager.iterateHTML.get is called, which is used to extract the state in the HTML form elements. Normally, when using the previous HTML form-submit technique, the browser manages the extraction of the state from the HTML form. It is more complicated to perform a custom extraction, but it does give the added benefit of being able to extract the state from other HTML elements, such as div or span elements. You need to think of a GET method call as a general state extraction that is assigned to a JavaScript object.

When the JavaScript object that contains the state has been created, you need to convert the object into a computer graphics interface (CGI)-encoded query string. The function Ops.serializeCGI carries out the conversion. Again, you need to perform a custom serialization, but you have the added flexibility of serializing to a CGI-encoded query string, a persisted JavaScript Object Notation (JSON), or even an XML string.

Then when you have the CGI query string, you use the remaining code in OnSubmit to POST the data to the server. Notice that the POST URL used is from the HTML form. Once the POST has been completed in the implementation of the onComplete method, the location.href is assigned the URL that was POSTed to.

Here is where you might get confused. Why first POST and then GET the same URL? It might seem more efficient to perform a single POST or GET. The reason for executing the two verbs is due to browser history. The POST is executed by the XMLHttpRequest object and thus not part of the browser history. The POST is used to create a state on the server, and then the browser executes the GET, so that the page is recorded in the browser history. As a result, the browser has two GETs in the history, instead of a GET and a POST, as was the case in the original HTML form example. When you have two GETs in the history, you don't need to send state to the server, as the state is retrieved.

The client still calls the same URL, but the functionality of the server URL has changed. In the modified HTML form example, the server has to react to a POST and a GET. However, the server must associate a state with the request, which was not necessary in the case of the original HTML form. In the original HTML form, the state was generated with every POST.

Associating a state with the request is not that difficult and only requires the use of the Web application-provided session mechanism. You have to change the server-side code so that the information generated by the POST is stored in the session and retrieved when the GET is called. The following code shows an extremely simple implementation of the original server-side code:

```
public void ProcessRequest(HttpContext ctx) {
    ctx.Response.ContentType = "text/html";
    ctx.Response.Write("<HTML><BODY>You wrote <b>" +
        ctx.Request["example"] + "</b></BODY></HTML>");
}
```

Here's the modified server code:

```
public void ProcessRequest(HttpContext ctx) {
    ctx.Response.ContentType = "text/html";
    if( ctx.Request.HttpMethod == "POST") {
        ctx.Session.Add( "example", ctx.Request[ "example"]);
        ctx.Response.Write("<HTML><BODY>You wrote <b>" +
            ctx.Request["example"] + "</b></BODY></HTML>");
    }
    else if( ctx.Request.HttpMethod == "GET") {
        ctx.Response.Write("<HTML><BODY>You wrote <b>" +
            ctx.Session["example"] + "</b></BODY></HTML>");
    }
}
```

The example is coded using ASP.NET, but even if you're not an ASP.NET programmer, you should be able to follow the explanation. In the original implementation of `ProcessRequest`, it was expected that you call the method using a `POST`. To generate the content, you extract the example variable using the method `ctx.Request`. As the original implementation of `ProcessRequest` is defined, there is no memory of having been called previously. The generated output is dependent on the parameters sent in the `POST`. The original code is considered unsafe, because a `POST` is assumed. If a `GET` is executed, then problems will occur, because an inconsistent state will be defined.

In the modified source code, you first test the HTTP verb that is being called (`ctx.Request.HttpMethod`). If an HTTP `POST` is called, then the generated content is like the original HTML form example, and the state is saved to the session (`ctx.Session`). If an HTTP `GET` is called, then the generated content is similar to the `POST`, except that the state is retrieved from the session.

POSTing Forms and REST

In the modified example, the URL uses `/ajaxrestrecipes/architecture/forms/AjaxPosted.ashx` and uses a session. The problem with this approach is that HTTP cookies are used to determine what content is generated. The solution is used to illustrate that you can relatively easily modify an existing application that uses a `POST` into one that uses Ajax-combined `POST` and `GET`.

Next, you modify the `POST` and `GET` combination to use no session variables. Or, to put it more succinctly, it's OK to use session variables as long as they don't use cookies. For example, in the ASP.NET architecture, it is possible to have the session variables modify the URL to include an identifier that cross-references to a session variable.

Having the infrastructure modify the URL makes it possible to bookmark the URL and reference it at some later point in time. However, you'll run into a problem if you use session variables that time out. A timed-out session variable, even if it doesn't use cookies, is problematic, because users might have bookmarked the URL and found out later that they cannot reference it. It is possible to just set the session variable to time out a very long time from now, but this doesn't solve the problem of the state eventually disappearing. In the case of this recipe, the last thing you want to happen is the disappearance of state.

Therefore, you need to re-architect the server to use a cache instead of session variables. The advantage of the cache is that it gives you the ability to control when a piece of state remains and is deleted. The next problem is a bit more complicated. In the modified example of the HTML form, the page `PostAjax.ashx` responded to either a `GET` or a `POST`. When the `GET` was called, the state of the HTML page and the HTML page itself were combined in one step. From Chapter 5, you know that combining the HTML page with its state is wrong. You want to be able to load the state as a Web service call. This means two URLs are necessary. The "Supporting HTML Pages with Relative URLs" section in Chapter 5 shows you how to manage the two URLs.

This recipe defines the two URLs, as Figure 8-5 illustrates.

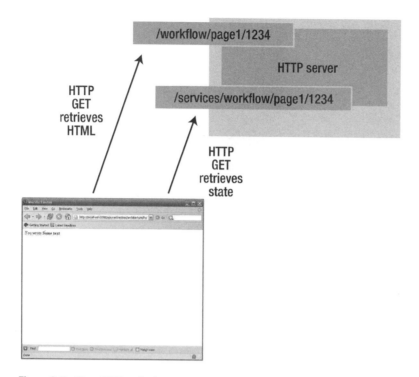

Figure 8-5. *Two-URL solution to processing a workflow application*

In Figure 8-5, the important pieces are the URLs, which are explained as follows:

- /workflow/page1/1234: This URL is used to download the HTML page that is displayed in the browser. The URL supports only the GET verb, as it is used to download the HTML content from the server.

- /services/workflow/page1/1234: This URL supports both the POST and GET verbs and is the state associated with the HTML page URL. The state URL is created using the techniques explained in the section "Supporting HTML Pages with Relative URLs" in Chapter 5.

Both example URLs are appended with the number 1234, which represents the unique cached data identifier used when loading the state.

In the state and HTML page solution, the state created by one HTML page is delegated to another page. Look back at the code of the modified HTML form example. The state of the HTML page is associated with the PostAjax.ashx page. With the state and HTML page solution, the state needs to be associated with the page, and thus the implementation of the modified HTML form example changes slightly to the following:

```
<html>
  <head>
    <title>Title</title>
  </head>
  <script language="JavaScript" src="/scripts/jaxson/common.js"></script>
  <script language="JavaScript" src="/scripts/jaxson/communications.js"></script>
  <script language="JavaScript" src="/scripts/jaxson/commonmorphing.js"></script>
<script language="JavaScript" type="text/javascript">
var representations = { };

function OnSubmit() {
    var obj = RepresentationManager.iterateHtml.get( representations,
        document.getElementById( "form"));
    var stringToSend = Ops.serializeCGI( obj);
    var asynchronous = FactoryHttp.getAsynchronous();
    asynchronous.settings = {
        onComplete : function(xmlhttp) {
            location.href = document.getElementById( "form").action;
        }
    }
    var obj = new Object();
    obj.data = stringToSend;
    obj.length = obj.data.length;
    obj.mimetype = "application/x-www-form-urlencoded";
    asynchronous.post(URLEngine.serviceURL(), obj);
}

URLEngine.serviceURL = function() {
    return "/services/" + this.requestChunks.slice( 0,
        this.requestChunks.length - 1).join( "/");
}

function Initialize() {
    var asynchronous = FactoryHttp.getAsynchronous();
    asynchronous.settings = {
        onComplete : function(xmlhttp) {
            var obj = Ops.serializeFromCGI( xmlhttp.responseText);
            RepresentationManager.iterateHTML.set( representations,
                document.getElementById( "form"), obj);
        }
    }
    asynchronous.get(URLEngine.serviceURL());
}
```

```
</script>
  <body onload="Initialize()">
    <form id="form"
      action="/ajaxrestrecipes/architecture/forms/AjaxPosted.ashx"
     method="POST">
      <input type="text" name="example" />
      <input type="button" value="Submit" onclick="OnSubmit()"/>
    </form>
    <div id="output"></div>
    <div id="error"></div>
  </body>
</html>
```

The bold code shows the additional pieces necessary to implement the state and HTML page solution. As explained in Chapter 5, when the page has been loaded completely, the body.onload event is triggered and calls the function Initialize. Calling Initialize results in the state being retrieved using the URL dynamically computed using the function URLEngine. servicesURL. When the state has been retrieved, it is deserialized and assigned to the HTML page using the methods serializeFromCGI and iterateHTML.set.

The implementation of OnSubmit stays the same, with a minor modification being the URL where the state is being POSTed. The POST URL must be the same as the one used to retrieve the data in the Initialize function. The next page that loads after the state stays the same; you can modify it to your liking.

The URL that determines the next page warrants a little discussion. In the case of the HTML code, the loaded URL is /ajaxrestrecipes/architecture/forms/AjaxPosted.ashx. The URL is not appended with a cache identifier, meaning that the URL is not associated with any state. In the modified HTML form example, a cookie defines the state that is associated with the URL. Since you're not using cookies, the URL has no state. If this is your desired effect, then you can leave the code as is.

However, this probably is not the desired effect, so you need to associate the cache identifier with the URL. Therefore, the URL must be /ajaxrecipes/architecture/forms/1234/ AjaxPosted.ashx or something along those lines. The important bit is that the unique cache identifier is included in the URL. However, the URL is hard-coded, so you need to modify it dynamically, much like the approach illustrated in Chapter 5. In a nutshell, you need to define groupings of URLs. For example, one workflow might have the URLs /workflow/app-name/page1, /workflow/app-name/page2, and so on. Each of the URLs would be associated with a cache identifier. Thus, whenever you navigate one of the URLs, you'll be navigating the cached data associated with the workflow application.

Recipe Summary

This recipe illustrated that you don't need to POST data via the Web browser—instead, you can use the XMLHttpRequest object. Remember the following points:

- Using the XMLHttpRequest POST and GET combination avoids the dreaded HTTP "Post data again" dialog box. You can rest easy that your clients won't be purchasing the same item twice.

- By having POST and GET as separate steps, you can optimize the efficiency of the Web application, because the data associated with the GET can be cached.

- You don't need to make huge changes to your Web application to take advantage of the separate POST and GET, as illustrated in the modified HTML form example.

- In a complete state navigation implementation, use a two-URL approach, where one URL defines the HTML page, and the second URL represents the state Web service called by the HTML page.

- In a complete state navigation implementation, the URLs for the state and the next page need to be algorithmically definable.

- You can combine this solution with the data-validation recipes illustrated in Chapter 3.

- To associate cached data with a URL, you should not use cookies, but instead use unique cached identifiers in the URL. This allows you to bookmark an HTML page and its associated state for later reference.

Index

Find it faster at http://superindex.apress.com/

forums.apress.com

FOR PROFESSIONALS BY PROFESSIONALS™

JOIN THE APRESS FORUMS AND BE PART OF OUR COMMUNITY. You'll find discussions that cover topics of interest to IT professionals, programmers, and enthusiasts just like you. If you post a query to one of our forums, you can expect that some of the best minds in the business—especially Apress authors, who all write with *The Expert's Voice*™—will chime in to help you. Why not aim to become one of our most valuable participants (MVPs) and win cool stuff? Here's a sampling of what you'll find:

DATABASES

Data drives everything.

Share information, exchange ideas, and discuss any database programming or administration issues.

INTERNET TECHNOLOGIES AND NETWORKING

Try living without plumbing (and eventually IPv6).

Talk about networking topics including protocols, design, administration, wireless, wired, storage, backup, certifications, trends, and new technologies.

JAVA

We've come a long way from the old Oak tree.

Hang out and discuss Java in whatever flavor you choose: J2SE, J2EE, J2ME, Jakarta, and so on.

MAC OS X

All about the Zen of OS X.

OS X is both the present and the future for Mac apps. Make suggestions, offer up ideas, or boast about your new hardware.

OPEN SOURCE

Source code is good; understanding (open) source is better.

Discuss open source technologies and related topics such as PHP, MySQL, Linux, Perl, Apache, Python, and more.

PROGRAMMING/BUSINESS

Unfortunately, it is.

Talk about the Apress line of books that cover software methodology, best practices, and how programmers interact with the "suits."

WEB DEVELOPMENT/DESIGN

Ugly doesn't cut it anymore, and CGI is absurd.

Help is in sight for your site. Find design solutions for your projects and get ideas for building an interactive Web site.

SECURITY

Lots of bad guys out there—the good guys need help.

Discuss computer and network security issues here. Just don't let anyone else know the answers!

TECHNOLOGY IN ACTION

Cool things. Fun things.

It's after hours. It's time to play. Whether you're into LEGO® MINDSTORMS™ or turning an old PC into a DVR, this is where technology turns into fun.

WINDOWS

No defenestration here.

Ask questions about all aspects of Windows programming, get help on Microsoft technologies covered in Apress books, or provide feedback on any Apress Windows book.

HOW TO PARTICIPATE:

Go to the Apress Forums site at **http://forums.apress.com/**.

Click the New User link.

You Need the Companion eBook

Your purchase of this book entitles you to buy the companion PDF-version eBook for only $10. Take the weightless companion with you anywhere.

We believe this Apress title will prove so indispensable that you'll want to carry it with you everywhere, which is why we are offering the companion eBook (in PDF format) for $10 to customers who purchase this book now. Convenient and fully searchable, the PDF version of any content-rich, page-heavy Apress book makes a valuable addition to your programming library. You can easily find and copy code—or perform examples by quickly toggling between instructions and the application. Even simultaneously tackling a donut, diet soda, and complex code becomes simplified with hands-free eBooks!

Once you purchase your book, getting the $10 companion eBook is simple:

❶ Visit **www.apress.com/promo/tendollars/**.

❷ Complete a basic registration form to receive a randomly generated question about this title.

❸ Answer the question correctly in 60 seconds, and you will receive a promotional code to redeem for the $10.00 eBook.

2560 Ninth Street • Suite 219 • Berkeley, CA 94710

eBookshop

THE EXPERT'S VOICE™

Offer valid through 6/18/07.